Science, Technology and Innovation Studies

Science, technology and innovation (STI) studies are interrelated, as are STI policies and policy studies. This series of books aims to contribute to improved understanding of these interrelations. Their importance has become more widely recognized, as the role of innovation in driving economic development and fostering societal welfare has become almost conventional wisdom. Interdisciplinary in coverage, the series focuses on the links between STI, business, and the broader economy and society. The series includes conceptual and empirical contributions, which aim to extend our theoretical grasp while offering practical relevance. Relevant topics include the economic and social impacts of STI, STI policy design and implementation, technology and innovation management, entrepreneurship (and related policies), foresight studies, and analysis of emerging technologies. The series is addressed to professionals in research and teaching, consultancies and industry, government and international organizations.

More information about this series at http://www.springer.com/series/13398

Tugrul U. Daim • Dirk Meissner
Editors

Innovation Management in the Intelligent World

Cases and Tools

Springer

Editors
Tugrul U. Daim
Portland State University Technology
Management Doctoral Program
Portland, OR, USA

National Research University
Higher School of Economics
Moscow, Russia

Chaoyang University of Technology
Taichung City, Taiwan

Dirk Meissner
National Research University Higher School of
Economics
Moscow, Russia

ISSN 2570-1509 ISSN 2570-1517 (electronic)
Science, Technology and Innovation Studies
ISBN 978-3-030-58300-2 ISBN 978-3-030-58301-9 (eBook)
https://doi.org/10.1007/978-3-030-58301-9

This Springer imprint is published by the registered company Springer Nature Switzerland AG.
The registered company address is: Gewerbestrasse 11, 6330 Cham, Switzerland

Acknowledgments

The book and the contributions of Tugrul U. Daim and Dirk Meissner to the book chapters are based on the study funded by the Basic Research Program of the National Research University Higher School of Economics (HSE) and by the Russian Academic Excellence Project "5–100."

A Broader Picture on Innovation from Case Studies

Over many years innovation has been an integral part of company strategies and increasingly entered public debates over the last decade. While it has been discussed on several occasions, used as an argument for marketing, and discovered as a theme for politicians in elections campaigns everywhere in the world, there is still little literature describing how companies handle innovation in case study format. The book contributes to the debate about innovation and provides a collection of case studies which help to understand the many different practical approaches to innovation by companies.

This book is a result of a collaboration across oceans and continents. The initial content was created in classes taught by Professor Daim at Portland State University's (PSU) Department of Engineering and Technology Management (ETM). PSU is located in what is called Silicon Forest where a high concentration of technology companies exists. ETM attracts professionals from these companies. Classes require students to team up and work on team projects. As a result, projects analyzing data from the Silicon Forest reveals new knowledge about managing technological innovation. Professor Meissner converted these project reports into chapters revealing critical lessons for professionals, researchers, and students.

The book is structured into three parts. The first part focuses on R&D portfolio management, partnerships, and R&D governance models in seven cases including Apple, Google, Intel, Nike, and Amazon. The second part introduces six cases on new product development in NASA, Daimler Trucks North America, Biotronik, and Thermo Fisher. The third part presents leadership strategies and roadmaps in six cases including TESLA and Hyperloop.

The first part on R&D portfolio management and governance models begins with a case devoted to strategies developed for determining product design. Apple provides an interesting case with its now established product range which is clearly aimed at user satisfaction with the product and consistency and coherence of all products in Apple's portfolio. This requires a dedicated approach toward product portfolio management and respective governance models. The next case highlights several aspects of Intel's new product development with emphasis on customer integrated design, accelerated innovation, product development strategies, tooling supplier integration, and understanding the technology life cycle of its products. This is further described in the third case which shows the impact of Intel's technology in the future of sports. The case highlights the use of Intel's technologies in Nike's products in the sports industry. The fourth case extends this view and analyzes the internationalization of research and development in the case of Google AI Research namely in light of research mission definition including research partnerships and R&D portfolio management. Next the Amazon case describes the Amazon internal technology development and the global organization of research and development centers. It presents the main drivers behind Amazon's international and industrial cooperation with partners from different sectors, different types of cooperation, and related strategic technology investments. The cases all shed light on the meaning and role of digital technologies for current and next-generation products which is why the concluding two cases take a conceptual approach toward ethical issues of data tracking and analytics (Chap. 6) and implications for regional development in the case of Silicon Forest (Chap. 7). The ethical dimension includes data collection, storage, analysis, and commercial exploitation which are subject to regulation. Until recently, many frameworks surrounding data ethics are in place in different regions of the world, but only limited regulation is established assuring that companies respect consumers rights. The seventh chapter deals with Silicon Forest which is located in Oregon and was understood to become an IT technology hub. This, however, has not been achieved yet. The case illustrates an analysis of past events and developments which provide an understanding why Oregon and Silicon Forest is not fostering as an IT technological hub.

The second part begins with a description of innovation at Nike in Chap. 8. It shows how innovation thinking was cultivated and incorporated in the company's culture and outlines the product planning, development, and technology integration strategies. Chapter 9 presents research and development portfolio management at NASA. It provides an understanding of the fundamentals of how NASA manages R&D roadmap strategy/project selection methodology, measures performance and risk, as well as human resources and capital. Chapter 10 is devoted to knowledge management and technology forecasting at Daimler Trucks North America namely by describing inside the company and across company borders sharing knowledge for different purposes. These knowledge management approaches are important ingredients for product development processes which are described in Chap. 11 in case of medical device development at BIOTRONIK and Micro Systems Engineering. The case describes a methodology for new product development by using fundamental tools and concepts in fulfilling the development process. The succeeding case in Chap. 12 extends the product development process toward manufacturing introducing an approach toward assessing suppliers in manufacturing, namely proposing qualitative and quantitative methods for the evaluation and selection of suppliers. Part 2 concludes with Chap. 13 which presents Thermo Fisher Scientific's innovation management framework including strategic planning and a strong focus on project management.

In Part 3, leadership strategies and roadmaps are presented. Chapter 14 presents leadership strategies together with innovation and portfolio management as applied in Elon Musk transportation projects. The succeeding case is also related to one of Elon Musk's endeavors—energy, e.g., Tesla Energy. The case describes the business model innovation which is behind the product innovation in smart grids. Hyperloop as a new means of transport is described in Chap. 16. The case focuses on the Hyperloop development roadmap namely on the vast range of determinants to consider in such a roadmapping undertaking. Another example for R&D management in highly specialized companies is the case of R&D in rare disease focused biotechnology companies in Chap. 17. It introduces related approaches and instruments for use in highly specialized conditions currently underserved by mainstream research and development. Chapters 18 and 19 have a special focus on barriers and obstacle for technology diffusion. The first of the two cases (Chap. 18) analyzes barriers which are preventing the implementation of an emerging energy sustainable source in the Pacific Northwest. Following this, Chap. 19 assesses barriers to electric assist cargo delivery technology and its implications in last mile logistics. It shows that strategic partnerships are one important element of the overall logistics business model.

The book is aimed for teachers looking for case study material which can be used in innovation management teaching, practitioners looking for inspiration for their daily work, and the general public interested in learning what is behind successful innovators. The cases provide a rich reservoir of material on all facets of innovation management.

The editors are grateful to all the contributors who made this book possible. Special thanks go to ETM students at PSU. We also acknowledge the help of John Tacco Melendez in the preparation of this manuscript.

Portland State University Technology Management Doctoral Program, Portland, OR, USA — Tugrul U. Daim

National Research University Higher School of Economics, Moscow, Russia

Chaoyang University of Technology, Taichung City, Taiwan

National Research University Higher School of Economics, Moscow, Russia — Dirk Meissner

Contents

Part I
Information Technology

Chapter 1
An Investigation of the Motivations and Strategies Behind Apple's Product Design

Brian Barley, Ande Kitamura, Thomas Loar, Edwin Ramon-Samayoa, John Yuzon, and Tugrul U. Daim

1.1 Resourced-Based Theory

1.1.1 Resource-Based View

"Strategy has been defined as the match between an organization's internal resources and skills and the opportunities and risks that its external environment creates. The major advances in strategic analysis during the 1980s centered on the link between policy and the external environment (Grant 1991)." Around the same time of this strategy development a new company was about to be founded, Apple, Inc. We are all familiar with Apple, Inc., "Apple Computers, Inc. was founded on April 1, 1976 by college dropouts Steve Jobs and Steve Wozniak who brought a vision of changing people's view of computers to the new company. Jobs and Wozniak wanted to make computers small enough to have people in their homes or in their offices. In short, they needed a user-friendly machine (Brashares 2001)." How did Apple go from two people in a garage to what it is today?

According to Apple, "The Company develops, produces, markets mobile communication devices, media and personal computers, and sells a range of related software, services, products, and digital content and applications from third parties. The Company's products and services include iPhone ®, iPad ®, Mac ®, Apple Watch ®, AirPods ®, Apple TV ®, HomePodTM, a portfolio of consumer and

B. Barley · A. Kitamura · T. Loar · E. Ramon-Samayoa · J. Yuzon
Portland State University, Portland, OR, USA

T. U. Daim (✉)
Portland State University Technology Management Doctoral Program, Portland, OR, USA

National Research University Higher School of Economics, Moscow, Russia

Chaoyang University of Technology, Taichung City, Taiwan
e-mail: tugrul.u.daim@pdx.edu

T. U. Daim, D. Meissner (eds.), *Innovation Management in the Intelligent World*, Science, Technology and Innovation Studies,
https://doi.org/10.1007/978-3-030-58301-9_1

professional software applications, iOS, macOS ®, watchOS ® and tvOSTM operating systems, iCloud ®, Apple Pay ® and a variety of other accessories, services, and support offerings. The Company sells and delivers digital content and applications through the iTunes Store ®, App Store ®, Mac App Store, TV App Store, Book Store, and Apple Music ® ("Digital Content and Services" collectively). The Company sells its products worldwide through its retail stores, online stores, and direct sales force, as well as through cellular network third-party carriers, wholesalers, retailers, and resellers. Additionally, the Company sells through its retail and online stores a range of third-party Apple-compatible products, including application software and various accessories. The Company sells to consumers, small and medium-sized enterprises, and customers of education, enterprise, and government. The Company's fiscal year is the 52- or 53-week period that ends in September's last Saturday. The Corporation is a California company founded in 1977 (Apple 10K 2018).

This diverse product portfolio, heavy investment in Research and Development, and key competitive advantage resulted in 2018 net income of $59.5 billion. As of September 29, 2018, the Company had approximately 132,000 full-time equivalent employees (Apple 10K 2018). Apple Inc. operated 506 retail stores in 25 different countries around the world as of 2018, including the USA, where it has retail stores in 44 of the 50 states, including the Columbia District. More than half of them (272) are in the USA (Farfan 2019). What strategy did Apple, Inc. employ to achieve this level of success?

The Resource-Based (RB) Theory can be seen as a method of formulating a plan inside out. We begin by looking at what the firm has the capital. Next, we evaluate their value-generating potential and end up defining a strategy that will allow us to capture the maximum value in a sustainable way. The process is the following:

1. Identify the resources of that company. Appraise rivals strengths and weaknesses. Identify opportunities for better resource utilization.

   Identify the capabilities of the firm.
   What can the company do more efficiently than its opponents.

2. Identify the inputs of capital for each capacity, and the complexity of each capacity.
3. Appraise rent generating resource and capacity potential in terms of

   a) Their competitive advantage potential for sustainability.
   b) Their returns are sufficient.

4. Choose a plan that better harnesses the strengths and skills of the company in relation to external opportunities.
5. Identify resource gaps that need filling. Invest in replenishing, expanding, and improving the company's resource base Competitive Advantage Capabilities Capital Strategy.

In result, a Resource-based Strategy Analysis is conducted which is described in the succeeding sections.

1.1.2 Resources

Just as the name of strategy formulation suggests, Resources need to be evaluated and analyzed. Resources are all assets (tangible and intangible), firm attributes (reputation and innovation), information, know-how controlled by a firm that enables to implement strategies that improve its effectiveness and efficiency (Barney 1991). Accordingly, the question needs to be answered which assets Apple possess or require to create Value Proposition for its customers?

1.1.2.1 Tangible Resources

According to Harness, "Tangible resources are physical items including cash, inventory, machinery, land or buildings. These items can be easily liquidated and have a set value. They are critical in accounting as they help a company understand it's financial standing when entered on balance sheets and financial statements. There are two types of tangible resources; fixed and current. These assets differ in how easily they can be converted to cash and how they are treated during the accounting process (Harness 2019)."

Apple possessed $131 billion in total current assets as of September 29, 2018. This total was comprise $25.9 billion in cash and cash equivalents, $40 billion in market securities, $23 billion in accounts receivables, $3.95 billion in inventories, $25.8 billion in vendor non-trade receivables, and $12 billion in other current assets. Apple possessed $234 billion in total non-current assets as of September 29, 2018. This was comprise $170.8 billion in marketable securities, $41 billion in property, plant and equipment, and $22 billion in other non-current assets.

1.1.2.2 Intangible Resources

Intangible resources are defined as, "Reputation, appreciation of the name, and intellectual property including knowledge and know-how. Intangible assets are an entity's long-term capital, which lack physical existence. We derive their value from intellectual or legal rights, and the value of the other properties we add. Intangible assets are generally classified into two broad categories: (1) Limited-life intangible assets, such as patents, copyrights and goodwill; and (2) Unlimited-life intangible assets, such as trademarks. Like tangible assets, fire, earthquake, or other events or disasters can not destroy intangible assets and can help build back lost tangible assets. These will usually not, however, be used as collateral to collect loans, and some intangible assets (for example, goodwill) can be lost by carelessness, or as a side effect of business failure. Assuming that tangible assets add to the current market value of a company, intangible assets add to its future value. The estimate of the monetary value of the intangible assets of a company is determined by deducting from its market value the net value of its tangible assets. In some situations (such as the Coca Cola mark), the value of the intangible assets of a business is far greater than the value of its tangible assets (Definition of Intangible Resources)."

The definition of intangible assets raises an interesting question; what is Apple's market value? According to Furhmann, "Brandz recently released their 2018 ranking of the most valuable brands in the U.S. Apple (AAPL) claims second place, with an estimated brand value of $278.9 billion. Apple's logo helps consumers identify its computers, tablets, and mobile. It's interesting to examine the brand—it's power in reach, utility and indeed necessity in today's landscape (Furhmann 2018)." Besides market value, what other intangible assets does Apple possess?

According to Walker, "Apple has more than 75,000 patents and filed for over 2200 more since the beginning of 2017 (Stokel-Walker 2018)." In addition to the lengthy number of patents, Apple possesses 192 registered trademarks (Apple Trademark List). Strategic partnerships with respect to Apple's supply chain is one of the company's most valuable intangible assets. According to Seth, "Apple's Efficient Supply Chain around two-thirds of its revenue comes from sales of iPhones." That massive size is because the tech giant is currently operating one of the most efficient supply chain management systems on the market. Analog Devices (ADI) provides the iPhones and Apple to watch capacitive touchscreen controllers. These components are supplied by the company from facilities based in Ireland, the Philippines, and the USA. ADI stock soared back in March 2015, after Barclays reported that Apple was considering using ADI as a source for its anticipated 3-D touch feature. Glu Mobile (GLUU) does not provide hardware to Apple but is a major provider of iOS apps and mobile games. Jabil Circuit (JBL) manufacturing plants are located in China and are listed on the NYSE. This allows for Apple phone casings. Jabil also produces a wide variety of electronic and manufacturing equipment such as numerical computer control tools and miniaturization of medical devices, and also provides services such as product design, design, development, and production. Micron Technology (MU) and its affiliates, such as Elpida Memory, are located in multiple locations across the USA, Taiwan, Singapore, China, and Japan. These provide for Apple devices with different memory modules such as DRAM, LPDDR3, and LPDDR2. Smartphones and electronic devices utilize these modules to effectively multi-task and run various applications. The recent iPhone 6 is using LPDDR3, whereas the company is currently testing the next version of LPDDR4, which is expected to be up to 60 percent faster and low on power. Murata Manufacturing Ltd. is based in Kyoto, Japan, and supplies to Apple from factories spread throughout China, Japan, Vietnam, Singapore, and Indonesia. Apple and Samsung are the top two customers of Murata, providing the company with ceramic capacitors. These electronic parts are used for and according to Reuters to control the flow of electricity in electronic devices. Japan-based Nidec has emerged as the technology's primary supplier for the much-awaited Apple Watch which came with a special device called a tap-tic engine that produces a sensation of being strapped onto the wrist. Qualcomm (QCOM) is the world leader in products and services for semiconductors, mobile devices, and telecoms. Multiple electronic components are known to be supplied to Apple, including Envelope Power Tracker,

Baseband Processor, Power Management module, and GSM/CDMA Receiver and Transceiver. These are various instruments that are used in the power management systems of computers and in mobile signaling. The cellular baseband modem is however the most important component missing from Apple's own A-chip processor. Qualcomm has filled up this important space for Apple devices, providing the modem technology needed. Samsung Electro-Mechanics Co., with three separate subsidiaries—Samsung Electronics Co., Ltd. Samsung SDI. Co., and Ltd. are headquartered in four different countries (South Korea, China, the USA, and the Philippines). Samsung is one of the major suppliers to Apple who provides multiple components, including flash memory, which is used for data content storage; Mobile DRAM, used for multitasking of different device applications and application processors responsible for controlling and maintaining the entire device. STMicroelectronics (STM) is a multinational electronics and semiconductor company based in Geneva, Switzerland. It supplies Apple with a low-powered, three-axis gyroscope and accelerometer, used to detect a mobile device's orientation and altitude. STM's top customers, along with Apple, include BlackBerry, Nokia, and Cisco. Resource of Texas (TXN) serves Apple through its multiple facilities spread throughout Taiwan, the USA, Malaysia, Japan, Mexico, the Philippines, Germany, and China. TI is expected to provide the current operational amplification system in the Apple Watch, which itself contains 30 different components. This includes the touchscreen controller, the power management chip, and a control panel for iPhones and iPads (Seth 2019).

1.1.3 VRIO Framework

What attributes do these resources require in order for Apple to acquire and maintain a competitive advantage? According to Barney, "It has been proposed that in order to understand the sources of sustained competitive advantage, it is important to create a theoretical model that starts with the premise that heterogeneous and immobile firm resources can be. Not all firm resources, of course, hold the potential for continued competitive advantages. A firm resource must have four qualities to have this potential:

1. it must be useful, in the sense that it exploits opportunities and/or neutralizes risks in a company's environment;
2. It must be rare among the current and potential competition of a firm,
3. it must be imperfectly imitated because of Causal Ambiguity, because of Path dependency, or because of Social Complexity, and
4. strategically equivalent substitutes for this resource can not be considered valuable but neither rare nor imperfectly imitative.

These attributes of firm resources can be seen as empirical indicators of how heterogeneous and immobile the resources of a company are and how useful they are to generate sustained competitive advantages (Barney 1991)."

Alternatives

Alternative	Score (0-100) Overall
Trademarks	100
Patents	100
Customer Loyalty	100
Supply Chain	100
First Mover Advantage	100
Brand Reputation	100
Software	74.45
Hardware	74.45
User Friendly Design	74.45
Innovation	74.45

Fig. 1.1 AHP resources (AHP Software)

Using the VRIO system, you can evaluate Apple's tools and expertise. The first question here is about meaning. Apple's resources and capabilities allow the company to take advantage of multiple opportunities and neutralize external threats. As previously discussed, Apple Inc. possesses numerous resources and capabilities with respect to technology, smartphones, computer tablets, and software. Its product design and brand recognition such as the iPhone and its iOS operating system has revealed a well-orchestrated marketing department and distribution strategy. Apple Inc.'s resources and capabilities are rare. Apple was the first company to popularize the smartphone regardless of the many competitors that existed in the market. Apple's products, including its design, consumer ecosystem, and operating systems, are an internally held resource, due to the many patents the company holds. Apple is constantly innovating its products and services. The cost of imitating Apple's resources and capabilities is high because there are many rivals and a large market share has been captured. Several rivals copied other features of Apple's products by direct copying but were unable to completely replicate it. Apple has developed a large music, media, and film ecosystem that does not have the ability to mimic its rivals. Apple iTunes is the result of a strategic partnership with record companies and music artists that can be easily integrated into many devices on Apple. Apple's organization is able to exploit its resources and capabilities to their full competitive potential. Apple has clear leadership with Tim Cook and has established a positive brand image with a positive company culture and is highly organized. This gives Apple the potential to realize a sustained competitive advantage.

The VRIO Analysis was conducted using an Analytical Hierarchical Decision Process Software. Ten Intangible Resources were evaluated based on their Value, Rarity, Imitability, and the Organizations exploitation of the resource. Each resource either possessed the characteristic, or it did not. Following Fig. 1.1 illustrates the Ten Resources and their overall scores.

Figure 1.2 below illustrates the VRIO scores:

Figure 1.3 below illustrates the radar chart of the ten resources:

Criteria weights

#	Criterion	Weight	
		Local	Global
1.	Imitable	16%	16%
2.	Organization	10%	10%
3.	Rarity	28%	28%
4.	Valuable	47%	47%

Fig. 1.2 VRIO scores (AHP Software)

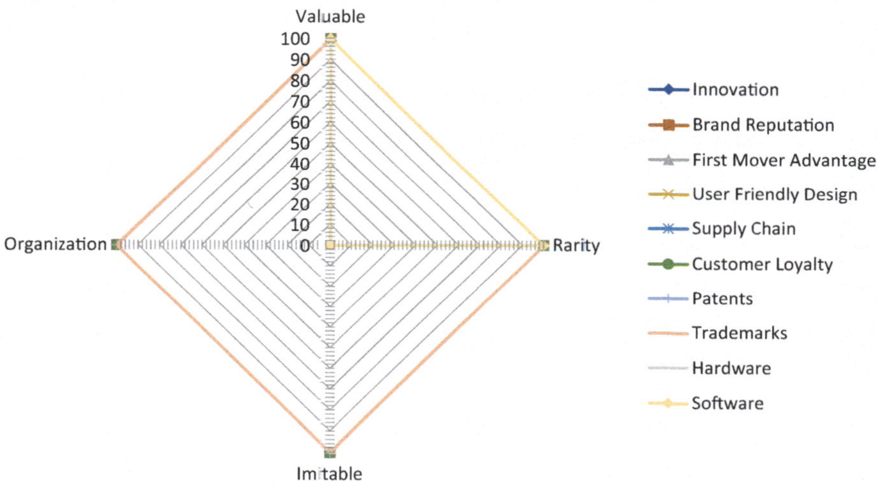

Fig. 1.3 Radar chart of resources (AHP Software)

Figure 1.4 below illustrates a bar chart of the scores of each Intangible Resource:

The Results of the AHP are summarized below in Fig. 1.5. If a resource scored 100, then the Intangible Resource provided Apple with a Sustained Competitive Advantage notated with an, S. If a resource scored less than 100, then the Intangible Resource provided Apple with a Temporary Competitive Advantage notated with an, T:

1.1.4 Sustainable Competitive Advantage

The key question that needs to be addressed is how Apple is able to sustain its competitive advantage? According to Markman, "Think about the landscape. In a world defined by shrinking prices, Apple casually charges more, for everything. Amazon and Alphabet recently announced lower-priced updates to their smart-speaker lineups. Apple entered the market with its own not-so-smart speaker, at a

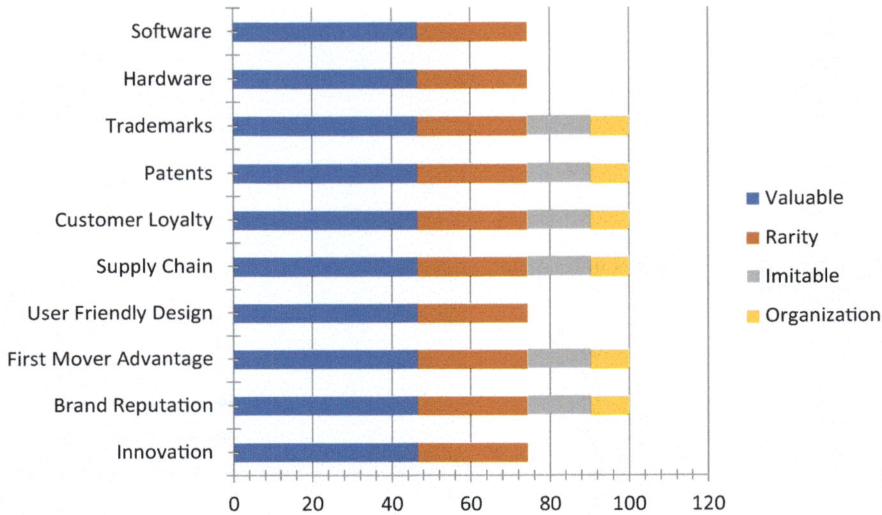

Fig. 1.4 Resource relative scores (AHP Software)

Resource	Valuable	Rarity	Imitability High Cost	Organization	Implications of Competitive
Innovation	Y	Y	N		T
Brand Reputation	Y	Y	Y	Y	S
First mover advantage	Y	Y	Y	Y	S
User Friendly Design	Y	Y	N		T
Supply Chain	Y	Y	Y	Y	S
Customer Loyalty	Y	Y	Y	Y	S
Patents	Y	Y	Y	Y	S
Trademarks	Y	Y	Y	Y	S
Hardware	Y	Y	N		T
Software	Y	Y	N		T

Fig. 1.5 VRIO analysis of Apple, Inc. Where *T* temporary, S sustained (Vargas-Hernández and Garcia 2018)

premium price of $200. New Macs, iPads and iPhones got a price bump, too. Because, hey, why not? And then there is the new, sexy iPhone X. It's the one causing plenty of buzz. It starts at $999, and that is only half the story. At around $1000, the iPhone X is Apple's priciest smartphone. Plus, it costs more to repair and to insure than any of its predecessors. Forget the pretense of a name that includes a roman numeral, Apple is jacking up the cost for out-of-warranty repairs and for insurance packages that cover repairs, like broken screens and glass backs. It's a great business plan. Stop making your flagship handset from durable metals. Switch to fragile glass. Then raise the cost of getting the thing fixed. It's hard to imagine any other consumer electronic company doing this. No other company could get away with it. That's not a criticism. On the contrary. It's what has made Apple a great investment. It is the ability to push price increases without alienating customers (Markman 2018)."

Based on the analysis discussed thus far, what strategies has Apple employed to sustain its competitive advantage? According to Meyer, "Apple uses Product Development as its main intensive strategy for growth. Product Development requires that the company develop attractive and profitable technology products to grow its market share and business performance. Apple implements this intensive growth strategy through innovation in its research and development processes. Apple Inc. uses Market Penetration as its second most significant intensive strategy for growth. Market Penetration involves gaining a larger share of the current market by selling more of the company's current products. Apple uses Market Development as a low-priority intensive strategy for growth. Using the company's competitive advantages, market development involves selling existing products in new markets (Meyer 2019)."

It is clear that Apple must rely heavily on it Research and Development team to implement its Product Development strategy. According to Rossignol, "R&D expenses rose nearly $3 billion: Apple spent $14.2 billion on research and development in its 2018 fiscal year, a nearly 23 percent increase over the $11.5 billion it spent in its 2017 fiscal year (Rossignol 2018)." With respect to product development being Apple's main intensive strategy for growth, a recent article states, "reportedly based on information from sources within Apple. The main news is that the Mac Pro is to come as a series of stackable modules, each only slightly bigger than the current Mac mini, letting customers choose the configurations they need (William and Wuerthele 2019)." This leads to an important crossroads in Apple's history. Will its Product Development shift to strictly modular in the future?

Does Apple actually manufacture their products, or do they just assemble them? In other words, does Apple employ a make or buy strategy (Park et al. 2018)? According to Kabin, "The company signs all its products, 'Designed by Apple in California,' but in the U.S., design is as far as Apple is willing to go. The tech giant outsources hundreds of thousands of manufacturing jobs to countries like Mongolia, China, Korea and Taiwan. But Apple apparently doesn't outsource these jobs to save money. Instead, it does so to save time (Kabin 2019)." It is clear, Apple employs a strategy of inhouse design with the intention of outsourcing the manufacturing process. As previously discussed, Apple relies heavily on its suppliers to deliver their final product.

1.2 Activity Network Process Models

1.2.1 Buyer–Supplier Network

An important determinate in new product design management is the buyer–supplier network and the relationships sustained between both parties. It is a mutual understanding of organizational aims, commitment, trust, and increased information sharing that motivate organizations to be highly committed to improve product performance, rather than pursuing their individual local performance objectives (Primo and Amundson 2002). Apple's supply chain has been ranked top five for sustained leadership over the last decade (Gartner Announces Rankings of the 2019 Supply Chain Top 25 2019) and is regarded as the industry leader for their supply chain capabilities due to the speed at which they can scale operations to fit market demands. Apple purchases materials from various suppliers, ships and assembles them in China and strategically warehouses products for distribution. It is within this supply chain that Apple can easily adapt to any market fluctuations. All aspects of the supply chain involve buyer–supplier relationships and ultimately its Supply Chain Management (SCM) success can be attributed to having built long-term relationships within the buyer–supplier network and the meticulous secrecy they employ and demand of their suppliers.

Tim Cook, Apple CEO, is a world-renowned supply chain expert and has Apple's supply chain operating as robustly as it has ever been. This is achieved by Apple's organizational structure that reflects high centralization in regards to buyer–supplier relationships. Centralization, in this context, refers to the level at which Apple controls and makes all the decisions on the product attributes with the purpose of improving the overall product. *Giannoccaro and Nair, 2016* (Giannoccaro and Nair 2016), found that high centralization is generally considered to be superior when efficiency is desired. This is due to the possibility of the buyer to take into account all interdependencies existing among the product design decisions. With efficiency being one of the main strategic objectives of Apple, high centralization will have to be accepted by Apple suppliers if they want to profit from being associated with the Apple brand and the innovation of new products that Apple so often delivers.

1.2.2 Apple New Product Process (ANPP)

Apple is a notoriously secretive company and information about Apple's design process is limited, but a book was written several years ago, "Inside Apple: How America's most Admired and Secretive Company Really Works" authored by Adam

Lashinsky (2012), provides some insight. At an organizational perspective, Jony Ive—former Chief Design Officer (CDO) at Apple—and his design team are separated and do not report to finance, manufacturing, or other business groups. This break from Apple's traditional hierarchical structure allows the design team to set their own budgets and create their own reporting structures that report directly to the executive team.

Once the design is underway, the Apple New Product Process (ANPP) begins. The Apple New Product Process is a step-by-step playbook spelling out everything that needs to get done to make the product (Lashinsky 2012).

When the product is ready to leave the conceptual design phase two key people take control of the system-level design: an engineering program manager (EPM) and a global supply manager (GSM). Their teams, the engineering corps, and supply-chain team are ultimately responsible for the materials sourcing, development, detailed design, and system integration of the product. Product assembly takes place in China, but the design process within Apple is not over at production as Apple runs many product iterations during the manufacturing process. The product is built, tested, and then reviewed by a cross-functional team of senior executives, and then the design will be improved upon and built all over again. These iterations take 4–6 weeks and can occur many times over a products development lifecycle (Apple's Product Development Process—Inside the World's Greatest Design Organization 2019). The ANPP finally wraps with a launch plan or action plan known as "the Rules of the Road" which entails all responsibilities and actions needed to be taken prior to bringing the product to market.

Apple takes a very nontraditional path with product design. Other companies generally attempt to perfect design and then outsource the manufacturing which in turn delivers the most cost-effective operation, but Apple iterates new product design *during* manufacturing which is often the least cost-effective approach. Apple is not perfect, but they are extremely successful in what they do and their success can largely be attributed to their ability to design, innovate, iterate, and bring high volume products to market.

1.3 DSM Applications and System Readiness Assessment

1.3.1 Design Structure Matrix

A way to look at information flows and other complex systems is through a design structure matrix—otherwise known as DSM. A DSM is a simple, compact, and visual representation of a system or project in the form of a square matrix and is used in systems engineering and project management (Browning 2016). DSMs are used to model the structure of complex systems or processes in order to perform system analysis, project planning, and organization design (Browning 2016) (Fig. 1.6).

There are three architectures DSMs can model: product, organization, and process (Browning 2016). Product DSMs focus on components and modules and how

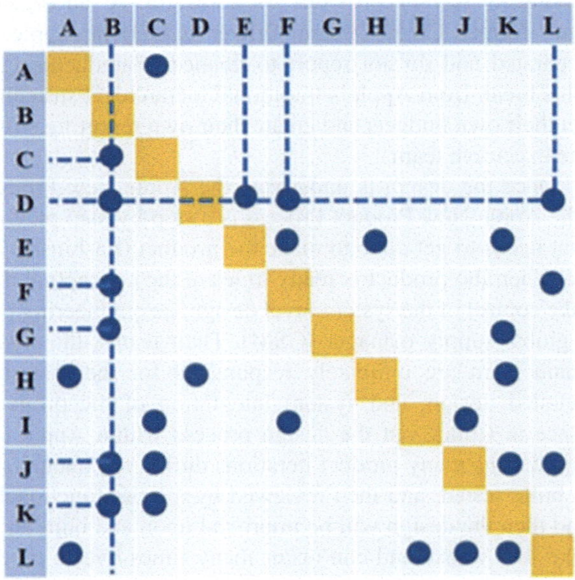

Fig. 1.6 An example of a basic design structure matrix (Tompkins 2018)

they converge and interact to perform specific functions (Browning 2016). Organization DSMs focus on networks of people (Browning 2016). Process DSMs focus on activities and their interactions comprising a project (Browning 2016). DSMs can be modeled in both a temporal and static model (Browning 2016). Process DSMs follow a temporal model while product and organization DSMs follow a static model (Browning 2016). A temporal model shows that the elements are placed in chronological order (Browning 2016). Static models are not put in chronological order so it does not matter the order in which the elements are placed.

Apple could utilize a process DSM for its Apple New Product Process (ANPP) using Microsoft Excel. Due to the extreme secrecy of Apple's organizational and process structure around its designing, the example DSM can only be a general outline of the actual ANPP (Lashinsky 2012). It would be recommended that Apple implements information regarding items such as pricing, marketing, and research for market trends, basic R&D, and other steps that may be missing from the ANPP due to secrecy. Due to process DSMs being temporal, the elements are inherently dependent on the previous elements so we highlight only the major dependencies in dark green and red. Light green represents how the elements are inherently dependent on the success and information of the previous elements in the process.

As previously stated in Sect. 1.2.2, much of the ANPP follows iterations (Lashinsky 2012). When a product reaches test and review it will go back to the engineering program manager and global supply manager to bring the product back to Cupertino for the input of the executives to make decisions as to whether the product needs to go back to design, production, or test/review (Lashinsky 2012). These iterations can be seen simply and concisely through a DSM. The DSM also

	Design	EPM/GSM	Production	Test	Review	Product Launch
Design	X					
EPM/GSM		X				
Production			X			
Test				X		
Review					X	
Product Launch						X

Fig. 1.7 An example of a process architecture DSM for Apple New Product Process

provides information on dependencies, interfaces, and interactions among elements (Tompkins 2018). Production is dependent on the information from testing as shown in the red square. The information that comes from testing is extremely important for how Apple continues to manufacture its product. Thus, a DSM can expose the structure of the ANPP architecture in a simple and concise manner that can show the lifecycle of the ANPP (Fig. 1.7).

1.3.2 System Readiness Assessments

System readiness assessment (SRA) methods offer a foundation for evaluating the existing maturity of systems under development (Tompkins 2018). SRAs use four types of measurements: two are assigned using inputs from subject matter experts (Tompkins 2018). These are the technology readiness level (TRL) and integration readiness level (IRL) (Tompkins 2018). TRL assesses the maturity of a particular technology and allows a consistent comparison of maturity between different types of technologies (Austin and York 2015). IRL measures the integration maturity between two or more components (Austin and York 2015). The other two measurements are calculated using various methods (Tompkins 2018). These two are component readiness level and system readiness level (SRL) (Tompkins 2018). SRL provides a snapshot in time of the readiness of the entire system (Austin and York 2015). Component Readiness Level is used to identify which system components are lagging or may be too far ahead in terms of their readiness and thus require Program Management and/or engineering attention (Austin and York 2015).

Apple is famously known to be secretive regarding new technology and products, so their SRA information is not readily available. On the other hand though, by looking at Apple's past products we can look at how technology readiness plays a role in learning from Apple's past failures.

1.3.3 Technology Readiness

Of the system readiness measurement methods, TRLs are most frequently used by technology companies to measure technology readiness (Technology Readiness and the Valley of Death). In general, TRL 6 is given to a technology when the technology is "proven" (Technology Readiness and the Valley of Death). Even when a product is shown to be "proven" it does not necessarily mean that it is ready for implementation—TRL 10 (Technology Readiness and the Valley of Death). There is a lot of cost and risk before a technology can be implemented and one of the risks is whether a customer is actually ready or not for the technology (Technology Readiness and the Valley of Death).

TRLs are given to a product based off of expert opinion from the company developing the new technology/product (Technology Readiness and the Valley of Death). Technology readiness can also be defined by the consumer by their general opinion about how technology achieves their goals in their daily and business lives (Başgöze 2015). An excerpt from the paper "Integration of the Technology Readiness (TR) Into the Technology Acceptance Model (TAM) for M-Shipping" by Başgöze describes consumer-based technology readiness as follows (Başgöze 2015):

"During the adoption stage of new technologies, consumers develop positive or negative feelings concerning the technological product, through their either positive or negative opinions regarding the product. These feelings are examined under four sub-dimensions as Optimism, Innovativeness, Discomfort, and Insecurity. Although optimism and innovativeness specify consumers' positive feelings, discomfort, and insecurity state negative feelings (Parasuraman 2000). Optimism dimension directs the consumer's confidence it feels in its ability to enhance the control, flexibility, and effectiveness in its life (Parasuraman 2000). Therefore it is defined as "the individual's tendency to believe that it will achieve good results throughout its life" (Walczuch et al. 2007). Innovativeness dimension directs an individual's lead about technological products (Parasuraman 2000). In other words, it measures the consumers' intention to try new products and services with high technology before others (Sophonthummapharn and Tesar 2007). Insecurity dimension covers the cases where the consumer does not trust a technological product and doubts about product fulfillment through its task (Parasuraman 2000). Doubt causes individuals to be in the tendency of avoiding computer use due to their innate fears from technology and this feeling may arise from their skeptical attitudes of individuals against new technologies (Walczuch et al. 2007). Consumers who are highly scored in the discomfort scale believe that their knowledge of technology is not sufficient and therefore they may feel depressed (Parasuraman 2000). This dimension represents consumers' anxieties in technological terms (Sophonthummapharn and Tesar 2007). For instance, when consumers come across a technological product, they may think that they will be unable to have sufficient expertise on the product, become worried, believe that the product is not designed for them, and therefore avoid purchasing the product (Sophonthummapharn and Tesar 2007).

In 1993, Apple came out with the Apple Newton MessagePad, which was profitably unsuccessful and was shortly discontinued only 5 years later (Technology Readiness and the Valley of Death). While the Apple Newton MessagePad paved the way for other personal digital assistant (a phrase coined by Apple CEO John Sculley during the introduction of the Apple Newton MessagePad) and touch screen devices, customers were not ready in the 1990s to pay the hefty $700 for this new technology

(Remembering the Newton MessagePad, 20 Years Later). While the Apple Newton MessagePad may have been proven to work in a given environment it did not mean that it was necessarily ready to go into manufacturing and marketed. In retrospect, some may argue that the Apple Newton MessagePad was not even TRL 10 since the writing recognition did not work well at all either (Remembering the Newton MessagePad, 20 Years Later). Altogether, the market was not ready for the Apple Newton MessagePad despite it being determined to be TRL 10.

In 2010 though, 17 years later, Apple came out with the iPad which was largely more successful and extremely popular and profitable—a time when customers were much more ready for this technology with the help of the iPhone's and other smartphone's huge successes (Technology Readiness and the Valley of Death; Remembering the Newton MessagePad, 20 Years Later). As some have noted regarding Apple Newton MessagePad's poor performance in the market in the 1990s, it "came too early for its own party"—showing that while proving that a technology can perform in its environment it does not mean that the technology is necessarily ready to be given TRL 10 (Technology Readiness and the Valley of Death). The readiness of the market and customer base needs to be accounted for as well.

Today, Apple has had large success in their final products that would be considered TRL 10 as seen in Apple's 2010 release of the iPad. Now Apple is soon to release what is being called a radical new design for its iPhone 11 on September 10, 2019, so it will be seen whether Apple's new technology in the iPhone 11 will be successful (iPhone 11 Release Date: Apple to Launch New iPhones in California on 10 September).

1.4 Assessment of Product Architecture

System architectures are a major consideration relative to product design, as both the needs of the end user and the values of a firm must be represented in such a way that a synergistic balance can be achieved. Further, considerations in product architecture have profound ramifications in development time and supply chain logistics that affect the overall time to market a particular product. In order to simultaneously develop a robust product framework as well as optimize the logistical end of the production line, there exist two primary formats that can be adopted to best fit meet these objectives: modular and integrated architectures. Each of these formats come with their own discrete benefits and shortcomings which may be adopted to best represent the aims and values of a firm and their product lines, and while Apple has historically favored one, (integrated structures), signs points to adoption or at least extension to the other.

1.4.1 A Primer on Modularity

Modular architectures are characterized by assemblies of easily interchangeable components with one or few functions; products are composed of 1:1 or 1:2 component to function mapped units (Cabigiosu et al. 2017). Modular systems are optimized by either isolating component function such that components may operate independently of one another, or by standardizing interfaces such that third-party vendors can generate modules and easily substitute with little to no integration effort (Wu et al. 2009).

Through this regimented compartmentalization, product functional aspects can be specifically tailored, the products as a whole are more adaptive, the development times and associated process innovation times are shorter, and valuations are made easy as they are broken down on a per individual functional area basis (https://images.adsttc.com/media/images/55c7/6a12/e58e/ce5c/7d00/01a3/slideshow/Screen_Shot_2015-07-08_at_21.39.11.jpg?1439132171). Additionally, modularity can have benefits with respect to supply-chain management via the mirroring hypothesis, which states that particular functional areas are addressed by subgroups within firms that are most optimized/suited to deal with those areas; function and firm structure are "mirrored" (Wu et al. 2009). In this respect, an internal intra-firm optimization occurs spontaneously, affording great benefit to the use and application of modules.

Lastly, modularity affords another benefit through the ability to re-use extant modules; application of the "re-use/redesign principle." This entails that per component generation, if the technology has not advanced to a level that is not yet appreciable enough to facilitate the development of a new component, a modular architecture can simply re-use the existing technology without having to go through the pains of integration. This affords incredible flexibility and the ability to selectively upgrade particular components within an assembly relative quickly with respect to new technological advancements, all the while performing precision cost-benefit analyses on the remaining assembly components.

1.4.2 Integrated Legacy

Despite the advantages of modularity, Apple has historically been a company that favors integrated frameworks in the design and manufacture of its products, their components, and hardware elements are often multi-functional and proprietary. With the benefits of modularity being well-known via ubiquitous build-your-own PC architectures, it is initially curious that Apple would choose this seemingly lagging mode of design. However, the statistics regarding performance as well as the weight of Apple's business values justify this decision in two regards: integration allows for higher optimization of a system architecture with respect to system parameters, and also adds a layer of intellectual property/brand perception protections that make Apple more desirable as a unique product.

An integrated system, being designed solely by one design team, has the benefit of being optimized for the other components on the board; the designers know what else is going on the board alongside their particular component, as well as the operation specifications of the system as a whole, allowing a for a design that exploits and operates within the system parameters to the best of its ability. Modular products, while advantageous on a component-to-component basis, may not have the luxury of being tuned for a system, often operating outside of idealized system parameters and thus degrading the system performance as a whole. In this respect, with every component being designed in-house, Apple has precision control over its user experience, a facet that has played into its brand legacy (https://www.zdnet.com/article/the-modular-mac-pro-is-the-solution-to-a-problem-that-apple-itself-created/). A rigorous example of this is the ubiquitous MacBook Pro, which features a fully integrated GPU, RAM, and SSD storage, aspects that are commonly upgrades in other brands that are essentially locked in Apple's case.

In addition to having control over user perceptions, integrated systems, and proprietary components add a layer of security to the integrity of the brand vision; intellectual property is protected. It is common that most computer-savvy users ponder upgrading their systems to achieve performance aspects not fully realized by designers. In this respect, lead users typically swap out components of their machines in order to beef up performance at the cost warranty voiding or possible malfunction due to the use of third-party hardware. Apple is notorious for resisting this, making their machines difficult to upgrade relative to standard PCs. While seemingly neglecting an entire market of users, this strategy has not actually impacted Apple in meaningfully negative way, rather, their products have found a home with many who have no desire to upgrade product performance and are satisfied with Apple's intents. As stated, this end user satisfaction with a product that came straight off the shelf is Apple's endgame, and it has worked to cult success.

1.4.3 Steps Toward Modularity

While largely an integrated company, it appears that Apple has taken notice of its modular market counterparts. June 2019 saw the announcement of a new Mac Pro, touted as being Apple's first fully modular product set to be released (https://www.zdnet.com/article/the-modular-mac-pro-is-the-solution-to-a-problem-that-apple-itself-created/). Boasting a variety of hot-swappable modules that were tuned to particular consumer needs and an ad campaign that took the pains to stress the new modularity of this offering, many begged the question: is this truly a modular product? While customizable to an extent, and modular in the idea that components could be swapped out readily, the Mac Pro was largely in-house designed, with proprietary data connections and hardware appearing all over the product; the symptoms of integrated architecture still lingered in this new pseudo-modular design.

While Apple has gone on record as saying that hardware licenses would be distributed to third parties for the development of modules, this would be an enormous step away from the legacy of end user perception control established by its mature product line and company philosophy. Further, the use of proprietary data connections and hardware appear to go against one of the major tenets of true modularity: interface standardization, which preaches the use of common connection points such that easy substitution/integration by external modules is made easy. In this respect, the adherence to these principles communicate that while steps are being taken toward modularity, the company seemingly remains a little guarded in incorporating more mainstream design elements, an understandable concern relative to desire to maintain a functional, as well as esthetic standard.

1.4.4 Design Philosophy

Apple has always maintained a brand tradition of artfulness and consideration in their product design, values reinforced by a set of core tenets parsed from interviews (https://www.fastcompany.com/1665375/the-6-pillars-of-steve-jobss-design-philosophy) strictly adhered to with respect to device architectures. The first is craft: the stipulation that every product must lay perfectly at the intersection of art and engineering. While the former may be (relatively) easy to achieve, the latter takes into consideration process flows with respect to product design; how much of this can be done in-house? The answer in Apple's case is, all of it, as they are hesitant to put an aspect of their product in the hands of a third part lest it is sullied in a way that degrades the product performance or perception overall. In this way, proprietary design is facilitated which in turn ups the propensity for Apple engineers to innovate; creative development is emphasized.

The second major tenet is simplicity. Apple understands that their primary demographic may not all be "lead users" and that some consumers are more casual, making purchase decisions on more primal, esthetic decisions with secondary needs in moderate performance values. In this respect, the decision for an integrated framework manifests itself: by lacking modularity Apple affords its consumers the complete removal of the paralysis of choice, a common dilemma plaguing those in the modification game. In this way, Apple products boast a more empathetic design relative to non-savvy users, with enough performance power to satisfy those who need it.

The last major tenet is the maintenance of the brand legacy of excellence. Apple is aware of its position in the market not necessarily as the performance brand, but rather the esthetic brand; the tool that "the artist chooses". In this way, integration plays a part via the prevention of uncertainty; by using in-house designs, the variability of sub-Apple standard third-party developers are completely removed, and Apple is able to determine its own end user experience through precision engineering and product testing.

1.4.5 Roots of Modular Apple

Interestingly, it should also be noted that this technically not Apple's first foray into modular product design. In 1985, a secret Macintosh prototype codenamed "Jonathan" was developed and reached late-stage prototyping phases (https://appleinsider.com/articles/19/02/21/apples-modular-mac-pro-design-may-mean-units-that-connect-like-lego-bricks). Rather than fitting its components into a single chassis, the Jonathan instead had several modules stacked horizontally, giving it a "books on a shelf" appearance. Unfortunately, this design was killed by Apple's then-CEO John Sculley as being "impractical" when compared to other emerging technologies. Now, in 2019 with modularity finally, on the docket for Apple, one is left to ponder what Apple would look like today if it had embraced modular design early on.

1.4.6 Ramifications

Apple's move toward modular architectures signifies a shift in paradigm that presents an interesting future for a once integration-centric firm. While small in the step, the departure from historic design principles coupled with the possibility of allowing third-party support relative to their system architectures spell Apple's acknowledgment for the need to adapt in the rapidly evolving tech marketplace. In this concession, we may expect some radical changes within Apple on the horizon; a truly modular product with actual third-party support. In this event, some customer perceptions would likely have to be surrendered as Apple would likely be unable to micromanage third-party sources to perform in an avenue of their standard, but the possibility certainly exists now that these steps are being taken.

With this adoption of a new modular architecture, we must speculate on potential changes in the process relative to product design and development. Apple is not known to make incremental improvements sporadically through a release year as expected of a product line featuring integrated technologies. Through the use of modular designs however, the exploitation of ever-evolving hardware choices is now on the table; the product architectures now being hot-swappable can now experience incremental improvement over time, necessitating a new approach to product releases on Apple's part as well as process procedurals.

This begs the question however, how will this impact Apple's brand legacy/product perception? One aspect of the Apple mythos is the cult-like race to attend the drop of new generations of iPhones and the latter, and while the iPhone is certainly not modular (yet) if it were to become so in the future the impact of the unveiling on the ravenous public would almost certainly be dulled, and thus the mystique and esthetic of Apple as the "artist's brand" would be cheapened. While not necessarily a consideration with respect to product design, for a brand like Apple, this is almost certainly something that must be attended to.

1.5 Life Cycle Assessment and Product Line Strategy

Environmental friendliness is an aspect important to any modern technology company. Focus on impacts made to the environment are ever more pressing with governments enacting regulations such as the Waste Electrical and Electronic Equipment directive, Restriction of Hazardous Substances directive, and the European Council's directive on energy-using products (Chan et al. 2013). These directives typically "bring . . . forward legally binding measures to step up Member States' efforts to use energy more efficiently at all stages of the energy chain" (Directive 2012/27/EU of the European Parliament and of the Council of 25 October 2012 on Energy Efficiency 2012). Another example includes the USA government-backed voluntary program called ENERGY STAR started in 1992 as a user-friendly approach to communicate to consumers the energy usage of products throughout its life (ENERGY STAR). A way to gage the impact on the environment is to use a life cycle assessment (LCA).

1.5.1 Life Cycle Assessment

There exists an Apple uses a full life cycle assessment when planning for new product offerings as well as its current product line offerings. This helps it stay as a leader in its field by applying high levels of environmentally friendly designs in all of its products. Some of the key aspects of its strategy are shared on its website (Environment—Answers). Apple relies on these categories when performing its LCA.

It can be estimated the greenhouse gas data emission from each product. A combination of Apple-specific and industry-average datasets for material production, manufacturing processes, electricity generation, and transportation along with offsets due to renewable energy usage (from Apple Supplier Clean Energy Program or suppliers' own independent program) are used to gage the impact of each Apple product. Data and modeling are then checked for quality and accuracy by Fraunhofer Institute in Germany. In any analysis of this type, there is a degree of uncertainty. Data limitations are overcome by developing detailed process-based environmental models with Apple-specific parameters and reliance on industry-average data and assumptions.

More in-depth replication on the exact numbers used in Apple data analysis is beyond the scope of this study. It can be said, however, that Apple has evolved in its use of LCA modeling. Based on an abstract from one of its industry conferences in

2018 it stated the following: "Over the past decade, Apple's use of lifecycle assessment (LCA) to measure environmental impact has rapidly evolved. Initially, LCA models focused on a limited number of representative products, utilized industry-average data, and were conducted after products had been designed. Today, LCA models are developed for every product, major components and materials are modeled using data from Apple's own supply chains, and modeling begins early in the design process. These changes have led to an increased role for LCA in influencing design and manufacturing decisions at the product level. Moreover, this evolution has enabled Apple to make strategic decisions on corporate environmental initiatives that have led to meaningful reductions in environmental impact" (Dahmus et al. 2018).

1.5.2 Product Line Strategy—Environmental Friendliness Approaches

Product line strategy implementation in the current context refers to the development of "environment friendly products for customers with different willingness-to-pay for the environmental attributes of a product" (Chen and Zhang 2013). A prime example would be the miles per gallon (MPG) of a car; generally, the smaller and lower weight will have a higher MPG in this tradeoff (Chen and Zhang 2013). However, for Apple, a tradeoff would mean offering an inferior product compared to itself so it would not offer to go in this direction. In addition, some of its core values are exemplified as being a responsible company. As such, analyzing Apple's product line strategy with respect to environmental friendliness skews in the direction of the mass-marketing strategy (one product offered to all markets) rather than the market-segmentation strategy (different products for each market) (Chen and Zhang 2013). As seen, Apple pushes the efficiency frontier of its products by investing heavily in R&D so that it offers the best products possible with cutting edge technology (Chen and Zhang 2013).

- Climate Change—"We take responsibility for the emissions associated with our own operations, as well as the entire lifecycle of all our products and accessories." (Apple 2019)
- Resources—"We believe in conserving Earth's resources when operating our facilities and making our products." (Apple 2019)
- Smarter Chemistry—"We believe that our products should be safe for anyone who assembles, uses, or recycles them." (Apple 2019)

As such, here are some examples of its approach to its business product line offering with respect to environment-friendliness (Apple 2019).

- Approach
  - Low-carbon design via low-carbon alternatives—Carbon footprint calculation

Corporate facilities
Product Manufacturing
Product Use
Product Transportation
Product end-of-life processing

- Renewable Energy

  100% renewable energy

  - Offices
  - Retail Stores
  - Data Centers

- Reduce total energy usage at its own facilities and those of its suppliers

  Designing—Total consideration of environmental impact along with cost, durability, form, and functionality
  Product
  Operating System
  Manufacturing process

It is evidently clear that Apple's strategy to environmental friendliness is to apply an equal green standard to all its products. It will not market explicitly a same product with less of an environmental friendliness aspect. The last 10 years have marked an average of 70 percent decrease in energy usage (Apple 2019). The 11-inch iPad Pro from Fall 2018 is 69 percent more efficient than the ENERGY STAR standard; iMac Pro uses 40 percent less power during sleep and off mode, and the MacBook Air uses three times less power in sleep mode than the previous generation laptop (Apple 2019). Apple also reduces the amount of silicon used in its chips; the A11 and A12 chips found in iPhone 8, X, XS, XS Max, and XR used this new design to lower the 2018 Apple footprint by 160,000 metric tons (Apple 2019). Aluminum is another material Apple has worked on reducing. It has partnered with Alcoa Corporation and Rio Tinto Aluminum on a new technology that eliminates direct greenhouse gas emissions from the traditional smelting (Apple 2019). Now, Apple utilizes 100 percent recycled aluminum for Macbook Air enclosures to reduce its carbon footprint in half. Other resource conservation highlights include updating its disassembly robot, Daisy, to recycle six more phones for a total of 15; reduced plastic utilization by 48 percent in the last 3 years; material recovery lab partnerships with industry experts and academia to innovate recycle methods; 11 products now use 100% recycled tin in the solder for logic boards; using recycled cobalt in batteries of new products; Apple refurbished 7.8 million devices and recycled 48,000 tons of e-waste in 2018 (Apple 2019). When Apple describes utilizing smarter chemistry methods it means the following. This includes updating the Apple Regulated Substances Specification to strengthen supplier requirements and restrictions on harmful substances, all supplier final assembly sites have adopted safer cleaners and degreasers, continued to expand Full Material Disclosure (FMD) program, and collect comprehensive chemical data for over 75% by mass of new iPhone, iPad, and Mac products.

From all the evidence presented, it is without a doubt that Apple goes beyond government regulations to ensure that its current product line offerings do not compromise on environmental friendliness. It balances its niche market of so-called high-quality products with high price tags to continue on this line of thinking (Chen and Zhang 2013).

Acknowledgement The book and the book chapter are based on the study funded by the Basic Research Program of the National Research University Higher School of Economics (HSE) and by the Russian Academic Excellence Project '5-100'.

References

AHP Software. https://content.transparentchoice.com/ahp-software/signup

Apple (2019) Environmental responsibility report. Progress report, Covering Fiscal Year 2018. https://www.apple.com/environment/pdf/Apple_Environmental_Responsibility_Report_2019.pdf

"Apple 10K 2018" https://s2.q4cdn.com/470004039/files/doc_financials/2018/q4/10-K-2018-(As-Filed).pdf

"Apple's Product Development Process—Inside the World's Greatest Design Organization" (2019) August 7. interaction-design.org. https://www.interaction-design.org/literature/article/apple-s-product-development-process-inside-the-world-s-greatest-design-organization

Austin MF, York DM (2015) System readiness assessment (SRA) an illustrative example, Elsevier,. Procedia Comput Sci 44:486–496

Barney J (1991) Competitive advantage, resource based theory of a firm. [Online]. pp 170–173. Moodle. Economics and the Organization of Economic Activity. Session 5: Resource Based Theory of the Firm.

Başgöze P (2015) Integration of the technology readiness (TR) into the technology acceptance model (TAM) for M-shipping. Int J Sci Res Innov Technol 2(3):26–35

Brashares A (2001) Steve jobs thinks different. Twenty-First Century Books, Brookfield, CT. LC Call Number: HD9696.2.U62 J633 2001 Catalog Record: 00057706

Browning TR (2016) Design structure matrix extensions and innovations: a survey and new opportunities. IEEE Trans Eng Manag 63(1):27–52

Cabigiosu et al (2017) Measuring modularity: engineering and management effects of different approaches. IEEE Trans Eng Manag 64(1):103–114

Chan K, Hing XW, White G, Yip N (2013) An extended fuzzy-AHP approach for the evaluation of green product designs. IEEE Trans Eng Manag 60:327–339. https://doi.org/10.1109/TEM.2012.2196704

Chen C, Zhang J (2013) Green product design with engineering tradeoffs under technology efficient frontiers: analytical results and empirical tests. IEEE Trans Eng Manag 60(2):340–352. https://doi.org/10.1109/TEM.2012.2212199

Dahmus J, Smith S, Arnold C, Santero N, Apple US, Ebert T, Apple DE (2018) Integrating lifecycle assessment into product-level and company-level environmental activities. Austria: Schoenbrunn Palace Conference Centre Vienna. Going Green CARE INNOVATION 2018. November 26–29. http://www.4980.timewarp.at/CARE/CI2018/PDFs/Program%20&%20Abstracts%20CARE%20INNOVATION%202018_26112018.pdf

"Definition of Intangible Resources" http://www.businessdictionary.com/definition/intangible-asset.html

"Directive 2012/27/EU of the European Parliament and of the Council of 25 October 2012 on Energy Efficiency" Build up—the European portal for energy efficiency in buildings. https://www.buildup.eu/en/practices/publications/directive-201227eu-european-parliament-and-council-25-october-2012-energy
ENERGY STAR. https://www.energystar.gov/about
Farfan B (2019) Apple's retail stores around the world. Dash. https://www.thebalancesmb.com/apple-retail-stores-global-locations-2892925
Furhmann R (2018) Why these are the most valuable brands of 2018. Investopedia. https://www.investopedia.com/articles/investing/072115/why-these-are-most-valuable-brands-2015.asp
"Gartner Announces Rankings of the 2019 Supply Chain Top 25" (2019) Gartner, Inc. (Press Release), May 16
Giannoccaro I, Nair A (2016) Examining the roles of product complexity and manager behavior on product design decisions: an agent-based study using NK simulation. IEEE Trans Eng Manag 63(2):237–247
Grant RM (1991) The resource-based theory of competitive advantage: implications for strategy formulation. Calif Manag Rev 33(3):114–135
Harness J (2019) Definition of tangible resources. Bizfluent. https://bizfluent.com/info-8127118-definition-tangible-resources.html
https://appleinsider.com/articles/19/02/21/apples-modular-mac-pro-design-may-mean-units-that-connect-like-lego-bricks
https://images.adsttc.com/media/images/55c7/6a12/e58e/ce5c/7d00/01a3/slideshow/Screen_Shot_2015-07-08_at_21.39.11.jpg?1439132171
https://www.fastcompany.com/1665375/the-6-pillars-of-steve-jobss-design-philosophy
https://www.zdnet.com/article/the-modular-mac-pro-is-the-solution-to-a-problem-that-apple-itself-created/
"iPhone 11 Release Date: Apple to Launch New iPhones in California on 10 September" https://www.expertreviews.co.uk/mobile-phones/1408263/iphone-11-release-date-and-price-rumours-leaks-features
Kabin B (2019). Apple's iPhone: designed in California but manufactured fast all around the World (Infographic). Entrepreneur. https://www.entrepreneur.com/article/228315
Lashinsky A (2012) Inside Apple: how America's most admired and secretive company really works. Business Plus, New York. Print
Markman J (2018) Apple still holds this key advantage. Forbes. https://www.forbes.com/sites/jonmarkman/2018/04/30/apple-still-holds-this-key-advantage/#2c2a45877824
Meyer P (2019) Apple Inc.'s generic strategy & intensive growth strategies. Panmore Institute. http://panmore.com/apple-inc-generic-strategy-intensive-growth-strategies
Parasuraman A (2000) Technology readiness index (TRI) a multiple-item scale to measure readiness to embrace new technologies. J Serv Res 2(4):307–320
Park W-Y et al (2018) How much does design internalization matter in the face of technological change? IEEE Trans Eng Manag 65(2):264–275
Primo MA, Amundson SD (2002) An exploratory study of the effects of supplier relationships on new product development outcomes. J Oper Manag 20:33–52
"Remembering the Newton MessagePad, 20 Years Later" https://www.macworld.com/article/2047342/remembering-the-newton-messagepad-20-years-later.html
Rossignol J (2018) Apple now has 132K Full-time employees, spent $14.2B on R&D in 2018 fiscal year. MacRumors.com. https://www.macrumors.com/2018/11/05/apple-2018-form-10-k-highlights/
Seth S (2019) 10 major companies tied to the apple supply chain. Investopedia. https://www.investopedia.com/articles/investing/090315/10-major-companies-tied-apple-supply-chain.asp
Sophonthummapharn K, Tesar G (2007) Technology readiness and propensity of cell phone users to subscribe to commercial messaging service. Mark Manag J 17(2):81–95
Stokel-Walker C (2018) Forget Apple vs Samsung, an even bigger patent war has just begun. https://www.wired.co.uk/article/apple-samsung-iphone-patents

"Technology Readiness and the Valley of Death" https://www.boeing.com/features/innovation-quarterly/may2017/feature-thought-leadership-newman.page

Tompkins Z (2018) Improving system maturity assessments by incorporating a design structure matrix. IEEE Trans Eng Manag, 1–19.

Vargas-Hernández JG, Garcia FC (2018) The link between a firm's internal characteristics and performance: GPTW & VRIO dimension analysis. Revista De Administração IMED 8 (2):222–235

Walczuch R, Lemmink J, Streukens S (2007) The effect of service employees' technology readiness on technology acceptance. Inf Manag 44(2):206–215

William G, Wuerthele M (2019) Apple's 'modular' mac pro design may mean units that connect like Lego bricks. Quiller Media. https://appleinsider.com/articles/19/02/21/apples-modular-mac-pro-design-may-mean-units-that-connect-like-lego-bricks

Wu et al (2009) Updating a modular product: how to set time to market and component quality. IEEE Trans Eng Manag 56(2):298–311

Chapter 2
New Product Development

Claris Leung, Andy Hsiao, Michael Hobernicht, Kevin Camp, Vanessa Kung, and Tugrul U. Daim

2.1 New Product Development Introduction

Since the industrial revolution, the global industrial economy continues to expand rapidly. The automotive industry enabled people to live outside of cities and commute in. The aerospace industry has linked not only states but entire countries. Henry Ford's assembly line revolutionized the way things were manufactured. At the heart of every successful design and manufacturing company is an efficient new product development process. This process allows engineers to understand their customers' desires and make quantitative and qualitative decisions about what features to design into their product. Companies that can rapidly innovate, deploy product development strategies, and integrate tooling suppliers are likely to gain and maintain market share.

The semiconductor industry is at the heart of the expanding digital world. The world's demand for silicon is on a steep positive trajectory. Silicon has many applications within the average consumer's life. From personal laptops, to data centers, the demand for more efficient processing and memory is continually growing. Intel Corporation is a major player in the semiconductor design and manufacturing industry. In order to stay competitive in the semiconductor manufacturing industry, Intel must focus on customer integrated design, accelerated innovation,

C. Leung · A. Hsiao · M. Hobernicht · K. Camp · V. Kung
Portland State University, Portland, OR, USA

T. U. Daim (✉)
Portland State University Technology Management Doctoral Program, Portland, OR, USA

National Research University Higher School of Economics, Moscow, Russia

Chaoyang University of Technology, Taichung City, Taiwan
e-mail: tugrul.u.daim@pdx.edu

T. U. Daim, D. Meissner (eds.), *Innovation Management in the Intelligent World*, Science, Technology and Innovation Studies,
https://doi.org/10.1007/978-3-030-58301-9_2

product development strategies, tooling supplier integration, and understanding the technology life cycle of its products.

2.2 Intel's Background

Founded in 1968, Intel changed the world dramatically with its revolutionary products, from the first microprocessor to miniaturized personal computers (NUC). Intel remained competitive in the semiconductor industry through clever marketing, high-quality research and development, superior manufacturing proficiency, an open corporate culture, and legal proficiency. Its wide range of products power not only computers, but also data servers, cloud services, memory systems, graphics, microarchitectures, media interfaces, and more. In addition, Intel has stayed on top of the changing world of technologies by accumulating acquisitions and partnerships in multiple industries over the years. One key aspect of Intel's continuous growth is its progressive, customer-oriented approach to product development, as discussed in this paper.

2.3 New Product Development Analysis and Discussion

2.3.1 Accelerated Radical Innovation

Intel has taken the lead in the semiconductor industry since day one. The innovator invented the world's first metal oxide semiconductor chip, replacing magnetic-core memory chips. In 1971, Intel released their first microprocessor, Intel® 4004, which was also the first general-purpose programmable processor on the market. At the time, the concept of microprocessors was still new to the general public. The 4004 was mainly for engineers to customize with software to perform different functions in a wide variety of electronic devices. After just 1 year, Intel released Intel® 8008, which was 8-bit instead of 4-bit, supporting significantly more random access memory (RAM). The 8008 was a tremendous success; it became widely used in hundreds of products in addition to the first microcomputer in the market, including traffic lights, cash registers, industrial machines, etc.

Starting the 1980s, personal computers (PCs) became common and without much knowledge of the product, people were focused on the software, specifications, or recommendations rather than the central processing unit (CPU) inside. Intel's market share was also eroding as manufacturers preferred upstart competitors for lower costs during the recession. This prompted Intel to launch a worldwide brand marketing campaign to help users identify PCs based on Intel's valuable processors. Intel Inside® became a label everyone looked for. One important aspect of radical innovation is the creation of new knowledge and commercialization of completely novel products and ideas. Intel no longer wanted to be seen as a highly technical company whose work only engineers or scientists could relate to, but also a prevalent name in every household. Prior to the campaign, Intel had been advertising the next chips or products or partnering with other companies such as HP, Dell, etc. Using their chips, Intel started a marketing strategy known as ingredient branding, which no other company had used. Intel invested in hundreds of millions of dollars in this incredibly novel approach of rebranding itself over a period of several years, with sales of only $500 million at the time. Its devoted efforts included half of the computer manufacturers' advertising costs, elaborate and immersive exhibits at the annual CES (International Consumer Electronics Show) and high-profile TV campaigns. Within just a few years following the campaign, Intel became the largest semiconductor of the world.

From the Intel 8008, the 10 μm process to Intel's latest released chip codenamed Coffee Lake, the 10 nm process, the company made amazingly significant progress. This progress follows the model of its co-founder, Gordon Moore, who predicted that the number of transistors in a chip double every 2 years. Rather than a force of nature of any sort of scientific law, this was Intel's commitment to continual progress due to their dedication. Moore's law went on to become the widespread business model of the semiconductor industry. With radical innovation defined as improvements in known performance features of five times or greater that could take decades, Intel's incremental increase of transistors on a chip 1000 times smaller after merely 40 years was an impressive feat. Its transistor density and chip size reduction have outperformed its competitors in the market. Intel has truly achieved what many other companies strive for—accelerated radical innovation. Intel has accomplished its innovation leadership since its very first processor and has been consistent throughout the years through meticulous analysis of scientific knowledge and telecommunication tools to precipitate the diffusion of its products in the market.

Rising to the top of a cutthroat competitive market is not merely about outperforming competitors, but also the company itself. Consumers must have the desire to not only stay loyal to the brand but also spend on an upgrade from the product's predecessor. A close evaluation of Intel's last two generations of microprocessors in the market indicates how the company is still able to be ahead in the market by attaining accelerated radical innovation. A comparison test amongst a pair of Acer Swift 3 notebooks, powered by eighth Gen Core i5-8250U CPU and a seventh Gen Core i5-7200U chip and a pair of Dell XPS 13 s, powered by eighth Gen Core i7-8550U CPU and a seventh Gen, Core i7-7500U processor, reveals that eighth Gen is ~80% faster than seventh Gen on average. In sub-areas like excel spreadsheets, video transcoding, and app load times, the eighth Gen is better than its predecessor by ~65, ~60, and 56%, respectively. Intel proves its commitment and propels its innovation forward by significantly boosting product performance with powerful enhancements from generation to generation.

Intel strived to achieve accelerated radical innovation from its first microprocessor with the Intel Inside® household name. Becoming an ingredient in someone else's recipe was never appealing to ambitious companies, however, Intel leveraged this opportunity and quickly established itself as a trusted brand with assured quality. The company made the endeavor to deviate from its traditional approaches, favor long-term benefits over short-term, consider its whole network of suppliers to manufacturers to consumers, and ultimately rewarded itself with a large, global consumer base. Intel products are incorporated in not only computers nowadays, but also in numerous other cutting-edge technologies, spanning from the semiconductor industry to entertainment, business, automotive, software, and more.

2.3.2 Product Development Strategies

Product development at Intel is multifaceted, employing multiple strategies to yield a plethora of product designs and increase manufacturing capability. These strategies include leveraging internal development/manufacturing capabilities to optimize Intel's product portfolio and acquisition of startups to enhance products in their portfolio and expand into high-growth markets.

As Intel's bread-and-butter PC market matured, Intel has been on the hunt for the next big market and finding related markets to expand into. Intel coined IoT (Internet of Things), opening doors for the company to grow into novel/high-growth market segments. IoT products encompass embedded electronic packages for a broad range of applications. Intel's decisions have begun to expand past the core silicon-based product focus, however, product offerings from Intel are still stayed true to the core integrated electronics focus and established R&D structure cultivated by manufacturing. The acquisition of companies such as Alterra and Mobileye demonstrates this divergence from the core silicon business while still staying true to the mission of selling silicon. The purchase of Altera has justifications in accelerating the product development process while mutually enhancing both companies' product lines. The acquisition of Mobileye demonstrates the acquisition strategy as a way of substantially accelerating product development through the purchase of a key player to gain foothold in a desired market segment.

2.3.2.1 Identifying Core Competency

Intel is an established international company with strong technical strengths. Intel was founded in 1968 and has been in the microprocessor industry since 1985. The company currently employs approximately 102,700 employees. Intel has nine major manufacturing and R&D sites and seven test assembly sites internationally with presence in 46 countries. Research and development expenditures reached over $13 billion in 2017. Intel took the fourth position for the number of US patent assignments over 2016 as well as 2017.

These core competencies integrate together in a model Intel calls "Virtual Cycle of Growth," meaning involvement of Intel projects in all parts of a system from data center devices to end-user devices of all kinds (PC, mobile, and IoT devices) can impact the company as a whole.

Intel is organized into five broad groups: Client Computing (CCG), Data Center (DCG), Internet of Things (IOTG), Non-volatile Memory Solutions (NSG), and Programmable Solutions (PSG). Each of these groups specializes in a related microelectronics related market focus.

The Client Computing Group has been responsible for designing and manufacturing Intel's Core-branded processor families, supporting Intel's notebook and desktop product lines as well as wireless and wired connectivity products.

Data Center Group specializes in data center platform advancement and supporting Intel's Xeon Scalable processor line for enterprise, cloud, and communication infrastructure market segments.

Internet of Things Group includes all IoT platforms for automotive, industrial, retail, and other markets with embedded applications.

Non-volatile Memory Solutions Group focuses efforts on developing and manufacturing memory technologies such as 3D NAND and Optane. These technologies have been implemented in the memory market in the form of solid-state drives.

Programmable Solutions Group is focused on programmable semiconductors such as field programmable grid arrays (FPGA) and related products for markets such as industrial, military, automotive, and communications.

Moore's law has been a major reference in semiconductor technology cadence since Gordon Moore, an Intel co-founder, published the observation in 1965. Moore's law states that transistor density should double approximately every 2 years. This is a cadence that Intel has aimed to achieve with every new iteration of transistor design, vastly changing the way the semiconductor industry has operated.

A less obvious analysis of Intel's position in the market is defined by the barrier to entry in semiconductor manufacturing. While the dense IC market prescribes to Moore's law on transistor density doubling, the trend for required resources in achieving this level of technological advancement in the last decade has been an opposite trend, requiring more and more R&D, test, and manufacturing cost. This observation of increasing the capital cost of semiconductor fabrication increasing over time has been dubbed Moore's second law or Rock's law. The rising cost creates a prohibitive wall around the manufacturing industry, limiting competitors to a select few: Samsung, Taiwan Semiconductor Manufacturing Company (TSMC), and GlobalFoundaries (GF); fewer which offer full-stack design-to-manufacturing capabilities similar to Intel.

2.3.2.2 Leveraging Core Competency

Intel utilizes its technical design and manufacturing capabilities with internally designed products as well as externally designed product manufacturing. Production manufacturing facilities are designed with a "copy exactly" method, which enables smooth technology transfer between manufacturing sites through the creation of a virtual fab environment. This design allows for better cost control and production capacity.

Product manufacturing process R&D on similar product lines are carried out concurrently. For example, referencing the transistor density, product R&D of 14 and 10 nm process nodes are stagger start but have periods of overlap in development to facilitate product release at the desired cadence described by Moore's law. This enables the company to have a fluid release of products by initiating technology research early enough to allow the technology to mature before releasing into retail products.

Leveraging internal resources has led to an expanded product portfolio outside of microprocessors. Intel has expanded to auxiliary microprocessor products such as motherboard sockets, thermal solutions, and motherboard reference designs as well as server products and assemblies, although manufacturing of some of these products is not done internally. Intel employs a multi-source strategy for supply chain to manufacture certain components such as connectivity, FPGA, networking, and memory products. These subcontractors help to augment internal production capability and capacity.

Taking advantage of the decades of technical experience, advanced production capabilities, and robust validation methodology, Intel offers custom foundry manufacturing for external design firms (known as Intel Custom Foundry (ICF)). The foundry business capitalizes on the fabless model employed by many other electronics design firms. This model is built upon design firms that do not have manufacturing capabilities to outsource production to an external foundry. The technology Intel offers to their foundry clientele capitalizes on performance-relevant matured process technologies. Intel is quiet about the success of ICF, however, ICF demonstrates a product optimization by leveraging Intel's technological lead over competitors with mature technologies and manufacturing resources of the company.

2.3.2.3 Enhancement of Core Competencies

A position Intel has taken to enhance their core competencies is through the acquisition of companies in target market segments supplemental to current Intel technologies and companies which are positioned in critical industries destined for future exponential growth. These companies provide Intel with the ability to foster growth within existing product lines as well as gain access and a technical foothold into new industries. Two recent purchases exemplify these different variations of this strategy: Altera and Mobileye.

Altera specializes in programmable logic devices, with their largest deliverable being field programmable gate arrays (FPGA). These devices are integrated circuits that can be configurable by the end user to cater to their product needs. FPGAs find purpose in integration in IoT devices: an industry that encompasses a broad range of products and applications such as data center sensor monitoring systems and health care monitoring systems. FPGAs function as sensor controllers and data acquisition tools which enable IoT systems to be developed and integrated into data analysis systems for connectivity.

Intel's purchase of Altera is a beneficial one that enhances its core competency while positioning Intel as a key player in the IoT device market. Intel has had prior experience with Altera's main product line, Stratix-10 FPGA, with a fostered relationship and familiarity through Intel Custom Foundries. Intel's expertise in microprocessor design and manufacturing coupled with Altera's market position as a major player in the FPGA market and designs enable mutual benefit to both organizations. Additionally, referencing the client-to-cloud strategy, the success of Altera would directly impact Intel's IoT market. As Altera establishes itself further as the choice for FPGAs by IoT device developers, Intel sees advantages directly through Altera sales while indirectly seeing demand increase in many related technologies also supported by Intel (data centers, wireless technologies, etc.).

The acquisition of Mobileye demonstrates a product strategy that diverges from the traditional silicon-based business Intel has pursued. Mobileye is a company that focuses on camera recognition software to enable autonomous driving vehicle abilities along with collaborations with governments and crowdsourcing for road data collection. The company has had its technologies implemented into over a million vehicles on the road today, spanning from Audi to Honda. These commercial technologies currently do not enable fully autonomous driving capabilities, however, it is the goal of the company.

This market has been identified by Intel to be a substantial growth market. Intel estimates the market can be worth up to $70 billion by 2030. The benefits, however, are mutual between the two companies. Mobileye brings to Intel new technologies and a leading position in the autonomous driving automobile market while Intel is able to supplement Mobileye's hardware efforts with their System-on-Chip (SoC) and FPGA product lines. Indirectly, Intel expects to see farther-reaching impacts into its data center market through an increase in demand for cloud computing resources. This purchase stands as staking a claim in a novel growth market that has benefits that span multiple business units within the organization.

2.3.3 Integrating Tooling Suppliers

The new product development process has many multivariable decisions embedded within it. When each one of these decisions arises, engineers and managers must hold design reviews to determine what the best solution is. Typically a decision matrix is used to decompose a decision. Key variables are assigned weightings, and the solution with the highest score is selected. This static method of decision support has its limitations. For one, this method is unable to account for uncertainty within weighting. Each weighting in reality is a stochastic random variable, taking on a range of values. Dynamic decision support is needed to understand the variability in the new product development process.

Thus managers and engineers can define probability distributions for the sub-variables and link them to the final variables. Monte Carlo simulation can be utilized to understand the probability of success of a product proposal. It should be noted that at Intel, many sub-variables are determined by their tooling suppliers. Product cost and available resources and affected by the wafer fabrication equipment used. The window of opportunity is affected by how quickly new manufacturing equipment can be developed. Product quality and margin rate are directly affected by the performance and quality of wafer fabrication equipment. Because of the importance of these sub-variables, it is vital that Intel integrates their tooling suppliers in its new product development process.

An important aspect of Intel's new product development strategy is understanding its suppliers of wafer fabrication equipment. Intel's corporate structure is designed to develop and manufacture new products. They act as a central integrator of new products and technologies. The wafer fabrication equipment used for etching and deposition processes is designed by tooling suppliers such as Lam Research, Tokyo Electron, ASML, and Applied Materials. Companies hold the majority of the wafer fabrication equipment market share. This competition between suppliers is advantageous for Intel because it promotes innovative design, and competition between companies to keep pace with Intel's innovation.

Intel and companies like Lam Research must have an ongoing dialog about the capabilities of the wafer fabrication equipment. For example, when Intel is developing a new advanced memory chip with copper interconnects, they are more than likely to purchase a Saber electrochemical deposition machine. The Saber machine can be used by Intel for "High-throughput, void-free fill with superior defect density performance for advanced technology nodes" Lam. The exact performance parameters of the Saber would need to be understood by Intel design engineers prior to finalizing their processor design. If an Intel engineer determines that small additional features are needed, often times they can be quickly added to the wafer fabrication equipment. However, for larger innovations, Intel will need to integrate their tooling supplier months, if not years, ahead of production to ensure the design criteria can be met. If Intel fails to align on a proper timeline with its tooling suppliers, they are setting up their new product launches for production failure.

2.3.4 Technology Life Cycle

2.3.4.1 Computer Processing Unit (CPU)

Intel's iconic microprocessor began with the first commercial 4004 processor in March of 1971. The release for the 33 years would be consistent and provide a prime life cycle of roughly 2–3 years per CPU. After the release of the next generation, CPU production of the last CPU will slowly be ramped down and prices will be cut. Driving the short relevant life cycle is the steadily increasing number of transistors available on every newer processor. This short life cycle makes the time an incredibly valuable asset in the release of microprocessors and establishes a barrier to entry to the industry. Each generation of microprocessors that reduces critical dimensions results in faster performance, reduced energy consumption, and a lower cost per transistor. These three items are the key performance indicators that PC and data center customers desire in processors. The expectations for the product development of the next generation of chips has been predictable for the research and development team.

This traditionally predictable product life cycle is simple in principle and heavily dictates every decision made in the industry about product life cycles. It offers the benefit of giving the industry leader a dominant market share but demands consistent innovation to retain market share. Intel maintained the improvement at consistent intervals with a "tick tock" model to vary the focus on each generation of microprocessor. The Tick model would represent a new manufacturing process resulting in a smaller critical dimension. The Tock model after would be the same gate size as the last Tick model but have a different microarchitecture on the chip. The new microarchitecture would squeeze the gate closer together to fit more transistors on the chip without shrinking the gates themselves. In the last decade, the thermal properties of silicon have reduced the gains expected in the clock speed of the chips. This forced companies to seek creative options in order to improve performance and resulted in more cores available in many consumer PC microprocessors. By sharing the workload in parallel across multiple cores the performance of the chips would increase with compatible software.

2.3.4.2 Internet of Things (IoT)

The IoT market is a new field for Intel where many different smart connected devices to provide innovation in a variety of fields. This field will require custom-built processors called Field Programmable Gate Arrays (FPGAs) in the devices and large data centers to interpret the information received. The data center side of the business will have predictable new product development expectations just like the rest of the CPU industry while the IoT devices themselves will vary. Countless devices will be connected to the internet and together they will solve engineering problems that currently seem impossible. Intel's business justification can be broken down into securely dealing with IoT devices, building an intelligent system, and providing customers end to end analytics. Developing IoT can provide Intel revenue directly from the services they provide and indirectly from the cloud analytics that will require additional server processors to review data.

Some IoT devices will power cheap sensors that monitor temperatures of homes, the humidity of rooms, and weather fridge doors are open or closed. Many of these devices will be cheap and have a low importance if they do fail. Certain IoT devices will be responsible for saving lives and require large amounts of validation and testing. Security will be a top priority for almost all data as companies and advertisers will view the data as valuable IP that may contain insight on consumers.

Autonomous driving is an incredibly new technology that will present unique challenges to product development and life cycles. The technology will continue to improve drastically over the next decade which will require consistent improvements in performance to remain competitive. The validation of the hardware will require external validation to ensure that the products are safe for the consumers. Cars themselves are driven for a long time after they are purchased with the average age of a car on the road in the USA being 12 years. Certain consumers will pay for the latest technology while others will use older technology to reduce the cost of the devices in their affordable cars.

FPGAs were a $6 billion industry in 2017 and are expected to grow to $10 billion by the year 2023. They represent a growing need for purpose-built chips that can efficiently, securely, and cost-effectively to accomplish device-specific tasks. Intel's acquisition of Aletra for $16.7 billion on December 28, 2015 help Intel gain the intellectual property needed to enter portions of the FPGA market. Companies want FPGAs that have a lower fixed initial design cost and a lower variable cost associated with manufacturing each. Having extra features on generic FPGAs can cost extra money per unit and result in poor performance. Generic FPGAs fail to do a very specific task well that certain devices need resulting in longer computational times and higher battery usage. Technology life cycles of FPGAs will vary greatly depending on consumer adoption habits and the demand of the device itself. Meaningful improvements in battery life, features, and security will drive demand for the latest model of FPGAs. The usable lifetime of specific devices will likely dictate how long the FPGAs will be expected to last. Cars may need reliable performance for 25 years while mobile.

2.3.5 *User-Centered Design of Products*

Companies' success is largely dependent upon the user-centered design of products and Intel is no exception. According to Intel company values, customer-centric work is based upon three pillars: why they do it, how they do it, and what they do. Intel believes "Design thinking" is the future of work. These kinds of design innovations can play an integral role by making human-to-device interactions more intuitive, individualized, and convenient. Creating superior user experiences can ultimately translate into a competitive advantage.

2.3.5.1 User-Centered Design Methods

Intel employs several methods in user-centered design of new products which include research studies, the Intel User Experience Lab, and various business acquisitions.

Intel was one of the first companies to research consumer acceptance in the self-driving car industry. In March 2017, Intel announced plans to purchase Mobileye, an

Israeli developer of autonomous driving systems. General acceptance of autonomous vehicles is low. This data is based upon two independent surveys conducted by Morning Consult in 2018. The polls show that mistrust in autonomous driving increased following two fatal accidents involving autonomous vehicles in March of 2018.

Even without technological flaws, acceptance, and adoption of technology are impossible if people are afraid to use the technology. Intel is an advocate for the social integration of self-driving cars. Intel conducted acceptance testing, a type of trial that is becoming more common in the food and software industries that analyzes consumer feedback on new products. Currently, no product in these industries is launched without extensive feedback from testers. In turn, developers are able to make products more user-friendly. Intel conducted this type of study to analyze consumer trust in self-driving cars. In general, people are wary of safety levels, surrendering control to a machine, and many must overcome psychological discomfort. Intel Autonomous Driving Group investigated whether participants who had never ridden in a self-driving car would change their mind after experiencing it first-hand. In the study, passengers were interviewed before, during, and after riding in an autonomous car in order to track any change in opinion. The cars used were Ford Fusion sedans that have a minimalist addition of a camera on the top roof of the vehicle. The following results were found: passengers reported that seeing the steering wheel moving without a driver contributed to anxiety; voice control between humans and machines eases feelings of lack of control; and passengers expressed concerns over the special needs of small children, the elderly, and those with disabilities. At the time, it was one of the first studies of its kind, but more research is to be done. Currently, there is no standardized testing model for self-driving cars, but one may be developed in the future to standardize testing methods.

In the Intel User Experience Lab, Intel products are researched with the consumer in mind; using technical equipment, the consumer experience is replicated by stimulating the senses of sight, touch, and hearing. Display testing is conducted using a variety of tools. A consistent pattern indicates a consistent picture, whereas a non-uniform pattern indicates an inconsistent picture.

Touch is analyzed using a robotic arm and display testing. The robotic arm lets researchers conduct tests in a repeated and controlled fashion, with the ability to simulate fast, slow, and erratic movements. A camera captures a video of the robot arm's actions. The footage is fed into a spreadsheet and analyzed to help researchers understand what needs to be improved to satisfy the user.

Sound is analyzed using a hemi-anechoic chamber, where in-depth testing is conducted on speech recognition, audio, and voice quality testing. A head-shaped device can measure pressure on the ear and distance from the mouth to understand ways that humans react with audio devices. Different voice types are simulated as well as background sounds such as forest environment, elementary school playground, and train stations among others.

Through numerous business acquisitions, Intel is capable of developing more user-centric products. In 2013, Intel acquired Omek Interactive, a company that develops gesture-based technologies; through this acquisition, Intel hoped to increase its capability of delivering more immersive perceptual computing experiences. In 2013, Intel acquired Indisys, a Spanish natural language recognition startup that developed artificial intelligence technology in the form of a human image that converses fluently in multiple languages across different platforms. In 2015, Intel purchased a 20% stake in Vuzix, a smart glasses manufacturer. In 2015, Intel purchased cognitive computing company Saffron Technology. In August 2016, Intel purchased deep-learning startup Nervana Systems.

2.3.5.2 Intel's User-Centered Products

In addition to fostering a creative, human-centered culture, Intel develops products that cater to the needs of consumers and industries alike.

Intel offers a wide range of CPU products suitable for different devices with their scalable processors. Intel Core processors can be chosen depending on the type of device and whether the customer prioritizes performance or mobility. Collectively, Intel Quark, Intel Atom, Intel Core, and Intel Xeon processors each support a wide range of performance points with a common set of code.

Intel has also worked to improve the user experience of virtual reality (VR) gaming. Intel designers worked to optimize the user experience and performance of Code51—the first worldwide mech arena VR game supporting Oculus Rift, HTC Vive, PSVR, and Pico VR platforms. The game has been released in over 3000 VR arcades in China and is targeted for release in PlayStation Store, Oculus Store, and Steam in Q2 of 2018. Intel enhanced visual and audial aspects of the game through the use of its Intel Core i7 processors and included features such as 3D audio, object destruction, enhanced CPU particles, and additional background objects. Intel achieved this improvement by utilizing seven design points of immersive VR games. First, they determined the choice of immersive motion tracking system to drive player movements in the virtual world of a game by comparing the tracking system's pros and cons with the game's mechanics. For instance, for Code51, the virtual cockpit tracking system was chosen for the ability to move continuously in VR, compatibility with current premium VR helmets, alignment with the "sitting down" style of the arena game, and to permit longer gameplay. Intel designers also worked to alleviate VR motion sickness through UI design, level design, rendering performance, reducing acceleration and angular velocity, and dynamically reducing the field of view. Steps were also taken to enhance the spectator viewing experience for e-sports. Another issue that was mitigated was the low sharpness of current VR HMDs compared to conventional displays. CPU performance was also optimized to prevent stalling the VR scene rendering. Lastly, the user experience of the VR game was improved by utilizing all available computational resources on a hardware platform as much as possible, resulting in a deeper immersive experience. These features significantly increased the immersion of Code51 on high-end CPUs without a performance drop, since most of the computation was offloaded to idle CPU cores.

Internet of Things (IoT) refers to the network of devices, vehicles, and home appliances embedded with electronics, software, sensors, and connectivity which enables these items to connect and exchange data without human interaction, resulting in many benefits such as improved efficiency, saved time and money, and reduced human exertion. This network of devices reinforces user-centered design by catering to the individual need of the user. Intel IoT products are present in every consumer and industrial application imaginable: retail digital signage and kiosks; retail analytics and operations; healthcare analytics, infrastructure, and products; financial services; smart cities, buildings, and homes; automotive and connected transportation; industrial automation; and energy. IoT devices cannot operate independently; significant data analysis—using servers—is necessary to run IoT systems. For instance, a self-driving car generates 4 TB per day and a plane generates 40 TB. Each of these systems needs to be connected in a feedback mechanism that can generate actionable intelligence, through AI or high-level data analytics. These IoT systems cannot run without powerful back end processing services. Smart homes, autonomous driving, industrial systems, and energy are utilizing an increasing number of sensors, but they cannot be enabled without a system to collect and analyze this data to make informed decisions. The recent restructuring of the Intel IoT group has shifted its focus to higher end and more compute-intensive applications such as autonomous vehicles, drones, and healthcare, with Atom, Core, and Xeon chipsets. Though this area is lower volume than "gadgets," it has better margins that better fit into Intel's strengths. These are areas where Intel has significant intellectual property to exploit: CPU, GPUs, storage, and connectivity for analytics, AI, ML, big data processing, and network operations.

2.4 Conclusion

This case study has identified five perspectives within the topic of new product development in which to analyze Intel Corporation. Intel focuses on accelerated radical innovation by meticulously investigating the product development process from initial concept to commercialization, adoption, and societal impact. Product performance increases substantially from generation to generation as a result of regimented innovative research process and implementation. Intel has defined product development strategies that include leveraging internal development/manufacturing capabilities to optimize Intel's product portfolio and acquisition of startups to enhance products in their portfolio to expand into high-growth markets. On the manufacturing side, Intel focuses on integrating tooling suppliers in their development process to ensure they have the manufacturing technology required. Collaboration between Intel and tooling suppliers allows for customer interactions and inputs in tooling supplier product design. This allows for improved product functionality custom catered to client needs.

Intel always understood where its products are in their respective technology lifecycles to understand the engineering expectations of their devices. User-centered product focus from the conception of a product is a key component of the methodology Intel employs in product feature design. Maintaining close ties to end users allow Intel to create products that better cater to customer needs. By employing these five strategies Intel has secured their place as a leader in the semiconductor design and manufacturing industry.

Acknowledgement Tugrul Daim's contribution to the book chapter is based on the study funded by the Basic Research Program of the National Research University Higher School of Economics (HSE) and by the Russian Academic Excellence Project '5-100'.

References[1]

8th Gen Intel Core Processors (2018, April). https://newsroom.intel.com/wp-content/uploads/sites/11/2018/04/8th-gen-intel-core-h-series-press-deck.pdf

Anthony S (2012, March 7) The future of computers: 3D chip stacking. https://www.extremetech.com/computing/119843-the-future-of-computers-3d-chip-stacking

Baldwin R (2017, August 24) Intel studies how to make people accept self-driving cars. Engadget. https://www.engadget.com/2017/08/24/intel-studies-how-to-make-people-accept-self-driving-cars/. Accessed 14 Aug 2018

Bers J, Dismukes J, Miller L, Dubrovensky A (2009) Accelerated radical innovation: Theory and application. Technol Forecast Soc Chang 76(1):165–177

Bessant J (2001) Radical Innovation: How Mature Companies can Outsmart Upstarts. Technovation 21(10):706–707

Bohr M (2017, May 8) Intel inside the package. https://semiengineering.com/intel-inside-the-package/

Deagon B (2018, January 9) IBM holds patent lead for 25th straight year. Samsung, Intel Follow. https://www.nasdaq.com/article/ibm-holds-patent-lead-for-25th-straight-year-samsung-intel-follow-cm902685

Hruska J (2016, October 10) Intel launches Stratix 10: Altera FPGA combined with ARM CPU, 14nm manufacturing. https://www.extremetech.com/computing/237338-intel-launches-stratix-10-altera-fpga-combined-with-arm-cpu-14nm-manufacturing

Int J Innov Technol Manag (2009) 6(2):135–153

Intel (2017, June 7) Enabling great user experiences with user-centered design. Intel Software Developer Zone. https://software.intel.com/en-us/articles/enabling-great-user-experiences-with-user-centered-design

Intel (2018, May 22) Optimizing the user experience of VR games on IA for E-sports. Intel Software Developer Zone. https://software.intel.com/en-us/articles/Optimizing-the-user-experience-of-vr-games-on-ia-for-e-sports. Accessed 14 Aug 2018

Intel (n.d.) Intel timeline: a history of innovation. [online] https://www.intel.com/content/www/us/en/history/historic-timeline.html. Accessed 2 Aug 2018

Intellectual Property Owners Association Recognizes Intel's Patent Prowess (2017, June 12). https://newsroom.intel.com/news/intellectual-property-owners-association-recognizes-intels-patent-prowess/

[1]Uncited references were used to develop this case.

Internet of Things (2018, August 14). https://www.intel.com/content/www/us/en/internet-of-things/products/programmable/overview.html

"Internet of Things Case Studies, Snapshots, and Blueprints" Intel. https://www.intel.com/content/www/us/en/internet-of-things/solution-blueprints-and-case-studies.html. Accessed 14 Aug 2018

Krzanich B (2017, December) 2017 Intel annual report. http://s22.q4cdn.com/548661872/files/doc_downloads/Intel_Annual_Report_Final-3.20.pdf

Krzanich B (2018, June 19) Safety is why Intel bought mobileye. https://newsroom.intel.com/editorials/safety-is-why-intel-bought-mobileye/

McCreay F (2018, March 15) Industry 4.0 demands the co-evolution of workers and manufacturing operations. https://newsroom.intel.com/wp-content/uploads/sites/11/2018/04/report-intel-manufacturing-research.pdf

McFarlane G (2018) Inside Intel: a look at the mega chipmaker. [online] Investopedia. https://www.investopedia.com/articles/markets/100214/inside-intel-look-mega-chipmaker.asp. Accessed 5 Aug 2018

Perry TS (2018, March 2) Hey big spender! (For Semiconductor R&D, That's Intel). https://spectrum.ieee.org/view-from-the-valley/semiconductors/design/hey-big-spender-for-semiconductor-rd-thats-intel. Accessed 8 Aug 2018

Piltch A (2017) Intel 8th Gen vs 7th Gen CPUs: Kaby lake refresh is a lot faster. [online] Laptopmag.com. https://www.laptopmag.com/articles/kaby-lake-refresh-8th-gen-vs-7th-gen. Accessed 10 Aug 2018.

Pressman A (2016, November 8) Intel may have new super-fast technology to connect chips. http://fortune.com/2016/11/08/intel-super-fast-technology-to-connect-chips/

Richter F (2018, April 6) Infographic: fatal accidents damage trust in autonomous driving. Statista. https://www.statista.com/chart/13450/perceived-safety-of-self-driving-cars/. Accessed 14 Aug 2018

Rohan (2018, August 14) FPGA market worth 9.50 Billion USD by 2023. https://www.marketsandmarkets.com/PressReleases/fpga.asp

SABRE Product Family (n.d.). https://www.marketsandmarkets.com/PressReleases/fpga.asp. Accessed 14 Aug 2018

Schaller RR (1997) Moore's law: past, present and future. IEEE Spectr 34(6):52–59. https://doi.org/10.1109/6.591665

Shapiro G (n.d.) The marketing backstory of how Intel became a household name. [Online] Fast Company. Accessed 5 Aug 2018

Staff, PCMag (2013, September 13) Inside the Intel user experience lab. PCMAG. https://www.pcmag.com/feature/315817/inside-the-intel-user-experience-lab. Accessed 14 Aug 2018

Stevens T (2018, May 16) How Intel and Mobileye are taking a simpler path to autonomy. https://www.cnet.com/roadshow/news/intel-mobileye-self-driving-car/

Surprising changes in semiconductor equipment market share in 2017 (n.d.). https://electroiq.com/2018/01/surprising-changes-in-semiconductor-equipment-market-share-in-2017/. Accessed 14 Aug 2018

Chapter 3
Impact of Technology in the Future of Sports

M. Krishna Priya, Raj Srinivasan, G. Harshitha, Shraddha Zingade, Nihal Jeena, Tugrul U. Daim, and Dirk Meissner

3.1 Impact of Digital Technology in Sports

Digitalization in sports provides a guide for future innovation showing the opportunities for innovation in sports sector. It defines a road map for R&D meeting health, social, environmental, and market needs. The effects of technologies such as mobile, cloud, artificial intelligence, sensors, and analytics are accelerating progress exponentially. Today, in sports sector right from organizing the event till broadcasting the sport everything is digitized which is redefining the traditional business. It is also creating a great platform for audience to discuss, share their opinions, and interact with their favorite player, sport, or team. Digital innovation increase fair play and good governance have success in revenues and expenses.

The case study focuses closely on the impacts of technology on sports.

As we are switching spotlight to science and technology, we explore the influence of digital technology in sports to help improve the athletes, sports, and gaming experience. While sports is gaining momentum there are so many factors that are digitally driven that is impacting the consumer, business, and the commercial aspects. For instance, the amount of people watching video streaming for sports on TV is declining and viewership is changing to mobile streaming for the first time.

M. Krishna Priya · R. Srinivasan · G. Harshitha · S. Zingade · N. Jeena
Portland State University, Portland, OR, USA

T. U. Daim (✉)
Portland State University Technology Management Doctoral Program, Portland, OR, USA

National Research University Higher School of Economics, Moscow, Russia

Chaoyang University of Technology, Taichung City, Taiwan
e-mail: tugrul.u.daim@pdx.edu

D. Meissner
National Research University Higher School of Economics, Moscow, Russia

T. U. Daim, D. Meissner (eds.), *Innovation Management in the Intelligent World*, Science, Technology and Innovation Studies,
https://doi.org/10.1007/978-3-030-58301-9_3

People are switching from subscribing to cable channels to Netflix and YouTube. Younger people are following their favorite gamers and gaming online and the growth has to come from digital means to attract new fans. Moreover, new digital technologies like GPS watches, Fitness trackers, Heart Rate Monitors, etc. have become the means of analytics that informs coaches, sports scientist, or medical staff making decisions about how to prepare and condition their athletes by capturing the data and insights of athletes and calculating their practice and work progress. With precise information by the use of advanced algorithms and metrics, it allows them to get the best out of the individual player with the team environment.

Intel's involvement in digital technologies like 360 replay, drone technology, True View technology, true VR technology has created a really dynamic way of viewing live events. Whether you are sitting at the stadium or at home, it allows a fan to see different replay angels with 3D footages, which is the most unique way to watch a game that they would have never able to see. Moreover, it allows players and coaches to learn from a 3D angle, to learn from their mistakes, and apply their learnings into the next game and become a game changer. These technologies have not only changed the viewing aspects but have also changed the way that everybody works within the team by contributing toward making more informed and more accurate decisions.

To sport fan's "Digital" is the sum of all on-demand ways they can interact with their favorite team, league, or event. Digital Technology has transformed the traditional way of watching the sport. Today, either for sport information or entertainment or for any sport event transaction everything is digitalized. Social media has become a major platform for fans to raise their voice and maintain relationship with their favorite sport or team or player. Social media—like YouTube, Twitter, and Facebook—has wide reach, technology, and money to interact with people. Few media channels like YouTube are winning the broadcast rights of a sport with their technological advancements and ability to serve the audience with services like Live streaming and on-demand services.

In the sports business, digital technology is like an iceberg imaginary, where only the tip is visible. That is audience enjoys a seamless digital experience delivered and relevant for fans. But, beneath the tip of this digital iceberg it includes many factors to be considered. Among them are finding a new strategy, governance models, cultural change, technology investment, and new approaches to innovation that create a digital line of sight through all operational areas.

Technology in sports is shrinking the gap between the spectator and their favorite sport or player by providing accurate and timely information. With this, the audience is able to see what is happening on the field of play or training pitch and could expect what is going to happen. Due to this audience is more connected, updated, and getting into the game rather than just being a spectator. It has augmented performance, pushed boundaries, and removed barriers.

Three areas in which digital technologies affected the most are:

1. Over the top content

   Today, we have several options for watching sports. We have a variety of options for screens through which we can satisfy our passion for watching it. We need not stick to the traditional TV broadcasting schedules.
2. Improving Performance

   Video technology-enabled coaches and athletes to better understand their own performances and provided a great platform to develop important gains and enhance their performance.
3. Electronic Sports

   E-sports is a competition with video games. It is played between individual players particularly professionals. Intel holds a tournament for e-sports called Intel Extreme Masters which provide live broadcasts of the competition, and prize money to competitors. Some of the e-sports sponsored by Intel include events like Starcraft II, Counter-Strike: Global Offensive, Quake Live, League of Legends, and Hearthstone: Heroes of Warcraft.

Innovation of Digital Technology has led to the conception of many mobile applications to track our health metrics. These applications are assisting athletes and coaches in their training for achieving better results. They are digitized and tracks athletes sport activities, nutrition, and strength. Which in turn helps coaches and athletes in improving their performance with good governance and fair play.

Market research conducted by ABI (2014) on digitalization in various fields like sports, health, clothing, and smart devices showed that there is significant growth for sport trackers in the coming years. Digital technology thus is very helpful for the sports industry and its need is growing rapidly in sports when compared to other industries.

Also, according to Business Insider (BI intelligence) in 2016, sports shifts its way to digital technology by 60% from 2005 to 2016.

3.2 Intel

3.2.1 Intel's Current Position in Sports

Intel's sports group was created in fall 2017 after Intel acquired the Virtual Reality startup company Voke. Intel is investing in what is changing the entire world, that is, digital transformation aiming to become a data company. When data is collected it should be analyzed and used later. As Intel was looking at many such opportunities where they can invest and get the highest ROI, sports emerged as a field with high opportunities for this goal. One such field with good opportunities for growth is the game viewing field. Thus, Intel aims at giving fans the best experience of watching any game in 3D and a virtually real environment (https://www.geekwire.com/2017/intel-investing-sports-tech-giant-sees-opportunity-help-athletes-fans-leagues/).

Intel introduced four major technologies to the world of sports, namely:

1. Intel True Virtual Reality
2. Intel 360° Replay (Intel True View)
3. Intel Drones
4. Intel 5G

1. Intel True Virtual Reality

   Intel True Virtual Reality was launched with the aim of giving all the viewers a front-row experience of watching the game. It requires the viewers to have a VR headset, a mobile device connected to Intel's True VR Technology. Using this, even from our couch, we are able to transport ourselves to the best seat in the stadium and enjoy the game in a virtually real environment from our own seat. Every stadium has 30–40 5 K cameras that capture the game from all possible views. 1 TB of images is gathered and processed to create one frame of image to show the viewers. In the Pyeongchang Olympics, True VR became very popular although it worked better for indoor games and smaller stadiums rather than outdoor games. It was successful in Ski Jumping and Figure Skating more than other games.
2. Intel 360° Replay (Intel True View)

   Intel True View was launched as a part of the Virtual Reality domain in sports to see all the key moments of a game from every possible angle be it from the viewer's point of view or the player's point of view, we can see both. To achieve this, Intel acquired the company Replay Technologies which was pretty well established in the field of Virtual Reality for sports. It uses high-resolution cameras that are installed in all arenas around the world. We can see highlights, replays, and all the key moments from 360° and enjoy the moment more. Currently, 360° technology is being adopted by all the major leagues in the world. This technology completely avoids any mistakes that can happen from referees and umpires. Currently, NBA stadiums, San Antonio Spurs, Golden State Warriors, and Cleveland Cavaliers stadiums have this technology installed (https://iq.intel.com/360-degree-replay-technology-brings-fans-into-the-future-of-sports/).

   Smallest detail of the game, be it LeBron James' angle of holding the ball or be it Messi's leg while kicking are broadcasted in real time to all the viewers to enjoy. It is assumed that once viewers get used to watching a game at 360° they will find it hard to go back.
3. Intel Drones

   Intel has created many varieties of drones for various purposes. Intel is expanding the potential of drones to solve issues related to oil and gas, energy, construction, and agriculture business. Intel has also designed a drone that is specifically designed for light shows. The aim of this technology is to redefine the entertainment business and create new experiences in the air. These new types of lighting drones are named as "shooting stars" as they look like stars when they are displayed in the night sky. These drones are lightweight and can only be used for lighting purposes. Intel has created multiple world records for their light show. Initially, they send 100 drones to the sky. The next target was sending 500 drones.

The light show has been conducted in many parts of the world, the recent being the Winter Olympics at South Korea.

During the Winter Olympics, Intel aimed at flying 1218 drones for the opening ceremony and created a world record for "most unmanned aerial vehicles airborne simultaneously." But due to the number of people present and safety concerns they aired a pre-recorded show. The concept of drone technology enables hundreds of Intel's shooting star drones to be controlled by one pilot.

4. Intel 5G

   Intel aims at bringing the worlds of wireless, computing, and cloud together in a seamlessly connected, very powerful 5G. With Intel 5G Viewers can control the time, target, even the angle of what they're viewing." By 2020, 50 million smart devices are expected to be in use of 5G. It will enable a variety of new capabilities, user experiences, and devices like self-driving cars. They have also promised that in 2020 5G is going to be fully operational.

3.2.2 Intel Collaborations and Vision

Intel established close links with many broadcasters during the various events. During Rio Games in 2016, NBC broadcasted the openings in virtual reality for the first time. In November 2017, Intel announced its partnership with Turner sports for a multiyear to broadcast NBA games in virtual reality using Intel True View technology. Intel has tie-ups with other broadcasters like Fox Sports, ABC, ESPN, CBS, Turner Sports that broadcast Intel's True View technology for highlights, and even for the whole games.

Intel's major long-term collaboration with the National Basketball Association (NBA) and National Football League (NFL) has brought upon installation of Intel's True View and True VR technology to major football and basketball games. Along with the Olympics, Intel also has tied-up with LaLiga, El Clasico, and UK's Golf Player's association to implement this technology. Currently, in all these stadiums 5 K cameras for broadcasting real-time games are being installed.

Intel's aim is to provide new viewing experience for sports enthusiasts and to compliment TV broadcasting coverage of sports with its technologies. Its goal is to develop ultimate fantasy sports experience. With Intel vision of sports immersion, everyone will be able to get into the game instead of just being a spectator. Intel is always moving forward in exploring new technologies that make sports immersion a reality within the next few years.

3.2.2.1 Future Plans

Intel is planning on introducing volumetric video for the next Olympics. Its aim is to do real-time 3D manipulation of all images and videos. Intel is already working on the technologies in its roadmap for the upcoming Olympics. They are also looking forward to expanding their partnerships with various broadcasters.

Along with the existing technologies, Intel promises a complete 5G experience until the next Olympics and will definitely have more innovative technologies to improve the sports experience more. As mentioned earlier, Intel also has ongoing research going with Stanford university to build a concussion mouthguard that analyses an athlete's hit better and helps doctors treat them. Although this is just a research project, whether Intel will expand more in the field of making athletes better is unknown. Intel has ongoing research to track the trajectory of a ball by embedding chips in balls to get a better look at how the ball moves in an ongoing game.

3.2.2.2 Nike

Nike Lacing Technology

It is the reality that people can actually feel with their shoes using adaptive lacing. It contains of a lace engine down at the bottom of the shoe with a housing engine so that it remains protected and attached to a fit system, a flywire that actually comes up through both sides of the shoe that goes and wraps around your foot. When the user steps in there is a heel sensor, that the lace engine will run and tighten down the fit system and it will sense a certain tension around your foot, and then it will stop. There are two buttons on one side of the shoe, minus (−) to loosen up and plus (+) to tighten up and to adjust it simply throughout your day which takes less than a second to adjust it, instead of tying your laces every time you want to make an adjustment. Also, the lights in the shoe tell you about when the battery is fully charged which is going to last through roughly about two weeks, so when your battery is full it becomes blue, when it is yellow which means you have few more days and when it is red you should get it to the charger right away. These products will change, adapt, and become more useful for performance from just being able to adjust it on the fly, for instance, at the beginning of a basketball versus the halftime, the beginning of a marathon versus the end of the marathon, the feet swell and sweat due to the environmental changes and these shoes allows you to have control of it and being able to adjust it when required by pressing the button quickly, making the quality of life just enormous.

Nike +

The connected products developed under the Nike+ umbrella leverage vast amounts of very accurate customer data.

- Nike Air VaporMax

  Nike uses a very new technology in shoes today. Vapormax sole is very complex but provides a very light and flexible shoes.

- Mercurial Superfly
  Nike used the flyknit technology on a soccer shoe creating a very efficient shoe.

3.3 SWOT Analysis

3.3.1 Intel in Sports

Intel created its sports division only two years back and they partnered with the Olympics only 8 months before the games. Thus, they are rather new in this area. Intel aims at being a data-driven company and not just a chip manufacturer. That is one reason why Intel entered into this business. Intel concentrated on inventing new ways of experiencing the game as they found that it was the aspect of sports in which technology could make a huge impact. Apart from creating a viewing experience for users, Intel is also involved in a research project which aims at the well-being of athletes. Intel is partnering with a prominent university to create concussion mouthguards for athletes.

Intel came up with a lot of amazing technologies for this Olympics: Intel True VR, True View, Drones, 5G, and has a lot more are on their roadmap for the next Olympics in Tokyo. Intel received mixed feedback for VR technology in the Olympics. They broadcasted 30 events with the help of VR technology. The feedbacks depended on the games that were broadcasted. For some sports which take place in a small area the feedback was not very positive. The most liked games were indoor games like Ice Skating and Figure Skating. Games with bigger stadiums or outdoor stadiums had a few negative responses.

3.3.1.1 Strengths (s)

One major strength Intel has is its brand advantage. Intel is one of the world's top semiconductor chip manufacturer. Intel acquired Nervana and Movidius to generate an AI portfolio. Nervana chips are 10 times faster than the traditional chips. Nervana chips can transfer in and out of 2.5 terabytes data per second.

Intel's vision for giving ultimate viewing experience is its great strength that builds confidence in them and encourage for new ideas.

3.3.1.2 Weakness (w)

Intel technologies are pretty expensive and have low demand due to high technology content. It needs further exploration of more valuable partnerships to gain footholds in new global markets. In addition, Intel needs to stay agile in risk-taking for more innovation.

3.3.1.3 Opportunities (o)

- IOC (International Olympic Committee) has announced Intel as its official partner through 2020 and was also announced as a partner for NBA. Intel helps athletes and coaches in their training programs with their wearable devices.

3.3.1.4 Threats (t)

The biggest threat found after using Intel's Virtual Reality is social isolation. Viewers can immerse themselves so much into the game that they lose grip with reality. The technology can be a fun and adventurous experience until it starts affecting the viewer's notion of what is real.

3.3.2 Nike in Sports

The impact of technology in the sporting industry targets all tiers of sporting people. The top levels of sporting people are the athletes followed by the people who play the sport casually. The next level is the lifestyle people who are more concerned on comfort more than performance. The top tier people are the premium athletes and technology helps them in winning competitions by improving their micro second's performance. The next set of people are the casual people who play sports casually and not play them professionally. It really helps them to get a sense of achievement by comparing their performances on a day to day basis. Technologies like wearables fit in this class. The last set of people are the ones who are mainly using technologies for lifestyle changes. Comfort shoes with best technology normally help them.

3.3.2.1 Strengths (s)

Nike has the best product quality which makes it a top brand across the globe. The distribution chain is very strong which makes the product available everywhere. It is one of the early leaders in the sports digital technology. A strong digital sports team funded with money and people which concentrates exclusively on digital products.

3.3.2.2 Weaknesses (w)

Nike is largely dependent on the footwear products while other branded products are not as strong. It possesses limited tracking technology and is not a technology company and has to rely on other technological companies.

Nike has a Semi-closed architecture.

3.3.2.3 Opportunities (o)

Nike has lots of available digital technological innovations that might open the gateways for further technological advancements. The data collected from NIKE+ and NIKE ID might help them to understand the customer needs and choices and might lead to new designs. It provides training and coaching advice where the data collected might help to understand the runner's performance and give training advice if needed.

3.3.2.4 Threats (t)

A new competitor entering the market will end up in stiff competition. Nike will have to maintain simplicity.

3.4 Conclusion

Intel has done wonders in the field of improving sports' viewing experience for their fans. They introduced the world to four major technologies namely—Intel True View, Intel 360 degree replay, Intel Drones, and Intel 5G. Intel's tie-up with the Olympics given them a broader platform to showcase their talent to the whole world and in turn make higher profits due to broader platform. Along, with the Olympics, Intel also has collaborations with National Football League (NFL), LaLiga, and UK's Golf Player's association and has Intel's high-resolution cameras installed there.

Intel has tie-ups with multiple broadcasters like Fox Sports, ABC, ESPN, Turner Sports that broadcast Intel's True View technology for highlights, and even for the whole games.

Intel has not entered the world of improving an athlete's performance as yet but has ongoing medical research going with Stanford university to create a concussion mouthguard that analyses the impact of an athlete's hit during the game. This research might help the doctors understand the impact of hit and the injury better and will allow them to treat the athlete better.

Nike provides skilled resources, budget, and coordination across the enterprise to support the digital transformation. Innovation groups investigate new digital technologies and practices to identify potential applications in products and customer engagement. They enabled new digitally enriched products to fit customers' tastes and needs. Nike plans to continue using technology to become ever-closer to each of its customers.

Acknowledgments Dirk Meissners contribution to the book chapter is based on the study funded by the Basic Research Program of the National Research University Higher School of Economics (HSE) and by the Russian Academic Excellence Project "5-100."

Chapter 4
Internationalizing Google AI Research Google AI

Aayushi Gupta, Binu Thomas, Fayez Alsoubaie, Harsita Gadiraju, Priyanka Patil, Tugrul U. Daim, and Dirk Meissner

4.1 Introduction

Internationalization is the trend that firms increasingly perform research and development activities outside their home countries. Reasons behind decentralized R&D are mostly related to faster learning of technology developments, customer needs, low costs, and globalizing the market. Capture knowledge and market opportunities internationally. The main goal of international cooperation is to capture knowledge that can be converted to profit through Technology exploration and Technology exploitation. The corporations were hesitant to internationalize their R&D work before the 1980s. The reasons for maintaining geographically clustered R&D are mostly related to maintaining optimum patterns of interaction. But market forces and the dissemination of technological know-how sources are forcing many companies to decentralize and internationalize their R&D labs. To order to stimulate this technical learning, businesses are internationalizing R&D to improve the process of technical learning and the management of the laboratory network.

One assertion could summarize the clearest drawback of regional decentralization as "communication difficulties." If a company's R&D activities are decentralized into geographically separate groups, this separation could result in less

A. Gupta · B. Thomas · F. Alsoubaie · H. Gadiraju · P. Patil
Portland State University, Portland, OR, USA

T. U. Daim (✉)
Portland State University Technology Management Doctoral Program, Portland, OR, USA

National Research University Higher School of Economics, Moscow, Russia

Chaoyang University of Technology, Taichung City, Taiwan
e-mail: tugrul.u.daim@pdx.edu

D. Meissner
National Research University Higher School of Economics, Moscow, Russia

T. U. Daim, D. Meissner (eds.), *Innovation Management in the Intelligent World*, Science, Technology and Innovation Studies,
https://doi.org/10.1007/978-3-030-58301-9_4

communication. Lack of communication also makes it much more difficult to adjust to each other through informal discussions, leading to difficulties in coordinating R&D activities. Distributing the development of technology can also lead to a reduction in the size of the individual entities. The laboratory's reduced size can reduce its impact on the local scientific community or government. R&D is basically a business of creating and creatively manipulating a know-how base within the company. Splitting the central laboratory into smaller hierarchical units risks splitting the know-how base and thus increasing its capacity for innovative growth and ideas fermentation. In addition, decentralization poses risks to protect proprietary information. However, despite these risks, offshore spending on R&D is increasing more rapidly than spending in the home country because of the benefits it has.

According to the National Science Foundation US companies "R&D spending abroad jumped 33 percent in 1986 and 1987, while the USA spending increased by only 6 percent in the same period. A survey of 20 Swedish multinationals found that, between 1980 and 1987, the share of international R&D as a percentage of total R&D spending rose from 20.6 to 22.8%". The reasons found for this increase were:

- Technology transfer from headquarters to major subsidiaries.
- A positive response to pressure from international host countries, promoting technological development localization.
- Public relations.
- Access to foreign talent and limited resources in engineering.
- Take advantage of cheaper engineering resources to lower development costs.
- Taking advantage of local ideas and products.
- A quicker production at the same time through several laboratories "parallel efforts."
- A greater sensitivity to the market.
- Continuation after acquisition and.
- Taking advantage of certain tax laws.

There must be some motivations behind the decision to go international. There are certain drivers that make that possible and interesting to choose a location along with the need for internationalizing. The quick increase in the stock of the existing knowledge can be a driver. People from different places may have different opinions and ways to perceive things; the knowledge and the tactics or techniques might differ too. Secondly, this diversity and internationalization could also increase the availability of resources to sustain innovativeness. Internationalizing would also increase the motivation of international managers and employees working for that firm. Meeting new people from different parts of the world, sharing ideas, and exchanging thoughts would also enhance their knowledge toward a common goal and would motivate them to bring new ideas to the firm or helping the firm in some way or the other. Another driver for internationalizing could be the increase or raising the opportunities for external collaboration with the local institution of foreign countries. This helps the company in finding new talent and also gives them a vast choice of candidates interested in their field, which might be useful for the company.

While choosing a location for the company, they predominantly look for places between high-income countries for increasing their chances of higher profit and they also look at the differences in labor costs between the home country and locations abroad. This saves them good about of money and increases productivity for the company.

4.2 "Artificial Intelligence" What Is it and Why it Matters

AI is becoming increasingly popular across the world. The term artificial intelligence was coined/in 1956, but today, due to increased data volumes, advanced algorithms, and computing power and storage improvements, AI has become more popular. Artificial Intelligence can be described as any task that is performed by a program or a machine. Amazon Web Services, Microsoft Azure, and Google Cloud Platform.

Amazon Web Services, Microsoft Azure, and Google Cloud Platform are some of the popular AI services available today. Big companies across all industries are trying to integrate machine learning into their products, from retail to agriculture. With the demand for the AI technology companies like Google, Intel, Apple, etc. are in rush to grab the Artificial Intelligence startups.

Google is the top acquirer of AI startups, with 14 acquisitions under its belt so far. In 2013, the University of Toronto's computer science department purchased "Deep Learning and neural network developer" DNN research. This acquisition is reported to have helped Google make significant upgrades to its image search function. Google also purchased DeepMind Technologies from the British company for $600 M in 2014.

4.2.1 Google AI

Google AI is a division of Google dedicated solely to artificial intelligence. It was announced by Google I/O in 2017. Google has rebranded its research division as Google AI indicating that its company's focus is all about Artificial Intelligence. Google is committed to progress in the development of AI and to share knowledge, research, tools, and other resources. Google Brain is a deep learning artificial intelligence research team at Google. Google Brain was formed in the early 2010s. It states its mission as "to make machines intelligent and improve people's living". The team focuses on constructing models with high degrees of flexibility that are capable of learning their own features and use data and computation efficiently.

Some of the AI projects from Google include:

1. Image Enhancement
2. Google Translate
3. Robotics

Google's latest experiments include

"Talk to books" which lets users talk to a learning-trained machine algorithm that surfaces answers to questions with relevant human-written text passages. Talk to Books allows us to make a statement or ask a question, and the tool finds sentences in responding books that do not depend on matching keywords. Another experiment Google is testing on is "Semantris." This measures word association features for users as the same technology that allows Talk to Books to rate and ranks on-screen words based on how well they fit user feedback responses.

In the light of opening the new research lab in Zurich and expanding more labs in the rest of the world, it is clear that Google pursues its mission of organizing the world's information and making it universally accessible and useful, as it is stated by the company itself ("About" 2018). Indeed, as it is highlighted by Patterson, Zurich is a powerhouse for university and industrial research; therefore, Google is promoting specialized talent in Zurich to strengthen its research center (Patterson 2016). Google itself acknowledges its concern regarding searching for talented and creative computer scientists, which drives the company to internationalize its R&D activities all around the world, including such centers as Zurich, Paris, New York, Mountain View, Israel, and Beijing.

4.2.1.1 Google R&D Framework

The R&D activities of Google are concerned with advancing the Artificial Intelligence technologies. As it is highlighted by the company itself, Google tries to help people solve problems in exciting new ways, which appears as the major driver of the company's research ("About" 2018). For this purpose, Google involves the whole range of available technologies, including software, hardware, and AI. For instance, the bright examples are TensorFlow used by a variety of organizations as an open-source machine learning library or Cloud AutoML, which allows researchers, developers, and businesses with limited AI expertise to establish their own models ("About" 2018). Also, Google is involved in researching the future place of AI in a variety of domains, including the critical problems of humanity, such as searching for sustainable energy sources. As a result, the Google AI R&D framework exists within the objectives aimed at reaching sustainability by means of advancing AI and related technologies.

In general, Google is involved in active Artificial Intelligence R&D activities, appearing as a leader among the other companies. According to Richter, Google is a leader among the other countries in terms of the number of Artificial Intelligence startups acquired (How Google Plans To Use AI To Reinvent The $3 Trillion US Healthcare Industry 2018; Join Us 2018). Also, Google is a leader in terms of patent application activity (Poutonnet 2018). Simultaneously, Google is highly concerned with its AI research and emphasizes its progress on machine learning much more than the other companies (How Google Plans To Use AI To Reinvent The $3 Trillion US Healthcare Industry 2018; Join Us 2018; Richter 2017).

Currently, the researchers across Google are conducting their activities in a range of fields and domains. For instance, Google is engaged in creating an open-source framework for NISQ algorithms, assessing cardiovascular risk factors with computer vision, developing People + AI Research (PAIR), generating Human-Like Speech from the text (Tecotron 2), developing the concept of federated learning by means of collaborative machine learning without centralized training data, advancing TensorFlow Lattice and Magenta, and many others ("Research") (Palmer 2018). On the other side, there are also some past projects that failed due to some reasons. For instance, recently, Google has pulled out its controversial military AI project with Pentagon named "Project Maven" after leaked documents revealed fears of public reaction to $250 m a year contract (Palmer 2018).

Alongside the conventional business instruments for assessing the performance, such as budget and schedule, Google clearly defines a set of expectations that should be met in terms of its every project. For instance, there is a list of specific objectives for AI applications, which states that AI should be socially beneficial; avoid creating or reinforcing unfair bias; be built and tested safety; be accountable to the people; incorporate privacy design principles; and uphold high standards of scientific excellence ("Principles" 2018). Simultaneously, as it is highlighted by Poutonnet, the company makes an emphasis on the creation of the customer value, trying to help efficiently incorporate the power of AI into the business applications (Poutonnet 2018).

Research Partnerships appear in two major spheres of Google Research Partnerships, which are in the spheres of education and business. In terms of education, the company develops a collaborative relationship in three major dimensions. The first one is about faculty engagement, which means supporting and participating in the academic research community through meaningful engagement with university faculty ("Outreach" 2018). In this context, meaningful engagement envisages funding for academic research and collaboration between faculty and Google researchers ("Outreach"). The second dimension refers to student support, including offering fellowships, scholarships, internships, and other student opportunities ("Outreach"). The third realm of education partnership is about global outreach, which means supporting the university research, academic development, and technological innovation that takes place across the globe ("Outreach").

The second realm of the Google Research Partnerships refers to the organization named AI Partnership, which appears as the partnership between the world-leading organizations involved in the AI R&D activities. In terms of the organization's focus, it aims at developing and sharing best practices, advancing the public understanding, providing an open and inclusive platform for discussion & engagement, and identifying and fostering aspirational efforts in AI for socially beneficial purposes ("About Us" 2018).

4.3 Google's AI Labs

We have seen Silicon Valley tech giants accelerate opening AI research laboratories around the world as they seek to gain traction among researchers and meet their international ambitions. Google has taken laboratories to China and France, Facebook has opened laboratories in Pittsburgh and Seattle, and Microsoft has revealed plans to open laboratories close to universities in Berkeley, California, and Melbourne, Australia. There are no signs of this trend slowing down. Google announced plans to open a laboratory in Accra, Ghana, the first in Africa for Google and perhaps the first in Africa for any tech giant.

Google's AI labs are located all over the world, including in New York, Toronto, London, and Zurich, all contributing toward the same goal of finding ways to improve AI for all.

4.3.1 Zurich Lab

Zurich is also a hub of the university and industrial study, widely recognized as a world banking base. Albert Einstein earned his PhD at the home of the Swiss Federal Institute of Technology in Zurich (ETH). A technically educated Cambrian (Cambridge person) relocated to Zurich would be familiar with his college-inspired community. Further, broaden its research center, Google is targeting an international pool of qualified expertise in Zurich. AI and machine learning are very scientific endeavors, with most work still being carried out in university laboratories. Google is searching for people with the right skills and education to help create a future with intelligent systems capable of perceiving, interacting, and engaging with the real world-like humans. AI and machine learning research's academic bias makes it essential to locate close to a leading technical university to recruit the best talent and foster ongoing research with university laboratories. Zurich was on a short list of locations considered by corporations when planning a new research facility in areas such as computer science, material science, biotechnology, and pharmaceuticals. Disney, Google, and IBM (for their work in their Zurich Lab, a four-time Nobel laureate) have invested in research centers there. Novartis, Hoffmann La Roche, and Biogen, representing the fields of pharmaceutical and biotechnology, also invested in large laboratories. Research is a big decision because big investments have to be made years and decades ahead of products that have to generate billions of dollars of revenue to return the investment. Switzerland ranks first in the Cornell University's 2015 Global Innovation Ranking. Zurich is also seen as an exciting place to move about. In the 2016 Mercer Value Living Index, Zurich ranked second among 230 cities worldwide, leading other AI and machine learning innovation hubs; San Francisco ranked 28th, and Boston ranked 34th. With more holidays and longer vacations, an expat can completely change his cultural surrounding with a short trip to another country. Flight time from Zurich to Paris is a little over an hour. The position of Zurich is generally not a source of friction when persuading well-educated and skilled citizens to move.

The close proximity of European cities and Switzerland's fantastic transportation system makes it possible to reach most European cities, except those in Scandinavia, in about an hour. This feature makes Zurich a true research hub because a researcher can conveniently collaborate with others in lab and university locations in other European cities with just a day trip.

4.3.2 AI Research Lab in Ghana

Throughout Africa we have seen people doing amazing things with the internet and technology—for themselves, their communities, and the world. Google is planning to open a research center for artificial intelligence in Accra, Ghana, the latest in a string of investments made by the tech company in Africa. Africa is the world's second-largest continent by landmass, and many people live in rural areas, so it might be worth pursuing AI solutions such as remote medical imaging or drone services (Google AI in Ghana 2018). Africa is also by far the youngest continent on the planet, so research that affects young people's lives, such as educational or personal finance applications, may also be appropriate.

Sixty percent of the population in Africa is under the age of 25. More than half the world's population growth will be in Africa by 2050, according to estimates from the United Nations. It already runs a training program for virtual skills that it hopes 10 million Africans will ultimately benefit (Google AI in Ghana 2018). Google also runs a separate initiative called Launchpad Accelerator Africa, which says it supports 100,000 developers and more than 60 technology startups in Africa.

The research center will focus on using AI in areas such as health care, farming, and education, said Google. They are committed to working with regional universities and research centers as well as focusing on the potential uses of AI in Africa with policy makers (Greg Sandoval 2018). The new Ghana AI center will open later this year and will include researchers and engineers in machine learning, Google said, thinking it provided details on the number of staff it will hire. During a trip to Lagos last year, Google CEO Sundar Pichai vowed that Google will continue to raise its profile on the continent. At the time, as part of the company's Launchpad Accelerator in Africa, Pichai announced a new investment in African startups (Greg Sandoval 2018).

Google's interest in Africa comes at a time when the continent is spreading a lot of international money. The United Nations expects Africa to be home to 25 percent of the world's 9 billion population in 30 years (Greg Sandoval 2018) This not only represents a huge market, but investors are planning for the day that the developing economies of Africa hit their pace. Russia is looking at investments in East Africa, and China has spent billions on infrastructure and other ventures there, according to recent reports.

More is said about the need to democratize AI, to include a diverse range of viewpoints, and to recognize how AI can shape the future and change humanity forever, particularly as AI spreads into parts of society beyond tech. If AI is the future, then perhaps no region has more the right to have a voice in that future than Africa (Johnson 2018). The opening of the laboratory in Ghana is a reminder that as AI laboratories are proliferating around the world, they can produce state-of-the-art AI research that advances common industry goals, but they can also carry out research that takes advantage of the unique characteristics and challenges that can be found in a different region.

Events such as Data Science Africa 2017 in Tanzania, South Africa's 2017 Deep Learning Indaba conference, and 2018 follow-up IndabaX events in multiple countries have shown an exciting and continuing growth of the African computer science research community (Johnson 2018). These are some crucial factors behind choosing Ghana as an upcoming AI center for Google.

4.4 Google AI R&D Portfolio

R&D portfolio provides a good insight into the focus areas of a company and serves as a reasonable indicator of its growth prospects. The amount of resources channelized toward specific research is directly associated with the company's roadmap in almost all cases. However, it should be noted that there exists research that is exploratory in many companies. Research areas and the amount of resources allocated for that area among the top leaders in the industry is also an indication of the maturity and prospects of that technological area.

Research is an inherent characteristic of Google and brings no surprise that it has a bigger research portfolio compared to others. With a vision for "bringing the benefits of AI to everyone," Google is betting heavily on AI R&D. Google AI R&D portfolio spans 22 research areas with 3700+ researchers across its 16 research centers globally.

4.4.1 Focus Areas

Google has identified nine focus areas (Research 2018) for research that is strategically relevant for its AI mission. The focus areas of research in Google and a short description of each focus area is stated below.

- *AI Fundamentals & Applications*: Create useful solutions to fundamental computational problems with an impact on Google's products and scientific progress.
- *Algorithms & Optimization*: Perform fundamental research in algorithms, markets, optimization and graph analysis and use it to solve challenges across the business of Google.
- *Applied Science*: Combining computer science with physics and biology to create breakthroughs that help the world.
- *Cloud AI*: The aim is to democratize AI and help clients by making AI more available to scientists, developers, and businesses.
- *Google Brain Team*: Make machines intelligent. Improve people's lives.
- *Language*: Advance state-of-the-art technologies in natural language and build systems that learn to understand and use language in context.

- *Network Infrastructure*: Design and build the world's largest, fastest, most reliable data center and WAN networks to enable non-existent computing and storage.
- *Perception*: Build systems for interpreting, explaining, and transforming sensory data.
- *Security, Privacy, and Abuse*: A team of engineers, researchers, advocates, and hackers who make the Internet safer for all users.

Google has other areas outside of its focus areas where research related to AI is conducted. Quantum A.I., Robotics, Education Innovation, Mobile Systems, Hardware and Architecture, Software Systems, Software Engineering are some of the areas where research is ongoing. Google has identified 22 research areas in total for doing its research. More than 3700 researchers combined are doing research in these 22 areas across different R&D centers globally.

Machine Intelligence has the largest number of researchers, followed by Machine Perception, which is among the focus areas of research. Exhibit 4.1 in the Appendix provides the list of 22 research areas in Google and the number of researchers associated with each of the areas.

4.4.2 Research Publications

Research Publications can be considered as a measure of prominence and maturity of the research area. Google has a large number of publications on its AI research areas. Google AI publications have increased substantially in recent years, starting with single-digit numbers during 1998–2002, and releasing more than 500 in 2017. Exhibit 4.2 in the Appendix provides the research publications in each area of research and the number of publications each year.

Transformation of research to real world products is a tangible measure to assess the outcome and relevance of research. As such Google has incorporated many of its AI research results into its own product solutions (Robson 2018). Exhibit 4.3 in the Appendix provides a list of AI solutions integrated to Google products.

4.5 Conclusion

Study of R&D and the relevance of internationalization in R&D based on the review of various technology companies strategies and focused study on Google AI R&D gives some key takeaways.

- Research is a key ingredient for growth in the top companies in the industry.
- R&D approaches differ but a high degree of similarity can be observed.
- Internationalization of R&D is adopted by most of the companies.
- Selection of Global R&D centers is a key factor for research.

- R&D portfolio selection and management are very important.
- Research collaboration with Universities and Research Institutes are standard.
- Hybrid approach for research is adopted by many companies.
- Open collaboration and people-oriented research is effective.

A Holistic Research approach, by strategic selection of research portfolios, internationalizing R&D, channelizing key resources, and hybrid approach with open collaboration as evaluated for Google AI R&D is recommended for other companies to propel growth and sustain with the state of the art technologies.

Acknowledgement Dirk Meissner's contribution to the book chapter is based on the study funded by the Basic Research Program of the National Research University Higher School of Economics (HSE) and by the Russian Academic Excellence Project '5-100'.

Appendix

Exhibit 4.1 Google AI research areas/teams

Research Team	Researchers
Machine Intelligence	641
Machine Perception	316
Algorithms and Theory	290
Distributed Systems and Parallel Computing	253
Natural Language Processing	253
Data Mining and Modeling	242
Human-Computer Interaction and Visualization	217
Software Systems	201
Information Retrieval and the Web	173
Security, Privacy and Abuse Prevention	147
Speech Processing	140
Software Engineering	134
Networking	128
General Science	108
Data Management	101
Economics and Electronic Commerce	82
Mobile Systems	75
Hardware and Architecture	66
Machine Translation	61
Education Innovation	32
Robotics	32
Quantum A.I.	24

Google AI Research Areas and Teams

Research Area	Publications
Machine Intelligence	1150
Algorithms and Theory	657
Machine Perception	521
Human-Computer Interaction and Visualization	460
Natural Language Processing	419
Security, Privacy and Abuse Prevention	294
Speech Processing	284
Software Systems	262
Data Mining and Modeling	227
Information Retrieval and the Web	222
Economics and Electronic Commerce	219
Distributed Systems and Parallel Computing	215
Networking	213
General Science	169
Data Management	118
Software Engineering	109
Mobile Systems	75
Hardware and Architecture	71
Machine Translation	52
Robotics	50
Quantum A.I.	36
Education Innovation	30

Google AI Research Area and Publications

Year	Publications
2018	373*
2017	542
2016	475
2015	377
2014	333
2013	358
2012	382
2011	332
2010	305
2009	323
2008	266
2007	213
2006	131
2005	56
2004	18
2003	14
2002	5
2001	5
2000	2
1999	2
1998	3

Google AI Research Publications History

Exhibit 4.2 Google AI research publications

Google Photos	Search (untagged) object of action	"dogs" or "hugs"
Google Play Music	Personalized recommendations	music for cooking dinner or watching the sunset
Pixel 2	Portriat Mode - background blur	pick out the subject of the photo and blur the background
Youtube Videos	Automatic captions	machine learning algorithms that transcribe speech in 10 languages
Gmail	Smart Reply	using AI to suggest three responses based on the email you received
Gmail	Nudging	uses AI to remind you to follow up or respond to messages that are older than two to three days
Google Play Protect	Automatic review	reviews more than 50 billion apps, and even devices themselves, everyday and takes action when it finds anything suspicious
Google Translate	Translate text on a sign or menu	Translate text on a sign or menu by holding your camera in front of it
Google Assistant	Conversations	conversation with your Google Assistant in more than a dozen languages
Google Maps	Park your car	estimate how hard it'll be to park your car on Google Maps
Google Maps	Find the right address	find the right address on Google Maps, using a system that learned to read street names and addresses from billions of Street View images
Google Lens	Search what you see	landmarks, books, artwork, or your neighbor's dog
Google Trips	Smart algorithm	help plan your next travel itinerary

Google AI Research in Products

Exhibit 4.3 Google AI research in products

References[1]

"About" (2018) Google AI. https://ai.google/about/. Accessed 13 Aug 2018
"About Us" (2018) AI partnership. https://www.partnershiponai.org/about/. Accessed 13 Aug 2018
Cbinsights (2018) The Race for AI. https://www.cbinsights.com/research/top-acquirers-ai-startups-ma-timeline/

[1]Uncited references were used to develop this case.

Enterprise edges (2018) Importance of AI. http://www.enterpriseedges.com/importance-artificial-intelligence
Google AI (2018). https://ai.google/research/join-us/. Accessed 13 Aug 2018
"Google AI in Ghana" (2018) Published Jun 13. https://blog.google/around-the-globe/google-africa/google-ai-ghana/
Greg Sandoval (2018) Google is opening an AI research center in Ghana. June 13. https://www.businessinsider.com/google-ai-research-center-ghana-africa-2018-6
"How Google Plans To Use AI To Reinvent The $3 Trillion US Healthcare Industry" (2018) CBInsights. https://www.cbinsights.com/research/report/google-strategy-healthcare/. Accessed 13 Aug 2018
Impact Hub Zurich (2018) Google for entrepreneurs exchange: AI & machine learning—impact hub Zurich. [online] https://zurich.impacthub.ch/program/gfe-aiml/. Accessed 14 Aug 2018
Johnson K (2018) AI weekly: Google's research center in Ghana won't be the last AI lab in Africa. June 15. https://venturebeat.com/2018/06/15/ai-weekly-googles-research-center-in-ghana-wont-be-the-last-ai-lab-in-africa/
"Join Us" (2018) Google AI. https://ai.google/research/join-us/. Accessed 13 Aug 2018
Nick S (2018) Google latest AI experiments. https://www.theverge.com/2018/4/13/17235306/google-ai-experiments-natural-language-understanding-semantics-word-games
"Outreach" (2018) Google AI. https://ai.google/research/outreach/. Accessed 13 Aug 2018
Palmer A (2018) Google pulls out of controversial military AI project after leaked documents reveal fears of public reaction to $250m a year contract. MailOnline. Accessed 13 Aug 2018.
Patterson S (2016) Why Google picked its Zurich lab to expand AI and machine learning research. Newtwork World. https://www.networkworld.com/article/3085427/internet/why-google-picked-its-zurich-lab-to-expand-ai-and-machine-learning-research.html. Accessed 13 Aug 2018
Patterson S (2018) Why Google picked its Zurich lab to expand AI and machine learning research. [online] Network World. https://www.networkworld.com/article/3085427/internet/why-google-picked-its-zurich-lab-to-expand-ai-and-machine-learning-research.html. Accessed 14 Aug 2018
Poutonnet P (2018) 6 must-see sessions on AI and machine learning at Next '18. Google Cloud. https://cloud.google.com/blog/products/ai-machine-learning/6-must-see-sessions-ai-and-machine-learning-next-18. Accessed 13 Aug 2018
"Principles" (2018) Google AI. https://ai.google/principles/. Accessed 13 Aug 2018
"Research" (2018) Google AI. https://ai.google/research. Accessed 13 Aug 2018
Richter F (2017) Google leads the race for AI domination. Statista. https://www.statista.com/chart/9443/ai-acquisitions/. Accessed 13 Aug 2018
Robson C (2018) Google AI, "13 ways you're using AI in your daily life". May 4. https://blog.google/technology/ai/13-ways-youre-using-ai-your-daily-life/. Accessed 13 Aug 2018
SaS Insights (2018) Artificial intelligence. https://www.sas.com/en_us/insights/analytics/what-is-artificial-intelligence.html
"Shaping the future of AI" (2018). https://www.technologyreview.com/s/610546/china-wants-to-shape-the-global-future-of-artificial-intelligence/
"Stories" (2018) Google AI. https://ai.google/stories. Accessed 13 Aug 2018
"Winners And Losers In The Patent Wars Between Amazon, Google, Facebook, Apple, and Microsoft" (2017) CBInsights. https://www.cbinsights.com/research/innovation-patents-apple-google-amazon-facebook-expert-intelligence/. Accessed 13 Aug 2018

Chapter 5
Amazon: Industrial/International Corporation and Dynamics

Deemah Alassaf, Lipishree Vrushabhendra, Nouf Alswine, Vidhi Chokshi, Tugrul U. Daim, and Dirk Meissner

5.1 Introduction

When businesses continually strive to access awareness and market opportunities globally, the globalization of R&D activities has continued its growth path. The main goal of international cooperation is to capture knowledge that can be converted to profit through two strategies: Technology exploration and Technology exploitation.

Amazon's immense evolution from merely an online bookstore to device manufacturer, from publishing platform to finding a global marketplace with fulfillment network and cloud computing is driven by their passion for pioneering and inventing on customers' behalf (Smart Insights 2017). Amazon today, works with the best and talented resources to build new technologies and platforms that improve the lives of customers ranging from consumers to sellers, from content creators to developers around the world. There are around 240,000 Amazon employees around the world, with most of the teams being small and operating much like a start-up enterprise (Smart Insights 2017). This means Amazon offers all team members equal opportunities to take on big challenges and make a difference. The company has emerged as one of the biggest innovation pioneers from Kindle to Amazon Prime and from

D. Alassaf · L. Vrushabhendra · N. Alswine · V. Chokshi
Portland State University, Portland, OR, USA

T. U. Daim (✉)
Portland State University Technology Management Doctoral Program, Portland, OR, USA

National Research University Higher School of Economics, Moscow, Russia

Chaoyang University of Technology, Taichung City, Taiwan
e-mail: tugrul.u.daim@pdx.edu

D. Meissner
National Research University Higher School of Economics, Moscow, Russia

T. U. Daim, D. Meissner (eds.), *Innovation Management in the Intelligent World*,
Science, Technology and Innovation Studies,
https://doi.org/10.1007/978-3-030-58301-9_5

Amazon Web Services (AWS) to Fulfillment by Amazon (FBA) (Smart Insights 2017).

Amazon strongly believes that "Technology infuses into all our teams, all of the processes, decision-making, and our approach to innovation in each of the businesses. It is deeply integrated into everything we do" (Smart Insights 2017). This shows that applying new technologies relentlessly gives Amazon a competitive edge. The company uses high-performance payment systems, dynamic rendering, and object storage with workflow and queuing systems, business intelligence and data analytics, machine learning and pattern recognition, neural and probabilistic networks, and a range of technologies that have made its goals and objectives a fact (Online 2017a).

All types of businesses can learn from their digital business strategy for their research and development efforts. From small businesses, startups, to large international businesses Amazon's focus is on the customer, testing market opportunities made available by digital technology and carry on further testing and analysis to improve results. The purpose of this chapter provides in-depth understanding of the R&D operations of Amazon, which is one of the most widely known R&D spenders among others in the global market in today's age. Amazon has dedicated its research and development activities in its R&D centers in the United States and the United Kingdom. The chapter focuses on the framework of different cooperation: International, Academic, Industrial, and sheds light on Amazon's practices, strategies, and goals on the same lines.

5.2 Amazon's Background

5.2.1 Amazon History

One of the biggest breakthroughs in today's time and age, the company Amazon was founded by Jeff Bezos in 1994. In 2008, Amazon was a global brand of accounts and order fulfillment from other 76 million active customers in over 200 countries. Given this volume of sales, Amazon had about 17,000 full-time and part-time employees at December 31, 2007. Amazon MP3, a la carte DRM-free MP3 music downloads that now contains over 3.1 million tracks from over 270,000 artists, was released in September 2007.

Amazon is now one of the biggest companies leading the online marketing arena. It started its business through book distribution which further evolved into sales of a variety of products. In 1988, the company launched its own online music and video stores which sold toys and electronics (Chauhan et al. 2017). Amazon is on the top of the list of highest R&D spenders in 2016 reaching 18 Billion Dollars. With around five research and development centers around the world, it has spent around 18 Billion Dollars.

Amazon describes there are three terms of product groups which are consumers, retailer customers, and customers of developers. There are more than 76 million customer accounts, but in its marketplaces there are only 1.3 million active seller customers, and Amazon is trying to increase that. For a retailer, Amazon is unique in defining "developer customers" using its Amazon Web Services, which provides access to software resources such as hosting that developers can use to develop their own web services. Customers are also encouraged to join Amazon Prime, a fee-based loyalty program in which customers receive free or discounted international shipping in the United States, United Kingdom, Germany, and Japan.

It follows that this culture of experimentation must be readily supported by the Amazon technology infrastructure and this can be hard to achieve with standardized content management. Amazon has achieved its competitive advantage by developing its technology internally and by investing heavily in this that may not be available to other organizations without the proper focus on the online channels.

As Amazon grew, its share price enabled its partnership or acquisition with a range of companies in different sectors. Amazon went on to partner with Drugstore.com in the pharmacy sector, Living.com in furniture, Pets.com for pet supplies, Wineshopper.com for wines, HomeGrocer.com for groceries, Sothebys.com for auctions, and Kozmo.com for urban home deliveries (Smart Insights 2017). Amazon purchased an equity stake in these partners, so that it would share their profits. The partners were also charged fees to support and drive traffic to their pages for placements on the Amazon site. Similarly, Amazon also charged publishers for prime-position to promote books on its site (Smart Insights 2017).

The market analysts refer to "Amazoning a sector" which means that one company becomes dominant in an online sector such as book retail that results in difficulty for others to achieve market share (Smart Insights 2017). In addition to developing, communicating, and delivering a very strong proposition, the company has been able to successfully consolidate its strength in different sectors through its partnership arrangements and through using technology to facilitate product promotion and distribution via these partnerships. The Amazon retail platform was also introduced, which enables other retailers to sell their products online using the Amazon user interface and infrastructure through their "Syndicated Stores" programme.

Toy store Toys "R" Us have an agreement identical to that. These alliances help Amazon expand its scope to other vendors 'customers, and consumers shopping in one segment, such as books, can of course be inspired to shop in other categories, such as clothes and appliances (Smart Insights 2017).

Another type of collaboration is the Amazon Marketplace, which allows Amazon customers and other sellers to sell their new and used books and other products in addition to regular retail offerings. Finally, Amazon has also facilitated the formation of partnerships with smaller companies through its affiliates programme. Amazon does not use an affiliate network that would take commissions from sale, instead it has created a tiered performance-based incentive to encourage affiliates to sell more Amazon products.

5.2.2 Amazon's International Cooperation

Apart from launching online music and video stores, Amazon started to expand its European reach by purchasing online bookseller Bookpage from the United Kingdom and Telebook from Germany along with acquiring Internet Movie Database. Amazon's key business strategy in terms of globalization deals was to spread its operations throughout the world. In this direction, the company began expanding in England, France, and Germany, and eventually targeted Japan and Spain (Chauhan et al. 2017).

5.2.2.1 Amazon's Seattle Center and Lab126

Amazon is the largest private employer in Seattle, with more than 25,000 employees and still growing. Amazon has developed its own internal development platform called "Weblab," which they use to test website and brand changes. In 2013, 1976 Weblabs are running around the world, up from 1092 in 2012 and 546 in 2011 (Smart Insights 2017). A new feature called "Ask an owner" is a recent example of how these are implemented. Customers can ask any product-related questions from a product page, Amazon then route these questions to the product's owners who answer them.

Amazon Lab126 is an innovative R&D agency developing and engineering high-profile consumer electronic products such as the Kindle brand family (Smart Insights 2017). Lab126 started as a branch of Online Electronics Shopping, Apparel, Computers, Books, DVDs, and more in 2004. The Amazon Kindle e-reader was published in 2007 after three years of research and development by Lab126. The latest model called the Kindle Oasis continues to be launched in mid-2016.

Instead of being a standalone company, it expanded to include international resources for management roles and test engineers to be the main interface among the internal engineering and operations teams as well as our OEM partners (Smart Insights 2017). It also recruited the key software development engineer for APIs who are expected to work with an experienced cross-disciplinary team to design and develop creative user technology solutions. In Asia, and especially in Japan, Amazon is also expanding the Data Center management team. This position requires a broad knowledge of the Data Center in as many specific fields as possible through Subject Matter Expertise (SME).

5.2.2.2 Amazon's UK R&D Center

Amazon launched a new R&D facility in London in 2013, focusing on developing products and APIs for the global market for TVs, game consoles, smartphones, and PCs. Amazon is expanding its development operations in Cambridge, opening up new facilities. Teams working on Amazon devices—like the Kindle and Echo—will be moved to the new facility. The existing Castle Hill facility would be primarily used for drone-related research and development.

The United Kingdom has become one of the most important research and development center for Amazon because it on the top 5 most attractive countries for foreign direct investment. The United Kingdom is a country that is well equipped with rich talent pools, a highly secure IP protection system, with fewer regulations for research and development activities and strong law enforcement in the country.

5.3 Drivers of International and Industrial Cooperation

There are several important drivers for international cooperation and the drivers vary from one organization to another.

5.3.1 Knowledge Spillovers

When big companies, like Amazon, expand their research and development facilities internationally, they stimulate economic growth generated by knowledge spillovers. International knowledge spillovers or the diffusion of knowledge throughout countries happens when the knowledge created by a country is used in the innovation process of other countries (Online 2017b). R&D activities as recognized create externalities. Other firms, industries, or countries could take advantage of research activities performed in a particular place and expanding their resources (Caniels 2003). In addition, international R&D investments have a fundamental role in encouraging productivity growth and promoting competitiveness in a global world where knowledge and innovation are critical factors for the advanced economies. Therefore, firms have been engaging in R&D international and industrial cooperation.

5.3.2 Technological Exploration

However, although the benefits from this type of cooperation are great, different firms have different motives for seeking an international R&D cooperation. When a company decides to open an R&D center in a new country, it has to have a strong purpose to validate this decision. Cheng and Bolon (1993) state that "motivations reflect the organizational benefits that a firm could expect to obtain from investing in foreign R&D" (Sciencedirect.com 2012). Studies have categorized R&D internationalization motives into sets, such as input- /output-oriented factors, push/pull factors, access to internal/external capabilities, demand-/supply-side factors, and so on (Sciencedirect.com 2012). The main argument around international investments in R&D can be restricted to couple of sides, between the technology-driven motive, to get access to technology in a new country, and the market-driven motive, to get access to the market of the new country. The technology-driven motive for R&D could be expressed as technological exploration which expanding the firm's technologies through having access to foreign technology and knowledge. More importantly, studies have shown that the main functions of international R&D centers are product adaptation and satisfying local customers' demand. The adoption of overseas R&D centers enables firms to attain external technological resources and produce new technological skills by obtaining foreign beneficial knowledge bases in diverse locations. Amazon's international R&D expansion to locations that are rich with scientific knowledge and technological resources such as Cambridge, UK, has been motivated by the need of getting advantage of these valuable resources (Lomas 2017a).

Additionally, companies with a strong technological base, as Amazon, are considered as technological creators/contributors where they gather strong technological skills and contribute to new knowledge-creation activities in host countries that, therefore, accompany their international existing knowledge supply (Sciencedirect.com 2012). Hence, several studies have shown that firms from developed countries engage in overseas R&D activities in grounds where they have a solid technological knowledge.

5.3.3 *Talents and Technologies*

Furthermore, pursuing external technological expertise and employing qualified local R&D people is a critical task, especially for companies adopting the technology exploration R&D. In Amazon's case, the cities where it expanded its R&D centers like Bangalore and Cambridge are highly intense with individuals that have advanced technological and scientific knowledge. Planning the R&D foreign location based on the accessibility to scientific resources and cutting-edge talents offers a variety of benefits, one of which is a competitive advantage. In addition, the most effective way for the R&D units to access the local knowledge environment is by utilizing local human capital with superior technological expertise (Sciencedirect.com 2012). Amazon's latest R&D center was announced to be located in Cambridge, UK. Cambridge is notable for its outstanding university, which performs as a center for concentrating science and technology talent, logically leading many startups revolution out from it (Lomas 2017a). Amazon is apparently aiming to get as much as it can from this local talent's opportunity (Lomas 2017a). Furthermore, since one of the primary focuses of Amazon's Cambridge center is speech tech, it had acquired the speech tech startup Evi Technologies originated in Cambridge as well. Making foreign acquisitions in the places, where the company has an R&D center, provides it with access to technology, secures research and development skills, and ownership of international brands (Sciencedirect.com 2012).

Furthermore, globalization provides opportunity to tap on talents and innovation clusters. Many giant companies have various R&D centers around the world with the aim of obtaining the best technological resources and complementary expertise. Even though locating R&D centers in foreign countries has its risks and cost, the returned advantages can exceed that and provide competitive advantages. It crafts a channel to transfer foreign technologies to home countries. Indeed, R&D location should provide accessibility to higher quality personnel and prestigious academic entities. Additionally, R&D internationalization enables companies to have access to new markets and be close to their potential customers. This closeness provides the ability to sense any different need should be accommodated to succeed in that market (Stewart 2017; Wernstedt and Hersh 2006).

5.3.3.1 Amazon Web Services

Amazon Web Services (AWS) commonly known as the AWS was launched in 2006 (Miller 2017). AWS began as a support arm for the company, but now it provides a comprehensive, fully-featured cloud-based technology infrastructure system consisting of a wide range of computing, processing, server, analytics, application, and delivery services. AWS customers today range from start-ups such as Pinterest, Dropbox, Airbnb, Supercell, and Spotify to large companies such as Exxon, BP, J&J, Philips, Verizon, Netflix, Google, Newscorp, The New York Times, and Major League Baseball (Online 2017f).

Before the launch of AWS, the teams spent up to 70% of their time recreating software infrastructure, such as a web-scale server, processing, queuing, and other resources in use in other business areas (Miller 2017). For the teams, this was extremely time-consuming task, impacting their quality on customer delivery. With AWS, Amazon teams would concentrate on their innovations by spinning an on-demand project of any scale and without upfront capital investment immediately. It also helped the teams to spin it down just as quickly to retool and then do it all over again. That kind of experimentation loop is particularly advantageous for large-scale innovations which include moving rapidly, experiment more, and keep low the cost of failure. Today, it is highly successful in its own right, riding a remarkable $10 billion run rate. In Amazon's fourth-quarter report-2016, it was announced that AWS generated $2.4 billion in sales, a 69-percent increase from 2015 (Smart Insights 2017).

5.3.4 Efficient Global Market Entrance

Likewise, acquisition in foreign countries is a helpful tool to ease the entrance to the foreign market. Some countries have different complexity levels of sociocultural or political–legal differences relative to the home country (Online 2017c). Thus, with the help of native resources, the transition and entrance to new markets should become smoother and faster. Looking at Amazon product's international presence, the movement toward international R&D centers could be a signal for the company's intention to accelerate the pace at which it rolls out products. Up to the present time, Amazon has been slow in taking its products internationally. For instance, it took nearly two years for Kindle to be offered internationally after hitting the US market. Besides, the Kindle Fire still has not gone to markets other than the United States. The App-store is still available only in the United States too. However, Amazon has been actively contributing more efforts to overcome this drawback. Thus, in June of 2017, it finally announced the international App-store portal for developers, as the first phase to expand the store outside the United States (Lunden 2017). Therefore, international cooperation could be considered as an opportunity to accelerate the expansion of the company's global markets.

5.3.5 *Regulation Flexibility*

Regulation plays a major role in R&D practice and innovation process. One motive of globalizing R&D activities is regulatory restrictions. If a country is permitted for R&D practices, internationalize these practices becomes a necessity. Also, the slow pace of allowing such activities, it would cause accumulative cost and slow down innovation process. In high rival environment, encountering these hinders would lead R&D entities to move to where it is more friendly places. Furthermore, the action of transferring R&D centers or cooperating with other countries to facilitate R&D practice has its impact on regulation. It is an interactive relationship where R&D internationalization can enforce regulators to reform the regulations. Furthermore, R&D globalization would impose regulation harmonization among countries. A country that has a leadership position for having the first R&D trails would be followed as a regulation model by other countries (von Zedtwitz and Gassmann 2002).

5.3.6 *IP Protection System and Law Enforcement*

For R&D centers locating in developed countries, the quality of intellectual property protection is most vital. The decision of relocating or open R&D centers should consider the similarities and differences between the home and host country in their IP protection system. Moving R&D to a similar IP protection system can provide advantages to the firms. It can help the firms transferring back R&D centers or technological innovation to home countries more effectively and manageable.

5.4 Analysis and Discussion

5.4.1 International Cooperation

Amazon announced in 2014 that a new R&D center would be opened in the United Kingdom with a budget of $8.3 billion aiming to have 400 scientists and engineers. The main reason for this site is to develop Prime Air, its program to use drones to deliver parcels to customers in 30 minutes (Mitchell 2017). Amazon applied for a permit to perform its drones testing activity in 2013, but the Federal Aviation Administration (FAA) did not grant permission until a year later. However, permit had some restrictions that limit drones testing such as drones must be operated within the eyesight of pilot and not fly over people who do not have a connection with drones' operations. However, Amazon decided to move the project to the United Kingdom, which has more favorable regulatory environment (Dunning and Lundan 2009). Amazon did not want to limit its drones' functions to accommodate US regulations to deal with FAA's slow pace for responding. It refused to restrict its technological advancement and functional performance. By doing so, it seems that Amazon launched a pressure to reform FAA regulations. As a result, R&D internationalization can be a strategy to enforce more friendly regulations reforms.

Amazon's decision to transfer Drones Project to the United Kingdom has multiple dimensions. Beside it was a tool to put pressure on regulatory restriction, it was a strategy to expand R&D testing to other countries. In the aim for future business expansion, Amazon wants to test other potential market environments to enhance its technological advancement. Since the nature of the project requires testing in different geographical environments, internationalizing the project would strengthen R&D activities. Furthermore, transferring Prime Air Drones to the United Kingdom would provide market access to Europe. Moreover, London is one of the places, which is home to some of the most talented, creative people. Utilizing this knowledge and pool of talents would provide great technological advantages. Therefore, the decision of internationalizing R&D taken by Amazon includes the quality of the input factor. Spillover knowledge is the leading factor for internationalization strategy. One of the reasons for opening R&D in London is reaching innovation cluster. In 2013, Amazon acquired a speech tech startup called Evi Technologies with the aim of advancing its speech recognition technologies (Lomas 2017b). This technology was developed in a university lab. To tap this speech recognition technologies cluster, Amazon sits its R&D center.

Furthermore, in developed countries, policy interest in internationalization of R&D is driven by the desirability to maintain their technological competitiveness. Another driver is being the global innovation location where exogenous and endogenous R&D is attractive to. Offshoring R&D operations can affect this position of being technologically competitive [n12]. Governments and policy makers respond to international R&D by seeking new ways to create or reform more friendly regimes that surrounding R&D (Recode 2017). For example, in the last high-tech summit, the US administration met Amazon CEO and showed its support to Prime Air Drones project. The administration was receptive to feedback about the need to accelerate flexible regulations creation and new rules crafting (Digitaltrends.com 2017). This shows how R&D internationalization can influence policy makers to create a more friendly innovation place. Even though it has been always considered that policies and regulations have power to hurdle R&D activities, R&D has itself power to influence policy adjustment.

5.4.2 Collaboration of Amazon with Academic Institutions

In terms of the academic sector of international innovation, the term university spin-off is widely used in the field of research and development. The article, "Entry by Spinoff in a High-tech Cluster" by Micheal Dahl et al., sheds light on the concept of the university spin-off with the high-tech firms, its origins, and benefits. Spinoffs evolve around the development of particular innovations. Innovation relates closely to the activities or development of parents and grows out of the research undertaken by the parents. However, spin-offs occur, when employees pursue new technological discoveries or innovation made in his/her own firm, labs, etc. (Online 2017e).

Another article, "The performance of university spin-offs: an exploratory analysis using venture capital data" by Jungu Zhang, gives more insight on the concept of the academic cooperation. Zhang states that, the universities, as the center of knowledge creation and a major force of technological innovation are recognized as an important driver of economic growth (Zhang 2008). From the data analyzed through the statistical analysis and experiments, Zhang provides three key concepts related to the university spin-off. Firstly, the venture-backed university spin-offs are common in certain industries. Many academic entrepreneurs are engineering professionals, and most of their companies are in the life science and IT industries.

Second, the transfer of technology through spin-offs from universities is a local phenomenon. Studies have shown that more than two-thirds of the spin-offs from the university are in the same state as the parent university.

Third, after studying the industry and other relevant factors, university spin-offs have a higher survival rate, but show no significant difference from other venture-backed firms in the amount of venture capital raised. Connecting the concepts and analysis to the Amazon company, the literature review provides some insight into Amazon's R&D sector in relation to the university.

According to the "TechCrunch" website, Amazon is expanding its R&D operations in Cambridge, UK with their plan to staff a large research lab. Cambridge is known as the world-class university that acts as a central place for concentrating science and technology talent, which is leading to many startups spinning out from it (Lomas 2017b). Amazon has expanded in Cambridge and uses candidates from Cambridge's talent pool. Some of the technological facility Amazon has been working on in their R&D sector with the university deals with the speech recognition in Echo product, and have existing researchers and startup players located in Cambridge which include computer vision technology and augmented reality.

Amazon lists the United Kingdom at the time. Research centers in London and Edinburgh, operating for its international blogs on digital media research and development and new technologies.

Also, the "Economic-times," Amazon opening a new Alexa R&D center in Cambridge. The new headquarters of Amazon in the city east of England, which is situated at the heart of a global innovation hub known as "Silicon Fen," will then be used to grow Prime Air. Prime Air was designed to use drones to deliver packages to customers in 30 minutes or less following the opening of the new tower. Amazon has pledged to create 5000 new roles across the country this year, bringing its workforce to 24,000 (Economic Times 2017).

According to the acmqueue site, the article, "A conversation with Werner Vogels" provides insight into Amazon's company and goals. Werner Vogel is the chief technology officer and the vice president of Amazon.com sheds light on how people in academia help Amazon and its current university situation (Queue.acm.org 2017). Werner Vogels states that Amazon does not look to academia to solve the challenges for them. They are building data sets in Amazon, however, to provide to academics so that they can get interactions going on some of the issues where they can contribute. Amazon has a number of internships and sabbatical positions where the PhD candidates and professors can spend time in a very high tech production environment. Vogel states that students who have come to Amazon for an internship find it extremely gratifying to build something real. He also encourages students that an internship at Amazon will help learn about building complex robust distributed services which is hard to learn with the university professors.

5.4.3 Amazon Industrial Collaboration and Cooperation

Amazon's current strategy is to concentrate its development efforts on continuous innovation by developing and expanding their business-specific, proprietary software, and licensing or purchasing commercially developed technology for other applications. It aims at primarily using its own proprietary technologies, as well as technologies licensed from third parties to implement numerous features and functionalities.

Engine Yard, established in 2006, offers a fully managed system delivery platform. This framework incorporates high-end clustering tools to run cloud applications for Ruby and Rails (CNET 2017). The firm, a provider of the best cloud platform and support for Ruby on Rails and headquartered in San Francisco, California has thousands of customers across 58 countries. Amazon has been delivering cloud-based services for more than two years and its presence is great for the role of Engine Yard at the forefront of two emerging markets-Ruby and Rails and cloud computing (CNET 2017).

Engine Yard, envisioned a project called Rubinius, to develop the next generation virtual machine for the Ruby programming language. This plans to implement Ruby as a core library, making a system available to build and extend. Merb is a light framework that is an ORM, JavaScript library, and agnostic language design framework. It has completed the second round of financing, from Amazon which has boosted Engine Yard's cloud computing effort with a capital infusion of $15 million (CNET 2017). This is an example of Amazon's strategy to collaborate with other firms and invest in the development of cloud computing solutions.

Ericsson, the Swedish company that manufactures most of the hardware infrastructure on which wireless networks run, plans to set up a team to help telecommunications around the world use the cloud (Greene 2017). Amazon has partnered with Ericsson aims to provide an improved infrastructure by encouraging telecommunications companies (telcos) to develop new technologies in the fields of internet, IoT, and big data analysis. The two firms aim to build "internet technology centers" that would help the telcos make the best use of the cloud as they adapt to a world changed by mobile networks and the Internet of Things (IoT). The company reported in Amazon's fourth-quarter report that AWS generated revenue of $2.4 billion, a 69 percent increase from last year's same time (Greene 2017).

5.5 Conclusion

Globalized firms tend to innovate more and therefore invest more in research and development activities that result in acquiring higher returns when compared to the purely domestic firms. The type of R&D activities can influence R&D locations as well as the regulatory, political, geographical, market aspects can have a major impact on establishing global centers for R&D This chapter presented a case study on Amazon, which is one of the fastest-growing online retailers in today's market. Amazon has successfully explored various sectors of businesses along with pioneering a few of the most revolutionizing technologies like the cloud computing services and the drone for transportation. The strategy that Amazon follows is to infuse technology in everything that they embark on and in everything that they innovate. Therefore, in the process, the company invests billions of dollars into research and development efforts in its development centers around the globe. Amazon has been successful in achieving international cooperation and the UK R&D center is one of the best examples of its development and testing activities outside of its headquarters in the United States. Amazon has also collaborated with academic universities in an attempt to forge ahead in innovation along with an intention of pooling in talent resources and increase internship and employment opportunities. Lastly, the study discusses that Amazon has not hesitated to collaborate with other firms and invest in research and development for continuous innovation. Amazon has always been successful in implementing its strategy of continuing its development efforts toward innovation, not only in its headquarters but also around the globe by collaborating with academic institutions and other industrial firms.

This study provides a great insight that globalized firms like Amazon envision innovation by continually investing more into research and development. Such firms always implement new strategies of international and industrial collaboration that fuel the pioneering of new technologies and innovation.

Acknowledgments Dirk Meissners contribution to the book chapter is based on the study funded by the Basic Research Program of the National Research University Higher School of Economics (HSE) and by the Russian Academic Excellence Project "5-100."

References[1]

Atkearney.com (2017) The 2017 Foreign Direct Investment Confidence Index—Publication—A.T. Kearney. [Online]. Available: https://www.atkearney.com/gbpc/foreign-direct-investment-confidence-index/publication/-/asset_publisher/oXeK018TjbvE/content/the-2017-foreign-direct-investment-confidence-index/10192

Caniels M (2003) Firm-level knowledge accumulation and regional dynamics. Industrial and Corporate Change 12(6):1253–1278

Chauhan A, Havugi V, Lin J, Kumte R, Valluri S (2017). Amazon.com

CNET (2017) Amazon invests in Engine Yard's cloud computing. CNET. [Online]. Available: https://www.cnet.com/news/amazon-invests-in-engine-yards-cloud-computing/

Digitaltrends.com (2017) [Online]. Available: https://www.digitaltrends.com/cool-tech/amazon-prime-air-delivery-drones-history-progress/

Dunning J, Lundan S (2009) The internationalization of corporate R&D: a review of the evidence and some policy implications for home countries. Review of Policy Research 26(1–2):13–33

"Economic Times" (2017) [Online]. Available: https://tech.economictimes.indiatimes.com/amp/news/technology/amazon-opening-a-new-alexa-rd-centre-in-cambridge/58530813

Greene T (2017) Amazon fights poverty with prime discount for those on food stamps. The Next Web [Online]. Available: https://thenextweb.com/insights/2017/06/06/amazon-fights-poverty-prime-discount-food-stamps/#.tnw_CnztvURf.

Hall BH (2006) The internationalization of R&D. [Online]. Available: http://www.international.gc.ca/economist-economiste/assets/pdfs/research/TPR_2011_GVC/09_Hall_e_FINAL.pdf

Lomas N (2017a) Amazon is expanding its R&D in Cambridge, U.K., with a focus on prime air drones and speech tech. TechCrunch. [Online]. Available: https://techcrunch.com/2014/11/11/amazon-cambridge-lab/.

Lomas N (2017b) [Online]. Available: https://techcrunch.com/2014/11/11/amazon-cambridge-lab/

London A (2017) Amazon opens new UK head office and reveals plans to double R&D roles in London—Housewares. Housewares. [Online]. Available: http://www.houseware slive.net/amazon-opens-new-uk-head-office-and-reveals-plans-to-double-rd-roles-in-london/

Lunden I (2017) Amazon ramps up global expansion, opens massive media R&D center in London. TechCrunch. [Online]. Available: https://techcrunch.com/2012/07/23/amazon-ramps-up-global-expansion-opens-massive-media-rd-center-in-london/.

'Masthead' (1975) The Journal of Organic Chemistry, 40(23);3A–3A

Miller R (2017) How AWS came to be. TechCrunch [Online]. Available: https://techcrunch.com/2016/07/02/andy-jassys-brief-history-of-the-genesis-of-aws/

Mitchell V (2017) Keeping up with the drones | Victoria Coren Mitchell. The Guardian. [Online]. Available: https://www.theguardian.com/commentisfree/2017/aug/05/keeping-up-with-the-drones-amazon

[Online] (2017a) Available: https://www.strategyand.pwc.com/media/file/2015-Global-Innovation-1000-Fact-Pack.pdf.

[1]Uncited references were used to develop this case.

[Online] (2017b). Available: http://homepages.vub.ac.be/~mcincera/research/CEB-169-MCBVP.PDF.
[Online] (2017c) Available: https://www.degruyter.com/view/title/506266
[Online] (2017d) Available: http://An analysis of R&D spillover, productivity, and growth effects in the EU.
[Online] (2017e). Available: http://vbn.aau.dk/files/202145375/ICTin_DK_Info.pdf
[Online] (2017f). Available: https://media.amazonwebservices.com/AWS_Overview.pdf
[Online] (2017g). Available: https://www.recode.net/2016/12/14/13955818/amazon-drone-delivery-uk-us-faa-testing
[Online] (2017h). Available: https://www.bloomberg.com/view/articles/2016-04-29/amazon-and-facebook-are-big-spenders-on-r-d
Queue.acm.org (2017) A conversation with Werner Vogels—ACM queue. Queue.acm.org. [Online]. Available: http://queue.acm.org/detail.cfm?id=1142065
Recode (2017) President Trump will talk policy with drone makers, wireless companies and tech investors on Thursday. [Online]. Available: https://www.recode.net/2017/6/21/15848456/trump-meeting-drones-wireless-investors
Reuters (2017) Alexa: where is Amazon opening a new R&D center? Cambridge, England. Reuters. [Online]. Available: http://www.reuters.com/article/us-britain-amazon-com-cambridge-idUSKBN180203
Sciencedirect.com (2012) Chinese foreign direct investment in R&D in Europe: a new model of R&D internationalization?—ScienceDirect. Sciencedirect.com. [Online]. Available: http://www.sciencedirect.com/science/article/pii/S0263237312000229
Smart Insights (2017). Amazon.com case study—Smart Insights Digital Marketing Advice. Smart Insights. [Online]. Available: http://www.smartinsights.com/digital-marketing-strategy/online-business-revenue-models/amazon-case-study/
Stewart J (2017) As Amazon's runs drone deliveries in the UK, America falls behind. WIRED. [Online]. Available: https://www.wired.com/2016/12/us-doesnt-want-drone-deliveries-amazon-took-england/
von Zedtwitz M, Gassmann O (2002) Market versus technology drive in R&D internationalization: four different patterns of managing research and development. Research Policy 31(4):569–588
Wernstedt K, Hersh R (2006) Brownfields regulatory reform and policy innovation in practice. Progress in Planning 65(1):7–74
Yurieff K (2017) Amazon patent reveals drone delivery 'beehives' for every city. CNNMoney. [Online]. Available: http://money.cnn.com/2017/06/23/technology/amazon-drone-beehives/index.html
Zhang J (2008) The performance of university spin-offs: an exploratory analysis using venture capital data. The Journal of Technology Transfer 34(3):255–285

Chapter 6
Ethical Issues of Data Tracking and Analytics

Aishwarya Joy, Tyler Stahl, Caitlin Mohnike, Rushikesh Jirage, Kate Darcy Kula, and Tugrul U. Daim

6.1 Introduction

On September 28, 2018, Facebook founder Mark Zuckerberg was in the uncomfortable position of having to announce the largest data breach in the social media giant's history (Isaac and Frenkel 2018). Hackers were able to obtain information on approximately 50 million Facebook users by exploiting a weakness in how accounts were linked to each other. Perhaps more amazingly, even 2 months after the hack, there is very little public information about what motivated the hack and what the hackers might have done with the information (O'Sullivan 2018). Adding to Facebook's woes is that this attack comes on the heels of the Cambridge Analytica scandal, where it was exposed that the research company had used data provided by Facebook to target political ads to Facebook users (Sherr 2018). While Cambridge Analytica attests that they legally obtained the data on approximately 87 million users, Facebook contends that the research company broke Facebook's data use policy. The question for consumers is, can they still trust Facebook with their data?

The onslaught of the information age has gotten most people used to the idea of trading their personal information for convenience. It could be as simple as sharing an email address in exchange for access to a website or as complex as sharing DNA profiles and family history in exchange for access to associated family data. By providing one's current location to Google, for instance, Google is able to provide a

A. Joy · T. Stahl · C. Mohnike · R. Jirage · K. D. Kula
Portland State University, Portland, OR, USA

T. U. Daim (✉)
Portland State University Technology Management Doctoral Program, Portland, OR, USA

National Research University Higher School of Economics, Moscow, Russia

Chaoyang University of Technology, Taichung City, Taiwan
e-mail: tugrul.u.daim@pdx.edu

T. U. Daim, D. Meissner (eds.), *Innovation Management in the Intelligent World*, Science, Technology and Innovation Studies,
https://doi.org/10.1007/978-3-030-58301-9_6

list of nearby gas stations, restaurants, and hospitals. By subscribing to a video streaming service, both the consumer and the streaming service are able to build a profile for that consumer and find associated content (and advertising) that the consumer will be interested in.

As the Internet of Things progresses, consumers seem eager to add more and more devices to their networks. From televisions, printers, and security systems, to the once analog domain of house lights, coffee makers, and cat food dishes, seemingly anything can be connected to the internet and consumers are both willing and eager to do so. However, while consumers seem to understand that they must hand over personal data in order for their network of things to work, they do not seem to question how this data could be used by anyone else.

After all, how can an application like Google Home, Instagram, or Pandora stay in business if they do not charge for the right to use their software? As the old adage from the 1970s goes, "if you're not paying for the product, you are the product" (Goodson 2012). In fact, for many of these companies, advertising is their main source of revenue. Even when they may not sell ads directly within their application, they are collecting data and/or building consumer targets to sell to advertisers. However, as Facebook can attest, when consumers are made aware that the information they have given away is being sold or otherwise used in a way that they are not comfortable with, it can quickly create hurdles for a company.

This paper aims to investigate the lifecycle of data in the relationship between businesses and consumers and the ethical implications of this collection and analysis. How is the data being collected, stored, and secured? What analyses can be done with data collected from the consumer? How does the marketplace of selling and buying data work? What steps must companies reasonably take to protect user information? Are companies staying within bounds of reasonable expectations for usage, or are they crossing the ethical line in their collection and analysis of our data?

6.2 Data Collection

The first step in discussing the ethics of using consumer data is to discuss how companies and organizations collect that data in the first place. Even when limiting the discussion to primary data collection methods, there is a large array of the types of data being collected as well as how it is collected from consumers. While the amount and types of data being collected may have proliferated in modern years, it is important to remember that data collection is nothing new.

Our most robust historical datasets tend to come from government sources such as census data, voter registrations, military service, and trial documents. In some countries, this information has been successfully retained for several hundred years. Most people would consider this type of data collection benign since it is necessary for the government to be able to do things such as allocate federal state resources based on population and identify tax payments from property owners. Interestingly, this type of data is not included when defining government surveillance and information and collection technologies (Nam 2018).

Rather, when news articles and academic papers are discussing privacy rights, the focus tends to be on more modern data collection approaches that have made it capable for governments to track individuals on both physical and transactional levels (Solove 2006). This data includes aggregate information such as how many people flew from PDX on Thursday to individualized tracking of "high-value" targets. Of course, it is harder to know how much information the government tracks on an individual level because it is generally classified.

A more upfront type of data collection is done on a financial level. Data is stored about an individual's financial record including the number of accounts, locations they have lived, and payments they have missed. Data is collected when credit accounts are opened or public filings, such as debt collections, are made. Similar to the government census, this data collection appears to be fairly benign for most consumers. The data is used to help verify the individual's identity and their creditworthiness and has been around for at least 50 years (Konsko 2017).

However, that is not the only data collected by financial institutions. Banks also keep a record of account transactions. While this is not new, the ability for companies to aggregate and trend transactions is. With modern computing capabilities, banks are now able to build profiles of their consumers. This can prove beneficial for consumers when a fraudulent purchase shows up that the bank is able to identify at the time of purchase and notify the account holder. Alternatively, the financial institution is also able to anonymize and sell this transactional data to other companies as discussed later in this paper (Cohan 2018).

Similarly, consumers give their personal data to their medical doctors. What they are less aware of, is that medical records are generally considered the legal property of the medical provider. This understanding remains legally murky, however, so the commercialization of the data collected has yet to materialize (Anon 2015).

Of course, government, financial, and medical records are all part of being a citizen. People tend to have them regardless of social or financial standing. There are plenty of opportunities, on the other hand, for consumers to accidentally opt in to data collection. One of the most pervasive areas for data collection is media usage. Cable providers have traditionally tracked television viewership via the set-top-boxes used to view content. The data-return capability also allows the company to troubleshoot software issues with the set-top box and verify subscription access. However, buried in the terms and conditions of the cable subscription contract is the opt in notice that the cable provider will collect data on what is being watched when (Comscore Grows TV n.d.).

Additionally, there is now legislation in place that allows internet providers to collect and sell data about what websites their consumers visit and what web apps they use (Fung 2017). This is on top of the data collected by website and web app owners. Sites commonly use internet cookies to help track where website visitors were before getting to a particular website and where they visit after leaving. Ironically, much of the information collected by websites is provided by the consumer themselves. Consumers have historically volunteered their personal information on sites like MySpace, Facebook, and Ancestry. They build their own profiles that the website is then able to sell.

Then, of course, there are the most recognizable sources for data collection, the market research firms like Nielsen. These companies are quite transparent about what information they are looking to collect and reward participation in surveys and studies with small financial or sweepstakes-style incentives. Data collection methodologies span from online surveys to data collection devices that the individual wears, referred to as a Portable-People-Meter. Originally designed to listen for digital tags in radio songs, these devices are now capable of passively collecting large amounts of environmental data (About Us n.d.).

Similarly, cell phones and wearable technology have evolved to collect and aggregate data both for the consumer and the manufacturer. Devices like Fitbit fitness trackers collect data on heartbeat, location, and sleep patterns. While consumers volunteer, and even pay, to have this data collected for them, companies are also able to collect additional revenue by selling the anonymized data (Fitbit Privacy Policy n.d.).

6.3 Data Storage

Data storage has become a huge industry as more companies are tracking and storing more and more pieces of data. Companies have a large responsibility to its users to keep their data safe. If users stop trusting companies with their data, then their business will begin to degrade. With this being such an important portion of their company, how are they storing our data, and how safe is it really?

6.3.1 Data Centers

To understand the enormity of the data storage problem, it is useful to understand how the biggest companies in the world are storing and securing their data.

In 2012, Google's data centers were reported to be indexing 200 billion web pages and over 3 billion search queries per day (Levy 2017). Google recently announced its latest data center in Henderson, Nevada. This $600 million data center (Hidalgo 2018) will be their 16th massive Google data center campus, adding to the current 9 in the United States, 3 in Asia, and 4 in Europe (Data Center Locations n.d.; Google Data Center n.d.). They employ extensive security to ensure that the data is secure. Over 550 security experts monitor Google's security protocols, looking for vulnerabilities and malware. To limit the physical vulnerabilities, they limit the number of people who have access to the actual site (Google Data Center n.d.). All data has levels of encryption, so that even if there was a breach, the data would be secure (Google Data Center n.d.). Devices that are to be decommissioned go through a multilevel process, ending with on-site shredding for devices that are not deemed to be fully wiped (Google Data Center n.d.; Kim 2015). Google keeps a tight lid on the exact configuration of their data centers, both on the location and the type of data centers that each campus has (Google Data Center n.d.). To validate the secureness of their campuses and data centers, Google uses Site Reliability Engineers. These engineers are "members of a geek SEAL team" (Levy 2017) whose sole responsibility is to attempt to hack into the data centers and disrupt the flow of data (Levy 2017). Each year they run a simulated war of sorts, called disaster recovery testing (DiRT) (Levy 2017). There are people within the centers whose job it is to respond to and fix whatever service the SREs are taking down, but they stop short of anything that will affect the users (Levy 2017).

Amazon has two layers of its data centers that are dedicated to security—the perimeter layer and the data layer (Data Centers n.d.). Access to the site is heavily monitored. Anyone without an ongoing need for access is sent through a visitor process and given temporary access. Badges are limited to spaces specific to the project that someone is working on (Perimeter Layer n.d.). They constantly monitor for intrusions with video surveillance and access log monitoring systems (Perimeter Layer n.d.). Their data layer is heavily armored, especially "Critical" devices that store customer data (Data Layer n.d.). All access points require multifactor authorization, monitoring can detect if someone attempts to take data, and if someone does manage to take a server it is automatically disabled (Data Layer n.d.).

6.3.2 Security Issues

The fact that there are so many levels of security surrounding these data centers is indicative of the threat level that companies with data face every day. Even with the amount of security surrounding data storage, there are countless examples of hackers getting access to data that is supposedly secure. There are stories of data getting accidentally published, employees losing devices with data on them, and even stories of passwords to secure servers being stored in un-secured environments (McCandless 2017).

The two main types of security threats that data centers face—malicious insiders and outside intruders (Vurukonda and Rao 2016). Malicious insiders are threats that are posed by employees or other people with access to the site itself (Vurukonda and Rao 2016). These attacks can be sophisticated, because of the level of knowledge the person has about the security and protocols (Vurukonda and Rao 2016). An outside intruder is someone who is attacking the data server from an external location (Vurukonda and Rao 2016).

Information Is Beautiful (McCandless 2017) has compiled a list of hundreds of data breaches where someone got ahold of more than 30,000 records. Here are just some of the examples they listed.

6.3.2.1 Malicious Insiders

One of the most well-known examples of data being stolen from a malicious insider is that of Edward Snowden stealing data from the National Security Agency. In 2013, Edward Snowden joined Booz Allen Hamilton with the intention of getting access to classified documents (McCandless 2017; Szoldra 2016; Edward Snowden 2014). Since joining starting work as a CIA technical expert in 2006, he had become more and more disillusioned with governmental work (Szoldra 2016). He began downloading data, amassing an estimated 1.5 million files that he eventually handed over to journalists in Hong Kong (Szoldra 2016). How was he able to access all of this data without anyone finding out? He was a SysAdmin with top-secret clearance on a system that utilized "thin clients" (a computer whose main processing power is housed on the server) (How Snowden did it n.d.). Those three items created a security hole, which meant he was able to have unfettered access to all files on the server and that his actions were not monitored or audited (How Snowden did it n.d.).

In September 2013, a contractor of Vodafone was able to steal data on all of its German customers, including their names, addresses, gender, birth dates, bank account numbers, and bank sort codes (McCandless 2017; Insider Steals Data n. d.). The attack was highly complex and sophisticated, and only possible because the user had heightened privileges and intimate knowledge of the Vodafone system (Kennedy 2017).

In 2008, an employee of a mortgage lender (Countrywide Financial Corp) was caught after downloading millions of borrower files onto thumb drives (McCandless 2017; Admitted Countrywide Data n.d.). The files, over 50,000 of which included social security numbers, were sold to other lenders (Admitted Countrywide Data n. d.).

In March 2012, Experian acquired Court Ventures (CV), a company that aggregates personally identifiable information from court records (McCandless 2017; Court Ventures n.d.). CV had a contract in place with USA Info Search (USIS) that allowed CV to query USIS for people's addresses so they would know which court records to search (Court Ventures n.d.). A user of CV's was eventually found to be reselling information found from USIS (Court Ventures n.d.). The hacker made more than 2 million dollars, and the identities of over 200 million Experience customers were stolen (Court Ventures n.d.).

6.3.2.2 Outside Intruders

On October 12th, WikiLeaks reported that they had a list of all Amazon Web Services data centers and their addresses (Sverdlik 2018). The released document listed over 100 centers, information that is closely held by Amazon. In practice, major companies like Google and Amazon keep the location of their data centers secret as a measure of security (Sverdlik 2018).

In March 2018, MyFitnessPal was hacked (McCandless 2017; Agencies 2018; Lamkin 2018). Over 150 million users' email addresses, usernames, and hashed passwords were stolen (Agencies 2018; Lamkin 2018).

In 2016, hackers were able to breach the FriendFinder Network and gain access to more data about more than 412 million users (Lamkin 2018; Dickey 2016). The hackers were able to take advantage of a "local file inclusion exploit" (Dickey 2016). The company was storing passwords in plaintext, kept logins for a site they do not run anymore, and retained emails and passwords for customers who had deleted their accounts (Dickey 2016).

That same year, hackers got access to 57 million names, email addresses, and mobile phone numbers of both riders and drivers of Uber (McCandless 2017; Uber concealed huge data breach 2017). In addition to that information, 600,000 drivers had their names and license details exposed (Uber concealed huge data breach 2017). It was reported that the hackers were able to find Uber's AWS (Amazon Web Services) password on a GitHub repository (Newcomer n.d.). Once on AWS, they found an archived list of riders and drivers and contacted Uber to ask for money to keep quiet (Newcomer n.d.). Uber complied, and paid the hackers $100,000 to delete the data (Uber concealed huge data breach 2017; Newcomer n.d.).

6.3.2.3 Mishandling of Storage Devices

In 2013, a hard drive that contained information on 70 million veterans failed (Singel 2017). When the drive failed, the agency neglected to destroy it, and instead returned it to the company that the bought it from for repair (Singel 2017). When the company determined it could not be repaired, they sent it to a third company to be destroyed (Singel 2017). This puts the data of millions of people at risk of being exploited.

In 2011, an unencrypted laptop storing 8 million user records was stolen from the NHS (McCandless 2017).

In 2014, 4 million patient names, social security numbers, addresses, and birthdates were accessed after 4 laptops were stolen from a building at the Department of Health and Human Services (HHS) (McCandless 2017).

6.3.2.4 Accidental Publishing

In 2013, Citibank published a published a set of court records on the Public Access to Court Electronic Records (PACER) system (McCandless 2017; Kovacs 2013). Unfortunately, they failed to redact consumer information (including social security numbers) of 150,000 clients who had undergone a bankruptcy between 2007 and 2011 (McCandless 2017; Kovacs 2013).

Due to a bug, in 2012 Facebook users who used the "Download Your Information" tool were also sent phone numbers and email addresses that were listed as private.

6.3.3 Is Your Data Actually Safe?

These examples and so many more should show you that no matter what companies do, the data that they are collecting is at risk of being accessed by people outside the company. If you consider that data is something that is constantly at risk, is it ethical for companies to keep extensive information on individuals? Even if they do everything possible to protect the data, should they also make sure that they are collecting and storing only relevant data to their app?

6.4 Data Brokers

6.4.1 What is a Data Broker?

Data brokers are businesses that collect information about consumers from a variety of different sources (Data Brokers and "People Search" Sites n.d.). Data brokers sell information to organizations, which can use it for their benefit, these sources can be public or non-public (Information Broker 2018). Public data is information that can be found on the open web and can be used by anyone. There is no evident link between the information being collected and the actual person's identity. Non-public data, of course is the opposite, this data can be linked back to the exact consumer. Some examples of this non-public data are personal identification numbers, credit history info, and loan details (Non-Public Personal Information (NPPI) n.d.).

6.4.2 What Data are They Collecting?

Going through your daily activities, think about all the data points that could be collected on you. Over time these data brokering companies create whole user profiles on people which adds immense value to companies selling various products. They can target and advertise directly to consumers that are more likely going to buy their goods and services. A report published by the Federal Trade Commission trying to uncover the data collecting industry provided a list of examples that include but are not limited to identifying, demographic, court records, social media, general interest, financials, vehicle, travel, and health (Mirani and Nisen 2014).

6.4.3 Data Brokering Companies

The top data brokering companies are Acxiom, Nielson, Experian, and Epsilon. Each company has their own role they play in the data brokering industry. Acxiom helps companies' market more effectively by using data to increase revenue and drive profits. They offer a variety of services that help their customers measure, track behaviors, demographics, and identity solutions. Acxiom serves a wide range of industries from automotive to insurance (Identity Resolution and People-Based Marketing n.d.). Nielson's focus is in the media industry, analyzing what consumers buy and watch. The main customers of this effort include advertisers, agencies, media owners, and fast-moving consumer goods (FMCG) retailers/manufacturers. In 2017 the "Watch" portion of their business accounted for 51% of revenue at 3.3 billion dollars, while the "Buy" earned 3.2 billion. Their marketing strategy revolves around the 3 R's of Reach, Resonance, and Reaction. "We help our clients "Reach" the most desirable consumers; gage the "Resonance" of their messages; and quantify consumer "Reaction" in terms of sales impact" (Stock Quote n.d.).

"Experian is a global leader in providing information, analytical and marketing services to organizations and consumers to help manage the risk and reward of commercial and financial decisions." They break their business into four key segments—credit services, decision analytics, marketing, and consumer services. Their main area of expertise is in consumer credit checks, where they hold information on over 220 million Americans as well as over 40 million US businesses. To put in perspective how much information that is, it equals 1.5 petabytes of data or over 1.5 quadrillion bytes; in comparison, it would be like taking 6000 pictures a day for the rest of your life. Last year their annual sales totaled more than 2 billion in North America (Experian's Corporate Fact Sheet n.d.).

Lastly, Epsilon, is a global leader in data-driven marketing, serving over 14 industries and assist 7 of the top 10 automotive manufacturers. The top products offered by Epsilon consist of transactional, demographics, and self-reported data solutions. They pride themselves in being able to gather data through various marketing channels such as email lists, digital, mobile, and social. Epsilon's customer base includes 15 of the top 20 global brands and 8 of the top 10 fortune 500 companies. An example of some of their work can be shown with how they helped Dunkin Donuts increase revenue through improved loyalty programs. In 2013, they revamped their comprehensive loyalty program to support real-time offers and incentives. With the adoption of DDPerks they had over 6 million people enroll and increased year over year spending by 40% (Abacus n.d.).

6.4.4 Future State of Data Brokering

The above enterprises are just the beginning of how data collection companies can customize marketing solutions to target customers and increase revenue. The goal for the future is going to be providing safety policies to ensure the amounts of data these companies are collecting are in safe hands and that there are safeguards if information does get hacked. Instances such as the large Experian data breach in 2013 that affected roughly 15 million people, 250,000 of which never even got notified that their information was not kept safe, can be taken as a lesson and improved upon so that this does not happen in the future (Krebs on Security n.d.). The top companies need to work together to keep data from being used wrongly and to keep improving the everyday lives of people around the world while not sacrificing user experiences.

6.5 Data Analytics

The availability of large amounts of computerized data in companies has steadily increased over the years, but recent progress in processing speed, cloud storage and increasing social networks has changed the ease of data access and the nature of data that can be captured and stored for later use (Earley 2015). The data that is collected must not only be collected but used for decision making. With the magnitude of the data that is collected, the speed and accuracy of analysis become valuable.

Data Analytics is the application of algorithms in order to analyze sets of data and extract useful and unknown patterns, relationships, and information (Adams 2010). Big Data Analysis technologies have been recognized as the "next big thing for innovation" (i.e., a potential source of business value and competitive advantage). It helps to enhance organizational agility and helps firms survive in competitive markets (Côrte-Real and Oliveira 2017).

The data available is in different forms and the method to analyze them depends on how the data is presented. There are three categories of data: Structured, Semi-Structured, and Unstructured, each requiring different analytic approaches. Structured data is collected via the internal and external business/ scientific systems. This data has well-defined variables, classifications, and classifications. They are usually accompanied by extensive metadata records. Semi-structured data contain information that is structured and unstructured. Examples are logs, emails, or tweets for transactions. The message may include the sender and receiver, origin, signature, date/time mark, header or subject line, etc. The unstructured part is the message's body, usually text or images. Unstructured data does not have a pre-defined template of data or is not predefined organized. Examples of unstructured data are digital images of historic documents, maps, blueprints, or books (Marsden and Wilkinson 2018). Common advanced data analytics methods are Association rules, Clustering, Classification, Decision trees, and Regression analyses. These techniques are used in the below-mentioned segments in a variety of industries to generate profit and reduce operational and material waste.

6.5.1 Customer Intelligence

Data Analytics is used in industries like retail, banking, and telecommunication for Customer Intelligence. Data is collected and analyzed to profile customers based on socioeconomic factors, customer satisfaction, and retention (Cebr Data Equity

2012). This information is used to help drive marketing decisions. It helps to identify influential individuals, can help organizations react to trends and perform direct marketing. In many cases, it leads to targeted promotions and customized advertising. Using sentiment analysis on this data, firms can be alerted beforehand when customers are turning against them or shifting to different products, and act accordingly (Elgendy and Elragal 2014). Amazon is the largest online retailer. It leverages its larger data system and customer base information to create a recommendation engine. Amazon launched Echo Look, a Hands-Free Camera, and Style Assistant that pairs with Alexa. Customers take a picture or video and upload it to Amazon's cloud. Amazon then offers recommendations based on current trends and what looks good on you. The theory is that they will look up what is the current trend and base recommendations based on it. But there is nothing stopping Amazon selling the rights to retailers to place their sponsored contents in the mix. In the end, we may be paying Amazon to show us advertisements (Markman 2017).

6.5.2 *Supply Chain and Performance Management*

Data Analytics is used in manufacturing, retail, as well as transport and logistics industries to improve their supply chain management. It can be used to forecast demand and adjust inventory based on supply chain trends. Also, by analyzing how the stock is utilized and the location of deliveries, organizations can automate replenishment decisions. This will reduce lead times, minimize costs delays, and process interruptions. Data analysis can also monitor performance, improve transparency and planning and management functions (Elgendy and Elragal 2014).

6.5.3 *Quality Management and Improvement*

The manufacturing, energy and utilities, and telecommunications industries use data analytics for managing quality. An example is that predictive analytics on big data can be used by providing early warning alerts to minimize performance variability as well as preventing quality issues. This in turn will reduce scrap rates and decrease market time by identifying any problems before they occur in the process. Data analytics also allows real-time monitoring as well as forecasting in response to external factors (Elgendy and Elragal 2014).

The latest hot trend in China is facial recognition. Through studying their faces, banks, airports, hotels, and even public toilets are all trying to verify the identities of individuals. Nevertheless, police and security are the biggest users of this software. They use facial recognition and artificial intelligence to analyze and understand the mountain of incoming video evidence; track suspects, detect suspicious behaviors and even predict crime; coordinate the work of emergency services; and monitor the coming and going of 1.4 billion people in the country, official documents and reports from the security industry show (China's Watchful Eye 2018). While on paper it may sound like an ideal system to reduce crime, it may be used as a away for the government to track people. In a country like China that has limited free speech, this system may be weaponized to target protestors, activists, or the press.

6.5.4 *Risk Management and Fraud Detection*

Industries such as Finance and Insurance have traditionally always used Data analytics to manage and mitigate their risk. They usually analyze the likelihood of gains vs the likelihood of losses (Elgendy and Elragal 2014). Healthcare industries used a lot of data to monitor their patients for risk assessment. Even government programs such as Medicare and Medicaid have made it mandatory for the digitalization of their records. This data is anonymized and made public so as to encourage analysis and app developers. It is also used in several sectors to detect and prevent fraud. Big data can allow them to match electronic data across several sources, between both public and private sectors, and perform faster analytics (Elgendy and Elragal 2014).

While data analytics is used by the big insurance provides to increase their profits it negatively harms the consumers who may fall under the high-risk category. This data analytics may end up disproportionately affecting people from lower income groups, minorities, and other high-risk sectors and causing them to pay higher for the same services. This practice is morally wrong and unfortunately enabled by the ease of data analytics.

6.6 Ethics and Privacy

Privacy, trust, and security are as closely intertwined as law and ethics. Privacy preservation and security provisions rely on trust. Violation of privacy is caused every time a security threat occurs. Under the guidelines of what is ethically and morally right, we can frame laws to protect citizens.

"Data Ethics" is a new branch of ethics that studies and assesses data-related moral issues (including generation, recording, curation, processing, dissemination, sharing and use) algorithms (including artificial intelligence artificial agents, machine learning and robots) and corresponding practices including responsible innovation, programming, hacking and professional codes), in order to formulate and support morally good solutions (e.g., right conducts or right values) (Wanbil and Lee 2018).

Data ethics builds on the computer and information ethics foundation, but at the same time refines the approach that has been endorsed in this field of research so far. It shifts the level of ethical inquiry abstraction from being information-centered to being data-centered. This change focuses on the different moral aspects of all types of data, including data that never directly translates into knowledge but can be used to support actions or produce behavior. It highlights the need for ethical analysis to focus on the content and nature of computational operations—hardware, software, and data interactions—as opposed to the variety of digital technologies that enable them. And it highlights the complexity of data science's ethical challenges. Therefore, data ethics should be defined as a macro ethic from the outset, that is, as an overarching philosophy that avoids narrow, ad hoc approaches and discusses the ethical impact and implications of data science and its implementations within a consistent, comprehensive and inclusive framework. Data ethics will provide solutions that maximize the value of data science for our societies, for us all, and our environments only as macro ethics (Wanbil and Lee 2018).

Lastly, the ethics of practices addresses pressing questions about the responsibilities and responsibilities of people and organizations responsible for data processes, strategies and policies, including data scientists, with the aim of defining an ethical framework for shaping professional codes on responsible innovation, development and use that can ensure ethical practices that promote both In this line of analysis, three issues are central: consent, user privacy, and secondary use (Floridi and Taddeo 2016; http://time.com 2018).

The European Union has implemented data regulation, the first significant regulatory policy in more than 20 years. The GDPR (General Data Protection Regulation) requires companies to ask consumers whether they can collect their data, answer promptly if asked what it will be used for and disclose significant data breaches within 72 h. Failure to fully comply could result in fines up to $23 million or 4% of the company's worldwide annual revenue of the prior fiscal year [R3]. In the future, E.U. plans to improve existing data protection rules. The following table shows several improvements to deal with data protection violations in the future.

In all, there is a need for stringent rules and regulations to handle the issue of data protection. The countries like the USA who are major contributor and data gathering sources need to establish, implement and comply with a data protection regulation to use of data by the industries as well as research organization to preserve the individual's privacy.

6.7 Conclusion

Data based analytics provide huge opportunities to improve private and public life, as well as our environment. Unfortunately, such opportunities are also coupled with significant ethical challenges. Data (often personal, if not sensitive) is extensively used to shape choices and to make decisions (including machine learning, artificial intelligence, and robotics). In addition, the gradual reduction of human involvement or even oversight of many automatic processes, among others, raises pressing questions of fairness, responsibility, and respect for human rights.

These ethical challenges can be addressed by fostering the development and applications of data processing systems that respect privacy and security as a human right. Alternatively, failing to constantly innovate the processes used in data gathering, storing, and analyzing would have severe setbacks. Companies that work with data must understand that they would gain social acceptability and, even better, social preferability if they make ethical choices as their guiding principles for any data science project.

Trust and transparency are also crucial aspects of the ethics of data. There must be active education to increase public awareness of the benefits, opportunities, risks, and challenges associated with data. For two major reasons, effective and pragmatic guidance is needed to develop data protection standards. The first is that the function of information security in a technology-driven information-intensive environment becomes more complicated due to new risks (e.g., socio-techno risk); the second is that data protection becomes a primary concern for information security management as an infringement of privacy occurs frequently and attracts wide media coverage.

Viewing privacy from an ethical perspective can help companies to set up and improve their code of conduct. Considering privacy from an ethical point of view and establishing a code of conduct makes the protection of valuable data accountable to all individuals in an organization, not just security personnel.

Acknowledgments Tugrul Daims contribution to the book chapter is based on the study funded by the Basic Research Program of the National Research University Higher School of Economics (HSE) and by the Russian Academic Excellence Project "5–100."

References

Abacus E (n.d.) The industry's most advanced data-driven marketing | Epsilon. https://us.epsilon.com/. Accessed 22 Nov 2018

About Us (n.d.). https://www.nielsen.com/us/en/about-us.html. Accessed 25 Nov 2018

Adams MN (2010) Perspectives on data mining. Int J Mark Res 52(1):11–19

Admitted Countrywide data thief gets 8 months in prison (n.d.). https://latimesblogs.latimes.com/money_co/2011/09/man-convicted-in-huge-countrywide-data-theft-gets-8-months-in-prison.html. Accessed 20 Nov 2018

Agencies (2018, March 30) Hackers steal data of 150 million MyFitnessPal app users. https://www.theguardian.com/technology/2018/mar/30/hackers-steal-data-150m-myfitnesspal-app-users-under-armour. Accessed 21 Nov 2018

Anon (2015, December 10) Patient records: the struggle for ownership. http://www.medicaleconomics.com/health-law-policy/patient-records-struggle-ownership. Accessed 25 Nov 2018

Cebr Data equity, Unlocking the value of big data (2012) In SAS Reports, pp 1–44.

China's Watchful Eye (2018, January 07). https://www.washingtonpost.com/news/world/wp/2018/01/07/feature/in-china-facial-recognition-is-sharp-end-of-a-drive-for-total-surveillance/?noredirect=on&utm_term=.e80cc368ec8b. Accessed 20 Nov 2018

Cohan P (2018, July 24) Mastercard, AmEx And Envestnet Profit from $400M business of selling transaction data. https://www.forbes.com/sites/petercohan/2018/07/22/mastercard-amex-and-envestnet-profit-from-400m-business-of-selling-transaction-data/#f130dfe77229. Accessed 25 Nov 2018

Comscore Grows TV Measurement Footprint to More Than 69 Million TVs in Over 31 Million U.S. Homes. (n.d.). https://www.comscore.com/Insights/Press-Releases/2018/2/comScore-Grows-TV-Measurement-Footprint-to-More-Than-69-Million-TVs-in-Over-31-Million-US-Homes?cs_edgescape_cc=US. Accessed 25 Nov 2018

Côrte-Real N, Oliveira P (2017) Assessing business value of Big Data Analytics in European firms. J Bus Res 70:379–390

Court Ventures (n.d.). https://www.cyberinsurance.com/breaches/courtventures/. Accessed 18 Nov 2018

Data Brokers and "People Search" Sites (n.d.). https://www.privacyrights.org/consumer-guides/data-brokers-and-people-search-sites. Accessed 23 Nov 2018

Data Center Locations—Data Centers—Google (n.d.). https://www.google.com/about/datacenters/inside/locations/index.html. Accessed 20 Nov 2018

Data Centers—Our Data Centers (n.d.). https://aws.amazon.com/compliance/data-center/data-centers/. Accessed 20 Nov 2018

Data Layer—Amazon Web Services (AWS) (n.d.). https://aws.amazon.com/compliance/data-center/data-layer/. Accessed 20 Nov 2018

Dickey MR (2016, November 13) FriendFinder Networks hack reportedly exposed over 412 million accounts. https://techcrunch com/2016/11/13/friendfinder-hack-412-million-accounts-breached/. Accessed 20 Nov 2018

Earley CE (2015) Data analytics in auditing: opportunities and challenges. Business Horizon 58 (5):493–500

Edward Snowden: A Timeline (2014, May 26). https://www.nbcnews.com/feature/edward-snowden-interview/edward-snowden-timeline-n114871. Accessed 21 Nov 2018

Elgendy N, Elragal A (2014) Big Data analytics: a literature review paper. Lect Notes Comput Sci 8557:214–227. https://doi.org/10.1007/978-3-319-08976-8_16

Experian's Corporate Fact Sheet (n.d.). https://www.experian.com/corporate/experian-corporate-factsheet.html. Accessed 24 Nov 2018

Fitbit Privacy Policy (n.d.). https://www.fitbit.com/legal/privacy-policy. Accessed 20 Nov 2018

Floridi L, Taddeo M (2016) What is data ethics?. Philosophical transactions. Series A, Maths, Phy Eng Sci 374(2083):20160360

Fung B (2017, March 29) What to expect now that Internet providers can collect and sell your Web browser history. https://www.washingtonpost.com/news/the-switch/wp/2017/03/29/what-to-expect-now-that-internet-providers-can-collect-and-sell-your-web-browser-history/?utm_term=.aff1ef3899d5. Accessed 23 Nov 2018

Goodson S (2012, July 31) If you're not paying for it, you become the product. https://www.forbes.com/sites/marketshare/2012/03/05/if-youre-not-paying-for-it-you-become-the-product/#5d72acf55d6e. Accessed 20 Oct 2018

Google Data Center FAQ, Part 2 (n.d.). https://www.datacenterknowledge.com/google-data-center-faq-part-2. Accessed 20 Nov 2018

Hidalgo J (2018, November 16) Nevada approves Google's $600M data center near Las Vegas, $25.2M in tax incentives. https://www.rgj.com/story/money/business/2018/11/16/nevada-approves-google-application-600-million-data-center-near-vegas/2026903002/. Accessed 20 Nov 2018

How Snowden did it (n.d.). https://www.nbcnews.com/news/world/how-snowden-did-it-flna8C11003160. Accessed 20 Nov 2018

"http://time.com" (2018) Time, [Online]. http://time.com/5290043/nazi-history-eu-data-privacy-gdpr/. Accessed 27 Nov 2018

Identity Resolution & People-Based Marketing (n.d.). https://www.acxiom.com/. Accessed 20 Nov 2018

Information Broker (2018, November 23). https://en.wikipedia.org/wiki/Information_broker. Accessed 25 Nov 2018

Insider Steals Data of 2 Million Vodafone Germany Customers (n.d.). https://www.securityweek.com/attacker-steals-data-2-million-vodafone-germany-customers. Accessed 19 Nov 2018

Isaac M, Frenkel S (2018, September 28) Facebook security breach exposes accounts of 50 million users. https://www.nytimes.com/2018/09/28/technology/facebook-hack-data-breach.html. Accessed 25 Nov 2018

Kennedy J (2017, October 06) Vodafone security CTO: 'High-profile data breaches are becoming the new norm'. https://www.siliconrepublic.com/enterprise/vodafone-security-infosec-data-breaches. Accessed 20 Nov 2018

Kim E (2015, June 30) Take a tour of Google's secretive data centers where all your photos and emails are stored. https://www.businessinsider.com/google-data-centers-store-all-your-photos-and-emails-2015-6#google-has-data-centers-in-14-different-locations-including-the-nether lands-singapore-and-chile-this-is-the-one-in-finland-1. Accessed 20 Nov 2018

Konsko L (2017, October 30) History of credit scores. https://www.nerdwallet.com/blog/finance/origin-credit-score-history/. Accessed 20 Oct 2018

Kovacs E (2013, July 22) Citi exposes details of 150,000 individuals who went into Bankruptcy. https://news.softpedia.com/news/Citi-Exposes-Details-of-150-000-Individuals-Who-Went-into-Bankruptcy-369979.shtml. Accessed 20 Nov 2018

Krebs on Security (n.d.). https://krebsonsecurity.com/tag/experian-breach/. Accessed 20 Nov 2018

Lamkin P (2018, March 30) Under Armour admits Huge MyFitnessPal Data Hack. https://www.forbes.com/sites/paullamkin/2018/03/30/under-armour-admits-huge-myfitnesspal-data-hack/#425de585cc54. Accessed 20 Nov 2018

Levy S (2017, November 10) Google throws Open Doors to Its Top-Secret Data Center. https://www.wired.com/2012/10/ff-inside-google-data-center/. Accessed 20 Nov 2018

Markman J (2017, June 05) Amazon using AI, Big Data to Accelerate Profits. https://www.forbes.com/sites/jonmarkman/2017/06/05/amazon-using-ai-big-data-to-accelerate-profits/#5a07b56b6d55. Accessed 20 Nov 2018

Marsden JH, Wilkinson VA. (2018) Big Data analytics and corporate social responsibility: making sustainability science part of the bottom line —2018 IEEE International Professional Communication Conference (ProComm). https://ieeexplore.ieee.org/document/8476826/authors#authors

McCandless D (2017, March 21) World's Biggest Data Breaches & Hacks. http://www.informationisbeautiful.net/visualizations/worlds-biggest-data-breaches-hacks/. Accessed 21 Nov 2018

Mirani L, Nisen M (2014, September 08). The nine companies that know more about you than Google or Facebook. https://qz.com/213900/the-nine-companies-that-know-more-about-you-than-google-or-facebook/. Accessed 21 Nov 2018

Nam T (2018) What determines the acceptance of government surveillance? Examining the influence of information privacy correlates. The Social Science Journal.

Newcomer E (n.d.). https://www.bloomberg.com/news/articles/2017-11-21/uber-concealed-cyberattack-that-exposed-57-million-people-s-data. Accessed 20 Nov 2018

Non-Public Personal Information (NPPI) (n.d.). https://rusecure.rutgers.edu/non-public-personal-information-nppi. Accessed 20 Nov 2018

O'Sullivan D (2018, October 04) Facebook's worst hack ever could get worse. https://www.cnn.com/2018/10/04/tech/facebook-hack-explainer/index.html. Accessed 25 Nov 2018

Perimeter Layer—Amazon Web Services (AWS) (n.d.). https://aws.amazon.com/compliance/data-center/perimeter-layer/. Accessed 20 Nov 2018

Sherr I (2018, April 19) Facebook, Cambridge Analytica, data mining and Trump: What you need to know. https://www.cnet.com/news/facebook-cambridge-analytica-data-mining-and-trump-what-you-need-to-know/. Accessed 23 Nov 2018

Singel R (2017, June 04) Probe targets archives' handling of data on 70 million vets. https://www.wired.com/2009/10/probe-targets-archives-handling-of-data-on-70-million-vets/. Accessed 20 Nov 2018

Solove DJA (2006) Taxonomy of privacy. Univ Pa Law Rev 154(3):477–560

Stock Quote (n.d.). https://ir.nielsen.com/. Accessed 20 Nov 2018

Sverdlik Y (2018, October 12) WikiLeaks Publishes what it says is a list of Amazon Data Centers. https://www.datacenterknowledge.com/amazon/wikileaks-publishes-what-it-says-list-amazon-data-centers. Accessed 20 Nov 2018

Szoldra P (2016, September 16) This is everything Edward Snowden revealed in one year of unprecedented top-secret leaks. https://www.businessinsider.com/snowden-leaks-timeline-2016-9?r=UK&IR=T. Accessed 21 Nov 2018

Uber concealed huge data breach (2017, November 22). https://www.bbc.co.uk/news/amp/technology-42075306. Accessed 20 Nov 2018

Vurukonda N, Rao T (2016) A study on data storage security issues in cloud computing. Proced Com Sci *92*:128–135

Wanbil F, Lee W (2018) An ethical approach to Data privacy protection. *Isaca.org*. [Online]. https://www.isaca.org/Journal/archives/2016/volume-6/Pages/an-ethical-approach-to-data-privacy-protection.aspx. Accessed 27 Nov 2018

Chapter 7
Silicon Forest, the Tier-2 Stagnation

Jessie Truong, Jose Banos Sanchez, Mohammad Al Gafly, Shreyas Vasanth, Smarajit Chakraborty, Tugrul U. Daim, and Dirk Meissner

7.1 Introduction

The term "Silicon Forest" refers to the Portland city and its metropolitan area. According to Wikipedia the definition is, (Silicon Forest 2018), "*...nickname for the cluster of high-tech companies located in the Portland metropolitan area in the U.S. state of Oregon, and most frequently refers to the industrial corridor between Beaverton and Hillsboro in northwest Oregon...*".

The nickname contains 2 words, silicon and forest. "Silicon" comes from the high concentration of silicon labs and companies related to microchips in the area. In order to do not imitate the "Silicon Valley" nickname, but with the clear roots on this nickname, the second word from the famous hub in California is changed to "Forest," looking into the West of Oregon abundance of forest. As a result, the nickname "Silicon Forest" tries to compress on it the dominant technology in the area and the landscape peculiarity in Oregon. The area has been slowly displacing lumber industry as the main industry and replacing it by high-tech firms that nowadays contribute to 1/5 of the State wealth. For all these reasons, Oregon State has a clear debt to high-tech industry and it must seriously commit to its future sustainability, which is undoubtedly related to Oregon future. But growth must not

J. Truong · J. B. Sanchez · M. Al Gafly · S. Vasanth · S. Chakraborty
Portland State University, Portland, OR, USA

T. U. Daim (✉)
Portland State University Technology Management Doctoral Program, Portland, OR, USA

National Research University Higher School of Economics, Moscow, Russia

Chaoyang University of Technology, Taichung City, Taiwan
e-mail: tugrul.u.daim@pdx.edu

D. Meissner
National Research University Higher School of Economics, Moscow, Russia

T. U. Daim, D. Meissner (eds.), *Innovation Management in the Intelligent World*,
Science, Technology and Innovation Studies,
https://doi.org/10.1007/978-3-030-58301-9_7

be done at any price and impact in the non-high-tech members of the society has to be considered too.

Political, economic, social, and technological (PEST) analysis is a powerful and commonly used analytical tool for understanding the complexity of regional development achievements. It works well especially when it is used on researches that follow a timeline evolution. Additionally to PEST, this research has added a subchapter for Business Observation Tool (BOT) in political analysis. BOT could be used as a completely separate analysis tool but the scope of the research would be lower.

Therefore, the model is divided into 4 main chapters and several subchapters inside with a final conclusion.

Political: It includes the Oregon's main political party evolution, Oregon State investment in infrastructures, Education, and the impact of the taxes to attract companies. All they together are finally reviewed from the BOT perspective (business observation tool).

Economic: Assessment through the factors that help to exam Oregon's economy such as inflation, interest rates, economic growth, and the unemployment rate. These factors will help in accessing the demand, cost of the product, expansion, and growth for Oregon's economy.

Social: The investigation of social aspect includes the study of population demographics, population growth, age distribution, and career attitude. These social factors help in gauging the potential size of the market environment for Oregon.

Technology: A look through the factors that help make assessment on positive or negative impact from technology to Oregon. These factors include technological advancements, lifecycle of technologies, diversity, and the spending on technology research by the government.

The four perspectives are interrelated to each other, and it is possible that some points analyzed in different perspectives may require a multi/dimensional analysis. This could be reviewed in future research. All perspectives are presented in the following.

7.2 Political Perspective

Looking into parallelism with plants and fertilizers, political decisions, and especially political long-term decisions represent the fertilizer to make plants grow and create a fertile land. Economic, technical, and social situations are in most of cases a later reflection or consequence of the political decisions previously done. Political decisions shape the short and long-term wealth of a state and therefore it should be a highly important topic and be present in our daily life.

7.2.1 History

Oregon is a very recent state with not a long history. It was formerly admitted to the US union in 1859 with certain peculiarities in its constitution that reflect a non-tolerant past in the State. According to (Novak 2015), "It was illegal for black people even to move to the state until 1926.". There are some reports that highlight the initial and lately longtime mentality in Oregon to be a pure-white State, in contradiction to the high number of immigrants that support and contribute to the wealthy economy in Oregon nowadays. But this could be analyzed more in detail in the social part.

Looking into the governor elections since the State joined the US union until the beginning of World War II, there is not a clear difference between the colors of the governor political party. Democrats and Republicans were alternating the State government with no clear side as preferred. It is after WW2 when republicans ruled the state continuously until 1991 with the only exception of two legislatures. After this election, it has been the other way around and democrats have been ruling the State continuously.

Among all governors in Oregon, there is one that could represent Oregonian mentality more accurately than the rest, even though he was not originally from Oregon. Tom McCall was the governor of Oregon for two consecutive terms, from 1966 till 1974, representing the Republican Party. He is very well known for two political decisions, and one popular quote (About Tom n.d.; Tom McCall 2018). His two decisions are still impacting Oregonian daily life:

1. He promoted a set of rules oriented to protect the environment. A couple of examples are the "Beach Bill" and "Bottle bill." He also created the Department of Environmental Quality. This environmental-friendly mentality is still a core in Oregonian politicians and Oregonian citizens. Their concern about the environment is probably the highest among the US states.
2. Establish the first statewide land-use planning system, which introduced the urban growth boundary around the state's cities. We could analyze whether this has an impact on the high cost of houses in the cities area.

Looking at his famous quote "We want you to visit our State of Excitement often. Come again and again. But, for heaven's sake, don't move here to live," we perceive the same feeling and mentality than current Oregonians. People in Oregon would love to keep living in a quiet and not stressful State. It may have a direct relationship with Silicon Forest stagnation because Oregon population does not want its State to be like California or Seattle metro area.

7.2.2 Education

Education is one of the core pillars for any society. It is not just an empty sentence but a fact that is behind some of the most recent and successful cases of developed countries. Looking into the list of most developed countries in the world we can find a common variable among them——high investment in the educational system. The world is changing and manual labor is less and less valuable year by year. The capacity and relatively easy ways for companies to move their manufacturing facilities from their home country to countries with lower wages make these types of jobs not anymore a competitive value and easily replaceable. However, the knowledge, the creativity, the entrepreneurship, etc. are the new values to generate wealth. We have seen how Scandinavian countries, South Korea, or Singapore are among the most competitive nations worldwide and one of the reasons for this successful transition to highly developed economies was and is their investment in education and not because of their lower wages. Even looking into the United States, as Bauer, Schweitzer, and Shane (2006) describe and conclude with a mathematical argumentation, during the XXI century the college attainment represents one of the most important variables to explain the salaries increases in some states above others.

But investment in education is not only worth from an economic point of view but from a social point of view too. It helps to reduce inequality, which leads to a higher middle class. According to (Bauer et al. 2011), there are direct benefits with an increase in higher education population like lower criminality, higher productivity among a long list of nonmonetary societal benefits from enhanced educational attainment has been documented. However, Oregon has not invested actively in the creation of a worldwide known university. The initial collaboration between Oregon State and education as mentioned by Heike (2001) was during 1999 when NEC was created as a lobby to promote the education investment in high tech. It was a private initiative that later on attracted state participation. OCKED (Oregon Council on Knowledge and Economic Development) was formed in 2000 as the first real step from the State government to promote and support High Tech in Oregon. Several other initiatives came along the first decade of the XXI century, but they were punctual collaboration more than a long-term program.

Comparing the invested share to US and similar states like Oregon, we can see a gap for Oregon being far from other States. There is a lower investment in education at K-12 and higher education levels. Oregon needs a top education system if IT technology pretends to become the future of the region. IT companies demand an educated source of workers capable to compete with knowledge and new developments with other regions in the United States and by extension in the world.

Looking at the rate of investment in Higher Education in Washington compared to Oregon, the difference is more than 10 percent. Therefore, the investment is lower not only for K-12 level but also for higher education. Looking at the last 6 years instead of increasing the percentage of incomes dedicated to funding higher education, the percentage has dropped (Oregon state budget and finances n.d.).

In conclusion, the Oregon State investment in education is a critical factor that could help to develop a higher amount of educated and competitive workforce in the State. However, the state's political decisions do not seem to be too concerned about the importance of such investments and therefore education costs are directly supported by families and companies.

It is critical that the Oregon government get involved in the university and higher education system in Oregon, promoting and sponsoring new ideas, helping to attract talent to the education system, and creating a strong ecosystem in education sector capable to support the requirements from the private sector.

7.2.3 Taxation

One of the first variables that come to our mind when we think about politics is the taxes. Taxes are the fuel that states and countries use to keep the engine running, to invest in infrastructures, pay public employees, and look for the wellbeing of the population (at least, in theory. . .). In the case of Oregon, taxation of companies has varied over the years and it has not always been as "company friendly" as it is nowadays, with high tax exemptions to corporations. Let us see how is the tax distribution system actually in Oregon before continue.

Corporate taxation is pretty low and foreign companies are almost exempt to pay taxes. Additionally to that, certain counties have the possibility to exempt big firms with additional exemptions. Therefore, and according to a study by Ernest Young in 2011 (Ernst Young 2011), it includes Oregon, among the top 5 most competitive States with the lowest combined state and local business taxes as a share of the economy among all the United States. However, it is interesting to realize that none of the states with Tier-1 higher-tech hubs is at the top of the list.

But until the middle 1980s, Oregon had a unitary taxation, which forced any company established in Oregon to pay in Oregon a portion of its total worldwide sales. This was clearly a stopper for abroad companies or even companies from other states to allocate their offices or subsidiaries in Oregon. The first time it was over the table and a modification was analyzed was during the 1980s when different Japanese companies tried to enter the United States and found out that Portland would be a good location to open a subsidiary.

However, looking into the individual taxation, we can see in the next figure, that there is not a clear benefit either comparing Oregon with Seattle or California, the neighbors and competitor states in terms of high-tech jobs.

According to taxes distribution, it seems more probable that most of the demanded high-tech professional, with a similar salary proposal, they will choose Seattle or California because of lower taxes. Considering only the incomes taxes deduction in Oregon, a salary in Washington compared to Oregon is around 10% higher.

Current taxation distribution and corporations' exemptions have been several times questioned from the Oregon government, who has tried to change it on

2 occasions with different results. They were in 2009 with Ballot 66/67 and more recently in 2015 with Ballot 97.

7.2.3.1 Ballot 66 and 67

In 2009, Oregon State was facing a serious problem with its debt and budget deficit. The solution from government was to increase the taxation to the personal incomes (ballot 66) and remove some of the corporate tax exemptions (ballot 67). Measure 66 proposed to increase the taxation to the highest rents by 11% and reduce it progressively to lower rents. By the other hand, measure 67 increased the taxes to corporations and reduce some of their exemptions.

Both measures were approved in 2010, but the forecasted incomes during the next years were shorter by 1/3 below the expected. Therefore, the initial plan by the Oregon government was not achieved. Additionally, there is no clear answer about the reason behind the change on migration trend but during 2009 the ratio of migrants from Oregon to Washington (where there were no income taxes) was the highest in the last decade. It is not possible to clearly find a correlation between the Ballot 66/67 approval and migration increase to Washington, because it could be motivated by the 2009 Great Recession too. In any case, the following chart shows an interesting increment of migrants from Oregon to Washington than more than double respect to the previous year in 2009 (Ernst Young 2011), just after higher individual taxation was approved.

7.2.3.2 Ballot 97

In 2015, Oregon State was back into trouble with its budget and the debt continued as a major issue as it was during 2009.

The Oregon's government proposed to increases the corporate minimum tax for "C" corporations with at least $25 million in Oregon sales. Actually, Oregon C corporations pay the higher of either an excise tax or a minimum tax based on the corporation's sales in Oregon. Oregon companies with sales under $25 million would not be affected (Oregon Tax Hike Vote n.d.).

In less than 10 years, Oregon government has proposed an increase in the companies' taxation two times. This unusual situation led the biggest companies to lobby against this measure and influence in politics for the first time. The companies raised a historical $28.13 million for the "No" support (The Jury Is Back 2011).

Voters soundly defeated Measure 97 on November 8, preserving the business taxes situation as it was and Oregon as one of the states that have some of the lowest business taxes in the nation. As a counterpart, the same election, left Oregon's schools among the worst funded in the United States.

7.2.4 BOT

To conclude with the political impact on the lack of high tech consolidation in Oregon, from business observation point of view, the biggest impact was and it has continued being the lucrative exemption on taxes to companies. There is no other major variable that could foster or detract companies to move in or leave Oregon.

Assessing the ballot impact, we can conclude that increasing the taxes as a solution to solve the State debt problems is not a positive long-term decision. Few years after Measure 66 and 67 were approved, the debt issues and deficit on budget were again over the table in Oregon State government. As a result, a second ballot was celebrated to decide whether big companies should pay more taxes or not through new taxes schema. Taxes are a solution, but never by themselves alone. They are a solution if they are combined with the proper political decisions or changes to solve the root cause that causes the problem and ended demanding taxes increase.

Finally, looking in terms of total state spending including federal and regional incomes, the amount of money spent per capita in Oregon is higher than other states competing to attract high-tech companies like Washington or California. Therefore, the question is where is the spending going and why is it not helping to promote the industry that right now represents around 20% of the state incomes? From the political point of view, it seems that money is not going into the right investments, neither schools are properly founded or IT sector promoted beyond the tax exemptions.

Nevertheless, political decisions are not the only reason why companies may decide not to establish their offices in Portland. According to the articles review and research done, political factor is not the biggest that prevent the establishment or creation of new companies in Oregon.

But there is a risk in Oregon's economy-related to politics. Oregon state has a huge debt, affecting the future of public workers pensions among others. Politicians tend to increase taxes in order to solve their mistakes or lack of capacity to solve the problems in a creative way. The risk in Oregon is that in order to cover the State debt crisis, politicians finally convince population to increase corporation taxes. It could create a cascade effect in the high tech industry in Oregon, starting with a bunch of companies leaving the state. As a second direct consequence, it will influence other foreign/national companies to do not move to a less competitive State from a tax point of view. Fewer companies in Oregon will be a direct cause for less hiring and fewer people having a job, and therefore fewer people paying taxes. Individual taxes means the highest percentage for Oregon state incomes, and hereby the situation in a few years could be even worse than the situation before the taxes were raised.

7.3 Economic Perspective

Oregon's economy is composed of various forms of agriculture, fishing, and hydroelectric power due to its diverse landscapes. The state is known for its large timber producer which dominated the state's economy in the twentieth century (Oregon Department of Land Conservation n.d.). The other major economic force for the state is technology, which beginning in the 1970s with the expansion of Tektronix and Intel. Oregon hit hard times in the 1980s led the state to grow more on high-tech sector. After many decades, the state has transitioned from traditional resource-based economy to a mixed manufacturing and marketing economy, emphasizing high technology (Oregon Blue Book n.d.). Oregon hit hard times for second time during the Great Recession. There were about 8% job lost and had caused a financial crisis to the state. Until today, Oregon has not only regained all those jobs but also increased by 6.5% from the pre-recession peak (Perkowski and Capital Bureau 2017).

7.3.1 Inflation Rate

According to report from the Oregon Office of Economic Analysis inflation for the Portland-Salem were followed the nation average trending over the past 27 years. It raised as nation raised and fall as nation falls. Although in the 1990s and early 2000s where the inflation for Portland-Salem were increased while US inflation was falling. Perhaps local inflation might have had economic policies that could fluctuate the state's economy causing the quirks and the different movements seen on the chart (Inflation, 2013 n.d.). And perhaps this might be one of the reasons why Oregon tends to fall deeper in recessions.

For the upcoming years, experts are expecting inflation rate to rise. The International Monetary Fund, who prepared the forecast for the US inflation projected two to three percent annual rise prices in general. This means that a product bought today for about $100 will cost about $102–$103 next year (Statista n.d.). Will Oregon be able to keep its inflation rate steady?

7.3.2 Mortgage Interest Rate

In 2013, there was a dip in mortgage interest rate because the Federal Reserve announced that it will maintain its bond-buying stimulus, which should help offset the house price gains and keep housing affordable at the time. The interest rate climbed after that which suggested that the Federal Reserve believed the US economy had improved enough to withstand the climbing rates. Currently, the mortgage interest rate for 30 years fixed is at about 4.43%, while the 10 years treasury rate is at 2.86%.

The Wall Street Journal's Economic Forecasting Survey projects that the 10 years treasury rate will increase to 2.90% by June 2018, and 3.13% by the end of 2018. Looking ahead to 2020, the rate is projected increasing to 3.54% (Economic Forecasting Survey n.d.). According to economic experts, mortgage rates are also expect rising to 5% by the end of this year, and to 5.7% by 2020 (Mortgage Interest Rates Forecast 2018, 2019, 2020, 2021 AND 2022 n.d.). Analysts believed that the Federal Reserve will raise the rates up again. So far the rate has not been close to where it used to be before the Great Recession.

Oregon's strong job growth has been attracting newcomers causing high demand for home to skyrocket. With mortgage interest rate expecting to rise, home buyers are in rush for purchasing. Will this cause the housing price in Oregon to soar like in Silicon Valley or Seattle, Washington?

7.3.3 Economic Growth

The state has been ranked third among other states with economic growth since 2001. Oregon ranks third among states in terms of economic growth since 2001. The state has grown more than double that of the national economy. Data from the Oregon Center for Public Policy showed that in 2015, the state's economy expanded to 56% while the national economy was at 26% ("Oregon's Top Performing Economy Can Offer Opportunity for All", n.d.).

Ringing in third place as one of the states with strong economic growth from the nation has create an attraction for people to move to Oregon. The state's population has reached 4.1 million in 2017, growing a total of 64,750 during the past year. A growth rate of 1.6%, combined with similar gains in 2015 and 2016, mark the largest population growth in the state since the 1990s. People come to Oregon for job opportunities and have opportunities to create jobs (Urness n.d.).

According to the report from 2001 to 2015, the national economy grew about 12% on a per person basis while Oregon's growth about 35%. Despite the growing population, Oregon's per capita economy grew nearly three times that of the national average, and remain in second place after North Dakota ("Oregon's Top Performing Economy Can Offer Opportunity for All", n.d.).

Although Oregon wage trends have been accelerated steadily for the past years; but it is slower than in the 1980–1990, and a bit better on an inflation-adjusted relative to the mid-2000s where Oregon's gains outpaced the nation. The average wage is at its highest point today since the 1980s but still lower than the United States overall. Similar situation is also seen with per capita personal income, while still lower than the United States overall, it is at its highest relative point today since the dotcom crash (Oregon Wages, A 2017 Update n.d.).

Wages and household incomes are rising, while poverty and caseloads for needs-based programs are falling. Oregon's economy continues to expand, but analysts believe it is finally getting to where the business cycle is at its "feel-good" stage, and that the state is approaching full employment, and entering to a more sustainable pace. They are expecting for these trends to continue until the next recession comes (Oregon Wages, A 2017 Update n.d.). According to state official analysts, there will be a slightly faster job growth this year. The unemployment rate is also expected to be slightly higher (Quality Information, Informed Choices n.d.).

7.3.4 Unemployment Rate

Oregon unemployment rate fell below 4% in mid of 2017 making a record low in history. While the national economy remains strong, Oregon's employment is even better. It has been a slow journey for the state to recover from the Great Recession. The state has rapidly added jobs and playing catch-up (Quality Information, Informed Choices n.d.).

As mentioned earlier, one of the State's budget comes from income tax. A low rate in unemployment means the State receive more money for their budget. This is one of the signs showing the economy is doing well.

7.4 Social Perspective

7.4.1 Population Demographics

Portland is a recent city, incorporated in 1851 with under 1000 people, it grew quickly. By 1879, there were over 17,000 inhabitants listed (Beebe 2016). This did not take into consideration any displaced Native tribes, but counted the people working to develop the area. Portland was competing with the growth seen up North in Seattle and winning. The two cities compete today in the areas of technology and growth. Looking at the historical aspects of the city growth will show trends in the development of the city's educational and work fields while also providing a measure to estimate where the region is heading for the future. Looking at the past, present, and predictions of the future helps people understand the total growth of the Portland region in Oregon. This State was begun as the "white's only" State in the Union (2018 World Population by Country n.d.-b), and is working to bring diversity and growth through the economic powers of education and technology.

While still predominantly white, Portland Metro is showing an increase in cultural diversity. In recent years demographics have shown that Portland is still a predominantly white city; however, this does not take into account the large educational population within the city due to the shifting numbers of visiting citizens listed as students. Looking at the demographic outline of Portland State University shows a more varied demographic (U.S. Census Bureau 2010).

The issues facing Portland in diversity are trending toward more balance within the colleges showing the natural pull of diversity to the area. Those who choose to stay are doing so for the aspects provided by the region and career opportunities.

7.4.2 Population Growth

Tracking of growth in Oregon's Portland Metro area includes Clackamas, Columbia, Multnomah, Washington and Yamhill counties, Oregon and Clark and Skamania counties, Washington (U.S. Census Bureau 2010). It is the increasing numbers of people in the area who are adding to the costs of living, educational means of the citizens, and the estimates of continued growth. Over 21, 000 people moved into the area from other US towns and cities. This is over half of the entire growth of 2014–2015; this trend can be traced to jobs provided by companies such as Tektronix, Intel, and Nike.

Yearly growth is consistently been more than 1% since 2010. This has placed Portland on the Forbes lists of one of the best cities in the United States.

7.4.3 Age Distribution

Portland is still a young city. With the median age in the 30s, this shows that people are able to work for a long time, provide toward the economic growth of the region, and bring population growth to the area as well. This will lend information toward estimates for the education, business, economic, and health needs for Portland's future.

Estimates for social services including housing, food, and medical use numbers such as these to determine the level of care and needs Portland has. The elderly generation is significantly less than the working population. The trend can show either the availability to survive to live in the area, or the number of people who leave for warmer climates in retirement ages. The averages in the college-age populus drops by approximately 20,000, which shows the normal trends for children leaving their parents and forging their own paths. What the age population does show is that the median age is steady, and the pool leaving is not above the normal expectations, which lends credence to the stability of Portland and its future.

7.4.4 Career Attitudes

According to national averages statistics Portland is getting expensive to live. Listed at approximately 10% of the national housing averages, the best businesses are bringing in the brightest people, and the demands are increasing. This trend is unlikely to change. The prognosis is in direct competition with the green and sustainable living Portland claims. The manufacturing industries will need to increase the technological aspects to improve green building components to maintain the city's quality of living and dedication toward green living. The college attainment group shows that out of the total citizen numbers less than half have obtained a college degree. This does not reflect the number of people who may have taken advanced classes, own small businesses, or are striving toward that degree. What it does show is that the city is unable to maintain the demands of the new graduates coming from the local colleges. Education is a high goal, but the area businesses are not growing fast enough to demand a larger portion of the graduating classes. The cost of living is high, this also may determine the number of entry-level positions available to those new graduates. The cost and availability of sustainable housing that would be in demand would overrun the market which would then again drive up the cost of living. There is a balance that Portland is not yet attaining due to its growth, age, and demographics.

7.5 Technical Perspective

7.5.1 Technological Advancements

Ever since tech giant Intel moved to Oregon, the state saw a significant rise in the technology companies in Oregon. Lots of small startups started budding and other big names started relocating to the state. Right now the area has around 400 high tech companies, including the startups. Even the company who sowed the seed of the Silicon Forest, Tektronix, recently revamped itself and is innovating constantly to stay as one of the biggest dominators of the area. Intel came to the Silicon Forest so it was closer to the Silicon Valley unlike its other quarters and built their biggest and most comprehensive research and manufacturing facilities in the world. It is the workplace of around 20,000 people. Intel created an ecosystem in Oregon, which drew other companies. FEI Company is one of those companies. FEI primarily manufactures high-end electron microscopes, which Intel uses for its submicron photolithography process and, in return FEI mimics Intel's idea and improves its market intelligence. Many metal sheet manufacturing companies started budding up in Oregon to provide for Intel's FABs (Bandlamudi et al. 2016). As a matter of fact, research says that 25% of the high-tech companies are dependent on semiconductors and software. With these companies creating a hub here, it has improved the high-tech employment rate of the state over the years. Back in the 1970s timber used to be the biggest source of income in the state and today it has exchanged places with high-tech employment, which was low back in the day (Oregon Office of Economic Analysis 2016).

The ecosystem created here has not only attracted companies to form ecosystems but also attracted big companies like eBay, Amazon, and Facebook to build huge outposts here along with new budding startups in the area. Recently an augmented reality-based startup, RealWear, moved their headquarters to the Silicon Forest and raised $17 millions (Rogoway 2018b). Apart from technology-based startups, even nontechnical startups that heavily rely on the Internet are increasing in number. Fleet, a shipping service company, owned by 22-year-old native Portlander, Max Lock, raised "*$14 million for technology to help small and midsize businesses ship or import products around the globe*" (Rogoway 2018a). With budding high-tech startups like RealWear, Fleet, Vacasa, Jama software, Opal, Drone Compiler, Levrum, etc. (bizjournals.com n.d.; 10 Best Tech Startups in Portland 2018) along with big business fished like Facebook, Amazon, Google, the Silicon Forest has turned into a high-tech business hub creating new ideas every day. As a matter of fact, the technology density, productivity, STEM concentration, and R&D intensity of Oregon has made the state the sixth most innovative state in the United States, as per Bloomberg's ranking of the most innovative US states (Here are the Most Innovative States in America in 2016 2016).

7.5.2 Lifecycle of Technologies

A technology life cycle has 4 distinct stages, the first being research and development of the technology, second stage is its ascent, third stage is the technology reaching its maturity, and the last one being its decline. The technologies also have adoption lifecycle. Empirical evidence generates a positive correlation between technological innovation and economic performance.

In the case of Oregon, they have invested a lot in the R&D, especially in the semiconductor industry which led to the creation of Silicon Forest. Now, it has hit the phase of maturity which is flat and likely to decline in the near future as we can see in Exhibit-14 where the total amount of jobs is stable since the dotcom crisis. This also looks like a good opportunity to invest in developing new technologies to balance the decline of current technology (semiconductor) (Foxley and Stallings 2014).

7.5.3 Diversification of Industries and Spending on Technology Research and Development

Diversification helped the state to eliminate any dependency on a particular industry, this kind of dependency on any industry can prove fatal in case that particular industry has recession or becomes obsolete. These diverse set of industries have become an unparalleled asset to the economy of the Portland metropolitan region and the state of Oregon [44].

Oregon has always been observed to spend less on higher education than its neighboring states. But in recent years, investment by the government in universities and community colleges has seen a slight growth. These high education public institutions include a huge number of high-tech graduates including engineers and technologists. At the same time investment by venture capitalists are close to double of what it was five years ago. Venture capital investment significantly in the year 2017 (Rogoway 2018c). As a matter of fact, Oregon startups got an investment of $1.7 millions at the Bend Venture Conference (bizjournals.com n.d.). With high-tech funding on the rise along with investment by capitalists in business, Oregon is providing a huge opportunity to startup aspirants to fulfill their dreams.

7.6 Discussion and Conclusion

- In the past, Portland was more green and friendly compared to now. The increase in companies and people moving in had impacted the area. Traffic congestion is getting worse, but more importantly, PDX is now extremely diversified. The largest industry is wood products and the largest company is Nike. Seattle has the technology and business density makes it a good place for relocation. Portland has created lots of tech jobs attracting a lot of outsiders but locals could not capitalize on this as they were not educated/skillful enough to compete for these jobs. Oregon has the third highest high school dropout rate in the country which is due to the level of funding received to the school districts in Oregon, which is very low compared to other states. This lack in high school education quality has underprepared people in this region to be not equipped to compete with the workforce to obtain these tech jobs. Education cost is increasing and the difference between rich and poor is also increasing.
- Oregon is one of the two states that does not have sales tax, this reduces the revenue of the state. Hence, calling for budget cuts on several things, one of them being education. Oregon does have an impact on the US economy as a whole but does not grow necessarily. It does not need to be fixed from that as it is not a "broken" state. Tax incentives and availability of talent are the most advantages/disadvantages for Oregon.

Political decisions like lowering the taxes during the 1980s and 1990s helped attract newer companies, but they were not enough to consolidate the expansion and sustainable growth of the industry in Oregon. Political decision cannot be the only responsible for the lack of growth on Silicon Forest but they are part of it. For any reason, the low taxes only attracted one huge company during the 1990s, Intel, but no other major companies decided to establish here its main office. Recently, some software companies opened offices here but they were subsidiaries offices employing less than few hundreds people. One remarkable example of the lack of attraction for big firms in Oregon was the recent search for a city to host its second hub announced by Amazon. Portland was never among the potential candidates to host this hub with an estimation of 50,000 new jobs.

A decline in unemployment rate was driven by the growth of startup sectors. Several startups were born here in Oregon, but the trend is that either they die here or when they grow enough they move to other states. No major startups have been able to flourish in Oregon. One of the reasons is short of resources. Entrepreneurs are hungry for talented employees, but with high demand, it can be difficult for them to find the right people for their open positions. Other factors might also have contributed to the fact that the consolidation is not happening and making startup to consolidate their growth elsewhere.

The existence of big firms seems to be the reason for other firms to move to Oregon and local firms growth based on supplying services to big firms. Additionally, there is an ecosystem of new companies built around a big central company from where spin-offs are created by individuals leaving these big companies looking for major challenges. In Oregon, as a big pure high-tech company there is only Intel, and it seems to be not enough to guarantee the expansion. Looking into a parallel case, we can see how companies related to sport sector have flourished around Nike, who attracted the Adidas North America headquarter and it has a direct impact on the creation of Columbia sports.

It is very risky to have all the high-tech jobs related to a single main industry, semiconductors. A good example is the Nokia case. Nokia impacted dramatically the job market and the economy of Finland when it felt as a consequence of their lack of capacity to adapt to smartphones new era. Oregon might fall into the same situation as Finland if Intel fell. A diversification toward software sector seems to be happening, leaving the strong dependency on microchips and hardware as less critical. In the recent years, hardware jobs' growth rate is almost flat, but software is increasing rapidly. Maybe this is a step to diversify the industry in the area and it may help to create a big firm that will attract other software companies and create a new ecosystem around it.

Education is the base for a healthy and wealthy society, and therefore it should be one of the top priorities for Oregon government. Education cannot rely only on private institutions or private companies to support it. A closer collaboration between them and the state is demanded for the long-term success of the region. This ecosystem university–private sector has proved its benefits leading other regions and countries in the world to become technological leaders. Additionally, the state obtains most of its revenue from income taxes, therefore, its best interest should be to create more high-tech well-paid jobs to collect more taxes. Oregon universities must create more professional programs to upskill students to satisfy the high skilled professionals demanded by companies from the state. Investment in education is a winning bet with a high return. The state should be involved in the quality and improvement of education.

Oregon's healthy economy's been very attractive for new businesses. There were lots of people moving to the state in the past recent years for job opportunities. This has caused the housing market price soaring due to high demand and low supplies. Inflation rate also increases in recent years forcing businesses to raise prices, and banks to increase the interest rate. These factors impact small business operations. In addition to the high real estate cost, small businesses are also affected by Oregon high-income tax, as well as some other taxes. Also, the state is protected by a lot of Environmental acts and even the residents here hate losing the green cover to give way for concrete structures. This limits the opportunity for businesses to expand.

During the research, we found very interesting parallelism between certain countries' economies evolution from development to pre-development and later on, the most complex, the evolution from pre-development societies to highly developed societies. This final step is in many cases a backward step or an eternal situation of no change. It is known as "middle incomes trap," and it is very well documented and described by (Foxley and Stallings 2014).

According to World Bank estimates, only 10% of middle-income economies in 1960 had become high-income economies by 2008 (Escaping the Middle Income Trap n.d.). It means that only 2 countries per decade are reaching the next level on economic evolution.

Acknowledgments Tugrul Daim and Dirk Meissner contribution to the book chapter is based on the study funded by the Basic Research Program of the National Research University Higher School of Economics (HSE) and by the Russian Academic Excellence Project "5-100."

References[1]

10 Best Tech Startups in Portland (2018) The Tech Tribune, 31-Jan-2018. [Online]. Available: http://thetechtribune.com/10-best-tech-startups-in-portland/. [Accessed: Mar-2018]

2018 World Population by Country (n.d.-a) 2018 world population by country. [Online]. Available: http://worldpopulationreview.com/. [Accessed: 02-Mar-2018]

2018 World Population by Country (n.d.-b) 2018 world population by country. [Online]. Available: http://worldpopulationreview.com/. [Accessed: 07-Mar-2018]

About Tom (n.d.). TomMcCall.org. [Online]. Available: http://www.tommccall.org/about-tom.html. [Accessed: 19-Mar-2018]

Bandlamudi M, Chieh LC, Daliparthi M, Fabini S, Kutgun H (2016) Driving factors for technology companies to establish an outpost in the silicon forest

Bauer PW, Schweitzer ME, Shane SA (2011) Knowledge matters: the long-run determinants of state income growth. *Journal of Regional Science* 52(2):240–255

Beebe C (2016) Portland region nears 2.4 million residents, growing by 41,000 last year, *Metro*, 25-Mar-2016. [Online]. Available:https://www.oregonmetro.gov/news/portland-region-nears-24-million-residents-growing-41000-last-year. [Accessed: 04-Mar-2018]

bizjournals.com (n.d.) [Online]. Available: https://www.bizjournals.com/portland/news/2017/10/26/1-7m-invested-in-8-oregon-startups-at-the-2017.html. [Accessed: Mar-2018]

Boundless Management (n.d.) Lumen. [Online]. Available: https://courses.lumenlearning.com/boundless-management/chapter/technology-and-innovation/. [Accessed: Mar-2018]

Brown DNL (2017) When Portland banned blacks: Oregon's shameful history as an 'all-white' state, The Washington Post, 07-Jun-2017. [Online]. Available: https://www.washingtonpost.com/news/retropolis/wp/2017/06/07/when-portland-banned-blacks-oregons-shameful-history-as-an-all-white-state/?utm_term=.79fb593c3ad7. [Accessed: 12-Mar-2018]

[1]Uncited references were used to develop this case.

Economic Forecasting Survey (n.d.) The Wall Street Journal. [Online]. Available: http://projects.wsj.com/econforecast/#ind=tenyear&r=16. [Accessed: Feb-2018]

Ernst Young (2011) Competitiveness of state and local business taxes on new Investment. http://www.cost.org/globalassets/cost/stri/studies-and-reports/competitiveness-of-state-and-local-business-taxes.pdf

Escaping the Middle Income Trap (n.d.) Global economic symposium. [Online]. Available: http://www.global-economic-symposium.org/knowledgebase/escaping-the-middle-income-trap. [Accessed: 19-Feb-2018]

Foxley A, Stallings B (2014) Economías Latinoamericanas: cómo avanzar más allá del ingreso medio. Cieplan, Santiago, Chile

Here are the Most Innovative States in America in 2016, (2016) Here are the most innovative states in America in 2016 | Mass Digital Health, 22-Dec-2016. [Online]. Available: http://massdigitalhealth.org/news/here-are-most-innovative-states-america-2016. [Accessed: Mar-2018]

Inflation, 2013 n.d. Oregon office of economic analysis, 20-Feb-2014. [Online]. Available: https://oregoneconomicanalysis.com/2014/02/20/inflation-2013/. [Accessed: Mar-2018]

Mayer H (2011) *Entrepreneurship and innovation in second tier regions*. Edward Elgar, Cheltenham, UK

Mortgage Interest Rates Forecast 2018, 2019, 2020, 2021 AND 2022 (n.d.) Long forecast. [Online]. Available: https://longforecast.com/mortgage-interest-rates-forecast-2017-2018-2019-2020-2021-30-year-15-year. [Accessed: 19-Feb-2018]

Novak M (2015) Oregon was founded as a racist Utopia, Gizmodo, 21-Jan-2015. [Online]. Available: https://gizmodo.com/oregon-was-founded-as-a-racist-utopia-1539567040. [Accessed: 19-Mar-2018]

Oregon state budget and finances (n.d.) Ballotpedia. [Online]. Available: https://ballotpedia.org/Oregon_state_budget_and_finances. [Accessed: 26-Feb-2018]

Oregon Tax Hike Vote, Measures 66 and 67 (January 2010) (n.d.) Ballotpedia. [Online]. Available: https://ballotpedia.org/Oregon_Tax_Hike_Vote,_Measures_66_and_67_(January_2010)#cite_note-20. [Accessed: 25-Feb-2018]

Oregon Blue Book: Oregon's economy: overview. (n.d.) [Online]. Available: http://bluebook.state.or.us/facts/economy/economy01.htm. [Accessed: Mar-2018]

Oregon Business Tax Increase, Measure 97 (2016)(n.d.) Ballotpedia. [Online]. Available: https://ballotpedia.org/Oregon_Business_Tax_Increase,_Measure_97_(2016). [Accessed: 25-Feb-2018]

Oregon Department of Land Conservation and Development Forest Land Protection Program (n.d.). www.Oregon.gov. [Online]. Available: http://www.oregon.gov/LCD/pages/forlandprot.aspx. [Accessed: Mar-2018]

Oregon Office of Economic Analysis (2016) Oregon's high-technology sector, LinkedIn SlideShare, 21-Apr-2016. [Online]. Available: https://www.slideshare.net/oregoneconomicanalysis/oregons-hightechnology-sector. [Accessed: Mar-2018]

Oregon vs Washington Taxes(n.d.) [Online]. Available: https://www.clarkcounty4sale.net/vancouver-wa-information/washington-vs-oregon-taxes/. [Accessed: 25-Feb-2018]

Oregon Wages, A 2017 Update (n.d.) Oregon office of economic analysis, 31-Jan-2018. [Online]. Available: https://oregoneconomicanalysis.com/2018/01/31/oregon-wages-a-2017-update/. [Accessed: Mar-2018]

Oregon's top performing economy can offer opportunity for all (n.d.) Oregon Center for Public Policy. Retrieve March 1, 2018.

Perkowski M and Capital Bureau (2017) Oregon has recovered the jobs lost during the 'great recession', Herald and News, 07-Feb-2017. [Online]. Available: https://www.heraldandnews.com/breaking/oregon-has-recovered-the-jobs-lost-during-the-great-recession/article_0c254c4b-b1be-54b9-b6d4-6e5b73f62f00.html. [Accessed: 19-Mar-2018]

Portland, OR (n.d.) Forbes. [Online]. Available: https://www.forbes.com/places/or/portland/. [Accessed: 19-Mar-2018]

Portland State University (n.d.) Forbes. [Online]. Available: https://www.forbes.com/colleges/portland-state-university/. [Accessed: 10-Mar-2018]

Quality Information, Informed Choices (n.d.) 2017 in review: job growth slows as unemployment reaches record low—article display—qualityinfo. [Online]. Available: https://www.qualityinfo.org/-/2017-in-review-job-growth-slows-as-unemployment-reaches-record-low. [Accessed: Mar-2018]

Rogoway M (2018a) Fleet, 22-year-old Portlander's startup, raises another $10 million, OregonLive.com, 24-Jan-2018. [Online]. Available: http://www.oregonlive.com/silicon-forest/index.ssf/2018/01/fleet_22-year-old_portlanders.html. [Accessed: 02-Mar-2018]

Rogoway M (2018b) Augmented reality startup raises $17 million after moving HQ from Silicon Valley to Vancouver, *OregonLive.com*, 02-Feb-2018. [Online]. Available: http://www.oregonlive.com/silicon-forest/index.ssf/2018/02/silicon_valley_augmented_reali.html. [Accessed: 14-Mar-2018]

Rogoway M (2018c) Oregon venture capital picked up in 2017—thanks to one company, *OregonLive.com*, 16-Jan-2018. [Online]. Available: http://www.oregonlive.com/silicon-forest/index.ssf/2018/01/oregon_venture_capital_picked.html. [Accessed: Mar-2018]

Silicon Forest (2018) Wikipedia, 06-Mar-2018. [Online]. Available: https://en.wikipedia.org/wiki/Silicon_Forest. [Accessed: 19-Feb-2018]

States in Motion: Visualizing how education funding has changed over time | EdSource. (n.d.) [Online]. Available: https://edsource.org/2015/states-in-motion-school-finance-naep-child-poverty/83303. [Accessed: 10-Feb-2018]

Statista (n.d.) All products require an annual contract. Prices do not include sales tax (New York residents only)., U.S.—projected inflation rate 2008–2022, Statista. [Online]. Available:https://www.statista.com/statistics/244983/projected-inflation-rate-in-the-united-states/. [Accessed: Mar-2018]

The Jury Is Back: Oregon's measures 66 & 67 were a disaster (2011) ValentineVentures, 05-Dec-2011. [Online]. Available: http://valentineventures.com/the-jury-is-back-oregons-measures-66-67-were-a-disaste. [Accessed: 25-Feb-2018]

Tom McCall (2018) Wikipedia, 16-Mar-2018. [Online]. Available: https://en.wikipedia.org/wiki/Tom_McCall. [Accessed: 12-Feb-2018]

The Oregon Encyclopedia (n.d.) [Online]. Available: https://oregonencyclopedia.org/articles/silicon_forest/#.WqBOB4Pwapo. [Accessed: Mar 2018]

Urness Z (n.d.) Oregon's population grows at fastest rate in 20 years, fueled by new residents, Statesman Journal, 17-Nov-2017. [Online]. Available: https://www.statesmanjournal.com/story/news/2017/11/16/oregons-population-grows-fastest-rate-20-years-fueled-new-residents/872884001/. [Accessed: Mar-2018]

U.S. Census Bureau (2010) Your geography selections, American factfinder—results, 05-Oct-2010. [Online]. Available: https://factfinder.census.gov/faces/tableservices/jsf/pages/productview.xhtml?src=bkmk. [Accessed: Mar-2018]

Part II
Leaders and Practices

Chapter 8
Sports Innovation

Achala Kaushikkar, Sema Kirkewoog, Erica Merckling, Sneha Prabhu, Tugrul U. Daim, and Dirk Meissner

8.1 Introduction

Nike was founded by Phil Knight in 1964 with the intent to distribute and eventually design and develop the best track shoes. The company went on to revolutionize the sportswear industry. At the time, Adidas dominated a vast majority of the industry market share. The company quickly developed a large following after bringing several innovative and technology-driven shoe designs to market. Soon Nike's brand became synonymous with high-performance sportswear and elite athleticism.

Extensive contracts with sports icons have elevated the Nike brand to become one of the most recognized in the world. The relationship between high-performance athletes and Nike was mutually beneficial; Nike gave the world's best athletes the necessary tools to be champions while the athletes would help the design and marketing of the company's products. This symbiotic relationship radically changed the face of sports. Nike's deep-rooted culture of innovation is highly conducive to collaborating with athletes to break boundaries in the realm of sports.

Additionally, Nike's global presence has allowed the company to excel in the design and manufacturing of athletic shoes, apparel, and equipment. Strategic portfolio management paired with athlete-driven collaborations and a strong

A. Kaushikkar · S. Kirkewoog · E. Merckling · S. Prabhu
Portland State University, Portland, OR, USA

T. U. Daim (✉)
Portland State University Technology Management Doctoral Program, Portland, OR, USA

National Research University Higher School of Economics, Moscow, Russia

Chaoyang University of Technology, Taichung City, Taiwan
e-mail: tugrul.u.daim@pdx.edu

D. Meissner
National Research University Higher School of Economics, Moscow, Russia

T. U. Daim, D. Meissner (eds.), *Innovation Management in the Intelligent World*,
Science, Technology and Innovation Studies,
https://doi.org/10.1007/978-3-030-58301-9_8

manufacturing base all gear toward innovation has allowed the company to maintain market leadership. Although Nike acknowledges the competition, such as Adidas, Under Armour, and Reebok, the company does not make or drive its decisions based off of the strategy of its competitors.

Nike's Research and Development (R&D) strategy is heavily dependent on product or service functionality, reliability, convenience, and cost. Nike's immense success can be attributed to its R&D strategy of continuous improvement and innovation that is driven toward creating new and industry-altering products and services. Sportswear technology incorporated into athletic shoes and apparel as well as software integrated technologies incorporated into wearables and application-driven products continuously changes the mechanism of traditionally defined sportswear research. Sportswear is an intrinsic component and instrument that can enhance an athlete's performance. The applied sports and human physiology components of Nike's innovation process have revolutionized the way performance is measured.

Nike's product strategy relies heavily on collaboration with elite athletes in order to understand how sportswear can improve the athlete's performance. Expert insight into specific sports, such as basketball, golf, and tennis amongst many others, allows experts to qualitatively understand and pinpoint potential gaps in the current and future capabilities of sportswear technology. Understanding these gaps translates to core innovations (products) and peripheral innovations (product enhancements) which are often driven on new and innovative materials.

Much of Nike's model of innovation is materials centric. A large portion of Nike's products are the result of intersecting technologies spanning from the material, knit, and overall durability. The overall process from an initial concept to product involves collaborative efforts between the athlete, R&D, materials, design, and merchandising.

Nike's global product reach stems from a clear understanding of their customers. When new products are conceptualized, they are designed for the specific athlete in mind which translates to the global market of everyday athletes. The mindset that what works for the most top-performing athletes in the world will also aid the performance of the everyday athlete has served the company well (Russell Watt 2016). Geographic specific customizations are also incorporated with the intention of localizing products and serving the everyday athlete across the globe. Localizing Nike's products to fit geographic needs allows for specific product optimization. Mass customization is a phenomenon that Nike continues to embrace in order to optimize products to geographic requirements and trends.

8.2 Innovation Strategy

The analysis that follows will detail Nike's innovation strategy in relation to product planning, development, and technology integration. This section provides the framework for the following analysis.

At the core of Nike's internal R&D strategy is athlete-driven innovation. Close collaboration with elite athletes has propelled the brand to be synonymous with high performance and successful technology transfer at Nike means successfully transferring innovations to industries and markets (Cormican and O'Connor 2009). Nike's process from the initial concept and ideation stage to a marketable product on the shelves involves a substantial R&D strategy based on innovative materials, design, manufacturing, and merchandising. Products are typically designed at the company's US-based headquarters, then outsourced for overseas manufacturing. Strategic outsourcing involves outsourcing particular processes. Outsourcing allows companies to focus resources on core competencies (Quinn and Hilmer 1994). Nike's R&D strategy predominantly involves innovating products within the company, then outsourcing manufacturing processes which are also considered an integral part of the company's success. Nike is the world's largest supplier of athletic shoes and solely relies on outsourcing production (Quinn and Hilmer 1994). The company's pre-production and post-production activities share a synergetic link. Pre-production R&D and post-production marketing are linked through the company's outsourced supply chain, manufacturing network, and global presence.

Transferring research from within an organization to outside an organization through commercialization involves deliberate technology transfer (Cormican and O'Connor 2009). The key to successfully transferring a product is to capture critical knowledge so that a facility can supply the market. Critical knowledge associated with the product can be integrated into future innovations (Cormican and O'Connor 2009). Nike's outsourced manufacturing methods incorporate methodologies relative to technology transfer.

Nike's innovation process reveals the close relationship between design and merchandising. Sportswear products range from a variety of categories including clothing, shoes, and accessories. Because Nike's innovation process is primarily centered on sportswear, there is a significant R&D emphasis on materials. Materials innovation can improve an athlete's performance which ultimately impacts Nike's aim to inspire the customer base to live the athletic lifestyle. The methodology of managing and protecting Nike's IP is also an integral part of the innovation process. Patent filing is incorporated early in the R&D process to protect the company's investment (Kaiser 2010). Internally managing IP poses a significant challenge to implementing and sustaining innovation (Kaiser 2010).

Strategically planning for future products comprises of understanding specific market demands (Grienitz and Blume 2010). Nike's anti-clog soccer cleats represent a comprehensible innovation which was a result of understanding market demands. Anti-clog technology is an example of Nike responding to specific market demands. Fully integrating product scenarios (PS) with product structure segment (PSS) components and product segment structure attributes (PSSA) sub-components coherently combine technologies while satisfying potential constraints (Grienitz and Blume 2010).

Nike's principal innovation portfolio encompasses a wide variety of materials innovations that are integrated into core products. Nike's R&D also involves the integration of peripheral innovations. Peripheral innovations include products that are offered as a detachable accessory. Nike's peripheral innovation portfolio involves technology integrated products. New product development decisions can be swayed by a company's existing portfolio (Venter and Van Waveren 2009). New product development is characterized by a tremendous degree of complexity and uncertainty (Venter and Van Waveren 2009). Although criteria in new product developments can vary in relation to specific industries, they generally involve technical feasibility, strategic fit, customer acceptance, financial performance, and market opportunity (Venter and Van Waveren 2009). The critical objective of new product development at Nike is swayed by the demands defined by their specifically distinct customer groups (Schilling and Hill 1998). Focusing on specific customer demands in sports-specific niches has allowed Nike to out-focus its competitors (Schilling and Hill 1998). Nike produces several hundred variants of athletic shoes in several sports categories to create a portfolio of products that has appeal to "every conceivable market niche" (Schilling and Hill 1998). New product development decisions can be swayed by a company's existing portfolio (Venter and Van Waveren 2009).

Large firms, like Nike, are in a better position to exploit the market potential of products (Love and Roper 1999). The brand's strength has a significant customer following resulting in continuous pressure to innovate new products. Companies that fail to innovate may put themselves at risk (Tsai et al. 2011). There is a positive relationship between external technology acquisition and product innovation performance (Tsai et al. 2011). Nike's brand strength makes them a target for competition, but also opens several avenues for acquisition as a part of the company's overall portfolio. Portfolio diversification therefore has a positive impact on product innovativeness (Tsai et al. 2011). Nike's historical acquisition of Converse and Hurley has unlocked opportunities into new consumer industries. Diversifying the company's portfolio through acquisitions has allowed Nike to maintain their market leadership.

Alliance strategy is also an integral component of Nike's market leadership success in the sportswear industry. Particularly, forming alliances with premier athletic organizations including the NBA, NFL, MLS, and NCAA. Forming strategic alliances creates a pipeline to enhance performance (Ahn et al. 2009). Alliances with organizations spark collaborative innovation efforts that intrinsically help both parties. Elite athletes provide an un-surmounted amount of insight into what can be done to improve their performance, while Nike can bring the athlete's vision to light. Integrating a product from concept to a globally marketable product is deduced through the process of mass customization.

Nike's innovation process highlights the importance of interfacing with the customer in order to integrate the user's insight into product design. The design is intended to incorporate both product and process (Russell Watt 2016). Specifically, innovating and designing for the user is a strategy that emphasizes product usability. R&D methodology emphasizes functionality, reliability, convenience, and price. The innovation of a new product is a multilateral process incorporating several interdependent decisions.

Nike products like the FuelBand are intended to "make more athletes" (Russell Watt 2016). The FuelBand was revolutionary at the time of its release because it was a manifestation of Nike's vision to motivate athletes. In his current position, he deals with reliability testing and more specifically testing products to failure. Durability and reliability testing typically comes second in the product development R&D process at Nike. Integrating testing earlier in the product development process is beneficial to incorporate design iterations and improvements.

Nike is situated in global products and merchandising which involves the important process of understanding product design, development, and market requirements. Applying analytical science incorporates the defining of products alignments, manufacturing methods, and overall fundamental product demands in order to satisfy the market. Data from pre-design, design, and sales numbers is reviewed to understand product specifications related to merchandising.

Pairing innovation with market trends is a balance. The position of innovation lead involves planning for future products from a strategic point of view. Great ideas exist but the difficulty arises when scaling the product. The concept of seek, scale, and maximize involves substantial consideration of the supply chain, seasonality of a product, manufacturing capacity, and raw materials availability (Hasan Boylu 2016). Learning from different industries incorporates a diverse spectrum of expertise which ultimately helps create the next generation of products.

Nike's innovation strategy incorporates a diverse spectrum of people from various backgrounds—athletes, scientists, engineers, designers, lawyers, and materials specialists. Diverse backgrounds promote an atmosphere that combines both the art and science required to solve problems. The ideation process can occur through various avenues but most often the idea comes straight from the athlete. Athlete-driven design is the foundation of the R&D innovation process with some solutions stemming from incubators such as the Nike Sport Research Labs (NSRLs). New products must be iconic with a tactile, clean, and immediately clear message to the consumer.

8.3 R&D Strategy & Integration

Nike has grown from a small track shoe distributor eventually moving to manufacturing shoes in waffle irons to a billion-dollar market leader in the sportswear and sports equipment industry through continuous cycles of innovation. Nike successfully benefitted from globalization by creating products within market niches that customers valued such as basketball, baseball, golf, and tennis markets. Successfully creating both performance and leisure sportswear, Nike continues to transform the sportswear industry (Hayes and Venkatraman 2016). Companies with substantial financial backing are often able to take more risks in supporting radical innovations. Nike's overall success was not by happenstance, it was a result of carefully considering consumer "needs" as well as "wants" (Hayes and Venkatraman 2016). Although Nike's sportswear innovations primarily involve athletic collaborative efforts, translating this to a consumer product also involves careful consideration of the intended consumer. For example, translating a product developed in collaboration with basketball icon Lebron James to improved performance may not necessarily be applicable to the general consumer base. It is crucial to understand the products overall function in order to understand its potential for mass market success.

Nike's user-centric innovation efforts focus on inspiring and enhancing athletic performance. Typical activities in the user-centered design process involve identifying the user, determining the user requirement specs, creating a prototype design, and application testing (Wood 1998). Innovation strategy in the sportswear industry involves continuous consideration of how specific materials or high technology fabrics and other innovative technologies will impact performance.

Innovation strategy involves a combination of core and peripheral innovation efforts. Nike continuously focuses on innovation in order to produce premier footwear, clothing, and athletic equipment (Ali Mahdi et al. 2015). These efforts are generally in line with improving performance, reducing, or eliminating injury, and maximizing overall comfort (Ali Mahdi et al. 2015). Product development heavily involves understanding the mechanics of material and the biomechanics of the athlete. Core products often involve the compilation of several materials innovations. For example, Nike's Flyknit shoe integrates engineered yarn material with ultralight flexible shoe soles. The formfitting technology produces a shoe that essentially feels like a sock. Additionally, Nike's radicalized the soccer cleat market by introducing Anti-Clog technology. The unique stud pattern eliminates surface areas where mud could potentially build up. Much of Nike's innovation strategy involves understanding its customers' requirements and offering innovative solutions.

Innovation centered around materials in fiber and the textile process are key strategies in the sportswear industry, an area where Nike excels. Redesigning materials and surface architecture has revolutionized how fabrics can improve performance. Fabric can be designed to be more aerodynamic, diffuse UV rays, and/or improve movement efficiency. It is widely unknown that Nike's Elite socks business is one of their highest profitable divisions. Socks can vary based on their specified application (Nitin Mayande 2016; Russell Watt 2016). Nike sought market opportunity in a product that was widely considered generic. R&D directly applied to the sock business opened opportunities to create application-specific socks—soccer, running, basketball, football, tennis, etc.

Nike also develops peripheral innovations intended to enhance products and experiences. Technology integration at Nike is applied with the intention of "making everyone an athlete." The FuelBand was developed to enhance the overall experience of exercising. Motivating everyone to be an athlete ultimately benefits Nike's bottom line. Technology integration in the sports industry will open avenues into new potential markets, such as health care. Integrating data gathered from technologies like the FuelBand could be integrated into the general health care system to track personal health. Designing for the future is at the core of Nike's innovation strategy.

With athletes being the muse and inspiration behind Nike's drive toward innovation, a keen understanding of the physiological aspects of athleticism is at the core of the design and development of Nike's most marketable products. Collaborating with these athletes is a testament to the brand's authenticity.

What motivates and drives the consumer? What challenges does the consumer face? What is a "must" and what is a "want?" How can we help? These are the questions that each designer, engineer, and scientist faces on a day to day basis. These questions drive development and athletes are at the crux of the R&D innovation process. Effectively producing for the athlete is where material and technology intersect. Take Ashton Eaton's "Cooling Helmet," for example, a product of an athlete collaboration and an NSRL endeavor. The decathlon athlete was looking for a way to "feel like you've just started on every event" of the decathlon which is a 10 event competition spread out over the course of two days (Nike News 2016a). Working with athletes such as Eaton means solving problems faster and more efficiently, getting the product in the hands of the end user much more quickly than had there been no athlete involvement. This ties in directly with the stages of the Nike R&D innovation process.

8.4 Product Development Lifecycle: Stages of the R&D Innovation Process

As previously discussed, the product development strategy starts with the athlete. Everything that follows is strictly driven by the needs, wants, and direction of the athlete. From the initial idea conception to the final end product, the athlete is constantly consulted and collaborated with. The process is heavily focused on prototyping, taking advantage of the latest technologies in 3D printing and additive manufacturing. On average it takes Nike eighteen months to design and manufacture a product. The lead time for manufacturing taken by traditional methods can be cut down significantly along with condensing the development cycle into smaller, more efficient design orbits (Russell Watt 2016).

The Nike development process does not only draw inspiration from the athlete but also looks outwards toward other industry trends and how they can utilize those technologies into creating better products. Looking into the medical industry for biometric screening and health-oriented wearable technology as well as the aerospace industry for new developments in material and textile technologies (Nitin Mayande 2016). Always asking the questions of how is this relevant to the consumer, how does this benefit the consumer, and can this be easily translated from the use of an elite athlete to the everyday athlete, keeps the end user at the forefront of the design and development process. And performance testing executed in the NSRLs does just that. Measuring performance in a quantifiable manner means analyzing speed, power, and stamina on the small scale of continuous improvement. Incremental improvements, even by microseconds, are at the core of the development process along with integrating new technologies discovered in the labs and elsewhere.

Nike's product portfolio features products that meet the physiological needs of the athletic world as well as products for the mass market. Various participants or athletes have different interests, and some tasks and development paths are more challenging than others. The projects are managed with a mindset of implementing the geographical trends, enriched technology for superior performance and manufacturing from sustainable materials. It so appears that most customized products designed specifically to meet athlete's needs, cannot be mass produced, due to its uniqueness such as a specialized shoe size or shape. This is when the merchandising department in close connection with the sales department manages the concept of mass customization. Product development of a customized design concept is extended to meet the customer perspective and demands of specific customer groups. This included product development for geographically dispersed athletes, sports clubs, or mass consumers. To manage and market the products on a more strategic level, the design of the product is given a geographical direction, localizing the product to meet the needs, trends, colors, and cultures of the location.

8.4.1 Technology Transfer

Technology transfer at Nike involves the deliberate act of scaling products for manufacturing. New product innovation involves the process of design by understanding user requirements. Iterations of product prototypes and application testing allow for a further understanding of whether or not the product can be scaled. Not all innovations have the capacity to be globally scalable. The process of seek, scale, maximize involves understanding whether a product is feasible (Hasan Boylu 2016). Considerations such as supply chain, seasonality, capacity, and raw materials must be inferred during the development of a new product (Hasan Boylu 2016). Technology transfer involves the deliberate transfer of technology (Cormican and O'Connor 2009). Nike's outsourced manufacturing methods involve methodologies similar to technology transfer. The process of innovating new products involves an understanding of whether it can be transferred for manufacturing scalability; a process of critical importance to successfully transferring knowledge from one team or department to another in terms of manufacturability in this case.

8.4.2 Globalization

Nike's products are globalized through the process of mass customization. Much of Nike's success is attributed to connecting with the consumers, bringing forefront solutions they want or they think they may want (Hasan Boylu 2016). This involves localizing products relative to trends, needs, and requirements. Geographically speaking, these aspects differ. Mass customization is a phenomenon that Nike continues to embrace in order to optimize products to its geographic requirements and trends. A soccer shoe designed for an MLS or FIFA athlete on a field 110–120 yards long by 70–80 yards wide will have different design requirements than a soccer shoe designed for a futsal athlete on an outdoor field or indoor field of 42–46 yards by 22–27 yards. These different design requirements call for a keen understanding of athletics on a global scale. This requires Nike to have a foothold in many different locations in the world in order to better address the needs of the global athlete. However, design and customization is not the only factor; as previously discussed, merchandising also comes into play.

Merchandising in the USA is a different game than that in Europe and Asia. An average sales price of a sneaker in Europe may not be tolerated in the USA. An average sales price of an article of clothing in the USA may not be tolerated in Asian countries. A color popular in the USA may be highly offensive in another country making the product a huge turnoff and deterrent to the brand. Again, this requires extensive front-end work from Nike. When in the planning and development stages of a new product, these factors are 'make it or break it' aspects that must be addressed. For a global brand like Nike, appealing to the global athlete is crucial to success.

8.4.3 Proximity Strategy

Nike's R&D and innovation efforts are primarily based in the Beaverton, Oregon World Headquarters. Nike's presence in the Portland Metro area has created a sportswear ecosystem consisting of Adidas, Columbia Sportswear and Mountain Hardware, and soon Under Armour as they build a major headquarters in the area. Nike was the first and the rest followed suit. This sportswear cluster allows for healthy, local competition. Although market competition is acknowledged, it is clear that this does not drive the strategy behind the company's innovation. Nike strives to lead new innovations, not copy them (Russell Watt 2016). Maintaining market leadership ultimately means being an expert in what the consumer needs as well as identifying where the market is heading.

As far as manufacturing goes, some processes occur at Nike's In House Manufacturing facility in Beaverton along with a few other key domestic facilities, but most of the manufacturing of Nike's products happens overseas. Nike has manufacturing facilities in Indonesia, China, and Vietnam. Coincidentally, protective labor laws are poorly enforced and cheap labor is commonplace in these areas. This ties directly into Nike's R&D product planning, development, and technology integration strategy but also poses as a potential threat to the brand.

Nike has received a lot of flak over the years on the lack of attention paid to the humanitarian aspects of these facilities. The labor is cheap and the laws are lax but, Nike has made significant efforts to improve the conditions of these work environments and continue to work on the personal relations aspect of working overseas.

Although not close in proximity to these facilities, Nike is able to fully leverage the capabilities of these plants by maintaining strong relationships. These facilities are run and overseen by Nike employees who are always held to the highest of standards. That being said, the financial aspect of working overseas is crucial to the profit margin of Nike's products. If all of Nike's products were produced domestically we would surely see a massive hike in sales price on the majority of their products due to the added cost of manufacturing in the USA.

8.5 Managing R&D

Innovation is a cornerstone of Nike's success. The company's portfolio of innovative products extends into designing and producing better, faster, and lighter products with elements of sustainability embedded into the business. As an industry and market leader, the ambitious vision of Nike's agenda calls for intensive management of design approaches, integration of new tools, metrics for innovative products and marketing of the product on a global platform which will be discussed in the following subsections.

8.5.1 Organizational Structure

Nike's organizational structure consists of both a vertical and horizontal configuration of departments, authority, and jobs. To ensure continuous innovation and improvement of the company's products, Nike has developed a strong and effective organizational structure. Every department at Nike has a leader who works under the authority of the Chairperson and board members. Such departmentalization involves grouping work and workers into separate business units with each unit responsible for their area of expertise (Organisation 2013). The use of functional and divisional structures ensures endless possibilities in regards to short term and long term goals among an organization. This means that Nike is set up as a Matrix Organizational Structure with multiple lines of authority. At Nike, employees report to team managers, who then have to report the progress to the department managers. Each department consists of separate managers who independently report to the CEO (Quaintance 2013). Specific product-related decisions are made by the employees and their managers while the department managers are in charge of policy-related issues. Thus the use of a Matrix structure allows Nike to make decisions and react quickly.

To manage and structure operations, Nike has split the management and functional responsibilities between its global headquarters in Oregon and regional headquarters in Europe (Brenner et al. 2013).

The company's organizational decision making, including design, R&D, and product development tasks are handled at the global headquarters in Oregon

(Brenner et al. 2013). Hence, the accountability for products is at the headquarters where the main decisions are made. Thus most global collections are a result of a joint effort made by global and regional designers via effective communication and cross-functional team collaboration (Brenner et al. 2013).

8.5.2 Innovation Management

Nike's aim has always been to provide customers with well-constructed and uniquely designed products (Marketrealist.com 2016). The company has laid the foundation that combines diverse spectrums of expertise including engineering and user-centered innovation in order to deliver the next generation of apparel, footwear, wearable devices, and sports equipment. The company invests extensively in R&D for new technologies and their applications for existing product lines, dependent upon the consumer's preferences. The strategy of Nike's innovation management in creating and commercializing sports goods has incorporated activities that generally flow in the following manner—concept generation, understanding market needs & market demands, customized new product development, prototyping, technology innovation infused in products and wearables, and mass customization and marketing.

The concept and ideation stage of Nike's R&D process begins with elite, top-performing athletes, and the everyday average sportsman. The complex process of product innovation and the subsequent R&D is managed with a vision to generate a product line that meets the performance needs of athletes as well as provide a line of lifestyle sports clothing for the mass market (Hasan Boylu 2016). Product design and development materializes by gathering analytical data from sales and pre-design teams that comprises focus groups intended to collect a customer perspective of their products. Nike's R&D portrays efforts of an intelligent team of researchers, that striving to understand the jobs what the customers are looking to accomplish and products willing to pay for. This encourages Nike to design and innovate customized sports products that have a perceived value of comfort, style, and innovation in order to enhance athletic performance. The management of innovation activities is optimized by close and personalized interaction with athletes to understand potential product gaps. Once gaps are understood, Nike designs products with the intention to accomplish better performance in the specific athletic activity. Product gaps are identified as potential design components not already addressed in the market that may improve an athlete's performance or experience. For example, Nike Studio Wrap shoes specifically designed for yoga were conceptualized and designed from the insight of experienced and professional yoga experts (Russell Watt 2016). Further, the research involves discovering new sustainable materials and knit for the clothing and apparel line.

8.5.3 Global R&D Management

The key practices adopted by Nike's R&D in its effective management on a global commercial platform is optimized by seeking market opportunities. Seeking R&D opportunity through design is managed by identifying objectives pertaining to next generation innovation, future trends, envisioning the future line of products and demands of athletes. Nike heavily invests in identifying future business opportunities and seeking the next big thing in the sportswear industry (Roussel et al. 1991). Nike follows a pattern to forecast the regional demand, place purchase orders regionally, and then manage purchase orders with the factories globally (Morrison 2012). Nike believes that incorporating the world's finest engineering and innovation techniques will influence the development of radical new products. Setting priorities strategically in response to market trends and competitive developments are key considerations in maintaining market leadership. The process of scaling and maximizing the product by extending the initial concept to a smaller subset of athletes (200–300 athletes) for product testing comes next in the new product innovation process (Hasan Boylu 2016). Finally, the element to maximization that has strengthened Nike's global presence is its retail and direct to consumer business policy. The products are marketed in stores dispersed across the globe and sponsored by various athletic groups and sports clubs (Nitin Mayande 2016).

Nike's brand has more reach, higher brand loyalty, and more market share than its competitors. This is because of their strong customer base, known market segments, and clear idea of establishing new markets. R&D plays an important role in facilitating the competitive global market surrounding innovative products and user-centered products. The success of Nike's diversification occurs through the monitoring and administering global trends and cultural inclinations (Nitin Mayande 2016). The legacy of innovation in search of better, lighter, faster product performance is spread across meeting the cultural and geographical attributes of every country. It can be implied that Nike is a successful global leading brand that expresses R&D objectives and business objectives via the common language of technology, lifestyle, and comfort. This common vision and language bring the innovation standards and business terms that are valued by customers and world-class athletes to light.

8.5.4 Integrating Sustainability with Supply Chain Management

By looking at Nike's growing global market share and the continual increase in economic value added each year, Nike's strategy has incorporated sustainability as a channel for growth. In 2010, World Cup football shirts were made from recycled plastic bottles and developed using the Nike Materials. Similar products like Nike's Flyknit is a result of sustainable innovation produced to deliver a lighter material shoe made from fewer quantity of material, also promising enhanced performance. The company teams are managed on a vision to increase the sustainability index, which pushes the design teams to pick on environmentally friendly and sustainable materials (Nidumolu et al. 2009).

Nike's supply chain on the other hand has gone above and beyond its efforts for consumers to enjoy the benefits of Nike's innovative new products and features. By prototyping and scaling sustainable sourcing, Nike aims to make its global supply chain "lean, green, equitable and empowered." "Nike ID platform allows consumers to make customized Nike shoes, gear, and apparel online with no minimum order quantity for a small premium above typical retail prices for non-customized goods" (Robinson 2016). As materials account for around 60% of the environmental impacts of the average shoe, Nike aims to use less and recycle more. In 2011, Nike used 7m kg of organic cotton, for example, and included recycled polyester in 31.5 million products (Balch 2012).

8.5.5 IP & Portfolio Management

Nike has invested heavily on innovation centered on the development of technical fabrics to improve performance (Russell Watt 2016). New product patents are continually reviewed in order to ensure that there are no existing patents that could potentially restrict or challenge Nike's intellectual property. The process of managing and protecting Nike's IP is an integral part of the innovation process. Patent filing occurs early in the R&D process to protect the company's investment (Kaiser 2010). Internally managing IP is a significant challenge to implementing a sustainable innovation (Kaiser 2010).

Nike was granted around 500 patents last year and ended 2015 with 5060 issued patents according to the USA Patent and Trademark Office (USPTO) (Low 2016). With a large number of innovations in manufacturing and design Nike has given major competition to its rivals Adidas and Under Armour in terms of patents. Nikes patents have nearly doubled since 2009 and are the third-largest USA portfolio of design patents (Low 2016).

Nike integration of new technologies discovered in the labs into marketable products is initiated from the human physiology that is extended to building sustainable and products from reused materials. The management of subsequent R&D projects is smoothened by applying characteristics like clear defined goals, target market research, and scheduled planning. The product development process is managed with the intersection is of many different technologies—material, knit, durability, and testing.

8.5.6 *Team Dynamics*

Nike is known for bringing athletes into its headquarters to optimize innovation activities, prototyping, and product testing. Inspiring employees and reinforcing the athletic environment within the company to create the next generation of sportswear and equipment has been a successful strategy adopted by Nike. Nike has infused the elements of internal branding of active sports within its employees that encourages an understanding of the brand value. In addition to the mission statement "to bring inspiration and innovation to every athlete," Nike expands the mantra further to inspire its employees and create an environment conducive to inspiring the workforce to see through the lens of an athlete. The innovation management of concept to product development is managed through close connections with sales, design and development teams, and physiology experts. Like all good values, Nike is encouraged to interpret the core management values whose principles include Leading, Coaching, Managing, and Inspiring (Waite 2014).

8.6 Alliance Strategy

Strategic alliances can be divided into three categories: non-equity alliances, equity alliances, and joint ventures. Companies aim to venture into strategic alliances when they do not have the muscle, knowledge, and brand to access unrelated markets. Nike has entered into alliances with autonomous companies as a way to market their brand. Their strategic partnership with Apple was mutually beneficial to both the companies, with Nike, expanding into the music world, and Apple attaining access in the sports industry. Nike has leveraged its core competencies by forming strategic alliances with Sina Corp, a leading marketing company in China that features and presents the latest sports content (M. Burress, M. Burress and V. profile 2011). Sina has three sub-business lines namely sina.net, Sina online, and sina.com and collaborates with Nike to provide the latest interactive news on stars and competition, sports team content, and fashion and sports gear. Nike's leading suppliers and merchandise manufacturers are located globally in Asia.

Forming strategic alliances and collaborating with athletes to develop, manufacture, and sell products is a critical component of Nike's corporate strategy. The non-equity alliance with Apple allowed both the companies to channel their expertise and popularity to tap new markets (J. B., J. B. and V. profile 2012). The shared collaboration of resources and skills gives them a competitive advantage to remain profitable and innovative. Nikes GPS enabled sports watches was a collaborative project with a Dutch-based satellite navigation company (J. B., J. B. and V. profile 2012). By forming such technological alliances Nike has ensured that they do not just adhere to their core products but also incorporate world-class technology to make their products more desirable.

Nikes equity alliances are dispersed globally in terms of manufacturing, marketing, and distribution. With major partners being Europe and Asia, outsourcing is done outside of the USA for low-cost affordability, access to new emerging markets, and also retract from declining markets. Nike also started a joint venture with Phillips electronics in creating the MP3 players back in 2004 (J. B., J. B. and V. profile 2012). This symbiotic relationship helped Phillips venture into American markets and Nike into electronics. Nike strategically seeks alliances to gain competencies in new product markets but also seeks acquisition opportunities to further the company's global reach.

Nike currently owns Converse, Hurley, and Umbro (J. B., J. B. and V. profile 2012). These companies strategically align with Nike's existing market. Nike has been continually looking out for channels to stay competitive. The merger and acquisition strategies enable economic value creation and gain competitive opportunities that are created via the acquired firms. These mergers facilitate Nike's aim to stay powerful in the product market. Large companies like Nike need to continuously find opportunities for further growth as well as brand reach which is a key component in their marketing initiatives.

Nike aims to be 100% sustainable by 2050 across key impact areas of climate and energy, labor, chemistry, water, waste, and community (Nitin Mayande 2016). To pursue this it has created strategic alliances with supply chain partners to co-develop supply chain solutions that offer both logistics and environmental benefits (Kumar and Malegeant 2006). A strategic alliance creates a green image for a company that can improve both the sales and the value of the company (Kumar and Malegeant 2006). Nike's other green partnerships include IKEA GreenTech and LAUNCH Nordic that focus on innovating sustainable materials and waterless dyeing systems (Nike News 2014).

To enhance their manufacturing business Nike recently announced its partnership with Flextronics, a world-class global manufacturer, to enable customized solutions and increased performance innovation (Investors.flextronics.com 2015). This business tie-up aims at delivering the footwear to the consumers more quickly by building an efficient manufacturing supply chain, customized solutions, and increased performance innovation.

8.7 Conclusions

Through the analysis of Nike's R&D strategy, a variety of relevant implications crossing several industries were uncovered. They are as follows.

1. **Athlete-Driven Innovation**

Athlete-driven innovation is an industry standard that most sportswear and sports equipment companies take advantage of. Athlete sponsorships not only allow the company to stay relevant and to address the needs of the elite athlete both in the short and long term over the course of the athlete's career but, they also propel the company's brand on a global stage. Athletes are typically viewed as role models in which the everyday athlete wants to emulate themselves after. An athlete endorsement drives the mass market consumer to the products their favorite athletes uses and promotes which in turn only makes the brand more recognizable and the loyal consumer base grow stronger.

2. **Sustainable Design and Manufacturing**

Companies are no longer discussing whether or not to focus on sustainability, but instead they aim to integrate the social, environmental, and economic impact into management decisions to achieve better financial performance. Organizations like Nike, Procter & Gamble, Home Depot, and Nissan are taking increased risks and creating new opportunities for innovation to solve social problems and improve sustainability locally as well as globally (Epstein and Buhova 2015). From designing better, faster, and lighter products Nike now wants to embed sustainability into their business. This broader vision requires new approaches to design, management, partnership, and new tools and metrics to support integration and adoption throughout Nike. Nike's core competency has always been in innovation and the shift into sustainability will act as a vehicle for growth.

As a commitment to innovation through the use of environmentally friendly materials, Nike in collaboration with the Massachusetts Institute of Technology (MIT) Climate CoLab is intended to innovation in materials to the forefront of the climate conservation It is also commitment to reach 100-percent renewable energy in company-owned-and-operated facilities by 2025 (Nike News 2016b). Companies are taking bold steps in manufacturing in order to become sustainable. Adidas and Nike are beginning to use carbon-based process that dye polyester without the use of water or chemicals in order to reduce water scarcity in the future (Nike News 2016b). Nike has re-invented the traditional practices of manufacturing by using reused and recyclable supplies in their products. For instance, Nike's Reuse-A-Shoe program recycles old worn-out shoes into a material called Nike Grind which is then utilized to create athletic material and playground surfaces (Nike Reuse-A-Shoe FAQs 2016). Some of its scrap material from its manufacturing facilities is used in new Nike products such as buttons and zipper pulls. Conclusion, Nike strives to continuously enhance the performance and experience of athletes through improvements in their clothing and equipment, while using as much sustainable materials as possible.

3. **Textile Innovation**

As consumers are becoming increasingly aware and clothing manufacturers are stepping up to become more environmentally accountable, huge advances are being made in textile design and manufacturing processes. To lead a company's vision toward a next generation innovation, it is important for companies manufacturers to understand and innovate the practices behind its production (Nidumolu et al. 2009). In 2009, Speedo's research team began to brainstorm innovative ways to help swimmers go faster. This research resulted in the breakthrough polyurethane bodysuit technology that contributed to an astonishing number of swimming world records. However, the bodysuit was deemed an unfair advantage by athletes who donned the polyurethane technology. They were later banned because they devalued overall athleticism in the swimming events (Morrison 2012). Wrangler introduced a collection of women's jeans with skincare ingredients like aloe vera, vitamin E, and fragrance infused into the fibers of the fabric via micro-encapsulation technology to refresh and revitalize the skin, giving more comfort.

Functionality is also evolving in the compression category to provide additional benefits beyond muscle support and soreness. With such a massive demand for performance-enhancing wearables, companies are drifting to trends in high-tech fabrics. This extends to textile innovation, where the advanced Materials in Textiles enable the power of collaboration to overcome common business problems such as design issues, IP shortages, manufacturing issues, and market intelligence. The future of textile innovation in sports implies technology working in sync with human physiology and environmental conditions to provide comfort along with enhancing the performance of an athlete.

There is a reason why Nike has maintained its market leadership position in the sportswear industry for more than 50 years. The special sauce or the differentiator is the constant drive toward innovation, toward discovering new technologies and materials and expertly integrating their findings into highly marketable products. Nike has mastered the art of strategic alliance and partnerships across the globe by pairing with the most elite, highest performing athletes. The brand recognition alone is so widespread and synonymous with winning on the world's largest stages, olympic stadiums, world-renowned tracks, and even high school gyms, that it is hard not to be inspired. "Just Do It!" is a simple motto but highly effective in relaying the simple message of perseverance. The swoosh is a symbol of the will to win, to push farther, harder, for just one more minute, one rep, one breath. The Nike brand is about constant innovation and reinvention deeply rooted in the all-inclusive drive to win. There is nothing that can stop you. As an Oregon track coach once said, everything you need is already inside.

Acknowledgment Tugrul Daims and Dirk Meissner contribution to the book chapter is based on the study funded by the Basic Research Program of the National Research University Higher School of Economics (HSE) and by the Russian Academic Excellence Project "5-100."

References

Ahn MJ, Meeks MD, Davenport S, Bednarek R (2009) Death of distance? – biotechnology agglomeration patterns, alliance proximity, and firm performance. Int J Innov Technol Manag 6(3):247–264

Ali Mahdi HA, Abbas M, Ilyas Mazar T (2015) A comparative analysis of strategies and business models of Nike, Inc. and Adidas Group with special reference to competitive advantage in the context of a dynamic and competitive environment. Int J Bus Manag Econ Res (IJBMER) 6 (3):167–177

Ashton Eaton aims for head start in Nike recovery prototype. Nike News. Web. May 21, 2016a

Balch O (2012) Nike reveals a new, innovative game plan for sustainability. The Guardian [Online]. http://www.theguardian.com/sustainable-business/nike-sustainability-report-social-environmental-impact

Brenner, Barbara, Bodo B. Schlegelmilch, and Björn Ambos. "Inside the NIKE matrix." (2013).

Cormican K, O'Connor M (2009) Technology transfer for product life cycle extension: a model for successful implementation. Int J Innov Technol Manag 6(3):265–282

Epstein M, Buhova A (2015) How sustainability leaders are implementing sustainability | The European Financial Review | Empowering communications globally. Europeanfinancialreview.com [Online]. http://www.europeanfinancialreview.com/?p=4359

Flex – NIKE's manufacturing revolution accelerated by new partnership with Flex (2015) Investors. flextronics.com [Online]. http://investors.flextronics.com/investor-relations/company-news/press-release-details/2015/NIKEs-Manufacturing-Revolution-Accelerated-by-New-Partnership-with-Flex/default.aspx

Grienitz V, Blume V (2010) Strategic planning of future products with product scenarios. Int J Innov Technol Manag 7(3):237–246

Hasan Boylu Nike Innovation Lead. Nike, Inc. Interview. Phone Interview. May 20, 2016

Hayes SG, Venkatraman P (2016) Materials and technology for sportswear and performance apparel. Taylor & Francis Group, CRC Press Boca Raton, FL

J. B., J. B. and V. profile (2012) Josh's Nike Inc. blog – MGMT 7160: Nike's strategic alliances. Joshsnikeblog.blogspot.com [Online]. http://joshsnikeblog.blogspot.com/2012/04/nikes-strategic-alliances.html

Kaiser L (2010) Management of intellectual property in research and development: a search for systems from the viewpoint of research and technology organizations. Int J Innov Technol Manag 7(3):263–272

Kumar S, Malegeant P (2006) Strategic alliance in a closed-loop supply chain, a case of manufacturer and eco-non-profit organization. *Dent Tech* 26(10):1127–1135

LAUNCH expands search for sustainable materials innovations (2014) Nike News [Online]. http://news.nike.com/news/launch-expands-search-for-sustainable-materials-innovations. Accessed 25 May 2016

Love JH, Roper S (1999) The determinants of innovation: R&D, technology transfer and networking effects. Rev Ind Org 15:43–64

Low E (2016) Why Nike has more patents than Lockheed, Ford and Pfizer. Investor's Business Daily [Online]. http://www.investors.com/news/a-nike-apple-watch-an-under-armour-baseball-line-patents-hold-secrets/

M. Burress, M. Burress and V. profile (2011) Marilyn Burress' blog: Nike strategic alliances. Marilynburress.blogspot.com [Online]. http://marilynburress.blogspot.com/2011/04/nike-strategic-alliances.html

MIT Climate CoLab and Nike Call for Materials Innovation to Combat Climate Change (2016b) Nike News [Online]. http://news.nike.com/news/nike-inc-and-mit-climate-colab-materials-innovation-to-combat-climate-change. Accessed 24 May 2016

Morrison J (2012) How speedo created a record-breaking swimsuit. Scientific American, a division of Nature America, Inc.

Nidumolu R, Rangaswami M, Prahalad C (2009) Why sustainability is now the key driver of innovation. Harv Bus Rev. [Online]. https://hbr.org/2009/09/why-sustainability-is-now-the-key-driver-of-innovation. Accessed 25 May 2016

Nike Reuse-A-Shoe FAQs (2016). Help-en-eu.nike.com [Online]. http://help-en-eu.nike.com/app/answers/detail/a_id/39600/p/3897

NIKE's global markets: top revenue earners – market realist (2016) Marketrealist.com [Online]. http://marketrealist.com/2014/12/nikes-global-markets-top-revenue-earners/. Accessed 25 May 2016

Nitin Mayande Sr. Data Scientist, Nike, Inc. Interview. Beaverton, OR. May 18, 2016

Organisation (2013) Nike Inc. [Online]. https://nike1020.wordpress.com/organisation/. Accessed 25 May 2016

Quaintance J (2013) Nike: organizational structure of Nike. Strategicmanagementofnike.blogspot.com [Online]. http://strategicmanagementofnike.blogspot.com/2013/04/organizational-structure-of-nike.html

Quinn JB, Hilmer FG (Summer 1994) Strategic Outsourcing. Sloan Manage Rev 35:4. Periodicals Archive Online p 43

Robinson R (2016) 5 things you need to learn from Nike's huge management changes. Brandid.com [Online]. http://www.brandid.com/5%20Things%20to%20Learn%20from%20Nike%20Management. Accessed 24 May 2016

Roussel PA, Saad KN, Erickson TJ (1991) Third generation R&D: management the risk to corporate strategy. Harvard Business School Press

Russell Watt Director of Product Integrity Nike +. Nike, Inc. Interview. Beaverton, OR. May 12, 2016

Schilling MA, Hill CWL (August 1998) Managing the new product development process: strategic imperatives. Acad Manag Exec (1993–2005) 12(3):67–81

Tsai K, Hsieh M, Hultink EJ (2011) External technology acquisition and product innovativeness: the moderating roles of R&D investment and configurational context. J Eng Technol Manage 28:184–200

Venter JP, Van Waveren CC (2009) New product development with dynamic decision support. Int J Innov Technol Manag 6(2):135–153

Waite (2014) Nike's management philosophy revealed

Wood LE (1998) User Interface Design: Bridging the Gap from User Requirements to Design. CRC Press LLC

Chapter 9
Managing Research & Development Portfolio at NASA

Bashair Al Saglab, Charles Asafo-Adjei, Shahram Khorasanizadeh, Stephan Hoo-Fatt, Tugrul U. Daim, and Dirk Meissner

9.1 Introduction

NASA stands for National Aeronautics and Space Administration. It is an indepen dent agency of the executive branch of the United States federal government responsible for the civilian space program, as well as aeronautics and aerospace research. Given the complexities and challenges involved in space and aeronautics explorations, how does NASA manages its technology roadmap as it relates to research and development activities?

One of the common myths in the area of managing R&D projects is the assumption that all R&D organizations and projects are managed with the same set of processes and techniques. However, in reality, R&D organizational practices vary from company to company and from project to project. Therefore, "one size does not fit all." This could not be far from the truth when it comes to managing R&D projects and practices at NASA. NASA embarks on research and development activities with applications for the general population including devices that improve health, medicine, transportation, public safety, and consumer goods. However, NASA's mission focus is to "*Pioneer the future in space exploration, scientific discovery, and aeronautics research*" with a vision to "*To reach for new heights and reveal the*

B. Al Saglab · C. Asafo-Adjei · S. Khorasanizadeh · S. Hoo-Fatt
Portland State University, Portland, OR, USA

T. U. Daim (✉)
Portland State University Technology Management Doctoral Program, Portland, OR, USA

National Research University Higher School of Economics, Moscow, Russia

Chaoyang University of Technology, Taichung City, Taiwan
e-mail: tugrul.u.daim@pdx.edu

D. Meissner
National Research University Higher School of Economics, Moscow, Russia

T. U. Daim, D. Meissner (eds.), *Innovation Management in the Intelligent World*, Science, Technology and Innovation Studies,
https://doi.org/10.1007/978-3-030-58301-9_9

unknown for the benefit of humankind." NASA achieves its mission and vision through a well-coordinated organizational structure depicted below.

The area of R&D technological development this paper focuses on is central to the Office of Chief Technologist (OCT). The Chief Technologist at NASA is the main Administrator's principal advisor and sponsor on matters concerning technology policy and R&D programs. The OCT provides the strategy and leadership needed to integrates NASA's technology development and open innovation projects. It coordinates agency-level technology roles with NASA Mission board of directors as well as field centers to align the NASA technology investments to meet mission requirements, anticipating future needs, and minimizing duplication of efforts. NASA technology integration and innovation consist of:

- **Strategic Technology Integration** which develops policy, requirements, and strategy for NASA's technology development activities and external organizations.
- As part of these efforts, OCT develops the **NASA Space Technology Roadmaps** and the **NASA Strategic Space Technology Investment Plan (SSTIP)**.

9.2 NASA R&D Projects Management

9.2.1 NASA R&D Roadmap Strategy

In 2010, the NASA published its first roadmap technology called the called NASA Authorization Act of 2010. In 2012, NASA drafted 14 Technology Areas (TAs) as part of its roadmaps strategy program. These 14 TAs help Guide NASA's Research & Development as well as its Open Innovation activities. Embedded into the TAs are the Technology Candidates (TCs) which outlined ideas that have the potential to evolve into actual technology for missions. In 2015 NASA expanded its Technology Roadmap areas as well as Technology Candidates with further details plus the addition of a 15th TA (Aeronautics). The 15 TAs are a set of documents for technology candidates and development pathways for the next 20 years. These documents are intended to be revised every 5 years.

Each TA is assigned with Chair as well as Co-Chair in collaboration with the Office of the Chief Technologist. Therefore, it is important to understand how NASA manages its technology investments through the above TAs.

9.2.2 Project Selection Methodology

Like any R&D organization, it is critical to have a defined process by which technological investments can be effectively managed. NASA R&D investments are managed through an integrated agency-wide technology portfolio management process. This process consists of Space Technology Roadmaps (STR), followed by the Strategic Technology Investment Plan (STIP) which is updated every two years. These two plans are then submitted to the NASA Technology Executive Council (NTEC) who makes decisions on project prioritization of investment plans. The NTEC channel these plans into the budget process for review and funding purposes prior to submitting them into a decision support software tool called TechPort—a centralized web-based integrated relational database where all R&D projects are kept.

The NTEC and other Executive bodies, make decisions on NASA's technology policy, prioritization, and strategic investments for efficient management of the portfolio contents in TechPort.

9.2.3 R&D Investment Budget

Funding for R&D projects it's an essential part of the critical resources needed in order to achieve organization mission and vision. The budget supports developing the technologies that will bring ideas from concept into a product. NASA budget fund a wide range of areas that covers R&D activities and others. For instance, a typical budget allocation maybe exemplify the 2017 budget covering the fiscal year (FY 2017 $19.0B).

These funding are allocated to make future space missions, aeronautics, and other explorations more capable and affordable. For example, the current budget keeps other projects on track such as the Webb Telescope for 2018; builds on scientific discoveries and achievements in space; and supports the Administration's commitment to serve as a catalyst for the growth of a national security.

9.2.4 Performance Measurement

NASA is known to be an organization that is based on performance, as they commit to managing specific, measurable goals based on a defined mission. They use performance data to continuously improve their operations. NASA's focuses lie in optimizing value for the American public and being results-driven while holding themselves accountable to the goals they've set through a transparent framework that guides how progress is measured.

The organizational structure of NASA was created to achieve its Mission through sound business, management, and safety oversight. NASA is headquartered in Washington, DC, where guidance and direction for the whole agency is emitted from. The Office of the Administrator provides top-level strategy and direction for the agency, while "the administrator and his staff give direction for NASA's missions and guide the operations of the Centers/NASA's Centers and facilities execute the mission work engineering, operations, science, technology development and supporting activities." Strategic management and accountability are ensured by NASA's performance management activities and depict the relationship between the three phases of the cycle.

NASA assesses its mission at different levels of the planning phase and adjusts as necessary while taking accounts for national priorities, laws, and other stakeholder input into consideration. During the evaluation, NASA internal reviews to evaluate the performance of program authorities and hold leadership accountable to help support management processes and decision-making.

This is typically done through reporting from management to senior leaders. The COO monitors progress toward their strategic objectives and looks at concerns that might affect performance. The performance determines the next steps and phases, a strategic plan performance frame.

Two sets of goals are set within the strategic plan:

- Short-term goals which target a 4-year time span.
- Annual goals which show progress within the budget year.

Agency and cross-agency priority goals are a subset of goals that receive additional senior management focus. To measure and or assess R&D projects progress, NASA uses the "traffic light rating system" to evaluate project statuses with **RED**, **YELLOW**, and **GREEN** color ratings. Success criteria are defined by program officials alongside NASA management and then these criteria are combined with explanations of the ratings and sources provided by the program officials, to review and validate each rating (NASA n.d.). Though many of the programs are assessed internally, external entities, such as science review committees and aeronautics technical evaluation bodies, further validate some of the ratings prior to publication by NASA.

Occasionally, the WHITE rating indicator is sometimes given to confirm whether a particular project is in canceled or postponed status. If labeled with a WHITE label, there is no development of measure-specific success criteria.

9.3 Risk Management (NASA 2011)

In a general point of view, risk administration and management can be seen as an arrangement of exercises aiming at realizing success and progression. This happens by proactively and actively coming up with risk-informed choices when dealing with risks and correctly chosen decision alternatives. In this paper, I will define risk management is a well-defined and expressed in regard to RIDM and CRM. NASA Procedural Requirements (NPR) archive NPR 8000.4A is the most recent handbook that was promoted in November the year 2011 to tackle the utilization of a number procedures and processes to the expenditure, security, and timed operation execution fields in the life span of projects together with involved activities, incorporating procurement and acquisition (National Research Council 2011).

NASA RM reforms and processes have been predominantly built on CRM, which focuses on managing hazards and risks amid the Implementation period of Project Life Cycle. To be precise, NASA didn't own any deliberate or formal RM process until midway 1990s. In the year 2008, NASA issued the Procedural Requirement handbook called the NPR handbook; which presented RIDM as an integral part of the CRM procedure. The CRM procedure involves an investigation of imperative in addition to direction-setting choices and decisions. Initially RM was viewed as being equal to CRM. However, RM comprised of CRM and RIDM, the different forms of Risk Management at NASA that are categorized under the two types of RM. The motivation behind incorporating RIDM alongside CRM is to promote practical risk evaluation and management to foster informed decision-making approaches using the risk information approach (Campbell and Borener 2004). After which in a viable manner overseeing the implementation of dangers and risks by utilizing the CRM procedure. RM is then centered on the standard execution necessities rising out of the RIDM procedures and processes. Inside RIDM procedures and processes, choices are made with respect to the results of the decision substitutes and alternatives to identify pertinent dangers and possible vulnerabilities. Therefore, CRM as a major aspect of the execution and implementation procedure is to discover those dangers and risks aiming at accomplishing the operation levels that propelled the selection of specific alternative (Risk Management 2017).

What NPR does is that it reinforces NASA's inner mechanism and exercises as indicated in the NPD handbook. Indeed, NPR's focus is to affect risk organization and management crosswise over budgetary and programmatic activities. The purpose of risk management is to set up an inward mechanism of mitigating and relieving known risks that may adversely impact the project outcome. The handbook PR 8000.4A provides good procedures regarding controlling project risks for NASA projects (Psenka 2008).

As per the NPR handbook, it is absolutely critical to review all risks in order to identify the probability of under-performance projects rather than acknowledging it later. Performance setbacks might affect mission execution or identified with at least one of the accompanying mission execution areas such as cost, protection, technically, and Schedule. The aim is to encourage the management of passive risk and critical risk as indicated in the NPR 8000.4A. This addresses RIDM reforms and Continuous Risk Management (CRM) in a solitary reasonable structure. The basic RIDM procedure tends to lean toward informed risks and solid choices in order to accomplishing defined goals. The CRM procedure tends to use the other selected options to ensure that necessities are met. The reason being is that in order to coordinate RIDM together with CRM into an eloquent system, you need to leverage the strengths of both methods.

As we later learned that the RM approach is mainly used in circumstances where basic NASA specialized achievement must be met within a set time stamp and specific budgetary cost. Although a part of RM is to not just explain projects expenditures, but also to identify ways that project cost can be minimized. Therefore, the techniques discussed in this paper are aimed to evaluate the way of analysis in order to oversee and analyze total costs. This is because the cost is enhanced by utilizing this approach, the expenditures reserved by settling risks before they move toward becoming issues that surpass the cost of actualizing and implementing the approach. Measuring performance can be described as a metric to quantify the degree to which a framework, process, or action satisfies its expected targets.

One of the key deciding factors for mission execution is safety performance. This may include evasion of damage, casualty, or demolition of key resources and assets. Specialized execution, for example, may help to decide whether NASA should push or yield a particular mission based on risk factors relating to the cost of execution or scheduled performance. NASA's choices for overseeing risk management includes the portrayal of the three fundamental segments of risk. The first scenario being reduced performance based on a single or many performance measures. For instance, situations that prompt damage, casualty, obliteration of key resources, or situations that lead to exceeding certain confinement limits. The second is anticipating the consequences, of a subjective or quantitative seriousness of observed performance scenarios that could come about. The aspect of risk management, especially at the Agency point, includes the full range of possible dangers and risks. Therefore proper handling of potential risks is vital to NASA. It is no surprise that NASA places a lot of emphasis on safety and risk assessment mechanisms such as RDIM particularly when it comes to space missions. RIDM process includes, Identification of various decision alternatives, perceiving chances where they emerge, and considering an adequate number and decent variety of execution measures to mitigate known risks. As a major aspect of the risk-informed procedures and processes, the entire measurement process is highly vetted to enhance decision-making in addition to seeking expert consultation (Flippen et al. 2002; Risk Management 2017).

NASA utilizes a particular procedure regarding the management of various risks in relation to the execution of plans, and procedures. These procedures are the main ventures in the CRM process which include: Identifying the main contributors and prerequisites to risk. Analyzing the estimate and likelihood and result segments of the risk through examination, by incorporating vulnerability in the probabilities and outcomes. Planning the risk mitigation procedures and methodologies and choosing a chronological order that will be followed. Tracking observables that can be identified with performance measures like the entire process execution data. Controlling the risk by assessing and following the risk information with the aim to check the adequacy of designs and making changes as needed.

9.4 Human and Capital Management, Partnerships, and NASA 2050 Vision

In terms of human capital, NASA places a lot of emphasis on preserving skilled workforce, controlling expenses, and giving viable oversight to essential initiatives. NASA's Human Capital community seeks to promote and encourage practices that foster creativity and innovation, from science to accounting to facilities management

(NASA 2011). NASA objective for the workforce is to create a vibrant culture that supports creative ideas and helps provide novel ways of working together in a dynamic work environment (NASA 2011).

Recognizing and Rewarding Innovative Performance is one of the initiatives NASA's uses to foster creativity, innovation, collaboration, and teamwork. This plan help employees to be more productive, get better results and operate more safely. Indeed, the program helps NASA to build an innovative and creative culture that embraces change, and practices that enhance collaboration and teamwork (NASA 2011).

NASA's efforts to reach beyond traditional boundaries and encourage partnerships and collaboration with a variety of organizations to solve the global issues (NASA 2014).

> NASA embraces participation from partners in industry, academia, and the larger aerospace community with mutual interests in development of breakthrough capabilities that support its aeronautics and aerospace goals, and national priorities. Strategic partnerships are designed to expand and strengthen NASA ability to execute its mission, and range from non-traditional partnerships to systematic engagements with local, regional, state, national, and international partners. These partnerships enable NASA to leverage funding, capabilities, and expertise within and outside NASA to address technology barriers and advance technology. (NASA 2014)

> Creating effective partnerships that bring their technical strengths, resources, and capabilities to bear will increase the robustness of optimal organizational architectures in ways that increase the probability of the project success. (Laurini 2011)

Although each section of NASA has their own partnerships and cooperation programs and activities, but mainly programs and offices that are responsible for partnerships and international collaboration are as follows:

- **Chief Technologist** has a section titled Partnership, Innovation, and Emerging Space.
- **International and Interagency Relations (OIIR)** "provides executive leadership and coordination for all NASA international activities and partnerships and for policy interactions between NASA and other U.S. Executive Branch offices and agencies. OIIR serves as the principal Agency liaison with the National Security Council, the Office of Science and Technology Policy, the Department of State, and the Department of Defense" (NASA, Office of International and Interagency Relations 2017).
- **Small Business Innovation Research and Small Business Technology Transfer (SBIR/STTR) Program** "engages small businesses in our Nation's space enterprise and infuse these products across NASA missions."
- **Mission Support Directorate** provides "effective and efficient institutional support to enable successful accomplishment of NASA mission objectives" (NASA, Mission Support Directorate 2017).
- **Goddard Space Flight Center** is "home to the nation's largest organization of scientists, engineers and technologists who build spacecraft, instruments and new technology to study Earth, the sun, our solar system and the universe" (NASA, About the Goddard Space Flight Center 2017).

- **Innovative Partnerships Program** offers "a variety of resources for collaborations that will advance technology and result in commercialization and technology transfer" (NASA, Innovative Partnerships Program 2017).

During spring 2017, NASA's Planetary Science Division (PSD) hosted a community workshop titled "Planetary Science Vision 2050 Workshop" at NASA headquarters in Washington, DC on February 27–28 and March 1, 2017. This workshop provided PSD with community input on a very long-range vision for planetary science in the future (Dirk Schulze-Makuch 2017; Planetary Science Vision 2050 Workshop 2017a).

According to NASA's 2014 Strategic Plan, as well as the outlines of the mentioned workshop, NASA is laying the foundation for further scientific advances and improved quality of life on Earth (NASA 2003; Planetary Science Vision 2050 Workshop 2017b). Some of the main future vision of NASA are summarized as follows (NASA 2014, 2015; Planetary Science Vision 2050 Workshop 2017b):

- Continuing the human and robotic exploration of space (discovery programs).
- Increasing cooperation with its traditional partners in industry, academia, and other national space agencies.
- More investment and innovation in scientific research, technology, new technologies, tools, and techniques.
- Expanding international collaboration.
- Consider the research and planetary protection in the context of human exploration.

NASA will require the following action plan for reaching its vision 2050 (Hofstadter et al. 2017):

- Investments in technology and ground-based science in the 2020s.
- Continuing technological development of both ground- and space-based capabilities in the 2030s.
- Data analysis and additional flights in the 2040s.

9.5 Conclusion

We learned a great deal about the pros and cons of what a good R&D organization and practices should be the case studies. These provided a good framework for researching NASA and its R&D practices. Based on our research and examination we gathered some key lessons learned and recommendations that are central to effective R&D management approaches. The following are our recommendations for some of the lessons learnt from our research study as well as recommended best practices of managing R&D organization.

- First the cultural diversity in R&D organizations fosters unique ideas and creative viewpoints that can spark innovation (Dubiel 2011). Global cultural contexts among R&D managers often highlights the beneficial impacts on the organization (Dubiel 2011; Greiman 2013; Thomke and Nimgade 2001). This goes hand in hand with the recognition of past experiences and partnerships, providing a good platform for building the relationships and trust needed to execute a project successfully and cost-effectively in open innovative projects (Laurini 2011). Namely the trust dimension is crucial for R&D related partnerships. In order to support a climate conducive research and development excellence, innovative approaches are essential to problem solving such as prizes, challenges, and collaborations. The third R&D controlling and monitoring needs to be kept to a minimum but rather expert oversights established to ensure R&D activities must be in-line with organizational vision, mission, and strategic goals while minimizing risks impact. Fourth effective decision-making mechanisms and tools are critical to the accessibility of data to facilitate monitoring/control of projects. Fifth a clear emphasis on technology development platform where various innovative applications can be created to benefit mankind is required together with project management sources such as the PMBOK Guide and Standards can have a significant impact on R&D organization effectiveness (Daim et al. 2014; Thomke and Nimgade 2001). Finally transparent communication and support of domestic and global partnerships that forge relationships of trust in order to work toward a common goal of achieving social and technological impact is an asset.

Acknowledgment Dirk Meissners contribution to the book chapter is based on the study funded by the Basic Research Program of the National Research University Higher School of Economics (HSE) and by the Russian Academic Excellence Project "5-100."

References[1]

2015 NASA Technology Roadmaps (2015). https://www.nasa.gov/sites/default/files/atoms/files/2015_nasa_technology_roadmaps_ta_0_introduction_crosscutting_index_final_0.pdf

Campbell BN, Borener SS (2004) Safety and business benefit analysis of NASA's aviation safety program. In: AIAA 4th Aviation Technology, Integration and Operations (ATIO) Forum, pp 1–12

Daim T, Pizarro M, Talla R (2014) Planning and roadmapping technological innovations. Springer International Publishing, London

Dirk Schulze-Makuch (March 5, 2017) A vision for planetary science in 2050. http://www.realclearscience.com/2017/03/05/a_vision_for_planetary_science_in_2050_275072.html

Dubiel A (2011) Successful new product development for international markets. Doctoral dissertation, A. Dubiel

Flippen AA, Navarro RJ, Larsen AM, Stamatelatos M (2002) The application of probabilistic risk assessment to habitable payloads: utilization of risk-based and traditional rule-based

[1]Uncited references were used to develop this case.

methodologies: a "first" for NASA. In: ASME 2002 international mechanical engineering congress and exposition. American Society of Mechanical Engineers, pp 1–6
Greiman VA (2013) Megaproject management: lessons on risk and project management from the Big Dig. John Wiley & Sons
Gunasekara SG (2011) "Other transaction" authority: NASA's dynamic acquisition instrument for the commercialization of manned spaceflight or cold war relic? Pub Contract Law J 40 (4):893–909
Hofstadter M, Simon A, Atreya S, Banfield D, Fortney J, Hayes A, Showalter M (2017) A vision for ice giant exploration. LPI Contributions, 1989
Laurini K (2011, August) International partnerships for space exploration. Ask Magazine. https://appel.nasa.gov/2011/08/01/international-partnerships-for-space-exploration/
NASA, About the Goddard Space Flight Center. (Last updated: August 3, 2017). https://www.nasa.gov/centers/goddard/about/index.html. Accessed 5 Aug 2017
NASA FY 2017 Budget Request (2017) NASA agency fact sheet. https://www.nasa.gov/sites/default/files/atoms/files/fy_2017_nasa_agency_fact_sheet.pdf
NASA Human Capital Plan: A Guide to Building a Highly Engaged Workforce (2017). https://nasapeople.nasa.gov/hcm/index_sbg.htm
NASA, Innovative Partnerships Program. (Last updated: November 19, 2017). https://www.nasa.gov/centers/dryden/news/X-Press/aerovations/dynamic_ipp.html. Accessed 5 Aug 2017
NASA, Mission Support Directorate (MSD) (Last updated: August 3, 2017). https://www.nasa.gov/msd. Accessed 5 Aug 2017
NASA, Office of International and Interagency Relations (OIIR) (Last updated: January 27, 2017). https://oiir.hq.nasa.gov/. Accessed 5 Aug 2017
National Aeronautics and Space Administration (NASA) (2003) 2003 strategic plan. NASA Headquarters, Washington, DC. https://www.hou.usra.edu/meetings/V2050/pdf/8079.pdf
National Aeronautics and Space Administration (NASA) (2011) NASA risk management handbook. NASA Headquarters, Washington, DC. https://ntrs.nasa.gov/archive/nasa/casi.ntrs.nasa.gov/20120000033.pdf. Accessed 11 Aug 2017
National Aeronautics and Space Administration (NASA) (2014) NASA strategic plan 2014. NASA Headquarters, Washington, DC
National Aeronautics and Space Administration (NASA) (2015) NASA's FY 2015 management and performance. NASA Headquarters, Washington, DC
National Aeronautics and Space Administration (NASA) (n.d.) NASA FY 2015 annual performance report and FY 2017 annual performance plan. NASA's Office of the Chief Financial Officer. https://www.nasa.gov/sites/default/files/atoms/files/nasa_fy2015_apr-fy2017_app.pdf
National Research Council (2011) Limiting future collision risk to spacecraft: an assessment of NASA's meteoroid and orbital debris programs. National Academies Press
Planetary Science Vision 2050 Workshop (2017a) Planetary science vision 2050. http://www.lpi.usra.edu/V2050/
Planetary Science Vision 2050 Workshop (2017b) Planetary science vision 2050 synopses. https://livestream.com/viewnow/vision2050/videos/150727850?t=1488290819199
Psenka CE (2008) A monumental task: Translating complex knowledge in NASA's human space flight network. Doctoral dissertation, Wayne State University
Risk Management (2017). https://sma.nasa.gov/sma-disciplines/risk-management
Thomke SH, Nimgade A (2001) Siemens AG: global development strategy (A). Harvard Business School Case 602-061 (Revised March 2002)
Ways the International Space Station Is Benefiting Earth (2015). https://www.nasa.gov/mission_pages/station/research/news/15_ways_iss_benefits_earth

Chapter 10
Technology Forecasting in the Automotive Sector

Colette Marthaller, Tanzila Akhter, Luciane Dolgos, Jessier Truong, Marthed Mohammed, Abdalilah Owaishiz, and Tugrul U. Daim

10.1 Introduction

Knowledge management is composed of tools and processes that are used to retain data and discoveries made by a multitude of individuals throughout the topic's community making the information easily accessible to all. Knowledge and discoveries must be managed so they are not lost, and that researchers are not "reinventing the wheel." When work is credited, it makes it easier to find experts in the field. This will allow work to continue to be built upon and furthered. If knowledge and discoveries are not properly managed and cited, they could be used by others allowing them to reap the benefits.

Technology forecasting is the process of cataloging current technology to discover gaps and use SMEs to predict future products or technologies, which can be incremental or disruptive to the current industry. It is useful to dictate where a company should invest next, and gives definition to the future of an industry.

To effectively manage R&D, organizations cannot neglect knowledge management and technology forecasting. There are many useful tools that help organizations in these two areas. This chapter will recommend the three tools to DTNA in hope to enhance their R&D management. The tools to be introduced are Diffusion Models, Reverse Salient, SNA, and Bibliometric Analysis.

C. Marthaller · T. Akhter · L. Dolgos · J. Truong · M. Mohammed · A. Owaishiz
Portland State University, Portland, OR, USA

T. U. Daim (✉)
Portland State University Technology Management Doctoral Program, Portland, OR, USA

National Research University Higher School of Economics, Moscow, Russia

Chaoyang University of Technology, Taichung City, Taiwan
e-mail: tugrul.u.daim@pdx.edu

T. U. Daim, D. Meissner (eds.), *Innovation Management in the Intelligent World*, Science, Technology and Innovation Studies,
https://doi.org/10.1007/978-3-030-58301-9_10

Daimler Trucks North America (DTNA) has long been at the forefront of industry-leading innovations. Their legacy is defined by a track record of technological advancements, including Intelligent Powertrain Management. The company has cutting-edge innovation when it comes to trucks. As the number one supplier of choice in the North American commercial trucking market, DTNA constantly pursues and achieves its goals of providing the best trucks on the road, delivering uncompromising value and customer satisfaction through technological innovation backed by superior engineering.

10.1.1 Diffusion Model

Technology forecasting may include many tools. Each tool brings something a little bit different. Together they help create more accurate "possible worlds" regarding products, components, costs, prices, units shipped, timelines, and other attributes.

A diffusion model is something that tries to predict how quickly the market will adopt a new technology. One of the dimensions of diffusion model is time, so the diffusion model creates a timeline. With a timeline, it is possible to make better decisions about planning. Comparing two technologies with a diffusion model can help decide many things, what kind of customer will adopt the technology when, time between multiple diffusions of similar technology, low and high estimates of diffusion, and which technology can take the market first are just some possibilities.

The diffusion models presented here can all be used to create S-Curve of diffusion, with time on the *x*-axis, and percent of diffusion on the *y*-axis. With the basic S-Curve graph, additional questions can be explored. Everett Rogers, for example, extend the graph with five divisions related to the type of person adopting the technology in some moment (Rogers 1983). This type of thinking can help companies to understand how to communicate with the adopters. For example, "Innovators" will naturally understand the new technology, they are the first to adopt. "Laggards" will need more explanation or incentive. They are the last to adopt.

Many diffusion models exist, two examples are the Fisher-Pry diffusion model and the Bass diffusion model (Bass 1969; Wolken et al. 2018). Both can be used to produce an S-Curve of diffusion. Different models need different parameters. A user may choose one model over another because of available data. Each model also can make different assumptions about the world. A user of a model must consider if the assumptions are correct in the real situation.

Consider the New Zealand Transportation Agency study of the diffusion of various technologies that can impact the agency's planning (Wolken et al. 2018). In their 2018 research report, they used the Bass diffusion model to consider the timeline of MaaS (Mobility as a Service). MaaS is services like Uber, Lyft, and Lime Electric Bikes. The NZ research group chose the Bass model because of an extension that allowed them to study successive generations.

Because the diffusion model considers time, it can be used to also compare multiple diffusions between generations of similar technology. The diffusion of autonomy of trucks is divided into three generations of the technology. Phases 1 and 2 are 12 years apart. Phases 2 and 3 are 14 years apart. A business using a diffusion diagram can make plans about when to adopt each phase. For example, if a phase one technology has a lifetime of 4 years, adopting Phase 1 technology in 2026 would indicate adopting Phase 2 very early or investing in Phase 1 again.

Each diffusion model has parameters and data to make the forecast. More advanced models can use assumptions about changing future conditions. For example, the cost of batteries for electric vehicles can change adoption. Different assumptions about how the decrease will happen can change the diffusion. The diffusion of L3 and L4 autonomy with different assumptions made by the authors (*Automotive revolution – perspective toward 2030, how the convergence of disruptive technology-driven trends could transform the auto industry* 2016). One group of assumptions for "high disruption" scenario, and another group of assumptions for "low disruption" scenario.

10.1.2 Reverse Salient Model

The reverse salient model is a subsystem that delivers low performance compared to other subsystems of the technological system. Also known as the unevenness in the subsystem, it hinders the performance of the system. It must be corrected in order to reach optimum performance as a system functioning as whole. Many models are integrated to define reverse salient in systems. The emergence of reverse salient is determined by developing absolute and proportional performance gap measures (Dedehayir and Mäkinen 2011). There are limitations on the literature review and systematic tools used to determine reverse salient in technologies.

Experts identify current and forecast future reverse salient from available information like standards and patent registries. (Dedehayir and Hornsby 2008) To obtain a competitive advantage in the market integration of models like Quality Function Deployment (QFD), bibliometric analysis, and Trend Impact Analysis (TIA) are needed. These models collected specific key performance indicators of reverse salient to identify the performance gap between current and market required production. Experts will be able to make a forecast about when reverse salient will be modified (Han and Shin 2014). Increasing citation analysis highlights the reverse salient theory to scholars and experts.

The reverse salient model is used by experts and scholars to apply technical as well as social, economic, and political approaches. Scholars must engage in a more theoretical approach to identify reverse salient (Dedehayir 2009). Politics have become reverse salient in innovation theory. Scholars are yet to discover politics and its security and complexities in general explanation (Taylor 2009). This relates to many fields like healthcare due to technological changes causing a gap between medical practitioners and the administrative management. Subsequently, it may be possible to correct the reverse salient and integrate different methodologies to reach the salient system.

10.1.3 Social Network Analysis Model

Social Network Analysis (SNA) is the study of structure based on theoretical constructs of sociology and mathematical foundations of graph theory. Because SNA focuses on network structure therefore the data required differs from a nonrelational analysis. In this model, the network structure refers to the regularities in the patterning of relationships among individuals, groups, and/or organizations. To perform a proper SNA, it requires not only attribute data, but a collection of relational data and these data can be contacts, ties, or connections, which relate one stakeholder in a network to another. These relational data cannot be reduced to properties of the individual stakeholders themselves but to a system or a collection of stakeholders. When applying SNA, the assumption is that network structure and its properties have significant implications on the outcome of interest (Mailman.columbia.edu 2018).

Researchers and scholars have been using SNA for varieties of studies, including technology forecasting, which is intended to find a future trend or a technology using analytical methods. A central technology forecasting model that uses SNA was proposed by the Department of Statistics, Cheongju University,Korea. The belief is that if the central technologies can be forecasted, organizations can effectively build their R&D policy on. The study was done by setting each technology as a node in an SNA graph and analyze the linkages between them, and forecast central technologies from SNA results (Jun n.d.). Another study was done by using SNA to build a model selecting sustainable technologies for Management of Technology areas such as R&D planning or new product development. In this model, technology is represented by a vertex in an SNA graph, and edges between the vertices represent technological relations. Patent documents were used in the study to illustrate how the model can be applied to a real-world problem (Park et al. 2015). These are just a couple of examples showing how SNA can be used as a tool when performing technology forecasting.

Knowledge Management has become more recognizable as a critical area by many organizations. Organizations are trying hard to implement different methods in managing knowledge such as enhance organizational learning, knowledge transfer, knowledge innovation, etc. A study was done to present the idea on how knowledge is disseminated effectively by the help of Social Network Analysis. SNA can help organizations to visualize and understand the details or relationships that can either facilitate or obstruct knowledge creation and transfer. With the help of SNA, organizations will be able to understand how information flow within their organization, whom people turn for advice, how individuals or groups are sharing what they know effectively and many more (Alamsyah 2013). SNA provides a method for expert localization, knowledge transfer, models of interpretation, and ways of interventions. SNA can be used as an effective knowledge management tool for any organization.

10.1.4 Bibliometric Model

Bibliometrics is the measurement of texts and information. In the past, bibliometric methods have been used to trace back academic journal citations. This way of using bibliometric has changed today. Now we use bibliometrics to understand the past and to forecast the future (Watatani et al. 2013). Bibliometrics helps to gather, organize, and analyze a lot of data then helping researchers to identify "hidden patterns" that may be very helpful, especially for decision makers.

Bibliometrics is extracting multiword from a large number of papers and determine what words came together and analyze these words to predict future technology or frequency of using certain words or phrases or authors using the Science Citation Index (SCI) and the Engineering Compendex (EC) databases. This analysis helps us to determine our experts to build a model and making the decision-making process more effective and useful. Then use other experts to evaluate this model (Daim et al. 2006).

Additionally, presented relevant papers in data mining using specialized software. Bibliometrics can be used in combination with other forms of technological evidence such as innovation forecasting. bibliometric applications are very important for the engineering and technology management field. With this model, bibliometrics helps researchers and R&D departments to identify hidden patterns classifying information by authors, organizations, countries, collaborations, co-citations, and also help businesses in technology forecasting (Daim et al. 2006).

10.2 Daimler Trucks North America

10.2.1 Company Profile

Daimler is a multinational automotive manufacturer that is leading the industry in fuel efficiency and technology. Within the current Daimler portfolio, there are passenger cars, buses, and multiple commercial vehicles. Daimler has entities in almost every continent and has major brands in Europe, Asia, North and South America. The business unit that this chapter will be focusing on is Daimler Trucks and more accurately Daimler Trucks North America. Daimler Trucks North America (DTNA) is a commercial vehicle manufacturer with five major brands; Freightliner, Western Star, Thomas Built Buses, Freightliner Custom Chassis, and Alliance Automotive Parts.

DTNA has been a leader in the industry in regard to alternative fuels and technological advancement. DTNA is the current market share leader and has been for over 5 years. They export globally with their major export markets in Australia, South Africa, and the Middle East. DTNA was the first commercial vehicle to get a license to test an autonomous driving truck and has a clean running Natural Gas truck in production. With the launch of the new Cascadia DTNA has the most fuel-efficient truck on the market and orders are booked out through the next year. So how has DTNA become such a technological leader? How do they know what is the next "big thing"? With all this technical knowledge, how do they ensure patent retention and best practice sharing?

10.2.2 Knowledge Management at DTNA

Knowledge management at DTNA is an active and growing process. Lessons learned after each project has been a DTNA staple for years, this ensures that project-specific knowledge and insights are not lost once a project has finished or a new product has launched. DTNA also partners with universities and within technical societies to recruit top talent and industry professionals to ensure that their technological personnel are industry and technology experts. A number of years ago, DTNA also launched a Technical Fellow career path with the purpose of developing individuals into industry leaders and experts in leading engineering topics. These technical fellows are responsible for not only leading the cutting edge technology at DTNA, but also publishing papers and giving lectures industry wide on technology. Daimler also has an inhouse "Think Tank" called Advanced Engineering that is responsible for looking for 20 years into the future, developing patents, and attracting talent to the organization. DTNA also has an extensive Intranet-based Wikipedia that is home to tribal knowledge, tips and tricks, best practices, and component knowledge that can be accessed by anyone within the company.

Sharing information on a global scale can be more difficult. In a company as large as Daimler, segmentation is expected. The organization of data for each business unit by nature is segmented as to not overwhelm simple search criteria. However, as the world is becoming more global and continuous improvement, cost reductions, and fuel efficiency topics are becoming more prevalent information needs to be shared. Global meetings and conferences have become the new normal at Daimler as all the business units strive to take each other's best practices and implement them within their regions. Global file share and Share Points are used to catalog and disseminate information of a technical nature to ensure that no business unit is starting from scratch with technology when another business unit is already knowledgeable.

10.2.3 Technology Forecasting at DTNA

Technology forecasting is a primary concern at DTNA. As DTNA attempts to focus on and anticipate customer needs, DTNA needs to keep abreast of all the up and coming technology and be able to integrate it at the right time for the market. DTNA has an annual roadmapping process to look at the technological readiness of new technology and decide what will go into production and when it will be available to customers. The roadmapping exercise takes input from key customers and market trends to identify the best time for a new technology. DTNA has also formed strategic partnerships with leading universities to tap into academic knowledge and research being performed. Since DTNA is a subsidiary of Daimler AG they also have the knowledge and foresight into what the passenger car market is expecting. The passenger car market is always ahead of the commercial vehicle market in regard to technology. Having this insight allows DTNA to pre-verify technologies and market acceptance of new technologies.

Other major drivers of future technology are suppliers Since DTNA is the market leader a supplier or technology company with a new product they strive to get it on DTNA's trucks. Suppliers are also stakeholders in industries that DTNA is not, for example, lighting. DTNA does not need to attempt to forecast the future of lighting because the suppliers already are and they are trying to be first to market with the newest technology in DTNA trucks. DTNA has always been at the forefront of alternative fuel technology with their range of Natural Gas trucks and now with the development of electric trucks and autonomous technology DTNA is helping to drive the future of the trucking industry.

10.3 Comparative Analysis

10.3.1 Knowledge Management

The electric truck is being developed to decrease greenhouse gas emissions and to meet the ever stringent EPA standards and the automated truck is being developed for the race to be leading the market. The CEO states that being at the forefront of the electric truck and automated truck fleets separately is the ideal approach (Daimler unveils two all-electric Freightliner trucks 2018). DTNA must develop the electric truck technology separately to be a main fleet manager. After developing the automated truck fleet and succeeding by being the biggest supplier of fleets worldwide DTNA can integrate the two technologies. Integrating both technologies currently would result in a reverse salient because both are still developing. With developing technologies risks occur and may delay the development of the system resulting in failure.

It is rather difficult to manage the knowledge and protect information as there is no historical data available (Social network analysis: a tool to improve understanding of collaborative management groups n.d.). In such cases, the use of bibliometrics and patent analysis has provided useful data. DTNA can use patent documents as a source of technical knowledge. These documents are always useful for R&D departments, especially in a huge company like DTNA. They have created a relationship map to identify the key persons and all these experts and data have been used to increase DTNA's knowledge and make the management of the knowledge easier and subsequently more successful, especially in high tech innovation (Social network analysis – QI toolbox – Minnesota dept. of health n.d.).

The importance of social networks has been discussed many times in the resources literature. It is essential for managing global resources, responding to natural disasters, and enhancing the resilience of social-ecological systems in the face of climate change. It also benefits organizations to manage natural resources effectively, and that desirable qualities for one network are not necessarily important to another (Social network analysis – QI toolbox – Minnesota dept. of health n.d.). DTNA can use SNA as a strategic tool for expert localization, identification of knowledge communities, and analysis of the structure of intra- and inter-organizational knowledge flows. For instance, DTNA can use SNA to map out their organization to find bottlenecks in the information or material flow, or silos where communication is completely absent. This can be done by performing a survey with their staff, understanding who they regularly work with generally or on a particular project, and then map out staff connections with arrows indicating directions of dependency. Different colors can be used to represent different attributes such as employee type, work unit, or level of knowledge on a particular topic. Once the network connections are established, DTNA will be able to identify places to create redundancies to get around bottlenecks, or identify area of experts with the right skills set for certain upcoming projects. This will help DTNA to maximize efficiency and collaboration (Reingold n.d.).

Not only SNA can help identify internal issues, it could also help identify external issues as well. Having a strong relationship with clients is essential for business success. SNA can help map out DTNA relationship with their suppliers/customers. This will enable DTNA to build strong and healthy relationships that will lead to generating more revenue, increasing returns for the company.

10.3.2 Technology Forecasting

Technology forecasting may include many tools. Each tool brings something a little bit different. The diffusion model helps predict technology adoption in the market. Together they help create more accurate "possible worlds" regarding products, components, costs, prices, units shipped, timelines, and other attributes.

Identifying reverse salients in research and development has become increasingly common due to the technological complexity and shortened life cycle of systems. Penetrating the market with new technologies like the electric Freightliner truck is challenging for DTNA. They will develop electric trucks and automated trucks separately. They have forecasted that developing the technologies together and integrating them right now would cause them loss. They will develop the technologies individually and maybe in the future there might be some interconnection between these technologies.

As mentioned in the previous section, Social Network Analysis and bibliometric have been put in use for technology forecasting. DTNA can apply SNA to help forecasting battery technology performance for their EV division and apply bibliometric to identify the keywords of certain technology and how the researcher predicts the new technology. Or they can also use both to forecast technology to improve their manufacturing sites.

It is very important for DTNA to know the experts in new product field and use them to build a decision-making model to choose a new product or even improve their process and make the picture very clear for decision makers to decide either short time plans or strategic plan. Using this method to improve automated R&D is a key point for DTNA, bibliometric helps DTNA to analyze a large number of researches and papers to capture the evolution of automation R&D new systems.

10.4 Conclusion

DTNA has created an automated research and development center at their headquarters in Germany to assist in knowledge management between their different companies and partners across the continents (Daimler talks truck sales, tariffs, and globalism 2018). For example, E-mobility (EMG) has been heavily researched and tested in Japan and Germany and Autonomous truck technology was first developed in Germany then brought to the United States. By leveraging the global work and knowledge DTNA is able to make it to market with new technology faster in all regions. DTNA solution is to go global with all development and to streamline the product offerings and leverage a global supply base (Daimler: Truck sales outlook positive, but tariffs a cause for concern 2018). Daimler is focusing on their innovation models and CASE strategy (connected, autonomous, shared, electric) that includes the autonomous self-driving trucks (Daimler net income, revenue down on soft total sales 2018). Daimler has also launched Project Future that will strategically align the different business units to be able to tackle innovative technologies in every region (Daimler net income, revenue down on soft total sales 2018). With the current focus on up and coming technologies using technology forecasting and the current continuous improvement and knowledge management culture at Daimler and DTNA have positioned themselves to be leaders in the industry for the foreseeable feature.

Acknowledgments Tugrul Daims contribution to the book chapter is based on the study funded by the Basic Research Program of the National Research University Higher School of Economics (HSE) and by the Russian Academic Excellence Project "5-100."

References

Alamsyah A (2013) The role of social network analysis for knowledge management. J Manajemen Indonesia 12

Automotive revolution – perspective toward 2030, how the convergence of disruptive technology-driven trends could transform the auto industry (2016) McKinsey & Company

Bass FM (1969) A new product growth for model consumer durables. Manage Sci 15(5):215–227

Daim TU et al (2006) Forecasting emerging technologies: use of bibliometrics and patent analysis. Technol Forecast Soc Change 73(8):981–1012

Daimler net income, revenue down on soft total sales, ttnews.com, Jul 26, 2018. [online]. https://www.ttnews.com/articles/daimler-net-income-revenue-down-soft-total-sales

Daimler talks truck sales, tariffs, and globalism, truckinginfo.com, Jun 7, 2018. [online]. https://www.truckinginfo.com/303985/daimler-talks-truck-sales-tariffs-and-globalism

Daimler unveils two all-electric Freightliner trucks, fleetowner.com, Jun 7, 2018. [online]. https://www.fleetowner.com/running-green/daimler-unveils-two-all-electric-freightliner-trucks

Daimler: Truck sales outlook positive, but tariffs a cause for concern, fleetowner.com, Jun 11, 2018. [online]. https://www.fleetowner.com/economics/daimler-truck-sales-outlook-positive-tariffs-cause-concern

Dedehayir O (2009) Bibliometric study of the reverse salient concept. J Ind Eng Manag 2(3):569

Dedehayir O, Hornsby A (2008) Staying at the technology forefront by spotting the reverse salient: the case of digital video broadcasting. 2008 IEEE international conference on management of innovation and technology, pp. 189–194

Dedehayir O, Mäkinen SJ (2011) Determining reverse salient types and evolutionary dynamics of technology systems with performance disparities. Technol Anal Strateg Manag 23 (10):1095–1114

Han K, Shin J (2014) A systematic way of identifying and forecasting technological reverse salients using QFD, bibliometrics, and trend impact analysis: a carbon nanotube biosensor case. Technovation 34(9):559–570

Jun S (n.d.) Central technology forecasting using social network analysis. computer applications for software engineering, disaster recovery, and business continuity, pp. 1–8

Mailman.columbia.edu (2018) *Social Network Analysis | Columbia University Mailman School of Public Health*. [online]. https://www.mailman.columbia.edu/research/population-health-methods/social-network-analysis. Accessed 9 Aug 2018

Park S, Lee S-J, Jun S (2015) A network analysis model for selecting sustainable technology. Sustainability 7:13126–13141. https://doi.org/10.3390/su71013126

Reingold J (n.d.) The hidden workplace. [online]. https://money.cnn.com/magazines/fortune/fortune_archive/2007/07/23/100135706/index.htm

Rogers EM (1983) Diffusion of innovation, 3rd edn. The Free Press, New York

Social network analysis – QI toolbox – Minnesota dept. of health (n.d.) [online]. http://www.health.state.mn.us/divs/opi/qi/toolbox/sna.html

Social network analysis: a tool to improve understanding of collaborative management groups (n.d.) [online]. https://www.joe.org/joe/2011december/rb7.php

Taylor MZ (2009) Conclusion: international political economy-the reverse salient of innovation theory. The Rev Policy Res 26(1–2):219–223

Watatani K et al (2013) Global competencies of regional stem cell research: bibliometrics for investigating and forecasting research trends. Regen Med 8(5):659–668

Wolken, AR, Smith, MJ, Kaye-Blake, WH, Curry, KO, Dickson, MC, Drummond, CE, Thomas, AL (2018) Driving change: technology diffusion in the transport sector. NZ Transport Agency Research Report 647

Chapter 11
The Process of Forming a Successful Medical Device

Raghav Gupta, Kyle Haston, Isaac Kreft, Obianuju "Uju" Obiano, Colin Owens, Colleen Salmon, and Tugrul U. Daim

11.1 Introduction

Different concepts and methods are used collaboratively in new product development to comprehend the totality of the project. Biotronik/MSEI accomplishes new product development projects with the use of pre-marketing analytics, knowledge communication, customer integration, network communication, breaking a project down, and analyzing risks in a project. Biotronik/MSEI, as well as many other companies, use data, information, knowledge, and other variables to predict the projects' technical and marketing values forming a pre-analysis of the products. Knowledge learned and obtained from new, old, or ongoing projects (especially the project being focused on) needs to be distributed with the use of a transactive memory system. The product will be analyzed through customer integration allowing for specific feedback and insight into the product to allow for solutions and innovations. The development of strong network capability enhances the product and technical innovation which will reliably improve performance. As products formulate the project needs to be simplified into task-oriented objectives; this is where design structure matrices are applied. Then all of the risks for the product are examined, broken down, and mitigated to establish a well-defined product. Intertwining all of these different methods throughout the project through a specific

R. Gupta · K. Haston · I. Kreft · O. Obiano · C. Owens · C. Salmon
Portland State University, Portland, OR, USA

T. U. Daim (✉)
Portland State University Technology Management Doctoral Program, Portland, OR, USA

National Research University Higher School of Economics, Moscow, Russia

Chaoyang University of Technology, Taichung City, Taiwan
e-mail: tugrul.u.daim@pdx.edu

T. U. Daim, D. Meissner (eds.), *Innovation Management in the Intelligent World*,
Science, Technology and Innovation Studies,
https://doi.org/10.1007/978-3-030-58301-9_11

methodology provides ideal focus, clarity, communication, and outcome for the project.

Biotronik/MSEI understands the importance of R&D with a new product being developed because the new product can become revolutionary or profitable. The different concepts and structures are all related in some ways if the new product will be successful in any company. Throughout the paper, Biotronik/MSEI methodology can align with the articles' key ideas and methodology created from those articles to develop a new product.

11.1.1 Learning Zone

Like analyzing baseball stats to get the best roster, or counting cards to increase the odds of winning, most subjective things can be broken down into science or math terms. However, some subjects are very hard to quantify. One such area is the "learning zone" or the environment in which one is most able to produce creative ideas to apply toward new products (Cui et al. n.d.). Nonetheless, academic researchers attempt to find quantitative correlations. There is a delicate balance between a bunch of important variables.

This data suggests that new information can be most utilized if one has a moderate amount of known market and technical knowledge. If one has too little known knowledge one has no way of understanding new information. However, if one has too much knowledge and they are given new information, their wealth of information is overwhelming, so their creativity is stunted. Since creativity is very important when developing a new product, having too much knowledge is actually more of a hindrance than having too little. In fact, the tricky part is trying to integrate another variable: product novelty. Novelty represents the originality of the new product. A product with high novelty is a very disruptive technology, whereas a product with low novelty is not very different from other products. An example of high novelty is when electricity was first invented, and it revolutionized the market. An example of a low novelty product is the iPhone 7 as compared to the iPhone 6, which was not terribly different.

There is no real way to quantify the learning zone as can be done for other stages of new product development. The most valuable thing to know is that there must be a mixture of seasoned and fresh minds to create a successful research and development team. The company needs the valuable information from the senior employees, as well as the creativity from newer employees.

11.1.2 Transactive Memory System

Due to the complexity of medical devices, medical device companies are faced with a number of internal and external challenges that require teams to respond and evolve during new product development (NPD). This is on the grounds that NPD groups are viewed as a significant working unit for an organization because of the constant change in new product development. Since NPD teams regularly include individuals with various perspectives, ideas, backgrounds, and knowledge, NPD projects require a socially well-structured and effective collective memory (transactive memory system (TMS)). Akgün et al. (n.d.) show that the ability to leverage a TMS is important in the new product development team because of its positive effect on team learning and product speed-to-market.

TMS could be either positive or negative due to environmental turbulence associated with the environment. However, the following hypotheses (Hx…), Akgün et al. (n.d.) explain the result of applying TMS on new product development teams:

H1: The TMS is positively associated with 1) team learning and speed-to-market. For example, throughout the formal and casual team meetings that accompany repeated joint actions during the projects, team members' respective knowledge is blended and leveraged. Therefore, H1 helps to uncover and address product-related issues, improve the teams' collective mind and product launch.

H2: The collective mind mediates the relationship between the TMS and (1) team learning and (2) speed to market. For example, if individuals on the team do not have a collective consciousness of what is important to their managers, the rest of the company and the NPD project, they could wind up committing errors or rehashing work that other colleagues have effectively done.

H3: The effect of team learning changes quadratically, according to Akgün et al. [7] with respect to environmental turbulence. For example, teammate 1's synthesis of a new specialized know-how that emerged from the environmental turbulence, the internalization of that knowledge initially slows down teammate 2, who turns to teammate 1 seeking the technical knowledge.

H4: The greater the environmental turbulence, the greater the negative relationship between TMS and speed-to-market. Team learning slows down within the team and launching a product into the market becomes delayed.

H5: *Process* effectiveness mediates the relationship between TMS and *product* effectiveness. The proper application of TMS to NPD will help a team establish team stability, team learning, familiarity with a project, and, at the same time, be beneficial to the company in achieving new product success.

11.1.3 Customer Integration

The consolidation and integration process between the new product and the customer provides valuable qualitative and quantitative information for the company. The customer process for new product development is significant throughout the entire project from how a product can be implemented, perceived, and the information gained. Acquiring different levels of expertise with customers can provide insight and feedback which can give a whole view of the product. These customers can be experts in the field, current users, ordinary users, or potential users of the product. The identification of what users should be selected for the product is important because the information needs to be accurate, valuable, supply creativity, and marketing, among other advantages for the product and future products. Collaborating with proper customers throughout the NPD process assists in the long run with products, future products, and regulatory authorities (FDA, etc.).

The phases and stages a company innovates through development of a new product determine the success between the customer and the product. All three phases represent important parts for the customer and product integration process. The discovery phase introduces searching, different types of thinking, and early learning of a product. In the incubation phase, product testing, and observations with customers are used to gain feedback as well as insight. Finally, the acceleration phase brings all of the integration together for the rollout process. The company and customer phases are used throughout the project to obtain a suitable product for the user which will be marketable for the company.

Each phase has been broken down for further diagnostic and relevance to customer integration in the bullet points below:

Discovery Phase: Innovating company searches for new business opportunities

- Exploratory skills, potential customer needs and solutions to problems
- Direct and indirect methods
- Gather inspirations

Incubation Phase: Develops initial ideas into proposals

- Reduce technical and market uncertainties
- Concept testing and exploring

Acceleration Phase: Prepares a radical innovation for rollout

- Internal and external phase for launch
- Predictable revenues, foreseeable future and compete
- Areas to understand better after research in the RNP phase for customer integration
- Need to relate to customers to address attractive markets

The learnings acquired from all the customer feedback of products, competitors' products, and the MAUDE database provide innovativeness for all products in generating ideas, concepts, and solutions. The successfulness of Biotronik/MSEI has with the customer integration process can provide potential customer needs, marketing visions, product solutions, and foreseeable future upon rollout.

11.1.4 Networking Capability

Modern theory regarding the *performance of* inter- and intra-firm collaboration is labelled "Networking Capability." These connections have prerequisites, advantages, and limitations. Information flows between parties via these often convoluted, often fragile connections. Not surprisingly, much has been learned from analyzing these links, and project success can be either helped or hindered by forming and growing connections.

In terms of New Product Development (NPD), there are five main benefits to cultivating and leveraging a healthy network:

1. *Interaction Cost Reduction* refers to both physical items like inventory and less tangible things like time spent getting teams all "on the same page." These costs are classified into three categories:

    a. Products
    b. Services
    c. Ideas

2. *Opportunity Discovery* refers to a firm's awareness of market/business/talent/production opportunities. Further, good awareness of what is available lends a confidence factor to the information surrounding each opportunity. In colloquial terms, this may be likened to "being an informed buyer."
3. *Resource Acquisition* dictates that by taking advantage of networking capability, not only can firms have a better understanding of where to turn for help when they need resources for NPD, but they may also better decide on how to acquire value-producing resources. Further, a firm may avoid accidentally acquiring value-destroying resources.
4. *Market Knowledge Generation* and *Technology Knowledge Generation* are often lumped together as "*Knowledge Generation*." There are obvious benefits to having up-to-date market knowledge as this can help steer strategic decisions. As we saw in the Intel case study (Case study: Intel Research – exploring the future n.d.), sometimes the "right" choice for a product that is ahead of its time is to cap it off and mothball the effort for later market reentry.

    Networking and the consequential functional blocks establish three things:

1. Networking capability is a reliable predictor of NPD performance.
2. The five benefits of networking capability (depicted in the middle) drive positive NPD performance.
3. Environmental dynamism acts as a moderating factor on the effect of networking capability on NPD performance. Specifically, when environmental dynamism is high, the effects are amplified positively (NPD performance is bolstered).

Put another way, firms can develop strong networking capability in order to enhance product and technology innovation.

All in all modern product development network is often times a *global* network. This is known as Global Product Development (GPD). There are three commonly recognized motives for implementing global product development (GPD):

1. Competence Seeking
2. Cost Savings
3. Development Capacity Hedging

Once the intent to form a globally distributed development network has been established, the next step for complex engineered systems (CESs) is to decompose either the processes, products, or some hybrid of both (processes and products) into design structure matrices (DSMs). The type of decomposition is influenced by GPD intent.

11.1.5 System Decomposition and Integration

Simple systems do not require much rigor to decompose, analyze, and reintegrate. When systems become more complex, with many nodes and multiple branching dependencies, more rigorous methods are needed to make sense of the system to form groups and allocate resources. This occurs regularly in the development of new, complex, and engineered products. A design structure matrix (DSM) as detailed in (Browning n.d.) provides a simple, compact, and visual representation of a complex system that supports innovative solutions to decomposition and integration problems.

The general idea of a DSM is simple. The steps to its successful implementation are:

1. Decompose the system into elements.
2. Understand and document the interactions between the elements.
3. Analyze the potential reintegration of the elements via clustering or diagonalization.

There are effectively four applications of DSMs that are covered in the following subsections.

11.1.5.1 Component-Based DSM

A component-based DSM seeks to present designs of systems according to their components. It is useful for modeling system–component relationships and facilitating appropriate architectural decomposition strategies. Component-based DSMs consider spatial, energy, information, and/or material dependencies between design components. Clustering can show how designs should be physically organized, electrically connected, or sequentially designed.

11.1.5.2 Team-Based DSM

A team-based DSM seeks to analyze organizational structures. It is beneficial for designing organizational structures that account for team interactions. Better understanding of organizational interfaces supports the application of appropriate integrative mechanisms (new organizational structures, interteam interfaces, colocation, special tools, common databases, etc.). The fundamental steps in these DSMs are to: decompose the organization into elements (e.g., teams) with specific functions, roles, or assignments; document the interactions between (the integration of) the teams; and analyze the clustering of the teams into "metateams" for a variety of resource allocation purposes.

11.1.5.3 Activity-Based DSM

An activity-based DSM seeks to analyze design efforts or process flows according to their inputs and outputs. Process structure or architecture affects process efficiency and effectiveness. The fundamental steps for these DSMs are to: decompose the process into activities, document the information flow among the activities (their integration), and analyze the sequencing of the activities into a (generally) maximally-feed-forward process flow. This can be done with diagonalization.

11.1.5.4 Parameter-Based DSM

A parameter-based DSM seeks to analyze design activities based on design parameter establishment. They are effective for integrating low-level design processes based on physical design parameter relationships. They can be thought of as a subcategory of activity-based DSMs. Many of the same methods can be applied between them. Cross-coupled individual activities in an activity-based DSM can be divided up into a parameter-based DSM with sub-activities with dependencies. When the macro-activities are decomposed in favor of the micro-activities, the micro-activities can be rearranged to maximize feed-forward and eliminate feedback.

11.1.6 Reducing Risk

In many cases, lack of value stems less from doing unnecessary activities and more from doing necessary activities with the wrong information (and then having to redo them). Design performance levels cannot indicate progress unless they include a notion of how much uncertainty remains. Risk decreases with the availability of useful information (Ahmadi and Wang 1999). Browning et al. (n.d.) provide a method for evaluating the customer value added in product development as a function of the generation of useful information that reduces risk.

Per Browning et al. (n.d.) state that to evaluate progress, one must define the *Technical Performance Measures (TPMs)* which are the metrics to plan and track the level of important technical performance attributes as product development unfolds.

The *Technical Performance Risk (R)* can be assessed by measuring the:

1. *Uncertainty*, i.e., the number of possible outcomes, cases, or situations that fail to meet requirements. For development of an aircraft, the aircraft's *range* in nautical miles is a TPM, which can have a probability distribution function. It has a required target set as per the customer's needs. The values below the target are all unacceptable outcomes. One needs minimum deviation from the desired range target but high range is desirable therefore the range function is a "larger is better" (LIB) type of parameter. This PDF can be simplified to a three-point estimate representing worst-case value (WCV), most likely value (MLV), and best case value (BCV) which gives a simplified TriPDF.

2. *Consequence or Impact* of each TPM. This consequence is a function of the gap between the utility of the outcome and utility of the target (U). The utility increases drastically as one approaches the target value from the left. Once the target is met the utility only increases a little, after which, it saturates.

By reaching the target requirement for a TPM one is meeting the demands set by the customer. Hence, they achieve customer satisfaction. At each interval, the range of rangeTPM is indicated. An overlay of risk associated with each assessment point is also provided. In April, the risk is low. This can be explained by the fact that the range of rangeTPM is smaller while the mean of rangeTPM is higher as compared to the February assessment point. In June, the risk increases. Changes made in the design caused the mean of rangeTPM to be lower than the target range value. However, in the following assessment in the month of July, the risk drastically reduces. This can be explained by observing that the rangeTMP reaches the target value as the designers must have resolved a major issue that was discovered in the last assessment. With an improved design and reduced risk, the following assessment is near the target value and almost zero risk.

Further, it should be noted that the assessment points must be strategically selected (Browning et al. n.d.). The first three points are 2 months apart each. During the initial phases of product development, it is necessary to give sufficient time to gather ample relevant data that will help in making sound decisions. Later, as the product development process matures, monthly assessments help to quickly troubleshoot any issues and test product performance.

It compares two points of assessment—February (t1) and August (t2), in terms of their TriPDF. In comparison to t1, t2 shows much sleek TriPDF indicating that due to improved product design and successful development, the probability of getting acceptable outcomes near the target value increases. Therefore, the associated risk (shaded region) reduces.

(a) Timely assessment of product performance. RangeTPM is measured over a duration and the risk associated with each analysis point has been overlaid. (b) comparison of two points of assessment—February (t1) and August (t2) in terms of TriPDF and associated risk (Browning et al. n.d.).

The information gathered during NPD could affect a TPM in various ways. It may cause MLV to go up or down and/or it may cause the bounds (BCV and WCV) to widen or narrow. These effects are categorized for a LIB TPM (Just exchange the first and third row labels in the figure for a "smaller is better" (SIB) TPM). Moreover, the magnitude of an activity's effect on a TPM could be small, medium, or large. The different steps in NPD are listed out and their impact on various TPMs is marked. Such an approach with regular assessment will help to analyze which TPMs are most affected by which step(s) of development and whether the overall product under development is reaching a low-risk state.

(a) Type of activity effects on TPMs. (b) Analyzing the effect of various steps in preliminary design process on different TPMs of an aircraft. Adapted from (Browning et al. n.d.).

The end goal is to identify what information should be created such that the overall risk associated is reduced. Thus, *proper activity planning* is crucial. In essence, project management is risk management. The above-mentioned approach helps in activity planning by highlighting the following:

1. *Early Estimates*: It is essential that the initial estimates used in NPD process are as close to actual values as possible in order to converge to the target value as the development progresses. In this way, the primary TPMs are also not overlooked. Thus, an early robust verification can be achieved.
2. *Prioritization*: The procedure helps to identify dimensions of a project that have the highest levels of risk. Thus, resources can be reallocated to target such dimensions first. Many times, a bundled approach could be utilized where several interdependent variables can be worked upon together.
3. *Post Analysis*: After the project has been completed, an evaluation to compare achieved TPM values with the targets is crucial to understand which areas might require improvement. This will help to re-evaluate plans and controls utilized in the next product development process.

11.1.7 R&D Methodology for New Product Development

Based on the learnings from research articles and case studies, an R&D methodology for new product development at a medical device company has been proposed.

Step 1: Identify Need to Innovate (Cui et al. n.d.)

- Carry out market and literature research to explore areas that have a need, which can be addressed through innovative products.
- Look into the products already available within the company for potential improvement.

Step 2: Action Plan (Tripathy and Eppinger n.d.; Mu and Di Benedetto n.d.; Browning and Eppinger n.d.; Akgun et al. n.d.; Jaber et al. n.d.; Browning n.d.; Case study: Intel Research – exploring the future n.d.)

- Decide upon an idea that best aligns with the business model after taking into consideration its capacity to be marketed, tested, and manufactured in high volume.
- At this stage, the product and technology roadmaps become fixed. Further, resources such as money, time, and human resources are allocated.
- Duties are delegated; management and development teams are finalized that will design and develop the product.

Step 3: Execute Plan (Schweitzer et al. n.d.; Tripathy and Eppinger n.d.; Browning et al. n.d.)

- An iterative process is used to reduce the risk associated with the product in order to meet target performance levels as desired by the customer.
- Customer feedback is taken into consideration while product design is refined.
- Patents are filed based upon intellectual property generated through research and development.

Step 4: Market Trends (Mu and Di Benedetto n.d.; Akgun et al. n.d.; Case study: Intel Research – exploring the future n.d.)

- Analysis of the upcoming trends in the market. Reassessment of market needs, refining marketing strategy, and fixing upon an ideal launch date.
- Knowing the status of product development by competitors. Assessing whether a symbiotic relationship could be made that will benefit all parties involved by overcoming an individual's challenges and helping the product reach the market faster.

Step 5: Testing (Case study: Eli Lilly and Co. – innovation in diabetes care n.d.; Case study: Vertex Pharmaceuticals – R&D portfolio management (a), product#: 604101 n.d.)

- Carrying out pre-clinical (benchtop, cadaver, and animal) and clinical (human) testing of product based upon regulatory requirements.
- If the product fails any testing or does not meet desired standards, it is critical to amend further development. The action plan needs to be revisited and strategies are devised to overcome the issue.

Step 6: High Volume Manufacturing (Case study: Intel Research – exploring the future n.d.; Case study: Eli Lilly and Co. – innovation in diabetes care n.d.)

- Once the product passes testing, factory level production is phased in.
- Quality needs to be assured throughout HVM.
- Timely meeting of product demand.

Step 7: Post-launch Assessment (Schweitzer et al. n.d.; Case study: Intel Research – exploring the future n.d.)

- Assessment if predicted sales and profits were achieved.
- Taking customer feedback into consideration to see if there is room for improvement in product design.
- Identifying opportunities to develop a product ecosystem based around the current product and/or to innovate a new product based upon the learnings from the current product.

11.2 Biotronik and Micro Systems Engineering, Inc.

11.2.1 Company Profile

BIOTRONIK is a multinational, privately held medical device company headquartered in Berlin, Germany with an annual revenue of about $500 million (https://www.owler.com/company/biotronik n.d.). They specialize in solutions for diagnosis, treatment, and therapy support in the areas of cardiac rhythm management, electrophysiology, and vascular intervention. The company began with the development of the first German implantable pacemaker in 1963 which was developed at TU Berlin by physicist Max Schaldach. In 1979, a site in Lake Oswego, OR, now called Micro Systems Engineering, Inc. was built which has become the company's American research, development, and manufacturing facility. Since the beginning, over 19 million BIOTRONIK devices in over 100 countries have been implanted. The company currently has around 9000 employees around the globe, with major centers in Germany, Switzerland, and Oregon. Significant achievements over the years include Closed Loop Stimulation (CLS), Home Monitoring®, ProMRI®, and the BioMonitor family of products.

11.2.2 R&D Strategies at Biotronik for New Product Development

11.2.2.1 Innovation at Biotronik

The research presented in (Cui et al. n.d.) generally stated an ideal learning environment for fostering innovation. Biotronik uses a variety of resources when trying to develop a new product idea. The company's Innovation Model supports employees going to research conferences, studying other fields outside of simply medical devices, and bringing in new minds. This last point relates well to (Cui et al. n.d.) because it allows for a range of experience levels among employees. The more experienced employees are, the less likely they can analyze new market and technical information in a positive way.

Also, having employees study fields outside of medical devices is another great benefit. While it might seem counterproductive, in the creative realm it is better to research a variety of areas sparingly than to go in-depth into any one subject. This is proved in (Cui et al. n.d.) as the ability to innovate positively goes down with increasing technical knowledge. If too much focus is put on one field, then they will be decreasing their ability to innovate effectively.

Another very important innovation factor is company culture. At Biotronik they facilitate a very open culture that supports the flow of creative ideas. By having this culture it helps new employees share their thoughts, and according to the Learning Zone, these are the minds that can utilize new information the most effectively in new product development. So Biotronik's model for innovation is very helpful in that regard. A more encompassing point is the effect of culture in the United States on innovation strategies vs. Germany's cultural effect. One of the interviewees, Java, stated that the US R&D culture tends to be more accepting of risky ideas than German R&D culture. In Germany, risk is considered above most other factors when choosing to develop a product. However, in the United States they explore great ideas no matter how risky. This helps people share their ideas even more, and sometimes the craziest ideas are the ones that work.

11.2.2.2 Planning and Collaboration at Biotronik

A Design Structure Matrix (DSM) model, as presented in (Browning n.d.) was applied abstractly, as a component-based DSM, to elements of the new product development process for medical device companies on the basis of our industry interviews and knowledge of the structure and function of traditional pacemaker implantable pulse generators (IPGs) (Fig. 11.1).

<--Depends on

Provides input to-->

	Battery	Module Layout	ASIC	Header	Frame	Feedthrough	Substrate	Software	Housing	Circuit design	Power system	Radio
Battery	■	•			•				•	•	•	
Module Layout		■			•	•	•					
ASIC	•	•	■					•		•	•	
Header				■		•			•			
Frame					■							
Feedthrough		•				■			•			
Substrate		•			•		■			•		
Software			•					■		•	•	
Housing	•	•			•	•			■			
Circuit design		•					•			■	•	
Power system	•	•	•							•	■	
Radio		•							•	•	•	■

Fig. 11.1 Generic, simplified, component-based DSM for the components of a traditional pacemaker

A generic, simplified, component-based DSM is proposed, for the components of a traditional pacemaker (specifically the Implantable Pulse Generator [IPG] of the pacemaker). Along the columns and rows are the major high-level components of a pacemaker, which must be designed or otherwise procured. Along any particular row, it can be seen to which components a particular component provides design input. Along any particular column, one can see upon which components a particular component depends. Some example observations can be made from this DSM, as presented:

- The “Radio” column has no dots but the “Radio” row has four. This reflects the fact that the radio is selected in isolation and then its selection informs four other component designs.
- The “Frame” column has four dots but the “Frame” row has none. This reflects the fact that the frame is custom-designed to fit the already-selected adjacent hardware.
- Module layout depends on eight components and informs three. This is why module layout is done iteratively.

The components are listed in an arbitrary order. Understandably, diagonalization and clusters are absent. If one were to apply a sophisticated clustering algorithm as in (Browning n.d.) to this DSM, one would probably see a high level of interdependence in the system as a whole and a moderate amount of upper-diagonalization occurring. Even without any such clustering algorithm, a natural grouping emerges with the electrical components in one group and the mechanical components in another. This pairs logically with the organizational grouping that

	Radio	ASIC	Software	Battery	Power system	Circuit design	Substrate	Module Layout	Housing	Feedthrough	Header	Frame
Radio					●	●		●	●			
ASIC			●	●	●	●		●				
Software		●			●	●						
Battery					●	●		●	●			●
Power system		●		●		●		●				
Circuit design					●		●	●				
Substrate						●		●				●
Module Layout	Electrical						●			●		●
Housing				●				●		●		●
Feedthrough								●	●			
Header									●	●		
Frame							Mechanical					

<--Depends on

Provides input to-->

Fig. 11.2 Reorganized by engineering discipline, generic, simplified, component-based DSM for the components of a traditional pacemaker

occurs with the designers of these components: electrical and mechanical engineering teams tend to organize along lines of engineering discipline (Fig. 11.2).

Not coincidentally, reorganizing the components of this DSM according to their primary engineering discipline is remarkably akin to sorting components according to the precedence of the tasks of their determination. When this is done with electrical engineering tasks taking precedence to mechanical tasks, we can see that a highly diagonalized (but still quite cross-coupled) quasi-activity-based DSM emerges.

Some observations can be made from this mostly optimized DSM:

- Tasks tend to cluster readily by engineering discipline.
- There is a specific sector of the design where significant interdisciplinary collaboration is required: module layout and substrate selection. This reflects real life, where these design decisions have many stakeholders from across the design teams.
- Adjacent tasks tend to be highly cross-coupled. This makes sense in such a complicated product. Much design collaboration and iteration are required. However, one could potentially apply a parameter-based sub-DSM to local instances of cross-coupling and decouple problematic cross-coupled activities.
- There exists a potentially very long feedback loop: battery selection/design depends on housing design and vice versa. This makes obvious sense, because the battery and housing need to fit together mechanically. Since batteries tend to be selected early (because their selection has a large impact on other electrical systems) care must be taken that housing design considerations are taken into account early to minimize costly iteration.

11.2.2.3 Application of TMS in Establishing NPD Teams at Biotronik

The application of TMS to Biotronik's new product development will help in facilitating an interpersonal awareness of who knows what and who has appropriate and adequate skills and expertise, and then receiving information from that person. TMS, in return, will help Biotronik/MSEI to develop a strong and compelling team with a collective mind as a mediating factor as well as positively influencing the team's learning and the product's speed-to-market. This system is beneficial to Biotronik/MSEI's new product development by helping team members to easily synthesize, analyze, and disseminate new knowledge and information in a shorter period. The group is able to grasp a shared comprehension of the NPD procedure rapidly, settle on choices about process, product, and procedure plans quicker, and solve procedure-related issues more in an auspicious way. However, trust can be a challenge between different teams in R&D organizations because of political reasons, according to Expert A, Manager of the ProMRI and RF Systems department. Trust can not only become an organizational dilemma but also a global and painstaking issue that restricts the flow of knowledge between teams. This issue can slow down the team's performance and disrupt the product's speed-to-market.

To establish an effective team, the method for success for trust in Biotronik/MSEI NPD is to integrate trust into TMS by selecting team members with different expertise, benevolence, and integrity. Consequently, teams who possess the mentioned skills are more likely to be sought after during knowledge transfer. Another important aspect of setting up a successful team is ensuring that each individual on the team has a thorough understanding of the task at hand, the objective, customer needs, the design target, and schedule. While the team is formed, product managers are required to build teams to recognize the interpersonal dynamics that exist within the group. The purpose of this training is to improve the team's performance, because individuals who spend time working independently might not do well in a team setting. In addition, managers will also empower and direct teams by providing direction and guidance to the teams. Moreover, product managers will invest in training and cross-training of the teams for team members to understand other aspects of the project. At the end of each fiscal year, team members should be reviewed for their performance and awarded for their hard work through either incentives or Biotronik recognition.

11.2.2.4 Collaboration Between Biotronik and MSEI

Effective collaboration feeds into the Action Plan for any Global Product Development (GPD) network. The Action Plan, in turn, feeds into:

- Market Trends
- Testing
- High-Volume Manufacturing

The resulting effect is that collaboration efficiencies and high-performance collaboration necessarily amplify New Product Development (NPD). In short, collaboration is critical to NPD.

BIOTRONIK and MSEI are separate companies for fiscal and regulatory reasons, yet they operate as one company when possible. BIOTRONIK serves as the "Manufacturer of Record" for regulators, meaning they submit the product for approval and sell it. They focus on designing the superset of regulations, which includes Europe, the United States, and Japan. They focus on the big picture, such as features and markets. They publish the "Lastenheft" (Market requirements). MSEI, on the other hand, provides input, determines detailed requirements known as Pflichtenheft (System requirements), and makes design decisions. While the two groups have distinct roles, the need for information flow between them is apparent. Strategic design decisions will often involve stakeholders from multiple design teams, spanning both companies.

Applying what we have learned from our texts and case study regarding Networking Capability in NPD ecosystems, we see how the BIOTRONIK/MSEI collaboration has leveraged several of the five main benefits of a healthy GPD network:

1. *Interaction Cost Reduction*:

- Products: Implant batteries and substrates are made in-house. This prevents the acquisition of critical teams by other firms, and ensures quality control.
- Services: Automated, rapid assembly competence sought out and established in the Silicon Forest area. This effort yields higher quality metrics, better repeatability, and longer reliability long term.
- Ideas: RF development competency sought and established in the Silicon Forest area.

2. *Opportunity Discovery* refers to a firm's awareness of market, business, talent, and production opportunities. MSEI benefits from the oversight provided by BIOTRONIK maintaining good awareness of market conditions. MSEI can also hold the information surrounding opportunities in higher confidence knowing it came from in-house (BIOTRONIK).
3. *Resource Acquisition*: MSEI serves as a value-producing resource for BIOTRONIK. And the oversight that feeds back from BIOTRONIK may prevent accidental acquisition of value-destroying resources at the MSEI site.
4. *Market Knowledge Generation* and 5. *Technology Knowledge Generation* come from BIOTRONIK and MSEI, respectively. Responses from our interviews detail an early venture in the monitoring market space with BioMonitor (2011) which was largely unsuccessful, but they leveraged the experience as a valuable learning opportunity, albeit costly. They re-entered the market at a later date with a revised product and BioMonitor 2 (2014) and BioMonitor 3 (2019) are both selling well. This method of rolling a failure into a future success does not happen without adequate awareness of market opportunities, or without the technical expertise to quickly revise design and speed it to market.

Given that BIOTRONIK and MSEI are part of a modern and global product development network, we also discussed the three commonly recognized motives for implementing GPD:

1. Competence Seeking
2. Cost Savings
3. Development Capacity Hedging

Two of these were directly confirmed by our interviewees: Originally BIOTRONIK sought competencies in both the Silicon Valley (Northern CA) and Silicon Forest (Portland, OR) areas, as well as in Texas. There was also an ecosystem for stent business in the Switzerland area that was tapped. Years later, sites have remained open in Oregon as a means of diversifying the manufacturing and R&D bases and to hedge production demands.

11.2.2.5 Risk Management and Incorporation of Customer Feedback at Biotronik

Strategic Utilization of Opportunity

Biotronik is a leading medical device company, which is privately owned. Annual revenue of about $500 million makes it a mid-size company (https://www.owler.com/company/biotronik n.d.). As a result, the company does not take upon very high-risk projects despite the fact that such projects have the capacity to yield higher returns. If the probability that a new product will make it to market is 30% or more, then the company might take the risk of going ahead with its development. However, in most scenarios, the company tends to be a "fast follower." For example, Cardiac Resynchronization Therapy (CRT) was a high-risk opportunity. Despite being aware, the company chose to miss out on this opportunity. Once the therapy was proven to be effective by competitors, Biotronik followed up with their product in the market.

Selected Biotronik products for Cardiac Resynchronization Therapy (CRT). CRT is used to treat the symptoms and complications associated with certain types of heart failure. It helps the pumping chambers to beat in a coordinated manner so that the heart works properly. By improving blood flow, CRT may reduce heart failure symptoms, improving patients' quality of life, and reducing mortality (https://www.biotronik.com/en-us/products/crm/cardiac-resynchronization n.d.).

Risk Matrix

During each stage of product design and development, several factors are taken into consideration to form a risk matrix that is checked off to assess product performance. For example, during development, design parameters such as product dimensions, its placement in the body, and the ease with which doctors can implant and handle the product are checked repeatedly so as to minimize risk to the patient.

BioMonitor for heart rhythm sensing. Reliable and early arrhythmia detection for atrial fibrillation (AF) (https://www.biotronik.com/zh-cn/products/crm/arrythmia-monitoring/biomonitor n.d.). BioMonitor 2: The next level of accurate arrhythmia sensing, detection, and remote monitoring. Precise AF capturing. Fast, easy, and flexible insertion is designed with the patient's anatomy in mind (https://www.biotronik.com/en-ch/products/crm/arrythmia-monitoring/biomonitor-2 n.d.).

Schedule Risk

The risk that the project takes longer than scheduled is checked at intermediate milestones by qualification and verification of the new product being developed. One of the ways to reduce schedule risk is by initiating work on the next generation of product, while the older generation is already under development. For example, development of BioMonitor 2 started at the same time when BioMonitor was being developed.

Customer Feedback

The *usability group* at MESI incorporates customer feedback during the design and development of a new product.

Formative studies are not required by FDA and other countries' medical regulatory authorities. However, these studies are used to get design input. Physicians are informally asked to provide feedback on product mock-ups, which are sometimes tested on cadavers. The feedback from physicians is then used for product design refinement.

Once the product design is finalized, validation, and verification studies are conducted. FDA and others make these studies mandatory. The product is validated through pre-clinical (benchtop, animal, and cadaver) testing conducted by a group of specialists, which handle and evaluate the product. Physicians are monetarily reimbursed for their time but not for their input. This information can be used to modify labeling, casing, use instructions, etc.

11.2.2.6 Market Trend Analysis at Biotronik

In the context of the wireless remote monitoring market, recall the primary differences in the roles of BIOTRONIK and MSEI: BIOTRONIK is charged largely with being aware of market opportunities and both directing and timing the NPD push to market, while MSEI is charged mostly with growing technical proficiency and maintaining technical ability. As we have gleaned from our case studies and interviews, management must know when to amplify certain efforts and when to bring an effort to a close (Case study: Intel Research – exploring the future n.d.). In NPD, the latter is not always seen as a failure, but as a re-entry point for future efforts (as often as possible). This market analysis lends the ability to:

- Analyze upcoming trends in the market
- Reassess market needs
- Refine marketing strategy
- Determine ideal launch dates

Our NPD framework addresses market analysis and trends, so we explored this topic in our interviews. On the topic of effort cessation due to sudden awareness of an unfavorable market, getting "too far ahead" of the market is a good reason to pause an NPD effort. Other reasons include lacking the necessary infrastructure and/or slow reimbursement. Regarding reimbursement refers to using low-risk products to build funding for higher-risk ventures. Companies we have studied thus far, including BIOTRONIK, practice this form of portfolio diversification as a form of risk mitigation.

Home Monitoring efforts began in 1999 with "perfect timing" because there was "nobody in that [market] space" and there was a need for such innovation. "BIOTRONIK Home Monitoring® allows clinics the capability to replace device interrogation during in-office follow-up visits and to provide early detection of arrhythmias. Today, BIOTRONIK Home Monitoring is available in over 55 countries, optimizing patient management in more than 3800 clinics around the world" [22]. This is an example of a significant feature achieving an "evidence-based" value-add with "obvious patient benefit." This was made achievable by utilizing new technology and which was developed by leveraging BIOTRONIK's highly capable global network.

Awareness of market opportunities also entails knowing the status of competitors' NPD. Sometimes a symbiotic relationship between competitors can benefit all firms involved by evolving the entire market space, thus allowing new products (even competing ones) to reach the market faster. They do not cooperate very often due to antitrust laws which serve to promote competition for the benefit of consumers and prevent market-disrupting collaboration such as price fixing. However, exemption is given for the formation of standards. Obviously, engineer-to-engineer cooperation at standards meetings is collegial as engineers frequently love solving standards-related problems [together].

11.2.2.7 Product Testing at Biotronik

As a medical device company Biotronik has a lot of regulations and requirements to comply with. Regulations depend on the country, the industry, the invasiveness of the product, and more. Specifically, Biotronik complies with the FDA and other countries' regulations as well as their own self-made, market-driven regulations. In the case of FDA regulations, it is important to understand the different classes of risk for medical devices:

Class I Medical Devices (~47% of medical devices today)

- Patient Risk: Low to moderate
- Example Devices: Elastic bandages, manual stethoscopes, and bedpans

Class II Medical Devices (~43% of medical devices today)

- Patient Risk: Moderate to high
- Example Devices: Powered wheelchairs and most pregnancy test kits

Class III Medical Devices (~10% of medical devices today)

- Patient Risk: High
- Example Devices: Implantable pacemakers and stents

Since the majority of Biotronik's products are invasive, they are mostly Class III medical devices. The FDA regulations for these Class III invasive devices are found in ISO 14117 (Active Implantable Medical Devices) [25]. Biotronik needs to comply with this ISO standard, but they also strive to comply with their own company's requirements. Company requirements or market requirements are desirable to comply with, but they are not mandatory like the FDA regulations. This means that, if a Biotronik product is FDA compliant, but they do not comply with their own company's stated requirements, then they have options. They can either modify the product or change their company's requirements to accommodate the new product. Conversely, actual lapsing of regulatory compliance is a more serious issue, which must be mitigated as a condition of bringing a product to market.

11.2.2.8 High Volume Manufacturing of Products at Biotronik

The BIOTRONIK organization is a highly vertically integrated medical device manufacturer. The company includes multiple business units that exist as totally integrated companies. As some examples, LITRONIK is the organization's in-house battery manufacturer and battery technology developer [20] and DYCONEX is the organization's in-house substrate manufacturer and developer [21]. As stated by the interviewees, this vertical integration serves two purposes. The first is protection against acquisition. If a company controls the critical components of its business (like implant batteries and substrates), it mitigates some of the business risk that would exist if they relied on suppliers who may suddenly shift to preferring to work with (or being integrated into) the competition. The second reason, the more promoted, is the protection of quality. Management believes in the high value of BIOTRONIK's quality record and chooses to keep these sectors if the business is totally integrated to ensure the continuation of this quality.

From the perspective of the technologies involved in HVM, several changes in the manufacturing environment have had related changes in the R&D side of new product development. Dr. Stotts pointed out that, with higher scale circuit integration occurring, manufacturing is becoming even more averse to defects. The larger-scale integrated circuits have led to greater amounts of computing power to exist in smaller packages. This has allowed BIOTRONIK to push the envelope in reducing device size and increasing feature assortment, both key marketing features. Another key trend in integrated electronics overall is decreased power consumption. The ability to manufacture tiny, high-performance, ultra-low-power ICs has greatly increased the expected lifetimes of BIOTRONIK's implants while reducing the size of batteries. This creates understandably huge benefit for the company's new product development capabilities. Likewise, the automation advances present in HVM (fewer human steps and more machine steps) have increased manufacturing quality metrics, HVM repeatability, and product reliability.

While these advances have boosted the R&D and new product capabilities of the company to new territory, they have introduced new challenges not seen by old products. Risky, advanced products tend to lean heavily on the success of better, newer, technologies: advanced chips, sophisticated batteries, ultra-low-power electronics, and new alloys. New engineering questions have arisen like "how do we get these flat, square silicon chips [and substrates] to fit nicely in narrow, round housings?

11.2.2.9 Postlaunch Analysis of Products at Biotronik

Products are thoroughly taken through a postlaunch analysis in determining learnings of process and improvements on product to re-enter the product development process, marketing explorations, and future exploration for the company. Traditionally Biotronik/MSEI develops cardiac devices with pacemakers and defibrillators but, as the company explores the future, their sights are set on pain therapies among other developmental products.

The different new products and ventures Biotronik/MSEI explores can have many multiple results but always can provide insight and feedback for current and future products. Biotronik/MSEI had a venture into the monitoring space with BioMonitor around 2011 which did not sell well and was costly. But, the company obtained numerous learnings from the product and used those learnings to create. The information Biotronik/MSEI collects from the projects provide customer insight and feedback all to further innovation of product development. All of these products are evaluated and these evaluations are passed along to Biotronik/MSEI engineering personnel to assist in further ideas and improvements. Through the evaluation of the Biomonitor product, Biotronik/MSEI re-innovated the product with a II model in 2014 and a III model in 2019, both of which are selling well.

11.3 Conclusion

In this case study, an R&D methodology has been proposed which a medical device company should incorporate while developing a new product. To test this methodology, a thriving medical device company—Biotronik/MSEI—was targeted. Information gathered via interview of three managers in the vertical hierarchy at the company helped to get an in-depth understanding of managerial decisions regarding R&D at each level of management. A 7-step evaluation of the proposed R&D methodology indicates that it aligns well with the process followed by Biotronik/MSEI in the development of a new product.

Biotronik/MSEI is keenly interested in improving the efficiency and effectiveness of the products they provide to their clients in order to gain a competitive advantage in the medical field. They constructed an intricate process to identify, formulate, and establish a new product with industry-standard approaches and specific methods. Throughout the report, key concepts, examples illustrating these concepts, and links of these concepts to the methodology employed by Biotronik/MSEI in the development of new products have been provided. First, "Identify Need to Innovate" is where the company explores the motivation behind research on current products or innovating new ones. During "Action Plan," the company will decide upon an idea/concept and build a project plan and methods to carry out the new project. In the "Execute Plan" stage, the company evaluates the product with customer feedback, mitigates risks, and resolves issues associated with the product design. The fourth step is "Market Trends" where the company reanalyzes the current status of the market for their new product and determines how to bring the product to market with success. Then, in the "Testing" phase, the product is tested per regulatory and marketing requirements and, if the tests fail, strategic decisions are made regarding further development of the product. Once tests pass, the product reaches the "High Volume Manufacturing" stage where factory level production of the product happens with a strong emphasis on product quality. Finally, "Post-Launch Assessment" of the product is carried out wherein the product performance, profits achieved, feedback from the customers, and ways to innovate for future products are evaluated.

Therefore, the procedure that is used at Biotronik/MSEI for the development of a new product strongly matches with the R&D methodology for NPD developed from the review of case studies and literature. This structuring and method used to develop a new product can be used by any company with minor tweaks. The key philosophies discussed in this report establish a robust structure for how the research and development of a new product should be managed at the company level to create a successful product.

Acknowledgments Tugrul Daims contribution to the book chapter is based on the study funded by the Basic Research Program of the National Research University Higher School of Economics (HSE) and by the Russian Academic Excellence Project "5-100."

References

Ahmadi R, Wang RH (1999) Managing development risk in product design processes. *Oper Res* 47 (2):235–246

Akgun AE, Byrne JC, Keskin H, Lynn GS (n.d.) Transactive memory system in new product development teams

Browning TR (n.d.) Applying the design structure matrix to system decomposition and integration problems: a review and new directions

Browning TR, Eppinger SD (n.d.) Modeling impacts of process architecture on cost and schedule risk in product development

Browning TR, Deyst JJ, Eppinger SD, Whitney DE (n.d.) Adding value in product development by creating information and reducing risk

Case study: Eli Lilly and Co. – innovation in diabetes care (n.d.)

Case study: Intel Research – exploring the future (n.d.)

Case study: Vertex Pharmaceuticals – R&D portfolio management (a), product#: 604101 (n.d.)

Cui AS, Chan K, Calantone R (n.d.) The learning zone in new product development

https://www.biotronik.com/en-ch/products/crm/arrythmia-monitoring/biomonitor-2

https://www.biotronik.com/en-us/products/crm/cardiac-resynchronization

https://www.biotronik.com/zh-cn/products/crm/arrythmia-monitoring/biomonitor

https://www.owler.com/company/biotronik

Jaber H, Marle F, Jankovic M (n.d.) Improving collaborative decision making in new product development projects using clustering algorithms

Mu J, Di Benedetto A (n.d.) Networking capability and new product development

Schweitzer F, Van den Hende EA, Hultink E-J (n.d.) There's more than one perspective to take into account for successful customer integration into radical new product innovation: a framework and research agenda

Tripathy A, Eppinger SD (n.d.) Organizing global product development for complex engineered systems

Chapter 12
Effective Qualification of Suppliers in Manufacturing

Sneha Prabhu, Tugrul U. Daim, and Dirk Meissner

12.1 Introduction

Supplier selection is an important function of a manufacturing company. The supplier choice directly affects the cost and the competitive edge in the market. But what happens when there are multiple suppliers, various criteria, and ambiguous parameters to be considered. Supplier selection can be defined as the process of finding the right suppliers with the right quality at the right price, at the right time, and in right quantities (Ayhan 2013).

The question is how to evaluate a good supplier and why is it important to maintain good and lasting relationship with them? Selecting and getting approval for a supplier is a laborious process, and it is disconcerting to find that the supplier is not the right one. Wrong suppliers get chosen due to issues such as lack of time to choose a supplier, or assumption that the parts ordered would work but end up not meeting the specification, i.e., the end product of the parts not meeting the expectations. The formalities of approving a supplier can be a long and time-consuming process (Lyons 2017). That is why it is better to select a supplier that fits the company's specification. Manufacturers often tend to be biased toward the existing suppliers (Lyons 2017), which is why it is critical to select the right suppliers and

S. Prabhu
Portland State University, Portland, OR, USA

T. U. Daim (✉)
Portland State University Technology Management Doctoral Program, Portland, OR, USA

National Research University Higher School of Economics, Moscow, Russia

Chaoyang University of Technology, Taichung City, Taiwan
e-mail: tugrul.u.daim@pdx.edu

D. Meissner
National Research University Higher School of Economics, Moscow, Russia

T. U. Daim, D. Meissner (eds.), *Innovation Management in the Intelligent World*, Science, Technology and Innovation Studies,
https://doi.org/10.1007/978-3-030-58301-9_12

also remove a supplier if the company experiences an issue with them. Because if a supplier is not removed, chances of ordering parts from that supplier by another division due to poor communications are high leading to waste of time and cost or compromising the end product.

Supplier selection mainly constitutes of two types: single sourcing, where one supplier meets all the needs, and multiple sourcing, where a single supplier cannot meet all the needs and thus the company splits the orders with multiple suppliers. Supplier selection is a multi-criteria decision-making problem that constitutes qualitative and quantitative factors which has led to the development of a number of methods and techniques to deal with the selection and evaluation of a supplier. But these multi-criteria come with trade-offs that need to be identified in order to achieve an effective supply chain system. The reason behind developing these methods is that choosing the right supplier for a project leads to reduced risk, adds value to the customer, and builds long-term relationships (Suranaree J. Sci. Technol. 15(3):201-208 A REVIEW OF SUPPLIER SELECTION METHODS IN MANUFACTURING INDUSTRIES n.d.).

With increased global competition and market demand, many manufacturers are compelled to be the best and it is imperative to not only build existing supplier relationship but also collaborate with new suppliers. This gradual increase in global competition has led to the complexity of supply chains with a heightened pressure to produce higher quality products with low cost and fast delivery times (Supply Chain Management 2017).

12.2 Critical Aspects of a Good Supplier

Identifying a good supplier right away is not easy, but based on the features below it should make it easier to make an initial selection. A supplier should not simply be qualified based on the prototypes/products that they display. Their ability to function and work effectively with a team must also be gauged and factored in. Below are some of the common supplier traits that will help a manufacturer sort the good from the bad supplier. These factors can change depending on the organization, but it is important to note that to make any decision one has to consider aspects other than price.

12.2.1 Communication

Ineffective communication can give rise to an array of problems such as delays and noncompliance issues. Communication becomes a particularly critical aspect if the supplier is overseas and does not speak English or if the manufacturer does not speak the suppliers' local language. Language and cultural barriers are grave challenges for manufacturers that have suppliers overseas. Hiring staff that speak a common language or have the basic understanding of English and constantly communicating are some of the ways to combat this problem. The communication needs to be open and direct. Misunderstandings happen all the time and are far more common when the supplier is overseas. Oftentimes suppliers hold information from the manufacturer because of fault on their part, for example if there is a production delay, rather than being direct and informing, a supplier might wait until the last minute.

12.2.2 Accountability

A good supplier takes responsibility to work through quality issues and works to rectify it instead of blaming others. Suppliers need to own up to their mistakes, the ones that do not hamper the company's success to meet deadlines. Accountability in suppliers must be looked for early on.

12.2.3 Quality

Bad quality product affects customer satisfaction and future opportunities and also increases the cost associated with the delivery. Research shows that supplier quality issues have three main root causes, namely: (1) Lack of collaboration in the design phase—the highest number of supplier quality issue occurs when the supplier is not involved during the design phase (McKinsey and Company 2017). This leads to the inability to fully understand the customer needs. (2) Lack of a robust quality system or the right key performance indicators (KPIs)—this can occur when there is a lack of data-driven root cause analysis of the KPIs which can lead to quality issues. (3) Lack of capabilities in manufacturing (McKinsey and Company 2017). An insufficient understanding of the manufacturing processes or an incompetent workforce can lead to the inability of suppliers to manufacture the required volumes or standards. These situations occur when the technology is newly adopted or the complexity in the product is something that they have never produced before. These quality issues can be avoided if the manufacturer is able to understand the supplier's knowledge, QA processes, and capabilities. There needs to be a well-designed set of standards for their suppliers.

12.3 Supplier Screening Process

The process of finding and finalizing viable suppliers is arduous, time-consuming, and expensive; therefore, large manufacturing companies have a long-term base of suppliers. Before extending a contract to a supplier, manufacturers must take steps to ensure that there will not be critical consequences such as supplier nonperformance.

Supplier nonperformance such as late delivery or delivery of faulty goods must be avoided. Another goal would be to get assurance from the supplier that they would be responsible and responsive as a business partner (Supplier Selection 2009). Below are some of the key aspects and questions that need to be asked before the selection of a supplier.

12.3.1 What Questions Need to be Asked by Manufacturers before Selecting a Supplier?

The supplier OEM partnerships tend to go on for a long time (MDDI Online 2017). When suppliers are chosen, the company generally plans on committing for a minimum of 3–5 years (MDDI Online 2017). Granted the selection process can be difficult but by asking the right questions such as what the companies needs are, what kind of work needs to be outsourced, and what is the project about and what type of suppliers will best suit the project, the process of choosing the right supplier can be simplified.

1. What Am I Looking For?

   A company must decide what is needed. The details of the document can be detailed or proposed (MDDI Online 2017). Once the requirements have been defined, the company can then narrow down the suppliers. Suppliers can be narrowed down by identifying specific ones that will be able to serve the competencies that meet the project.

2. What Phase Is the Project In?

   Depending on what phase the project is in, the importance of factors such as cost, quality, and speed to market plays a role. For example, during the design phase, the company must focus on the speed to market and how well the supplier adheres to the quality standards (MDDI Online 2017). In the development stage, talks about cost begin and speed to market is an important factor here. During the manufacturing stage, volume, quality, and cost are the most important factors. Maturity: At this stage, the products sales have peaked and the products cost is a concern. End of life/ Phase out: At this point quality and cost are major factors; due to competition the products cost is made so low that the companies move it to off-shore locations to handle the low costs. Some suppliers can handle all the phases of the products' life cycle. There are some suppliers that collaborate with only one phase which is why products move from one supplier to the next (MDDI Online 2017).

3. Who will be Part of the Supplier Selection Process?

   Apart from the manufacturing teams, it is important to have the presence of other departments during supplier selection. The engineering team knows the product completely. Finance will be able to determine whether the deal that is being made is good for the company. Quality ensures that the quality standards are met and documentation team ensures the document system used by the company and the supplier is compatible. Other stakeholders such as regulatory, quality, manufacturing, procurement, marketing, and materials must also be fully involved in the selection process to provide inputs. The final decision must be a collective effort from all teams not just one functional group (Dr. Christopher Joseph Devine President 2017).

4. How Is the Fit?

Understanding if the supplier that is selected has similar experiences in the past. The supplier needs to be able to understand the requirements and be capable of performing. If the supplier has had expertise working on similar domains, then they would be able to better understand the complexities. Another important area to focus would be to find out if the supplier can handle the volumes when the product goes in full production. In addition, they must also be able to keep up with sudden increased volumes. If a supplier gets appointed to start the production and cannot handle the volumes, then the manufacturer would have to move to a different supplier and switching suppliers can be a tedious task (MDDI Online 2017). Being culturally aligned is also an important part. Both the supplier and the company need to be in sync with each other's beliefs such as corporate culture and treatment of employees (MDDI Online 2017). Important decisions could get affected if both parties have their own set of values as this can result in conflicts.

5. What Else Does the Supplier Bring to the Table?

In the medical device industry, it is fundamental that the potential suppliers understand the processes, quality systems, and record keeping. Medical device companies must hire suppliers that have experience in medical manufacturing; this way the company does not need to spend time explaining the standards of medical device manufacturing (MDDI Online 2017). It is also important that the supplier has a wide range of manufacturing services to provide all the services in-house. The chances of abnormality are reduced when all the parts are produced by a single supplier. It is critical that the supplier is financially sound and does not go bankrupt in the middle of the process. The supplier's financial resources need to be in place to avoid delays and for the product to be successful.

6. How Was the Visit?

By visiting the facility, it can be determined if the facility is well maintained and clean. This is critical especially in the medical device industry. A visit also gives a chance to interact with the personnel that would be working for the project and answer any questions that they might have.

Visits allow for a firsthand view and must be included in all the phases throughout the supply chain. A visit during the selection stage allows the manufacturers to understand the unique selling point of the supplier and features that the manufacturer was not previously aware of and that could potentially be in favor of the selection process. By touring the premises of the supplier facility gives insights into the actual physical conditions of the facility. A visit may also unravel negative impacts on the working conditions of the workforce.

7. What Did the References Say?

Getting in touch with customers the supplier has worked with can lead to useful information. The references can share experiences they had with the supplier, good and bad, the way the supplier handled pricing, and if the delivery was handled on time. Situations where the supplier handled unexpected situations and how well they were resolved and if the supplier adhered to the code of conduct and the terms of agreement. Was the vendor capable of understanding the business needs, clarity with communications, and the satisfaction with the services provided, or was there any aspect that the supplier needed to improve on? These are some of the questions that can be addressed while communicating with a reference.

8. Do You Want to Go Offshore?

Many companies decide to manufacture outside the country to cut down on costs. If the supplier is also located in that country, it would be economical to do so. Other factors are also taken into consideration while making this decision. A product that is less complex to produce and has high volumes. If the size of the product is large, then high shipping costs are incurred (MDDI Online 2017). Intellectual property also plays a role and the protection rights differ in different countries making it difficult to produce it if the product involves IP (MDDI Online 2017).

9. Is the Supplier Financially Stable?

Price often plays an important role in the selection of a supplier if the company has a strict budget. But it must be noted that suppliers that offer a low bid might not be fully equipped to handle all the requirements. The company must watch out for these loopholes before agreeing to finalize a supplier. Such risks associated with financial stability can be avoided before entering into partnership. It is very critical to check the supplier's financial stability before entering into partnership leading to project delays, damaged reputations, lost revenues, and wasted time (Cite a Website 2017).

Organizations that are unable to dedicate time to review and monitor the financial stability of suppliers should consider partnering with a third-party solution, which will gather, validate, and track supplier financial information and other pre-qualification and compliance data (Cite a Website 2017). Constantly ensuring the supplier's financial stability and keeping this data up to date may take a lot of time and resources. If the manufacturer has the budget, they can hire a third party to assess the financial information that is needed to screen suppliers. These third-party companies provide data such as annual revenue, the possibility of going bankrupt, and financial ratings (Cite a Website 2017). By gathering key supplier financial information such as revenue and "continuously updating the supplier risk profiles—organizations can ensure they minimize the threats introduced to the business when partnering with a third-party firm" (Cite a Website 2017). In order to build long-term business relations, it is necessary to know that the firm is financially sound.

10. Does the Supplier Already Belong to the Company's Supplier List?

Instead of going to new suppliers if there exist suppliers that the company has worked with, then it is best to work with the same suppliers. They will be aware of the policies and standards and the company's culture. As long as the supplier is technically qualified to supply the product, there should be no reason to look for a new supplier.

11. Did You Take Enough Time to Make the Right Choice?

Oftentimes companies take a hasty decision in the selection to stay on schedule (MDDI Online 2017). Supplier selection is a lengthy process involving a lot of documentation. Making a hasty decision the company has chances of running into problems mid-way. Manufacturers must ensure that the supplier is capable of handling its requests on time and is conforming to its quality standards. Delays in production can cause shortages, and supplying noncompliant products tarnishes the company's reputation and costs the manufacturer millions of dollars in recalls and also affects the sales potential in the future. It is always better to take extra time look for the best supplier than facing the consequences halfway through the process.

12.4 How to Create a Supplier Base?

Factors such as quality, regulatory and compliance, manufacturing capabilities, technology, capabilities, customer service, delivery and cycle times, and lifecycle management are the key aspects of the selection process. Besides this, business risk, regulatory risk, and risk of product failure must also be measured (Dr. Christopher Joseph Devine President 2017). A third aspect is an effective supplier survey to evaluate a supplier in a way that would reflect the manufacturer's preferences (Supplier Selection 2009). Lastly, all the supplier selection processes must be documented for FDA and regulatory bodies as proof of events (Dr. Christopher Joseph Devine President 2017).

12.5 Identify the Supplier

The selection team must reach out to a few suppliers and discuss the specifications of the product, evaluate their competency, and understand their pricing. Companies must not look at finding the cheapest supplier but rather look at properties such as reliability, delivery commitments, customer service, and communication. Supplier selection should not only be driven by the cost factor. During this process, the opinions of stakeholders should also be accounted. Stakeholders can be personnel from the marketing, quality assurance, development teams, and other teams that are involved in the supplier chain department.

12.6 Performance

The company should have a well-developed audit system to monitor and examine the supplier company. Audits help identify a supplier's strengths and weakness; if the number of weakness outweighs the strengths, then it probably is a red flag indicating that it is not the right choice of suppliers. The production of top-quality products should be a company's top priority, and the supplier must be often scrutinized for any quality failures. Audits must not be only limited to before the selection process (Food Safety Magazine 2017). By conducting audits throughout the different stages during the manufacturing process will ensure that there are no serious compliance issues. A supplier's performance can be tracked for positive as well as negative trends over a period of time. If the supplier's performance shows a strong and continued positive trend, it can enhance the relationship between the companies for future partnerships.

12.7 Supplier Assessment and Feedback

With a heightened dependence on suppliers to meet the customer expectations, companies are always under pressure to avoid problems in their products. One of the tools that can be used to improve the supplier performance is by using a self-assessment feedback form which would give the suppliers a chance to understand their own processes and get a better perspective. Companies with multiple suppliers often use a single model to assess their suppliers (Dr. Christopher Joseph Devine President 2017). This system can be inefficient; the requirements might differ from supplier to supplier, the inspection methodologies might be different, and these differences must be handled separately and not follow the same model of assessment. Depending only on a single model to assess the supplier base does not appear to be an efficient and proactive approach for supplier management (Dr. Christopher Joseph Devine President 2017). Even though the basic quality systems are uniform, manufacturing processes and inspection methodologies might differ widely, thus demanding a customized model for the purpose of assessment. For non-critical components that do not need an on-site assessment, a well-designed survey which takes into account the necessary business and quality information can be an inexpensive tool for assessment.

12.8 Developing Partnership

Developing a strategic partnership means that the supplier can anticipate the companies' needs in advance and start preparing for the production; there is trust that is built and the supplier does not hesitate to inform the manufacturer if there are any issues in quality and production, and an enhanced communication such as letting the company know if there is going to be a delay. A strategic partnership facilitates a level of commitment which should be strived for by all organizations.

12.9 Risk Assessment

All business–supplier partnerships present risk (Cite a Website 2017). With increased global competitive changes, companies depend more and more on their suppliers. These dependencies have made companies more vulnerable to uncertain events, thus making risk management an integral part of supplier selection. When it comes to companies that are globally located, issues such as time zones and regulations can be a hindrance. Uncertainty in data documentation also poses a risk. Manufacturers should identify the critical risk, have consistency in planning and mitigating risks, and have a methodical approach for examining the risk. Risk is present in every degree of supply chain. Due to globalization, increased outsourcing, and shorter product life cycles, the traditional supply chain's focus on cost, quality, and time is shifted to risk management (Micheli et al. 2008) .

Risks are present in all stages of supply chain that threaten the company's success and profitability. Companies must utilize an approach to estimate risks in order to analyze potential suppliers by considering risks such as market risks, country-specific risks (external), and supplier-specific (internal) risks (Ruhrmann et al. 2014). Organizations must associate suppliers with categories based on risks and the organizational needs. The selection and evaluation process for a certain medical device, for example, an insulin pump, will differ significantly to that of an allergy mask. Categories such as requirement for quality assessment, on-site assessment, and annual assessment mandatory—due to risk and schedule (Dr. Christopher Joseph Devine President 2017)—must be linked to suppliers and are ruled by the requirements of the organizations. Another factor relating to risk is the potential failure of a component and its adverse after-effects on the medical device. To avoid such accidents, medical device companies must adhere to failure modes and effects analysis (FMEA) (Failure Modes and Effects Analysis (FMEA) Tool 2017) to identify where and how a process might fail to assess its relative impact, so that those parts of the process are scrutinized and investigated thoroughly.

Customer service can drastically be improved if the delivery risk is lessened. When project deliverables do not meet the deadline, it not only disrupts the relation between the investors and stakeholders but also its customers. Reducing downtime and delays can lead to happier clients and a better reputation, which in turn results in new and/or repeat business (Cite a Website 2017). By not being able to satisfy the customers and not being committed to the agreement with the clients can damage the reputation, thus impacting the end product and the brand name. By being able to identify the supplier's weakness or conditions that the supplier might be susceptible to, the manufacturer should be able to handle the risks in order to reap benefits.

12.10 Negotiation Process

The best way to negotiate with a supplier is by getting quotes by other suppliers. This shows that the manufacturers have other options and increases competitive pricing. In addition companies must not have multi-year contract as these tend to favor the suppliers (Digikey.com 2017). Having an annual renewal contract results in lowering the cost of the goods procured. Conducting regular spend assessments gives an idea of how much is spent over time. Companies need to take control of the situation by assessing what other suppliers in the marketplace are charging and if the supplier will be able to meet their commitment for an affordable price (Digikey.com 2017). Companies can gain better negotiating power by aggregating volume buys. For example a company has two divisions and each division orders similar products from different suppliers; by choosing a single supplier to meet those needs will achieve discounts by aggregating the purchase. Communicating and collaborating with suppliers in helping them work efficiently, for example, by suggesting better material option or a cost-effective way in transportation, also plays a role in negotiating. Exploration of alternative options also helps gain insights into the latest availability and thus facilitate price reductions. In order to create a win outcome with the supplier, demanding to cut cost is going to be ineffective. Instead, recommending affordable manufacturing processes, transportation options, or material choices shows that the suppliers also get a good deal.

12.11 Supplier Selection Methods

As the selection process involves considering various criteria and supplier aspects, it can be called a multi-criteria decision-making problem. There are several decision-making methods that have been recommended to solve the multi-criteria problem. The model or method chosen have a significant influence on the results of the selection. Companies choose a single method or a combination of methods to cater to their business needs. This chapter includes briefly some of the important methods used in the industry but covers AHP and fuzzy AHP method in detail.

Over the years, several supplier selection methods have been developed. The type of method chosen plays an important role in the final supplier selection result. Manufacturing companies often combine two or more methods that have different strengths to meet their specific needs (Suranaree J. Sci. Technol. 15(3):201-208 A REVIEW OF SUPPLIER SELECTION METHODS IN MANUFACTURING INDUSTRIES n.d.). The total cost model quantifies all costs related to the supplier by taking the cost ratio and total cost of ownership. This model is considered flexible but requires a cost accounting system. It is expensive and time-consuming (Suranaree J. Sci. Technol. 15(3):201-208 A REVIEW OF SUPPLIER SELECTION METHODS IN MANUFACTURING INDUSTRIES n.d.). A more quantitative approach includes principal component analysis (PCA) that is capable of handling multiple conflicting attributes and artificial neural network (ANN) which is a cheaper and faster method but needs subject matter experts and a software to use it (Suranaree J. Sci. Technol. 15(3):201-208 A REVIEW OF SUPPLIER SELECTION METHODS IN MANUFACTURING INDUSTRIES n.d.). The multi-attribute utility theory (MAUT) method allows the supply chain team to design sourcing strategies and can handle multiple conflicting criteria (Suranaree J. Sci. Technol. 15(3):201-208 A REVIEW OF SUPPLIER SELECTION METHODS IN MANUFACTURING INDUSTRIES n.d.). This method is widely used when the supplier is based overseas and the environment is interlaced and risky. The fuzzy logic method evaluates the suppliers on their performance (Suranaree J. Sci. Technol. 15(3):201-208 A REVIEW OF SUPPLIER SELECTION METHODS IN MANUFACTURING INDUSTRIES n.d.). But one of the most widely used selection method has been the analytical hierarchical process (AHP). AHP is a decision-making method that prioritizes alternatives when there are multiple criteria to choose from by structuring complex problems in the form of hierarchy (Suranaree J. Sci. Technol. 15(3):201-208 A REVIEW OF SUPPLIER SELECTION METHODS IN MANUFACTURING INDUSTRIES n.d.). It has been widely used due to its simplicity, and it uses both qualitative and quantitative criteria. In AHP, the decision maker structures the criteria in a hierarchy that includes goals, criteria, and alternatives. Depending on the importance of the criteria, the suppliers are ranked according to their relativity to the criteria. It also includes alternative actions to be ranked based on the importance of each criteria. The results of the alternatives are analyzed to compute the relative importance of each alternative in meeting the goal. "Managerial judgments are used to drive the AHP approach" (Suranaree J. Sci. Technol. 15 (3):201-208 A REVIEW OF SUPPLIER SELECTION METHODS IN MANUFACTURING INDUSTRIES n.d.). The judgments are done in pairwise comparisons on each level of hierarchy with respect to their impact on the next higher level. Each comparison is the ratio of the weights of the two criteria being compared. These weights represent the importance of the criteria in meeting the goal of the hierarchy. AHP allows uncertainties and the application of experience and insights in a logical manner (Suranaree J. Sci. Technol. 15(3):201-208 A REVIEW OF SUPPLIER SELECTION METHODS IN MANUFACTURING INDUSTRIES n.d.).

However, AHP does have disadvantages. The implementation of this method becomes inconvenient when there are an extremely large number of criteria to choose from. Moreover, there can be complications when there are multiple people involved, with the opinions on weight of the criterion. AHP cannot be followed with a subject matter expert. Risks and uncertainties of the supplier's performance are not considered while using AHP.

Over the years, these methods have been classified into broader categories. After the year 2003, the focus was shifted on qualitative criteria. Prior to that, time, cost, and quality were given attention. Importance to qualitative criteria has begun only recently with methods such as AHP and fuzzy AHP that help the decision makers to make the supplier selection with their simple nature.

Fuzzy AHP uses the concept of fuzzy set theory and hierarchical structure analysis.

Even though AHP is considered one of the widely used multi-criteria decision model and the best way to utilize the subject matter expert's knowledge, it still cannot fully demonstrate human thinking style (Kahraman and Ulukan 2003). Thus, fuzzy AHP was developed to address the fuzziness in the hierarchical problems. In fuzzy AHP, the data that is already existing is combined with the preferences over each of the criteria by the decision maker. The pairwise comparisons in the matrix are fuzzy numbers as per the inclination of the decision maker toward the criteria (Kahraman and Ulukan 2003).

It expands the standard AHP method into fuzzy domain by using fuzzy numbers for calculating instead of real numbers (Ayhan 2013). The basic AHP has been improved from the fuzzy approach as it includes vagueness for personal judgments. There are many other techniques for MCDM such as TOPSIS, ELECTRE, PROMETHEE, DEMATEL, and ANP, but the analytical hierarchy process technique combined with a fuzzy approach is the most preferred as the decision-maker choices include both tangible and intangible criteria (Ayhan 2013).

12.12 Medical Device Industry Issues within a Complex Supply Chain

The medical device industry has evolved in the last decade with the inclusion of technologies such as big data, IoT, and cloud, but at the grassroots level the foundation is the same, i.e., patient safety. Thus, improving the quality of the supply chain processes is pivotal in medical device manufacturing. Quality cannot be compromised in any area of medical device production. This includes the quality control standards in place from the development of each part until the device reaches the intended healthcare facility or hospital. It begins with production and manufacturing that ensures minimum downtime during use (Mypurchasingcenter.com 2017).

Medical device companies need to be aware of the entire system starting from the development stages to the point when it is delivered to its customers. Quality and safety of consumer are paramount in the medical device industries; thus, choosing the right supplier is a critical business decision. Suppliers play a crucial part in the process as companies need to ensure that the parts are compliant with standards and regulations. The landscape of medical device manufacturing is so complex, with the ecosystem ranging from OEM and suppliers to smaller enterprises. One of the challenges that the medical device industry is facing today is the improvement in the control of supply chain system. The unstable global demand is thus compelling the medical device industries to gain visibility into supplier qualification, selection, and communication (A Blueprint for Optimizing Supply Chain Control within the Medical Device Industry 2017). This additional visibility would let the OEMs quickly respond to any number of unanticipated activities that could disrupt the demand chain. Processes that have been approved and tested must be implemented by medical device companies to control their supply chains by also making sure that the quality and speed of operations are not compromised.

Quality defects can impact patient safety. With the increase in globalized supply chain, quality cannot be constrained with the boundaries of an organization. With heightened complexities, and multiple suppliers involved in the production of a single device, there is always a chance that one of these suppliers may not adhere to quality standards in order to cut costs, thus leading to a defective product and posing a threat to the end user and tarnishing the device company's reputation. But mistakes in any organization are imperative and require measures such as CAPA and SCAR in place if quality standards are not met (Managing Medical Device Quality Issues within a Complex Supply Chain 2017) .The supplier must make sure that the quality standards align with that of the main device manufacturer. Focusing on quality and efficiencies is a must for medical device companies. A medical device manufacturer must ensure that the supplier can follow the regulatory and product quality requirements. According to the *Medical Device and Diagnostic Industry journal*, a major source of quality failures is due to poor material used by the suppliers which led to 20–30 percent of recalls in the recent past (Challenges with medical device 2017). *Medical Design Technology* published that "28 percent of medical device companies experienced more than one recall, and one company had 23 recalls during the third quarter of 2015 alone" (Challenges with medical device 2017). According to the FDA, the warning letters to the medical device industry have increased by 104 percent from the year 2007 to 2012 (Managing Medical Device Quality Issues within a Complex Supply Chain 2017). These statistics clearly indicate that there needs to be tremendous improvement in quality management in the medical device industry.

The medical device manufacturers are always under pressure to make sure that they maintain the quality of their products. Thus, the application of a good EQMS gives the company an overarching view of the supplier information and quality issues (Managing Medical Device Quality Issues within a Complex Supply Chain 2017). EQMS connects all the internal departments and the suppliers and gives insights into the workflows and processes and triggers warnings early in the manufacturing process (Managing Medical Device Quality Issues within a Complex Supply Chain 2017). Medical device manufacturers must take proactive actions to prevent quality issues by looking at the root cause. By conducting training programs for their suppliers, ensuring that the activities are completed on schedule and tracked till the completion phase and maintaining quality standards throughout the device life cycle will enable in building a safe product for the end user no matter where in the world the device was manufactured. The supplier must be able to meet the OEMs quality and engineering requirement along with cost and capacity (Supply Chain Strategies for a Challenging MedTech Landscape 2017). Using the right quality management, systems will allow visibility across all levels of supply chain operations and help mitigate quality issues.

As the medical device industry is highly dynamic, it comes across challenges such as shorter product life cycles, managing strategic partnerships, and frequent FDA checks. In the recent past, the US FDA has increased its inspections (A Blueprint for Optimizing Supply Chain Control within the Medical Device Industry 2017). With the rise in these regulatory checks, a supplier evaluation process that is well implemented helps manufacturers produce, manage, and track products effectively in order to deliver safe, reliable, and high-quality medical devices to the end user (Managing Medical Device Quality Issues within a Complex Supply Chain 2017). "Ensuring suppliers have performed adequate and appropriate validation studies, inspecting Critical to Quality (CTQ) attributes—manufacturers shouldn't assume that all specifications are tested or inspected by their suppliers and implementing methods for documenting oversight, such as balanced scorecards" were some of the key supplier issues and processes for the supplied parts that were identified by the FDA in the recent past (A Blueprint for Optimizing Supply Chain Control within the Medical Device Industry 2017). These processes need to be handled with caution as documentation and collection needs a commitment to maintain reliable data about the suppliers as globalization of supply chains in medical devices demands for constant real-time data without any inconsistencies.

Apart from the regulatory challenges, supplier diversity also plays a role in making the supply chain more complex in the medical device industry. The language barriers, multiple time zones, and multicultural workforce play a part in this highly convoluted business. Efforts should be made to make a more unified supply network which will result in better qualification of suppliers, transparent communications, and continuous improvement on a single platform.

There are no compromises made when it comes to quality and the measures that are taken to ensure that there are no issues when it comes to the quality of the product. If a supplier stands a risk, then new suppliers are sourced; some of the other risks that are considered are transportation, union v/s non-union, size of the company, financial position, public v/s private, and industry certifications (ISO, FDA approved, etc.). With the increased complexity due to globalization, quality and reliance are top selection criteria followed by cost.

12.13 Sustainable Supplier Selection

Only by assimilating sustainability in every stage of an organization's supply chain, true sustainability can be achieved (Sustainable Supplier Selection in Medical Device Industry: Toward Sustainable Manufacturing n.d.). This also includes the procurement of sustainable units/components by the suppliers. In recent years, a lot of focus is being put on sustainable supplier selection in many organizations. The goal is to become a sustainable manufacturer by using sustainable procurement.

Today's global and dynamic complexities often frustrate and curb the good sustainability intentions that manufacturing companies create using user-friendly and technology-filled supply chains. In the past, lack of supply chain intelligence has created havoc for some of the biggest companies in the world. Apple iPhone's reputation was tainted when in 2012 they were exposed of using unfair and unsafe labor practices by their suppliers in China (IndustryWeek 2017). Similarly, in 2007 Mattel had to recall almost 1 million toys because they contained lead-tainted paint from a supplier in China (IndustryWeek 2017). The examples above suggest that a sustainable supply chain is only as good as the worst supplier. Even if there is one supplier that delivered materials or engaged in practices that were dangerous or unacceptable, it will eventually surface and cause detrimental damage to the manufacturer.

As the supplier–manufacturer dependency is increasing more and more, the direct and indirect ramifications of bad decisions making become serious (de Boer et al. 2001). The inclusion of new criteria and decision making directly increases the complexity and criticality of supply chain. This increased and complex development claims for the requirement of highly systematic and understandable decision making with regard to the supplier selection.

Manufacturing of a sustainable product will not be achieved unless all the components that the product is composed of are sustainable. This can be attained by working with suppliers that include the TBL (triple bottom line) concept in their manufacturing environment. Even though most of the manufacturing organizations have taken the initiative to introduce sustainability, a lot of them face a barrier of not having total control over the completion of their final product. As much as 70% of product sustainability comes from suppliers, who are significantly lagging in the implementation of sustainability in their processes (IndustryWeek 2017). Manufacturers must make stronger efforts to improve the supplier's sustainability performance by providing them with training programs and incentives and monitoring their progress. They need to identify the worst suppliers and eliminate them and work with the suppliers that are able to comply with the manufacturer's sustainability requirements.

For a versatile sustainable supplier selection, the environment, social, and economic factors must be considered. To enhance the supply chain performances due to the environmental awareness, many manufacturers are embracing green practices (Govindan et al. 2015). The environmental aspect has only been interspersed within the supplier selection process since the last decade. The introduction of new criteria has created complexity in the decision models that have been traditionally used. These new criteria even include some uncertain aspects such as the social impact and the company's reputation (Govindan et al. 2015). Thus, there needs to be a reassessment of some of the traditional and well-entrenched selection models. There have been new developments in the introduction of sustainable multi-criteria decision models such as the application of fuzzy theory which has helped when there is fuzziness and uncertainty involved during the selection of intangible criteria.

12.14 Conclusion

Purchasing of goods makes a major portion of a product's cost and thus selecting the right supplier reduces costs, improves the competitive edge, and augments user satisfaction. Ensuring that the supplier management procedure is followed with characteristics such as constant communication, doing a good background research and building a relationship of trust and respect and conducting regular audits is imperative, especially in the manufacturing of high-quality medical devices. The process of supplier selection in the medical device industry is almost neglected in the literature. The limited research is due to the confidentiality in the sharing of data.

Supplier selection should not only be based on the cost factor but also by strategically considering criteria such as quality, capabilities, organizational structure, and the suppliers' overall capabilities. Suppliers play an important role in terms of cost, quality, and service which directly affect the outcome in the buyer's company .Supplier selection still needs further attention in order to bring consensus between the quantitative and qualitative criteria in order to receive the best results. As many suppliers are still lagging behind in the sustainability curve, manufacturers must act as agents and aggressively implement sustainability initiatives.

With the evolution of sustainability, criteria such as price quality and service that were considered competitive have taken a back seat, while the focus has now shifted to the incorporation of sustainable services in all phases of supply chain and manufacturing.

There have been many single and unified MCDM approaches proposed for supplier selection. The criteria selection depends on the priorities of the company. It was noticed that none of these research papers included sensitivity analysis and its impact on the supplier selection decision. This can be part of the future research. By taking into account the changing weights and paying attention to the changes in data, the selection of a wrong supplier can be averted. A fair amount of focus has been given on quantitative methods in the literature, while there is barely any work focusing on the qualitative methods that are critical to the supplier selection

Future research can be guided by critical analysis and will be able to identify capabilities and limitations of the tools in sustainable selection models. However, the scale of this literature review does pose a limitation, thus opening doors for new investigations; especially the literature on green supplier selection is considerably limited. It can be concluded that the supplier–manufacturer relationship is symbiotic; both can benefit if there is trust and commitment. There is no single all-encompassing technique of selecting a supplier; the final process is premised on organizational need. Firms need to know what their own needs are and then make an informed choice by asking the right questions.

Acknowledgment Tugrul Daim and Dirk Meissners contribution to this chapter was prepared within the framework of the Basic Research Program at the National Research University Higher School of Economics.

Glossary

MCDM	"Multiple criteria decision making (MCDM) refers to making decisions in the presence of multiple, usually conflicting, criteria"
FMEA	"Failure modes and effects analysis is a step-by-step approach for identifying all possible failures in a design, a manufacturing or assembly process, or a product or service. "Failure modes" means the ways, or modes, in which something might fail.. FMEA is used during design to prevent failures"
TBL	"Triple bottom line is an accounting framework with three parts: social, environmental and financial. Some organizations have adopted the TBL framework to evaluate their performance in a broader perspective to create greater business value"
EQMS	"EQMS is an emerging enterprise software category that manages content and business processes for quality and compliance across the value chain. It can be viewed as a quality management platform with an integrated with IT architecture and data model that facilitates cross-functional communication and collaboration"
OEM	"An Original Equipment Manufacturer is a company that produces parts and equipment that may be marketed by another manufacturer"
CAPA	"Corrective and preventive action (CAPA, also called Corrective Action / Preventive Action, or simply Corrective Action) are improvements to an organization's processes taken to eliminate causes of nonconformities or other undesirable situations"
SCAR	"SCAR Systems are designed by industry practitioner for automating the Supplier Corrective Action Request process in any organization. A SCAR system is the crux of any quality and compliance process"
QA	"Quality assurance (QA) is a way of preventing mistakes or defects in manufactured products and avoiding problems when delivering solutions or services to customers; which ISO 9000 defines as "part of quality management focused on providing confidence that quality requirements will be fulfilled"
FDA	"The Food and Drug Administration (FDA or USFDA) is a federal agency of the United States Department of Health and Human Services, one of the United States federal executive departments. The FDA is responsible for protecting and promoting public health through the control and supervision of food safety, tobacco products, dietary supplements, prescription and over-the-counter pharmaceutical drugs (medications), vaccines, biopharmaceuticals, blood transfusions, medical devices, electro magnetic radiation emitting devices (ERED), cosmetics, animal foods & feed and veterinary products"

Source: Wikepedia.com

References

Ayhan M (2013) A fuzzy AHP approach for supplier selection problem: a case study in a Gearmotor Company. International Journal of Managing Value and Supply Chains 4(3):11–23

Lyons, J. (2017) Fundamentals of supplier management for medical device companies. [online] Blog.greenlight.guru. Available at: https://blog.greenlight.guru/fundamentals-of-supplier-management-for-medical-device-companies Accessed 21 Nov 2017.

Suranaree J. Sci. Technol. 15(3):201-208 A REVIEW OF SUPPLIER SELECTION METHODS IN MANUFACTURING INDUSTRIES

"Supply Chain Management | Medical Device Manufacturing Services", *Lso-inc.com*, (2017). [Online].Available:http://lso-inc.com/medical-device-manufacturing/supplychainmanagement.html.

de Boer L, Labro E, Morlacchi P (2001) A review of methods supporting supplier selection. European Journal of Purchasing & Supply Management 7(2):75–89

McKinsey & Company (2017) Supplier quality management: a proactive and collaborative approach. [online] Available at: https://www.mckinsey.com/practice-clients/operations/supplier-quality-management-a-proactive-and-collaborative-approach.

Supplier Selection by Damian Beil Stephen M. Ross School of Business July 2009

MDDI Online (2017) *12 Key Questions for Selecting a Supplier*. [online] Available at: https://www.mddionline.com/12-key-questions-selecting-supplier. Accessed 21 Nov. 2017.

Dr. Christopher Joseph Devine President Devine Guidance International Dr. Christopher Joseph Devine is the President of Devine Guidance International (2017) *Column | For an Effective Supplier Selection Process | MedTech Intelligence*. [online] MedTech Intelligence. Available at: https://www.medtechintelligence.com/column/devine-guidance-for-an-effective-supplier-selection-process/.

"Cite a Website—Cite This For Me", *Media.cygnus.com* (2017) [Online]. Available: http://media.cygnus.com/files/base/SDCE/whitepaper/2014/05/browz-whitepaper-assessing-sup_11445606.pdf.

Food Safety Magazine (2017) *Supplier Management: Six Steps to Selecting the Right Supplier*. [online] Available at: https://www.foodsafetymagazine.com/magazine-archive1/augustseptember-2012/supplier-management-six-steps-to-selecting-the-right-supplier/.

Micheli G, Cagno E, Zorzini M (2008) Supply risk management vs supplier selection to manage the supply risk in the EPC supply chain. *Manag Res News* 31(11):846–866

Ruhrmann S, Hochdörffer J, Lanza G (2014) Assessment of dynamics and risks in supplier selection processes. *Procedia CIRP* 25:2–9

"Failure Modes and Effects Analysis (FMEA) Tool", *Ihi.org* (2017) [Online]. Available: http://www.ihi.org/resources/Pages/Tools/FailureModesandEffectsAnalysisTool.aspx.

Digikey.com (2017) *6 Steps to More Effective Supplier Negotiations | DigiKey*. [online] Available at: https://www.digikey.com/en/articles/techzone/2013/nov/6-steps-to-more-effective-supplier-negotiations.

Kahraman UC, Ulukan Z (2003) Multi-criteria supplier selection using fuzzy AHP. *Logistics Information Management* 16(6):382–394

Mypurchasingcenter.com (2017) *Procurement Revisits Supplier Selection Criteria for Medical Devices*. [online] Available at: http://www.mypurchasingcenter.com/purchasing/industry-articles/price-pressures-curb-innovation-medical-devices/. Accessed 21 Nov 2017.

"A Blueprint for Optimizing Supply Chain Control within the Medical Device Industry", *Emergo* 2017 [Online]. Available: https://www.emergogroup.com/blog/2016/11/blueprint-optimizing-supply-chain-control-within-medical-device-industry.

"Managing Medical Device Quality Issues within a Complex Supply Chain", *Medical design.com* 2017 [Online]. Available: http://medicaldesign.com/contract-manufacturing/managing-medical-device-quality-issues-within-complex-supply-chain.

"Challenges with medical device supply chain quality | IQS, Inc.", *IQS, Inc.* 2017 [Online]. Available: http://www.iqs.com/challenges-medical-device-supply-chain-quality/.

"Supply Chain Strategies for a Challenging MedTech Landscape", *MDDI Online* 2017 [Online]. Available: https://www.mddionline.com/supply-chain-strategies-challenging-medtech-landscape.

Sustainable Supplier Selection in Medical Device Industry: Toward Sustainable Manufacturing

IndustryWeek (2017) Sustainability starts with the supply chain. [online] Available at: http://www.industryweek.com/supplier-relationships/sustainability-starts-supply-chain.

Govindan K, Rajendran S, Sarkis J, Murugesan P (2015) Multi criteria decision making approaches for green supplier evaluation and selection: a literature review. *J Clean Prod* 98:66–83

Chapter 13
Innovation Management Framework at a Medical Devices Company

Kevin D'Souza, Jesse Fritz, Gwendolyn Jester, Jacqueline Nayame, Janet Rosenthal, Matt Yamamoto, and Tugrul U. Daim

The company in this case applies a dedicated elaborated innovation management framework including strategic planning and a strong focus on project management. Foresighting innovation is among the central elements of long-term strategic planning, which results in dedicated roadmaps for all technology domains. The company uses a moderate share of external inputs for its innovation activities but emphasizes the importance of internal competences strongly and assures that external sources for innovation are well incorporated in its own activities.

13.1 Introduction

Management of technological innovation is a unique field of study that focuses on a technology company's ability to grow through activities relating to advancement of R&D, new product development, new technological knowledge creation, and improvements to existing products and processes. Management of technological innovation (MTI) involves strategic alignment of business goals with opportunities for innovation using tools of forecasting, planning, and market adoption. Although data and analytics play an important role in making decisions, the people aspect must be highly regarded throughout all processes. Impacts on organizational culture,

K. D'Souza · J. Fritz · G. Jester · J. Nayame · J. Rosenthal · M. Yamamoto
Portland State University, Portland, OR, USA

T. U. Daim (✉)
Portland State University Technology Management Doctoral Program, Portland, OR, USA

National Research University Higher School of Economics, Moscow, Russia

Chaoyang University of Technology, Taichung City, Taiwan
e-mail: tugrul.u.daim@pdx.edu

T. U. Daim, D. Meissner (eds.), *Innovation Management in the Intelligent World*, Science, Technology and Innovation Studies,
https://doi.org/10.1007/978-3-030-58301-9_13

internal capabilities, and external networks must be considered as to not create any additional barriers to the innovation process. "Technological barriers are those instances where the use of the technology is perceived as not being sufficient to perform the tasks or accomplish the objectives for which the technology was initially utilized" (Paul et al. 1999). Many industry experts agree that real value is created by the people, and technological innovation can ultimately become self-sustaining by maintaining knowledge creation and motivation within a properly selected working group or organization (Nonaka and Konno 1998).

Modern Innovation is historically considered to have evolved through 5 generations. A 6th generation is currently still being openly debated as to what it is as well as if/when it begins. Since the early 2000s researchers have been writing about different concepts for a 6th generation. Some proposals for the 6th generation of innovation include; sustainability, data analytics, Internet of Things (IoT's), a combination of generations, and even reverting back to the original form of innovation. The "notion of R&D generations is a difficult term, especially since most companies constitute a mixture of the generations and since the relevant time period for them most likely differs depending on industry segment, demographics, company age, research intensity, legislation demands, etc" (Nobelius 2004). The generally accepted generations of innovation are:

1. 1950 to mid-1960s—Technology-Based Innovation (Technology Push)
2. mid-1960s to early 1970s—Demand-Oriented Innovation (Market Pull)
3. mid-1970s to mid-1980s—Hybrid Innovation (R&D/Marketing)
4. mid-1980s to early 1990s—Integrated Business Processes (Efficiencies)
5. 1990s to ?—Open Network Innovation (Ecosystems)
6. TBD

13.1.1 Framework

Through a literature review, a framework was developed identifying major themes concerning management of technological innovation (MTI). Reoccurring themes of forecasting, planning, and matching market needs were identified as consensually agreed upon by experts in the field. These themes were probed through the lens of the "Know Model" to include the people aspect of MTI and incorporate information beyond just analytics. The "Know Model" includes the human process and reasoning behind decisions that companies make to help achieve their mission (Garud 1997). The principles of the Know model and the resulting MTI Framework.

13.1.2 Company Background

With over half a century in the medical device industry, Case Company has not only existed during the multiple historical innovation eras but continues to this day growing its market position. Currently, Case Company has 5000+ scientists and engineers and invests $1 billion annually in R&D. As a large scientific company, Case Company grows its technology roadmap through strategic technology acquisitions as well as internal investments.

An evaluation of the corporate financials over the last decade shows that Case Company's R&D expenditures increased from 2010 to 2018 with some years flatter than others. R&D expenses as a percentage of revenue show a consistent 3% to 4%, which means that Case Company is consistently balancing their R&D investments with their growth versus over (or under) investing. There are many different methods to measure the return on investment for R&D expenditures, one being the percentage of expenditures against revenue. Some tech companies such as Intel spend as much as 20% of their annual revenue on R&D expenses (Intel, Inc. 2019). Alphabet, Inc. (Google's parent company) spends approximately 15% of their annual revenue on R&D expenditures (Alphabet, Inc. 2018). From an outside perspective, Case Company's corporate investment in R&D may appear quite low compared to the pure high-tech companies. But, this number actually represents a composite index across products from legacy products that have little-to-no R&D up to new complex or strategic technologies that are well over 10%. Thus, Case Company balances its portfolio and strategically invests its resources in the promising future technological development.

This case study applies the framework developed under the theme "Managing Technological Innovation" to Case Company's Materials and Structural Analysis Division. The products specifically coming out of this division are various types of electron microscopes, which are sold to diverse customers from universities and government labs to private industry in markets ranging from life science to semiconductor. As mentioned previously, since MSD, as well as other divisions, operate somewhat independently of the parent organization, it means the focus of this study can be solely on how MSD manages technological innovation without being muddled by how other divisions manage their innovation. Of course, best practices for one division are typically shared across the global company, but applying the authors' framework to MSD narrows the focus.

13.1.3 Applying the Framework to the Company

A representative from Project Management Office serves as the connection between R&D, the business managers (i.e., marketing), and executive leadership. The individual helps facilitate the annual planning and forecasting for future products, and thus allowed the research team to gather insights into how Case Company manages innovation.

The company defines three key roles in the managing of technological innovation: System Architect, Marketing Manager, and Program Manager. These roles fall in line with our formulated framework (know-what, know-why, and know-how) of the themes from managing technological innovation (forecasting, planning, and market adoption). It might be easy to say that each role represents one aspect of the model, but in reality this triumvirate of individuals must keep each aspect in mind. And, in fact, the collaboration of these individuals is what really drives innovation management.

The definition of these roles and the aspects they represent are not just unique to Case Company. In our research, we've seen this pattern present in other models such as Scaled Agile Development that defines the roles of system architect, product management, and release train engineer (Scaled Agile Inc. 2019).

13.2 Forecasting

The human aspect of forecasting relates to the "know what" of the framework. Learning by using and understanding the innovation worth pursuing is a key element of the Case Company innovation strategy. MTI literature tells us forecasting undoubtedly benefits from collaborative open forums of visionaries and experts. Traditional technology road mapping and product characteristics' influence on portfolio management heavily rely on views of expected future diffusion of innovations and market evolution (Kanniainen et al. 2011). Analytical forecasting models can help a company quickly react to foreseeable changes but may not reveal competitive dynamics that could be identified through open expert communication. In addition, unanticipated or dramatic changes to a heavily analytical forecast would require new model creations and simulations. Fostering an innovative environment for internal researchers and developers at Case Company is considered just as if not even more important than market analytics. The open forum method is heavily emphasized to encourage progressive discussion coupled with healthy criticism. It is well known, and often reinforced by company leadership, that all employees are expected to drive innovation. To foster this effort, barriers related to fear of being negatively impacted for stating one's opinions or ideas are fully eliminated. This is further bolstered and connected to the vision of the company through constant communication from leadership with regard to the strategic plan.

For Case Company the split of identifying innovative opportunities is about 90% internal and 10% external. The view of the company is the best way to avoid dramatic changes and disruptions is to be ahead of the competition or be the disruption. Being caught off guard is considered as a failure to identify and supply resources to a new opportunity. Being caught off guard also forces changes to a plan and reallocation of resources. New technological innovations are shared/proliferated throughout the organization through:

a. Open discussion/hallway talk
b. Managerial meetings/summits
c. Top-down inquiries and pre-approvals—linking groups and forums together
d. Bottom-up proposals

The organization guards against disruptive technologies from competitors by asking internal questions in terms of the competition, "What would the competition do?". Tradeshows and industry publications offer Case Company large sets of information with regard to competitors' strategic directions but not all of the competitors' innovation should be considered a disruptive threat. A major benefit of the internal expert forum method is being able to separate real market signals from market "noise." After determining what the competition is doing, the next internal question is "Are we currently doing something better?".

Analytical methods of forecasting and modeling are not typical practices at Case Company. Continually chasing data and updating forecasting simulations is considered an inefficient use of time and quite possibly even a barrier to innovation. The opinion is the speed and foresight of expert people will offer greater results with less effort. They justify this by maintaining market share through continually innovating and offering technology with low risk for disruption.

13.2.1 Mechanisms for Supporting Innovation

Case Company provides a number of methods for fostering innovation in the company through official processes.

- *Internal Grants*—An internal grant program allows developers and scientists to submit ideas to a review board. Awards are granted on an annual basis.
- *University Research Grants*—Like many large companies, Case Company supports research jointly developed between the company and universities. In some Case Company divisions, an investment of 20% or more of division R&D budget might be made in custom collaborations with external science researchers.
- *Internal Idea Crowdsourcing*—Case Company originated an internal crowdsourcing program to promote collaboration for building out innovative ideas across the company. Ideas are posted on an internal board monitored by Case Company R&D and Product Development teams, which route the ideas to different business units for further review.
- *Technology Conference*—Case Company Materials and Structural Analysis Division hosts a technology conference every other year that allows developers and scientists to showcase their research projects with the intent of sparking new ideas or collaborations through sharing of knowledge.
- *Customer Innovation Days*—In the past, Case Company has hosted Innovation Days where customers meet with Case Company scientists, engineers, and management through a type of external technology conference.

Despite these official processes, many innovative ideas are sparked simply from hallway conversations.

13.3 Planning

While forecasting is the practice of knowing the short- and long-term "What" of a company's technology sector, planning is all about the "How"—specifically, how a company plans to turn an uncertain technological roadmap into good bets for commercial success.

13.3.1 Strategic Planning

One of the themes drawn from the article group Managing Technological Innovation was the importance of planning, specifically long-term or strategic planning. Kostoff and Schaller (2001) state that strategic planning can be driven by either technology push, starting with where we are today as the foundation, or requirements pull, starting with a desired goal or future state and mapping the path forward toward that goal. Regardless of their differences, both inherently are focused on the long-term vision, the output of which is a technology or product roadmap.

Like many technology companies, Case Company engages in a strategic planning process. Strategic planning or roadmapping can span 5, 10, or more years. Although Case Company does have a 15–20 year "vision" of where it wants to be, from a practical standpoint, it chooses to plan on a rolling 5-year roadmap. This roadmap then feeds into the annual operating plan for the next year.

The company's annual strategic planning process starts by soliciting input from key contributors. These contributors are typically technologists or architects familiar with the current technology and potential future innovative product technologies. They also include marketing managers and business leaders who are in tune with market dynamics, the competition landscape, and customer needs. Finally, it includes program managers and project managers who are in charge of currently running projects and portfolios. And, of course, it includes the division's executive team and financial representatives.

The contributors weigh the projects, which can be in any particular stage of development from concept to established platform, based on several key equally weighted business drivers. Within each business, driver is a defined meaning for what a particular score means with respect to that driver. The output of the process is a prioritized list of projects to invest in. The process repeats itself annually, which means projects that may not be heavily invested in one year, may get more attention in the following years as market conditions change.

HDM breaks down a complex multi-criteria decision problem into smaller components and forms a multilevel hierarchical structure.

13.3.2 Phase Gates

Managing technological innovation means knowing not just which projects to invest in, but also assessing the project or technology readiness. As presented in class, Case Company executes a phase gate approach to manage risk in technology innovation. The phase gate approach is not unique to Case Company but rather best practice according to the Project Management Institute, which describes the purpose of gates as a means to address the two main causes of project failure: scope change and risk (Project Management Institute 2019).

When evaluating new innovative projects, Case Company conducts phase gate meetings with a project review board, which include approvers selected by upper management. The four possible outcomes of a phase gate evaluation are to proceed, proceed with conditions, defer, and terminate. The gate presentations at the product review board meetings provide management the opportunity to assess project progress. Project teams must retire risk and demonstrate progress (e.g., technical feasibility, project readiness, and manufacturability) at each gate. Depending on the particular focus of the gate, different review members may be required for sign-off.

After a project team receives the initial approval to proceed, Case Company makes a commitment to the team by providing funding and dedicated managers (Program, Marketing, and Systems) to the project.

13.3.3 Flexibility in Planning

Just as good forecasting accounts for uncertainty, good planning must account for uncertainty as well. As explored by Galbraith & DeNoble, 95% of venture capital bets fail, and focused experts tasked with the prediction of the commercial success of technologies have "generally low predictive power." Predicting the success of any particular technology is chronically difficult (Galbraith et al. 2012). Expert assessment is rarely better than chance, and the predictors commonly cited by experts often show zero (or even negative) correlation with the actual success of a particular technology. With such high failure rates in even the best predictive practices, it is important for a company to not only do the best they can in selecting initial efforts, but be prepared to—and plan to—change the strategic plan when encountering inevitable curveballs.

13.3.3.1 Pruning of Old Projects

The achievement of key milestones is one of the strongest early indicators of which technologies will have commercial success and which will not (Galbraith et al. 2012). By employing a stage-gate technology funnel, Case Company is following good practice to ensure funding is targeted on the most effective bets. Additionally, by allowing unexpected events to fold into their product lines, such as the emergence of new customer needs, the unexpected innovation of their engineers, or insights of their market analysts, Case Company is maintaining the flexibility necessary to stay on top of changes in an inherently difficult to predict market landscape.

13.3.3.2 Introduction of New Projects and Adaptation of Technology Plans

Case Company uses four triggers for inserting new innovation into their product lines:

- Ah-ha moments from any level of staff
- Technology forums
- New customer needs
- Competition

Case Company's open culture of communication, as explained in the prior section on forecasting, provides many benefits to the responsiveness and accuracy of the R&D organization's planning. As explored by Vojak and Suarez-Nunez, having strictly regulated, one-directional information flows expose that information to risk via a "telephone effect," where attributes of a technology, market, or product can get increasingly variable as the number of steps in the information chain increase (Vojak and Suarez-Nunez 2004). By having both formal and informal methods of syncing these plans against technology and market forecasts (managerial meetings, technology forums, and bidirectional information flow up the management chain), mis-understood or mis-communicated information has more opportunities to correct itself. However, while additional formalized methods of checking current plans against technology and market forecasts may exist, Vojak notes that they generally slow cadence of these meetings can cause significant shortfalls in planning accuracy (Vojak and Suarez-Nunez 2004).

Having too many processes will make any organization too slow and bureaucratic to respond quickly, and the selection of good people is paramount to overcome any gaps that may exist in established processes. In other words, Case Company balances its cadence of such meetings by hiring "the right people," and this acts as a failsafe for information that comes in between the cadence of more organized, rigorous examination. This analysis would recommend that Case Company, if it has not already, takes steps to ensure that any failures in "the failsafe of good people" will be caught, and that business leaders are held accountable if their people-networks are not communicating well enough to keep product plans reasonably in sync with variable technology and market forecasts.

13.3.4 Selection of Initial R&D Efforts

In the identification of which emerging technologies to invest research and development dollars toward, Case Company prioritizes projects by scoring identified market drivers. Additionally, Case Company evaluates the "strategic value," defined as an assessment of how hurt they will be if the option is left on the table. While this definition of strategic value can take many forms, Case Company appears to have a focus on market potential for these initial selection of R&D projects.

The previously cited analysis by Galbraith provides strong evidence that expert estimation of the market potential of an early-phase technology exhibits very little (or even negative) correlation with the technology's actual generation of revenue in the future marketplace. While market analysis is an inaccurate predictor in early-phase R&D projects, for later stage-gates the results of such predictions are far more relevant. For initial R&D selection, a focus on core technology is the most consistent predictor of commercial success (Galbraith et al. 2012).

A focus on core technology seems to be overshadowed by Case Company's market focus for early selection of R&D projects, and it is tempting to recommend a realignment of early-stage evaluation priorities. The question of "How does Case Company identify emerging technologies it needs to invest research dollars in pursuing?" implies very early stage-gates. However, further consultation with Case Company would be appropriate. The definition of "emerging technologies" is subjective, and the funding stage might be further along in the process than where Galbraith's data holds relevance. That is to say, by this point in Case Company's selection, the core technologies being chosen between might be fully fleshed out, and this decision is at the stage of "which of these technologically solid choices is the best."

Between the ambiguity of the term "emerging technology," as well as ambiguity of "how hurt Case Company will be" in the evaluation of strategic value, any recommendations to focus less on marketing and more on core technology in early technology funding is more highlighting an area that might warrant a closer look, as opposed to a specific criticism.

13.4 Market Adoption

Market adoption incorporates the "know why" of the framework and is important for Case Company's R&D management because it allows the firm to meet its main objective of establishing a permanent relationship with their customers by fully understanding the underlying reasons for the innovation. The firm differentiates themselves by learning through studying the customer and focusing their resources on markets and customer needs that are related to their strategy. Case Company focuses on strategic marketing, by aligning their organizational strategy with their marketing strategy. This is achieved by clustering the projects in the NPD portfolio into target niches and brands. By dividing the new product development portfolio budget according to targeted niche, the firm can better direct its development efforts and resources to fulfill customer needs and thereby react to new market trends quicker (Santiago and Soares 2020).

Case Company's market adoption strategy focuses on people. They rely on their marketing and product managers to attend trade shows and infiltrate competitive intelligence for effective market adoption. Case Company is rarely surprised by the competition. Their goal is to have less than 10% of its R&D influenced by surprises in the market. Three to four marketing directors attend trade shows to gather intelligence. They bring back customer and competitive information that determines if there is an immediate product development need. If it is determined that there is no immediate need, they focus on their five business drivers, and how these products rank among them. In regard to competitive intelligence, they look at that as a spectrum. They look at 5 business drivers and assign a score. By using this scoring system with drivers, it is not just "how many dollars do I get" by developing this product. They continually look at strategic value. If the value is on the high end of a driver, they ask themselves the question "how badly will I be hurt if I don't do something for this?".

In order to understand the needs of customers better, Case Company utilizes the early adopter strategy to test new products. The early adopter program gives Case Company an opportunity to test their ideas and understanding with a group of end users, who with their constructive feedback and insights will help the project team to ensure the project being developed meets the needs of the customers. Along with the early adopter program, Case Company can also utilize pre-prototype testing, as this would allow for more flexibility to make modifications to the product compared to the costs incurred once a working prototype has been developed. A research conducted by Davis & Venkatesh (2004) found that "behavioral intention and perceived usefulness measured before hands-on experience with a software product were highly correlated with, and not significantly different from the same measures taken after months of hands-on experience with the system."

13.5 Discussion and Conclusions

13.5.1 People Versus Process

Creating and maintaining a continually innovative environment where people can talk openly and express their ideas without barriers is of paramount importance to realize the full potential from the human aspect of the "know" framework. Case Company justifies the success of relying on the people aspects of their strategy, rather than analytical modeling, by being continually innovative, a world market leader, and offering technology that is low risk of disruption.

There are many case studies highlighting failure to regard the human factor in innovation management being detrimental to a project or product line but there are few cases about companies relying so heavily on it. Forecasting tools, such as the Bass diffusion model, use mathematical formulas to predict the market adoption of new products. The Bass diffusion equation relies on the coefficients of innovation and imitation that are based on the market adoption of similar products, whereas Case Company bases decisions on the experience of their management team. Typically, when the human aspect is highly critical to success there are still some academic methodologies used in combination to aid in decision-making and planning. Compared to the literature review, the Case Company process is atypical of a large successful technology company.

13.5.2 Marketing Focus Versus Core Technology

- Key performance measurements of innovation for Case Company is market share and prevention from being disrupted. External drivers for innovation should account for less than 10% of innovative projects.
- Aligning organizational strategy with strategic marketing is important to ensuring an organization is up to date with customer needs.

Case Company may or may not be overvaluing market predictions and undervaluing the quality of core technology decisions of which emerging technologies to fund. While a focus on marketability in later stages of technology development is appropriate, early-stage expert evaluations of market potential are negatively correlated with commercialization success. Quality of core technology is the strongest early-stage predictor of future commercialization.

When prioritizing the selection on innovative projects, Case Company currently utilizes internal subject matter experts (SME) to weigh each project against business drivers during strategic planning process meetings. A similar expert opinion-based approach can be used to quantify how well a project meets customer needs. Quality function deployment matrix, in which experts rate how well product features meet customer needs. The customer needs are weighted and the cumulative score can be used to identify product features that need to be developed further to compete in the market. The formal structure of a QFD matrix is recommended to provide consistency in the decision-making process and to standardize the selection tools used by R&D managers across Case Company's multiple R&D locations.

The Case Company R&D selection process currently takes place during in-person strategic planning meetings. Decision making through the opinions of internal subject matter experts is a main aspect of Case Company's organizational culture, but can introduce power influence and bias by senior management. To maintain the historical business model of relying on internal subject matter experts and to minimize groupthink, the use of an HDM model is recommended. The experts can complete the pairwise comparisons of the HDM model and the results can be gathered and synthesized prior to a strategic planning meeting. HDM models have the benefit of being easily adaptable and have the ability to isolate variables for sensitivity analysis. Any inconsistencies in the expert opinions will be identified in the results summary and can be used as a discussion point during the strategic planning meeting.

Acknowledgments Tugrul Daims contribution to the book chapter is based on the study funded by the Basic Research Program of the National Research University Higher School of Economics (HSE) and by the Russian Academic Excellence Project "5-100."

References

Alphabet, Inc. (2018) "Annual Reports". [Online]. https://abc.xyz/investor. Accessed Sept 2019

Davis FD, Venkatesh V (2004) Toward preprototype user acceptance testing of new information systems: implications for software project management. IEEE T Eng Manage *51*(1):31–46

Galbraith CS, DeNoble AF, Ehrlich SB (2012) Predicting the commercialization progress of early-stage technologies: an ex-ante analysis. IEEE T Eng Manage 59(2):213–225

Garud R (1997) On the distinction between know-how, know-what and know-why. Adv Strateg Manage *14*:81–101

Intel, Inc. (2019) "Annual Reports". [Online]. https://www.intc.com/investor-relations/financials-and-filings/annual-reports-and-proxy/default.aspx. Accessed Sept 2019

Kanniainen J, Mäkinen S, Piche R, Chakrabarti A (2011) Forecasting the diffusion of innovation: a stochastic bass model with log-normal and mean-reverting error process (May 1, 2011). IEEE T Eng Manage 58(2):228–249. Available at SSRN: https://ssrn.com/abstract=2168049

Kostoff R, Schaller R (2001) Science and technology roadmaps. IEEE T Eng Manage 48 (2):132–143

Nobelius D (2004) Towards the sixth generation of R&D management. Int J Proj Manag 22 (5):369–375. ISSN 0263-7863

Nonaka I, Konno N (1998) The concept of "Ba": building a foundation for knowledge creation. Calif Manage Rev *40*(3):40–54

Paul D, Pearlson KE, Mcdaniel R (1999) Assessing technological barriers to telemedicine: technology-management implications. Eng Manag IEEE Transactions 46:279–288. https://doi.org/10.1109/17.775280

Project Management Institute (2019) "Project Gates – 'Chutes and Ladders®' for project managers". [Online]. https://www.pmi.org/learning/library/contemporary-gate-philosophy-implemented-outcome-7786. Accessed Aug 2019

Santiago LP, Soares VMO (2020) Strategic alignment of an R&D portfolio by crafting the set of buckets. IEEE T Eng Manag 67(2):309–321

Scaled Agile Inc. (2019) "Scaled Agile Framework". [Online]. https://www.scaledagileframework.com. Accessed Sept 2019

Vojak BA, Suarez-Nunez CA (Aug. 2004) Product attribute bullwhip in the technology planning process and a methodology to reduce it. IEEE T Eng Manage 51(3):288–299

Part III
Emerging Technologies

Chapter 14
Elon Musk Transportation Projects

Briana Tran, Dawei Zhang, Mohammad Al Gafly, Tanzila Akhter, Jillrietnefertiti Lilithcleopatra, Tugrul U. Daim, and Dirk Meissner

14.1 Introduction

R&D management is one of the important activities for any company. It is a process where technology change results in a product; for that change there are several steps need to be done. A company's success depends on its R&D management. If a company does a great job on R&D, there is a big chance to get prosperity. Though lots of facts are conditional to the word "success," a company needs to fulfill its R&D requirement like technical, markets, etc.

People have much interest to know how a company or a person manages his R&D, especially when it comes to Elon Musk, one of the most successful business persons in the world. Might be many competitors of Elon Musk or his followers want to know what process Elon Musk takes for his R&D management; how much money he spends for his several transportation projects Tesla, SpaceX, and the Boring Company. People might be curious that Elon Musk can give similar attention to all of his transportation projects at a time or not.

B. Tran · D. Zhang · M. Al Gafly · T. Akhter · J. Lilithcleopatra
Portland State University, Portland, OR, USA

T. U. Daim (✉)
Portland State University Technology Management Doctoral Program, Portland, OR, USA

National Research University Higher School of Economics, Moscow, Russia

Chaoyang University of Technology, Taichung City, Taiwan
e-mail: tugrul.u.daim@pdx.edu

D. Meissner
National Research University Higher School of Economics, Moscow, Russia

T. U. Daim, D. Meissner (eds.), *Innovation Management in the Intelligent World*, Science, Technology and Innovation Studies,
https://doi.org/10.1007/978-3-030-58301-9_14

14.2 Elon Musk

14.2.1 Projects

14.2.1.1 SpaceX

The first of Elon Musk's projects in transportation is SpaceX. SpaceX was founded to revolutionize space technology with the ultimate goal of enabling people to live on other planets. They were the first to be able to return a spacecraft from low Earth orbit, and the first to design and build a spacecraft that was able to transport cargo to and from the International Space Station. Currently, SpaceX offers launch services for their Falcon 9 and Falcon Heavy rockets. The Falcon Heavy is able to lift more than 2x the payload of the closest operational vehicle and the Delta IV Heavy at one-third the cost (SpaceXcmsadmin 2012a). SpaceX is currently working on a new set of fully reusable launch vehicles that can carry humans to Mars and other destinations in space (Spacexcmsadmin 2012b).

14.2.1.2 Tesla

After his start with SpaceX, Elon Musk joined the Tesla's board of directors in 2004. Tesla Incorporated, previously Tesla Motors, is an electric vehicle, lithium-ion battery storage, and solar panel manufacturing company. The driving force behind Tesla is to move away from utilizing petroleum or hydrocarbon-based energy toward a solar electric economy, as it is a more sustainable solution. So the Tesla Roadster was born; it was designed to be comparable or better than gasoline sports cars and have greater efficiency than current electric vehicles. The goal is to put all the free cash flow from sales of the roadster toward R&D of a lower cost family car. To sum up, Tesla is using its more sporty and high-performance roadster to help it move into larger markets at lower price points (The Secret Tesla Motors Master Plan 2012).

14.2.1.3 The Boring Company

Musk's most recent transportation-related venture is the Boring Company. Citizens that drive in the city of Los Angeles, CA, USA, have to deal with one of the worst traffic situations in the country daily. LA ranks number one of cities in the USA with an average of 104 hours stuck in traffic a year (Jones 2017). The idea behind the Boring Company is to remedy this issue; they need to increase the commuting space and the only real option is to either build up or down. Building up leads to many challenges such as weather complications, building and regulating flying vehicles, FAA restrictions, and more. That leads to the other option of building down. According to TBC, building tunnels would allow for unlimited layers of tunnels, they are weatherproof, and tunnel construction and operation are silent and invisible to anyone on the surface. Currently, building tunnels requires lots of resources and time with cost being the biggest factor. Typically tunnels can cost as much as $1 billion per mile of tunnel. TBC's solution is to make a smaller tunnel, effectively reducing the boring cost and increasing boring speeds by increasing power, continuous tunneling, going electric, automated tunnel boring machines, etc. (FAQ 2018). Loop will be the underground high-speed transportation system that will transport passengers on autonomous electric skates traveling at 125–150 miles per hour. Each skate will be able to carry 8–16 passengers or a single passenger vehicle.

14.3 R&D Management

14.3.1 Leadership Strategies

14.3.1.1 An Effective Leader

One of the key factors of effective management of research and development is leadership. To be an effective leader, there needs to be a focus on the personnel and open communication must exist. The manager needs to be able to influence the attitude and commitment and create a work environment that challenges and motivates the members with drivers such as each member's personal interests, personal and work challenges, accomplishments, and recognition. An effective leader also must be able to identify and build teams with traits of a high performing team. Traits that are important in high-performing teams are traits such as self-directed, effective communication, innovative behavior, high need for achievements, quality oriented, and enjoy work. See the image below for more traits that all contribute to a high-performing effective team.

Four conditions to building an effective team are (1) a professionally stimulating work environment, (2) good project leadership, (3) qualified personnel, and (4) a stable work environment (Hans 2009).

14.3.1.2 Elon Musk's Leadership Strategy

Elon Musk's style of leadership is based on 10 principles (Top 10 in Leadership from Elon Musk 2017):

1. Lead by example: Elon Musk expects that leaders must work harder than all those who report to him or her. Must always make sure their needs are taken care of before yours.
2. Lead with purpose: Needs to believe that there is potential for a great outcome and believe in the leader of the company.
3. Be creative: Having a process inhibits creativity, which affects progress and innovation.

4. Be collaborative: Sense of pride in team success has to start with the leadership. Elon Musk leads by demonstrating rather than telling.
5. Encourage innovation: Failure is an option.
6. Be decisive: Must commit to acting in the present. Strategy and action lead to results.
7. Be comfortable with change: Successful leaders are able to adapt in any situation and continue pushing forward toward their teams goals.
8. Hire carefully: Elon Musk personally interviewed the first 1000 people at SpaceX and still interviews all engineering candidates. He believes that hiring great candidates is 90% of the solution.
9. Set exceptionally high standards: His goals for each of these companies are extremely innovative. For SpaceX, he wants to make Mars habitable for humans. For Tesla, he wants to make electric vehicles the standard reducing the world's carbon footprint. Finally for the Boring Company, his vision is to mitigate or remove the traffic issue, by building downward. Best leaders are self-aware. They understand the power of adjusting their behaviors and leadership style to inspire their people.
10. Put the right people in the right role: Assign roles that fit each individual's work style and passion.

14.3.1.3 Leadership Analysis

The management structure in all three of these companies has a relatively flat structure: anyone can contact anyone, even Elon Musk himself. With this method, everyone is involved and integrated so all communications occur quickly and efficiently. When there is an issue or problem, Elon Musk would inquire what help is needed and provide them as quickly as possible to resolve the issue. By eliminating roadblocks and providing the necessary resources, he is ensuring that his employees are able to work without major disruptions. In addition, Elon Musk forms and develops high-performing teams; he hires individuals that are extremely self-motivated, such as in the case of Josh Boehm (https://www.forbes.com/sites/quora/2017/11/08/i-worked-at-spacex-and-this-is-how-elon-musk-inspired-a-culture-of-top-performers/#321810af438f n.d.). During his time at SpaceX, many employees consistently put in 50–60 hours of work a week, not because they were forced to, but because they enjoyed their work and were motivated to get things completed. Overall, all three of these companies have similar management structure, so there is no project that dominates in terms of leadership strategy and success.

14.3.2 Budgeting Investments

When deciding the budget for R&D, management concerns itself with a variety of questions. R&D is a key driver for the company because it is related to the future revenues. While we tend to think R&D is mostly connected to new products and new services, a lot of R&D investments go through processes and the outcomes of these investments may not be visible for most of the people. Third, there is a time lapse between revenue and the budgeted expense. Current profits have a close connection with yesterday's R&D budget. Fourth, typically, in R&D budgeting process, a central question emerges. What would be a recommended level of R&D funding? Well, there is no direct answer to this question because many factors have influence, for example development risk. Another factor could be the objective of the company regarding strategic positioning or product or service life cycle.

14.3.2.1 Tesla

"Tesla's R&D expenses in 2018 stood at 1.38 billions which was more than 5 times that in 2011. In 2012 its R&D expenses were only 273 millions. For both 2017 and 2016, Tesla's R&D expenses were 12% of the entire revenue whereas in 2015, it was 18% of the entire revenue" (Tesla Inc 2018; Bloom 2018). "The Research and development ("R&D") expenses include the personnel costs of its engineering and research teams, manufacturing engineering and manufacturing test organizations, prototyping expense, contract and professional services and amortized equipment expense."

14.3.2.2 SpaceX

In July 2017, the company raised US$350m at a valuation of US$21 billion (Crane 2017) According to other leaked company financial documents published in the *Wall Street Journal* in January of 2017, SpaceX had "operated on total funding of approximately $1 billion in its first ten years of operation. Of this, private equity provided about $200M, with Musk investing approximately $100M and other investors having put in about $100M" (Crane 2017). The remainder came from progress payments on long-term launch contracts and development contracts. By March 2018, SpaceX had contracts for 100 launch missions (Sheetz 2018). SpaceX has an advantage in the private space industry because its research and development costs are relatively low.

14.3.2.3 The Boring Company

Budget information is estimated here from a recent April 2018 filing with the US Securities and Exchange Commission (SEC) revealed that the Boring Company has raised $113 million. More than 95 percent of this money came from Mr Musk (Nicoli 2018). The SEC filing revealed that no outside investors contributed to the funding, with the rest of the money coming from early employees at the company. Elon has made public statements which reveal what he considers the profitability opportunities of this company. “If you were to do a risk-adjusted rate of return estimate on various industry opportunities, I would put building rockets and cars pretty much at the bottom of the list,” said Musk to an audience at the SXSW festival in Austin, Texas, June 2018 (CNBC 2018). Musk told the audience that he did not start SpaceX with the idea of profitability, but rather to force NASA’s space exploration budget to be bigger (CNBC 2018).

14.3.2.4 Analysis

Based on the above discussion, the study finds that SpaceX has the most promising outlook with respect to return on investment (ROI) for R&D expenses. This conclusion has arrived by evaluating estimates of short- and medium-term operating costs as well as projected profitability investments. While Tesla has increased its R&D substantially over the decade since its inception—making up over 12% of revenue in 2017—Tesla has not yet made economic profit. The Boring Company boasts its first contract with Chicago municipality which is expected to receive over 140 million in operating profit (Nicoli 2018). R&D expenditure estimates for this venture are currently unavailable. SpaceX has a targeted estimate of 30 launches in 2018 which will net it close to 2.14 billion in profit. Of this expected revenue, R&D expenses account for only 4% of entire revenue (Parnell 2018).

14.3.3 Timeliness

Compressed timing enables products to be produced and offered for sale more quickly and has the potential of locking in the most profitable customer. Elon Musk has used the time compression strategy in all his business endeavors in order to increase the timeliness of his offerings. Time compression is the reduction of wasted time throughout a business in order to improve its competitiveness. The primary goals of time compression are to increase productivity, improve quality, reduce cycle times, and speed innovative products to market.

Another timing strategy Musk has frequently used to increase timeliness is bringing previously unimagined, risky, raw, fresh ideas to life, before competitors can even grasp them—let alone mobilize to beat them or even recreate them (Business timeliness n.d.; Muoio 2017).

14.3.3.1 The Boring Company

The Boring Company will team with Tesla in order to improve its timeliness through the use of Tesla’s existing resources. Investors initially believed that the Boring Company would use Tesla’s electric powertrain and possibly its autonomous driving software (much simpler to do in a tunnel and on a rail than on the open road) to create its high-speed, tunnel-traveling pods. However, Musk says that Tesla will make the entire pod, rather than just components for it. Musk's stated ultimate goal is for the Boring Company to build an underground network that "includes as many as 30 levels of tunnels for cars and high-speed trains such as the Hyperloop." Timeliness is inherent in this goal, since the Boring Company is the only company to have undertaken such feats.

14.3.3.2 Tesla

As for Tesla, its timeliness in offering customer-friendly long-range electric vehicles well ahead of its competitors, as well as concurrently creating a comprehensive, nationwide fueling infrastructure where none existed, has been the key to its success in its stated mission of accelerating the world's transition to sustainable energy. Recently, its Gigafactory has been making strides in terms of energy density and battery pack cost breakthroughs in order to lower vehicle prices and extend vehicle ranges even further. Tesla plans to open a new R&D center in Athens in order to be close to the technology centers that have produced some of its brightest design engineers. This is a timely maneuver, as Tesla is poised to research the employment of AI in the onboard computers that aid its autopilot feature and to further refine its motors to respond appropriately. The head of the Hellenic Entrepreneurs' Association has offered huge incentives (free healthcare for a year and free industrial plant for 10 years) to Tesla to undertake Tesla Greece in the hope that Tesla's involvement in the Greek economy will rescue Greece from its current economic slump in a timely manner.

14.3.3.3 SpaceX

Timeliness is also essential to SpaceX, regarding its stated mission of revolutionizing space technology with the ultimate goal of enabling people to live on other planets. Musk is concerned about the near extinction of the human race should WWIII break out. He would like to colonize the Moon to counter this potential issue, but is afraid that the Moon itself might be damaged by being too close to the battles. He thinks that Mars would be the most practical place to raise humans to re-seed the Earth after WWIII. He believes this is the best way to avoid a plant-wide Dark Age on Earth after WWIII. To that end SpaceX's R&D is aimed at developing a BFR rocket to colonize Mars, and in situ resource utilization (ISRU) to refuel the BFR rockets for their return trips once they reach Mars. The best timing of this project is uncertain, because politics and other world events will dictate when and if WWIII ever breaks out. However, timeliness is applicable to this issue because the sooner Mars is colonized, the better the chance the human race will survive should it be practically wiped off the face of the Earth.

14.3.4 Innovation management

Innovation is important to companies, from the very beginning to the whole developing period. A startup normally starts with a good idea fitting in a big market potential or a good idea to change the world; this not only gains financial supports from capitals, but also attracts attention from talented people to join in.

Later when companies are in their developing stages, innovation management helps companies to track their roadmap by building long-term strategic plan, and to improve their efficiency by exchanging knowledge with their partners and contractors, which could result in a form of partnership or outsourcing.

14.3.4.1 Good Ideas

All three companies we discussed here have good ideas at the beginning.

- SpaceX company was started in 2001 with Elon Musk's concept of *Mars Oasis*, a project to land an experimental greenhouse and grow plants on Mars; now their ultimate goal is enabling people to live on other planets (Miles O'Brien n.d.).
- Tesla was founded in July 2003 by Martin Eberhard and Marc Tarpenning and later had a Series A round of investment led by Elon Musk; the company was started after GM recalled all its EV1 electric cars and then destroyed them; Tesla has a primary goal to commercialize electric vehicles (LaMonica 2009).
- The Boring Company was introduced in December 2016 by Elon Musk, it is claimed by digging tunnel under cities; the trip will take five minutes, compared to normal driving that can take up to 45 minutes in normal traffic to go from LAX to Westwood. The company is trying to solve the problem of "soul-destroying" traffic (Hawkins 2017).

All three companies were headed by Elon Musk, who has a background in physics and economic knowledge; he dropped out from his Ph.D. in Stanford after two years studies and started his entrepreneurial career. Elon Musk made a great contribution to all these three companies in terms of the initiative ideas.

14.3.4.2 Innovative Technologies and Strategies

Having good ideas is a good start, but not good enough to consolidate a startup company; to implement those ideas, innovative technologies and strategies play a big role.

> SpaceX hard-headed itself against a reusable launching system, which reduced launching cost significantly by recycling the booster stages. (Satellite Technology n.d.) Tesla adopted an opposite strategy to implement electric car, instead of competing with other car manufacturers on the mass-production vehicles, it focused itself to build a luxury sport car *Roadster* to establish its brand. Later when the company had more resources and technologies, it shifted efforts to build mass production version, *Model 3*, instead. (Bryant 2016)

Boring company also took a innovative method to accelerate the boring speed, by reducing the tunnel diameter, adding more power, automating the machine, etc. (FAQ 2018)

To build a prototype is one thing and to achieve mass production is another; companies need innovative strategy and technologies to accomplish it step by step.

14.3.4.3 Partnerships

Partnerships can compensate and complement shortcomings of companies, thus contributing a lot in innovation management.

SpaceX's partnership with NASA not only enables more financial investment, but also expands the company's market to US Air Force. The strong partnership could also give more competence to the company, to compete with other competitors, like Blue Origin (SpaceX n.d.).

Tesla's partnership with Panasonic is critical since the electric cars need electric power batteries from the partner (Panasonic and Tesla Sign Agreement for the Gigafactory 2015). Tesla also partners with grocery stores, hotels, gas stations, etc. to build their destination charger stations; thus, it can share more confidence to its customers with adequacy of chargers (Tesla, Inc n.d.).

Powered by partnership with Chicago government and LA Metro, the Boring company gains more endorsement from public and regulation support (F. Lambert, Fred, and Electrek 2018), (F. Lambert, Fred, and Electrek 2018).

A good partnership can strengthen a company's technology, finance, and marketing and sometimes help eliminating regulation barriers.

14.3.4.4 Outsourcing

Outsourcing should also be considered in companies as part of innovation strategies; concentrating on the companies' main strength and delegating tasks to other companies is an efficient way to reduce cost and improve productivity, but all three companies discussed here did not adopt this very much.

For SpaceX, the company would rather build roughly 80% of the parts for its rockets to reduce their costs (SpaceX n.d.). Neither Tesla outsources much, by building the battery packs itself, e.g., from their Gigafactory, the cost could be cut for extra 30%. Besides, Tesla insources its production streamlines and even sales forces; it stands when the results showed the efficiency was quite improved for both production and distribution (Supply Chain Resource Cooperative 2016). Given the Boring company is still in an early stage; their main focus is still on developing the high-speed TBM (tunnel boring machine); there is not much that can be outsourced so far.

The reason Elon Musk's companies do not do outsourcing much could be related to their business models; costs reduction is one of main competitive advantages of these companies, plus Elon Musk has more technical sense to improve the process and structure, and considering there are rare companies outside having similar expertise to be outsourced, the situation sounds reasonable.

14.3.5 Portfolio Management

One of the important elements of R&D is portfolio management. Without portfolio management, it is not possible to take decision to prioritize the project. HDM is one important tool to portfolio management (Supply Chain Resource Cooperative 2016).

14.3.5.1 The HDM Model

A HDM model was created for Elon Musk's Transportation Projects which is adapted from Edwin's work to be published. The model was created using ETM HDM software tool. The detailed model, expert panel, and the data collection are described in this section. The model takes account of the technical, market, organizational, financial, and environmental/regulations dimension.

The **technical** dimension assesses:

- *Technical success*: Technical success means that technology works according to the specified design.
- *Existence of required competence*: What accessories are needed for a project or a technology, e.g., compact battery pack for Tesla.
- *Availability of resources*: It is important for a business to have enough resources to go for a project, for example, money and space. Or if they do not have money, they should have sufficient partners to run the business.
- Criteria for assessing the **market** dimension are *potential size of market*: potential size of market means potential revenues generated due to the project for a specific time.
- *Time to market*: Business should have an estimation how long it will take from product development to final product, and they must be sincere about this time frame.
- *Market risk*: Due to several factors or sometimes rejection by customers, an investment value could be decreased.

The **organizational** assessment includes:

- *Knowledge/skill availability*:

  Businesses need experience staff

- *Strategic fit*: Organizations need to match its resources and capabilities with external environment.
- *Available facilities*: For managing R&D, some facilities like space, tools, etc. are very important.

Financial assessment is carried using the following criteria:

- *NPV*: Business successful or failure is measured by it NPV.
- *Valued added of target products*: A product that adds value to the business and opens a new market.
- *Project cost*: How much money needs to be spent on the project.

Criteria for assessing **environment/regulation** include:

- *Economic regulation*: Application and enforcement of law by government for various purposes like protecting the environment, etc.
- *Environment policy*: Country-specific laws/policies and regulations business must meet.
- *Technical standard policy*: Any standards that the product must comply with, like emission requirements, speed limits, etc.

The assessment was done by an experts panel whose members have gained knowledge about HDM, Elon Musk, and the R&D process of those transportation project from the literature review and online research.

14.3.5.2 Data Analysis and Result

The technical dimension is the most important criteria with an overall weight of 0.24 followed by the market dimension with weight 0.22.

Inconsistency in each expert's judgment is within the <0.1 limit which is acceptable. Disagreement is defined as the way to identify generality among experts in pairwise comparison. A value near zero indicates that the experts are close to unity. Disagreement value is just 0.039 which gives a good indication that the experts' opinion about the decision was very close. Low values of both Inconsistency and disagreement highly support our model and illustrate its reliability. From the final result Tesla Inc. has higher mean value than other two transportation projects which indicates experts agreed that Elon Musk did a better job on Tesla Inc. than SpaceX and the Boring Company.

14.3.5.3 Sensitivity Analysis

After completing the HDM model, sensitivity analysis is done for all the experts based on all the five criteria. The ranking results were different depending on which criteria were weighted most heavily. Also, the calculations for the base values and the sensitivity analysis for all five criteria for Expert 4 are included in Appendix A.

- Expert 1's highest ranked company is Tesla based on the HDM model, but after the sensitivity analysis SpaceX got the highest ranking for criteria 2 and 5. All of the companies are equally ranked for criterion 3.

- Expert 2's highest ranked company is SpaceX, but after the sensitivity analysis Tesla got the highest ranking for criterion 1. All of the companies are equally ranked for criterion 3.
- Expert 3's highest ranked company is Tesla, but after the sensitivity analysis SpaceX got the highest ranking for criteria 1 and 5
- Expert 4's highest ranked company is Tesla, but after the sensitivity analysis, the Boring Company got the highest ranking for criteria 2 and 5, and SpaceX was ranked highest for criterion 4.

14.4 Conclusion

In this analysis, we examined the R&D management of three transportation projects headed by Elon Musk: Tesla Motor Company, SpaceX, and the Boring Company. R&D management entails a diverse set of concerns which include the strategies employed by company leadership, budgeting strategies, timeliness of projects relative to market events, as well as portfolio management. Under each of these categories, the expert panel who authored this analysis considered the countervailing factors.

For company leadership, the authors considered the benefits of Elon Musk's use of flat organizational structure and accessible management style across all three companies. For budgeting strategy, the authors considered the fitness of R&D budgeting and, focusing strictly on available quantitative data, found that SpaceX is the major preferred alternative in terms of budgeting prioritization. The authors discussed Musk's use of the time compression strategy across all three companies, finding that Musk's unique ability to bring the once inconceivable to market is crucial to his reputation and success. Innovation management concerns raised some interesting findings; our expert analysts found unique cost advantage opportunities available in partnership and outsourcing options. The individual findings of this report culminated in a portfolio management analysis using the HDM model (or hierarchical decision framework). Using the HDM framework, the team of experts provided an overarching cumulative analysis favoring Tesla as the major preferred innovation alternative.

While the research here is oriented toward crafting a research framework to formulate innovation strategies in dealing with the uncertainties of technology development, the authors maintain some hesitation in the strength of their conclusions at present due to the paucity of full company information. This predicament is underscored by the fact that two of the three companies under analysis (SpaceX and the Boring Company) are presently privately held companies and hence ambiguity remains over some relevant data points.

Acknowledgement Tugrul Daim and Dirk Meissner's contribution to this book chapter was prepared within the framework of the Basic Research Program at the National Research University Higher School of Economics.

Appendices

Appendix A: Sensitivity Analysis for Expert 4

Alternative	Alternative Project Title	Value
Alternative 1	Project 1	0.28
Alternative 2	Project 2	0.37
Alternative 3	Project 3	0.34

Base Value

Criteria		Sub-criteria		Alternatives		
	Value		Value		Relative Value	Relative Value rescpect to Mission
C1	0.21	SC 1	0.42	Alternative 1	0.32	0.0282
				Alternative 2	0.26	0.0229
				Alternative 3	0.42	0.0370
		SC2	0.21	Alternative 1	0.35	0.0154
				Alternative 2	0.29	0.0128
				Alternative 3	0.36	0.0159
		SC 3	0.37	Alternative 1	0.29	0.0225
				Alternative 2	0.5	0.0389
				Alternative 3	0.22	0.0171
C2	0.2	SC 4	0.27	Alternative 1	0.2	0.0108
				Alternative 2	0.49	0.0265
				Alternative 3	0.3	0.0162
		SC 5	0.36	Alternative 1	0.26	0.0187
				Alternative 2	0.29	0.0209
				Alternative 3	0.45	0.0324
		SC 6	0.38	Alternative 1	0.3	0.0228
				Alternative 2	0.25	0.0190
				Alternative 3	0.45	0.0342
C3	0.26	SC 7	0.31	Alternative 1	0.23	0.0185
				Alternative 2	0.43	0.0347
				Alternative 3	0.34	0.0274
		SC 8	0.29	Alternative 1	0.27	0.0204
				Alternative 2	0.38	0.0287
				Alternative 3	0.35	0.0264
		SC 9	0.4	Alternative 1	0.21	0.0218
				Alternative 2	0.51	0.0530
				Alternative 3	0.28	0.0291
C4	0.15	SC 10	0.33	Alternative 1	0.31	0.0153
				Alternative 2	0.48	0.0238
				Alternative 3	0.22	0.0109
		SC 11	0.36	Alternative 1	0.26	0.0140
				Alternative 2	0.41	0.0221
				Alternative 3	0.33	0.0178
		SC 12	0.31	Alternative 1	0.31	0.0144
				Alternative 2	0.47	0.0219
				Alternative 3	0.23	0.0107
C5	0.17	SC 13	0.33	Alternative 1	0.36	0.0202
				Alternative 2	0.26	0.0146
				Alternative 3	0.39	0.0219
		SC 14	0.29	Alternative 1	0.33	0.0163
				Alternative 2	0.33	0.0163
				Alternative 3	0.33	0.0163
		SC 15	0.38	Alternative 1	0.37	0.0239
				Alternative 2	0.21	0.0136
				Alternative 3	0.42	0.0271

Alternative	Alternative Project Title	Value
Alternative 1	Project 1	0.31
Alternative 2	Project 2	0.36
Alternative 3	Project 3	0.33

Criteria 1
Technical

Criteria		Sub-criteria		Alternatives		
	Value		Value		Relative Value	Relative Value rescpect to Mission
C1	0.96	SC 1	0.42	Alternative 1	0.32	0.1290
				Alternative 2	0.26	0.1048
				Alternative 3	0.42	0.1693
		SC2	0.21	Alternative 1	0.35	0.0706
				Alternative 2	0.29	0.0585
				Alternative 3	0.36	0.0726
		SC 3	0.37	Alternative 1	0.29	0.1030
				Alternative 2	0.5	0.1776
				Alternative 3	0.22	0.0781
C2	0.01	SC 4	0.27	Alternative 1	0.2	0.0005
				Alternative 2	0.49	0.0013
				Alternative 3	0.3	0.0008
		SC 5	0.36	Alternative 1	0.26	0.0009
				Alternative 2	0.29	0.0010
				Alternative 3	0.45	0.0016
		SC 6	0.38	Alternative 1	0.3	0.0011
				Alternative 2	0.25	0.0010
				Alternative 3	0.45	0.0017
C3	0.01	SC 7	0.31	Alternative 1	0.23	0.0007
				Alternative 2	0.43	0.0013
				Alternative 3	0.34	0.0011
		SC 8	0.29	Alternative 1	0.27	0.0008
				Alternative 2	0.38	0.0011
				Alternative 3	0.35	0.0010
		SC 9	0.4	Alternative 1	0.21	0.0008
				Alternative 2	0.51	0.0020
				Alternative 3	0.28	0.0011
C4	0.01	SC 10	0.33	Alternative 1	0.31	0.0010
				Alternative 2	0.48	0.0016
				Alternative 3	0.22	0.0007
		SC 11	0.36	Alternative 1	0.26	0.0009
				Alternative 2	0.41	0.0015
				Alternative 3	0.33	0.0012
		SC 12	0.31	Alternative 1	0.31	0.0010
				Alternative 2	0.47	0.0015
				Alternative 3	0.23	0.0007
C5	0.01	SC 13	0.33	Alternative 1	0.36	0.0012
				Alternative 2	0.26	0.0009
				Alternative 3	0.39	0.0013
		SC 14	0.29	Alternative 1	0.33	0.0010
				Alternative 2	0.33	0.0010
				Alternative 3	0.33	0.0010
		SC 15	0.38	Alternative 1	0.37	0.0014
				Alternative 2	0.21	0.0008
				Alternative 3	0.42	0.0016

Criteria 2
Market

Criteria	Value	Sub-criteria	Value	Alternatives	Relative Value	Relative Value rescpect to Mission
C1	0.01	SC 1	0.42	Alternative 1	0.32	0.0013
				Alternative 2	0.26	0.0011
				Alternative 3	0.42	0.0018
		SC2	0.21	Alternative 1	0.35	0.0007
				Alternative 2	0.29	0.0006
				Alternative 3	0.36	0.0008
		SC 3	0.37	Alternative 1	0.29	0.0011
				Alternative 2	0.5	0.0019
				Alternative 3	0.22	0.0008
C2	0.96	SC 4	0.27	Alternative 1	0.2	0.0518
				Alternative 2	0.49	0.1270
				Alternative 3	0.3	0.0778
		SC 5	0.36	Alternative 1	0.26	0.0899
				Alternative 2	0.29	0.1002
				Alternative 3	0.45	0.1555
		SC 6	0.38	Alternative 1	0.3	0.1094
				Alternative 2	0.25	0.0912
				Alternative 3	0.45	0.1642
C3	0.01	SC 7	0.31	Alternative 1	0.23	0.0007
				Alternative 2	0.43	0.0013
				Alternative 3	0.34	0.0011
		SC 8	0.29	Alternative 1	0.27	0.0008
				Alternative 2	0.38	0.0011
				Alternative 3	0.35	0.0010
		SC 9	0.4	Alternative 1	0.21	0.0008
				Alternative 2	0.51	0.0020
				Alternative 3	0.28	0.0011
C4	0.01	SC 10	0.33	Alternative 1	0.31	0.0010
				Alternative 2	0.48	0.0016
				Alternative 3	0.22	0.0007
		SC 11	0.36	Alternative 1	0.26	0.0009
				Alternative 2	0.41	0.0015
				Alternative 3	0.33	0.0012
		SC 12	0.31	Alternative 1	0.31	0.0010
				Alternative 2	0.47	0.0015
				Alternative 3	0.23	0.0007
C5	0.01	SC 13	0.33	Alternative 1	0.36	0.0012
				Alternative 2	0.26	0.0009
				Alternative 3	0.39	0.0013
		SC 14	0.29	Alternative 1	0.33	0.0010
				Alternative 2	0.33	0.0010
				Alternative 3	0.33	0.0010
		SC 15	0.38	Alternative 1	0.37	0.0014
				Alternative 2	0.21	0.0008
				Alternative 3	0.42	0.0016

Alternative	Alternative Project Title	Value
Alternative 1	Project 1	0.26
Alternative 2	Project 2	0.33
Alternative 3	Project 3	0.41

Criteria 3
Organizational

Alternative	Alternative Project Title	Value
Alternative 1	Project 1	0.24
Alternative 2	Project 2	0.44
Alternative 3	Project 3	0.32

Criteria		Sub-criteria		Alternatives		
	Value		Value		Relative Value	Relative Value rescpect to Mission
C1	0.01	SC 1	0.42	Alternative 1	0.32	0.0013
				Alternative 2	0.26	0.0011
				Alternative 3	0.42	0.0018
		SC2	0.21	Alternative 1	0.35	0.0007
				Alternative 2	0.29	0.0006
				Alternative 3	0.36	0.0008
		SC 3	0.37	Alternative 1	0.29	0.0011
				Alternative 2	0.5	0.0019
				Alternative 3	0.22	0.0008
C2	0.01	SC 4	0.27	Alternative 1	0.2	0.0005
				Alternative 2	0.49	0.0013
				Alternative 3	0.3	0.0008
		SC 5	0.36	Alternative 1	0.26	0.0009
				Alternative 2	0.29	0.0010
				Alternative 3	0.45	0.0016
		SC 6	0.38	Alternative 1	0.3	0.0011
				Alternative 2	0.25	0.0010
				Alternative 3	0.45	0.0017
C3	0.96	SC 7	0.31	Alternative 1	0.23	0.0684
				Alternative 2	0.43	0.1280
				Alternative 3	0.34	0.1012
		SC 8	0.29	Alternative 1	0.27	0.0752
				Alternative 2	0.38	0.1058
				Alternative 3	0.35	0.0974
		SC 9	0.4	Alternative 1	0.21	0.0806
				Alternative 2	0.51	0.1958
				Alternative 3	0.28	0.1075
C4	0.01	SC 10	0.33	Alternative 1	0.31	0.0010
				Alternative 2	0.48	0.0016
				Alternative 3	0.22	0.0007
		SC 11	0.36	Alternative 1	0.26	0.0009
				Alternative 2	0.41	0.0015
				Alternative 3	0.33	0.0012
		SC 12	0.31	Alternative 1	0.31	0.0010
				Alternative 2	0.47	0.0015
				Alternative 3	0.23	0.0007
C5	0.01	SC 13	0.33	Alternative 1	0.36	0.0012
				Alternative 2	0.26	0.0009
				Alternative 3	0.39	0.0013
		SC 14	0.29	Alternative 1	0.33	0.0010
				Alternative 2	0.33	0.0010
				Alternative 3	0.33	0.0010
		SC 15	0.38	Alternative 1	0.37	0.0014
				Alternative 2	0.21	0.0008
				Alternative 3	0.42	0.0016

Overal Importance of Alternatives with Respect to the Mission

Alternative	Alternative Project Title	Value
Alternative 1	Project 1	0.45
Alternative 2	Project 2	0.26
Alternative 3	Project 3	0.30

Criteria 4
Financial

Criteria		Sub-criteria		Alternatives		
	Value		Value		Relative Value	Relative Value rescpect to Mission
C1	0.01	SC 1	0.42	Alternative 1	0.32	0.0013
				Alternative 2	0.26	0.0011
				Alternative 3	0.42	0.0018
		SC2	0.21	Alternative 1	0.35	0.0007
				Alternative 2	0.29	0.0006
				Alternative 3	0.36	0.0008
		SC 3	0.37	Alternative 1	0.29	0.0011
				Alternative 2	0.5	0.0019
				Alternative 3	0.22	0.0008
C2	0.01	SC 4	0.27	Alternative 1	0.2	0.0005
				Alternative 2	0.49	0.0013
				Alternative 3	0.3	0.0008
		SC 5	0.36	Alternative 1	0.26	0.0009
				Alternative 2	0.29	0.0010
				Alternative 3	0.45	0.0016
		SC 6	0.38	Alternative 1	0.3	0.0011
				Alternative 2	0.25	0.0010
				Alternative 3	0.45	0.0017
C3	0.01	SC 7	0.31	Alternative 1	0.23	0.0007
				Alternative 2	0.43	0.0013
				Alternative 3	0.34	0.0011
		SC 8	0.29	Alternative 1	0.27	0.0008
				Alternative 2	0.38	0.0011
				Alternative 3	0.35	0.0010
		SC 9	0.4	Alternative 1	0.21	0.0008
				Alternative 2	0.51	0.0020
				Alternative 3	0.28	0.0011
C4	0.96	SC 10	0.33	Alternative 1	0.31	0.0982
				Alternative 2	0.48	0.1521
				Alternative 3	0.22	0.0697
		SC 11	0.36	Alternative 1	0.26	0.0899
				Alternative 2	0.41	0.1417
				Alternative 3	0.33	0.1140
		SC 12	0.31	Alternative 1	0.31	0.0923
				Alternative 2	0.47	0.1399
				Alternative 3	0.23	0.0684
C5	0.01	SC 13	0.33	Alternative 1	0.36	0.0012
				Alternative 2	0.26	0.0009
				Alternative 3	0.39	0.0013
		SC 14	0.29	Alternative 1	0.33	0.0010
				Alternative 2	0.33	0.0010
				Alternative 3	0.33	0.0010
		SC 15	0.38	Alternative 1	0.37	0.0014
				Alternative 2	0.21	0.0008
				Alternative 3	0.42	0.0016

Criteria 5
Enviornmental regulation

Criteria		Sub-criteria		Alternatives		
	Value		Value		Relative Value	Relative Value rescpect to Mission
C1	0.01	SC 1	0.42	Alternative 1	0.32	0.0013
				Alternative 2	0.26	0.0011
				Alternative 3	0.42	0.0018
		SC2	0.21	Alternative 1	0.35	0.0007
				Alternative 2	0.29	0.0006
				Alternative 3	0.36	0.0008
		SC 3	0.37	Alternative 1	0.29	0.0011
				Alternative 2	0.5	0.0019
				Alternative 3	0.22	0.0008
C2	0.01	SC 4	0.27	Alternative 1	0.2	0.0005
				Alternative 2	0.49	0.0013
				Alternative 3	0.3	0.0008
		SC 5	0.36	Alternative 1	0.26	0.0009
				Alternative 2	0.29	0.0010
				Alternative 3	0.45	0.0016
		SC 6	0.38	Alternative 1	0.3	0.0011
				Alternative 2	0.25	0.0010
				Alternative 3	0.45	0.0017
C3	0.01	SC 7	0.31	Alternative 1	0.23	0.0007
				Alternative 2	0.43	0.0013
				Alternative 3	0.34	0.0011
		SC 8	0.29	Alternative 1	0.27	0.0008
				Alternative 2	0.38	0.0011
				Alternative 3	0.35	0.0010
		SC 9	0.4	Alternative 1	0.21	0.0008
				Alternative 2	0.51	0.0020
				Alternative 3	0.28	0.0011
C4	0.01	SC 10	0.33	Alternative 1	0.31	0.0010
				Alternative 2	0.48	0.0016
				Alternative 3	0.22	0.0007
		SC 11	0.36	Alternative 1	0.26	0.0009
				Alternative 2	0.41	0.0015
				Alternative 3	0.33	0.0012
		SC 12	0.31	Alternative 1	0.31	0.0010
				Alternative 2	0.47	0.0015
				Alternative 3	0.23	0.0007
C5	0.96	SC 13	0.33	Alternative 1	0.36	0.1140
				Alternative 2	0.26	0.0824
				Alternative 3	0.39	0.1236
		SC 14	0.29	Alternative 1	0.33	0.0919
				Alternative 2	0.33	0.0919
				Alternative 3	0.33	0.0919
		SC 15	0.38	Alternative 1	0.37	0.1350
				Alternative 2	0.21	0.0766
				Alternative 3	0.42	0.1532

Alternative	Alternative Project Title	Value
Alternative 1	Project 1	0.35
Alternative 2	Project 2	0.27
Alternative 3	Project 3	0.38

References

SpaceXcmsadmin, "Falcon Heavy," SpaceX, 16-Nov-2012a. [Online]. Available: https://www.spacex.com/falcon-heavy. Accessed 13 Aug 2018.

Spacexcmsadmin, "Company," SpaceX, 28-Nov-2012b. [Online]. Available: https://www.spacex.com/about. Accessed 13 Aug 2018.

"The Secret Tesla Motors Master Plan (just between you and me)," Tesla, Inc, 29-Jun-2012. [Online]. Available: https://www.tesla.com/blog/secret-tesla-motors-master-plan-just-between-you-and-me. Accessed 13 Aug 2018.

Jones C, "La La Land has the world's worst traffic congestion," USA Today, 20-Feb-2017. [Online]. Available: https://www.usatoday.com/story/money/2017/02/20/los-angeles-new-york-and-san-francisco-most-congested-us-cities/98133702/. Accessed 13 Aug 2018.

"FAQ," The Boring Company. [Online]. Available: https://www.boringcompany.com/faq/. Accessed 13 Aug 2018.

Hans J (2009) Thamhain leadership lessons from managing technology-intensive teams. Int'l J of Innovation and Technology Management 6(2):117–133

"Top 10 in Leadership from Elon Musk," Predictive Success, 19-Oct-2017. [Online]. Available: https://www.predictivesuccess.com/blog/elon-musk-top-10-leadership-lessons/.

https://www.forbes.com/sites/quora/2017/11/08/i-worked-at-spacex-and-this-is-how-elon-musk-inspired-a-culture-of-top-performers/#321810af438f n.d.

Tesla Inc (2018) Form 10-K 2018. Retrieved from Mergent Online database. Winkler, Rolfe & Paztior Andy (2017, 13 January) Exclusive peek at SpaceX data shows loss in 2015, heavy expectations for nascent internet service. Wall Street Journal. Retrieved from https://www.wsj.com/articles/exclusive-peek-at-spacex-data-shows-loss-in-2015-heavy-expectations-for-nascent-internet-service-1484316455

Bloom M (2018, May 3) What every major Wall Street analyst had to say about Tesla's results, Musk's peculiar call. CNBC Investing. Retrieved from https://www.cnbc.com/2018/05/03/what-wall-street-thinks-of-teslas-quarterly-results-earnings-call.html

Crane L (2017) What billionaires are really doing in space. New Scientist 233(3116):25

Sheetz M (2018, 13 April) Latest SpaceX valuation shows 'an unlimited amount of funding' available in private markets, Equidate says. Retrieved from https://www.cnbc.com/2018/04/13/equidate-spacex-27-billion-valuation-shows-unlimited-Private-funding-available.html.

Nicoli A (2018, 18 June) Musk's The Boring Company just got less boring. The Street. Retrieved from https://www.thestreet.com/investing/the-boring-company-just-got-a-bit-less-boring-14625278.

CNBC (2018) Elon Musk's Boring Co. raises 113 million in venture capital funding. Retrieved from https://www.cnbc.com/video/2018/04/16/elon-musks-boring-co-raises-113-million-in-venture-capital-funding.html.

Parnell, Brid-Aine (2018, 22 June) SpaceX grabs $130M military contract after just one Falcon heavy test flight. Forbes Magazine. Retrieved from https://www.forbes.com/sites/bridaineparnell/2018/06/22/spacex-bags-130m-military-contract-after-just-one-falcon-heavy-test-flight/#3762dfde1e37

"Business timeliness: the intersections of strategy and operations management," n.d. *Emeraldinsight*. [Online]. Available: https://www.emeraldinsight.com/doi/full/10.1108/01443570410538131.

Muoio D "Elon Musk has ambitious plans for his tunneling company—here's what we know," *Business Insider*, 01-Nov-2017. [Online]. Available: https://www.businessinsider.com/elon-musk-boring-company-tunnels-facts-2017-8.

"Miles O'Brien," n.d. Polybius at The Clickto Network. [Online]. Available: https://web.archive.org/web/20170323235120/http://milesobrien.com/elon-musk-unedited/.

LaMonica M "Tesla Motors founders: Now there are five," CNET, 21-Sep-2009. [Online]. Available: https://www.cnet.com/news/tesla-motors-founders-now-there-are-five/.

Hawkins AJ "Elon Musk's new video of his underground tunnel project will make you nauseous," The Verge, 12-May-2017. [Online]. Available: https://www.theverge.com/2017/5/12/15629754/elon-musk-boring-company-tunnels-watch-first-route-la.

"Satellite Technology n.d.," TMCnet—World's Largest Communications and Technology Community. [Online]. Available: http://satellite.tmcnet.com/topics/satellite/articles/222324-spacex-plans-test-reusable-suborbital-vtvl-rocket-texas.htm.

Bryant C "Germany Wakes Up to Tesla and Elon Musk," Bloomberg.com, 14-Sep-2016. [Online]. Available: https://www.bloomberg.com/gadfly/articles/2016-09-14/tesla-too-tempting-for-germany.

"SpaceX: 10 Facts to Know," Time. n.d. [Online]. Available: http://time.com/space-x-ten-things-to-know/.

"Panasonic and Tesla Sign Agreement for the Gigafactory," Tesla, Inc, 06-Jan-2015. [Online]. Available: https://www.tesla.com/blog/panasonic-and-tesla-sign-agreement-gigafactory.

Tesla, Inc. n.d. [Online]. Available: https://www.tesla.com/destination-charging.

F. Lambert, Fred, and Electrek, "Elon Musk's Boring Company announces 'partnership' with LA Metro for its tunnel network under Los Angeles," Electrek, 18-May-2018. [Online]. Available: https://electrek.co/2018/05/17/elon-musk-boring-company-partnership-with-la-metro-tunnel-network-los-angeles/.

"Supply Chain Resource Cooperative," Supply Chain Resource Cooperative What is Supply Chain Management SCM Comments, 04-Apr-2016. [Online]. Available: https://scm.ncsu.edu/scm-articles/article/outsourcing-tesla-is-bucking-the-trend.

Chapter 15
Tesla Energy

Tina Matthews, Mrunal Hirve, Yuqian Pan, Dao Dang, Elia Rawar, and Tugrul U. Daim

15.1 Introduction

Solar energy is one of the clean and green energy sources that has received increasing popularity in recent years together with wind and to a lesser extent hydro. Till recently solar panels for power generation and lithium-ion batteries for storage were expensive and not easy to use or install. However, Tesla says the challenge is being addressed with a fleet of battery systems targeted at consumers, companies, and utilities. (Tesla Ventures Into Solar Power Storage for Home and Business. Cardwell, Diane 2015). Tesla's products for the solar storage market include rechargeable lithium-ion battery packs that can mount to a home garage and large battery blocks big enough to smooth out fluctuations in the grid (Tesla Ventures Into Solar Power Storage for Home and Business. Cardwell, Diane 2015). According to Tesla, they worked to build a world-class battery that would be a super-efficient and economical way to store power. It is just that most of the time they have installed the battery in vehicles (Tesla Ventures Into Solar Power Storage for Home and Business. Cardwell, Diane 2015).

With Tesla bringing out its latest products for solar energy storage, the future seems to look brighter for solar power. According to company sources (Battisti and Giulietti 2015), Tesla is not just an automotive company; it is an energy innovation company. Tesla Energy provides high-capacity installed batteries to store

T. Matthews · M. Hirve · Y. Pan · D. Dang · E. Rawar
Portland State University, Portland, OR, USA

T. U. Daim (✉)
Portland State University Technology Management Doctoral Program, Portland, OR, USA

National Research University Higher School of Economics, Moscow, Russia

Chaoyang University of Technology, Taichung City, Taiwan
e-mail: tugrul.u.daim@pdx.edu

T. U. Daim, D. Meissner (eds.), *Innovation Management in the Intelligent World*, Science, Technology and Innovation Studies,
https://doi.org/10.1007/978-3-030-58301-9_15

solar-generated power for later use. Tesla Energy is expanding its efforts to accelerate the transition from fossil fuels to a sustainable energy future with Tesla Energy. Tesla batteries make it possible to store sustainable and renewable energy in homes, businesses, and utilities.

However, whether solar energy has won the battle against alternative clean energy technologies and against fossil fuel remains to be seen (Battisti and Giulietti 2015).

15.2 Energy Market features

15.2.1 Energy Products

15.2.1.1 Powerwall

Tesla's battery storage system is not an innovation that is radically different from what is already on the market for energy storage (Battisti and Giulietti 2015). But, according to Elon Musk, it is not always the best technology that wins the innovation race, but it is often the one that best suits existing dominant technologies (Battisti and Giulietti 2015). The Powerwall is the battery on the market that provides an easy-to-use, easy-to-install solar energy storage solution, relatively inexpensive to maintain, and more attractive than existing home bat. Their first product is the Powerwall, a lithium-ion rechargeable battery designed to store residential energy for solar power generation load shifting, backup power, and self-consumption (Laposky 2015). The Powerwall consists of a lithium-ion battery pack from Tesla, a liquid thermal control system, and software that receives dispatch commands from a solar inverter. The unit mounts on a wall and is integrated with the local grid to harness excess power and provide flexibility for customers to extract energy from their own reserve (Laposky 2015).

The Powerwall provides power for household or business (Laposky 2015):

- The battery can provide its owner with financial savings by changing the load, i.e., charging during low-rate times when electricity demand is lower and discharging during higher-rate periods when the demand for electricity is higher.
- It can store excess solar energy that is not used at the time it is produced, but is used it later when the sun does not shine.
- It can be used as a backup power supply in the event of a power outage.
- It can be used to charge an electric vehicle from a Tesla owner, or any other electric vehicle.

The Powerwall is available in 10 kilowatt (kWh) hours, optimized for backup applications, and 7kWh, optimized for regular applications. Both can be connected to the solar system or the grid and both can provide backup power (Laposky 2015). The 10kWh Powerwall is configured when the grid goes down to provide backup. The 7kWh Powerwall can be used in daily cycling when combined with solar power to extend the solar energy's environmental and cost benefits into the night when sunlight is not available (Laposky 2015).

15.2.1.2 Powerpack

The Powerpack combines batteries, power electronics, thermal management, and controls into an easy-to-install turnkey solution for businesses and utilities (Tesla Powerpack 2018a). There are 16 individual battery pods in each Powerpack, each with an integrated DC-DC converter. Pod architecture and onboard power electronics optimize array-wide performance and make it easy to switch at any time (Tesla Powerpack 2018b). Powerpack features a new power module and electronics, and incorporation into several grid rates is more seamless. Powerpack fits a new inverter designed by Tesla and manufactured in Sparks, Nevada, at Gigafactory 1 (Tesla Powerpack 2018a). This inverter has the lowest market cost, the highest performance, and the highest utility-scale power density. The installation process of the entire Powerpack system is also significantly simplified by integrating a number of previously independent components into the inverter itself (Tesla Powerpack 2018a). A Tesla inverter can connect between one and 20 Powerpack systems, and larger systems can easily accommodate multiple inverters, allowing flexible system sizing and design for any project (Tesla Powerpack 2018a). Powerpack is the new standard for industrial and utility battery solutions, which can be scaled from 200 kWh to 100 + MWh.

Powerpack enables companies to gain greater control, efficiency, and reliability across the electrical grid to (Tesla Powerpack 2018a):

- Avoid peak demand charges
- Buy electricity when it is cheapest
- Participate in grid services
- Back up critical business operations in the event of a power outage
- Maximize consumption of on-site renewable power

15.2.1.3 Solar Roof

The Solar Roof is a complete roof that consists of extremely durable glass tiles uniquely engineered so that the photovoltaic cells are invisible (Tesla Powerpack 2018a). While the entire roof looks the same, customers can choose which sections of their roof will contain the hidden solar technology. The solar roofs provide homes, battery storage systems and the grid with renewable energy seamlessly, saving owners (Tesla Powerpack 2018a). According to Tesla, when paired with Powerwall, Solar Roof can power an entire home with 100% renewable energy (Tesla Powerpack 2018a).

15.2.1.4 Tesla Gigafactory

The Gigafactory was set up to provide sufficient batteries to support the projected demand of Tesla (Tesla Powerpack 2018a). At Gigafactory 1, battery production hit an annualized rate of approximately 20 GWh in mid-2018, making it the world's highest-volume battery plant (Tesla Powerpack 2018a). With the Gigafactory increasing production, Tesla's battery cell costs will decline substantially through economies of scale, creative manufacturing, waste reduction, and easy automation by bringing all manufacturing processes under one roof (Tesla Powerpack 2018a).

The Gigafactory manufactures a cell designed and engineered by Tesla/Panasonic called a "2170 cell," since the diameter is 21 mm in height x 70 mm. The cell offers the best performance metric optimization required for an EV at the lowest cost of production. The size also works well for other large battery packs, such as power devices from Tesla, Powerwall and Powerpack. In December 2016, production of 2170 qualification cells began and mass production began in January 2017. Today's cells coming off the line are used in the energy products of Model 3 and Tesla's Powerwall and Powerpack (Tesla Powerpack 2018a).

15.2.2 Product Strategy

Tesla's battery plan is to provide benefits to households and business customers who have already built solar panels and maybe own an electric vehicle from Tesla. It would allow storage of energy produced during the day for evening and early morning use (including vehicle charging) (Battisti and Giulietti 2015). This allows Tesla's batteries to be associated with an established technology (solar power) so that the two technologies begin to spread together and eventually become a new technical standard adopted by most households and businesses (Battisti and Giulietti 2015).

To support this strategy and encourage adoption, both companies have planned not only to work together but also to expand their activities to control costs and make their customers more affordable with solar energy (Battisti and Giulietti 2015). Tesla's $5b Nevada plant, together with Panasonic, and SolarCity revealed the same project for large-scale solar panel production in Buffalo County, New York. SolarCity imports heavily subsidized solar energy on the rooftop from China to help make the energy source more affordable. Despite the potential benefits provided by the complementarities and the interdependence of technology with solar power, the strategy of Tesla involves risks. The business may become critically dependent on solar power's successful growth, but is the bet worth solar power (Battisti and Giulietti 2015)?

Another strategy that Tesla plans to implement is to triple the volume of its energy deployments in 2018 compared to 2017 (Tesla Plans to Triple Energy Storage Deployments in 2018 2018). The company deployed 143 MW of energy storage projects in its fourth quarter, with a 100-MW energy storage project in South Australia. According to company sources, the South Australia project is already generating “substantial benefit” and has significantly increased the company’s Powerpack energy storage system (Tesla Plans to Triple Energy Storage Deployments in 2018 2018).

Tesla is also working with the Southern California Edison’s grid and completed a 20-MW energy storage system to ensure power storage reliability for the grid (Tesla Completes Energy Storage Project for Southern California Edison 2017). The battery storage system includes two 10-MW systems, each of which contain 198 Tesla Powerpacks and 24 inverters (Tesla Completes Energy Storage Project for Southern California Edison 2017). More projects like this will allow Tesla to be the preferred company for reliable power storage by public utility commissions in other states as well.

15.2.3 Market shift

15.2.3.1 From the Central Station Model to a Two-Way Electricity Flow Model

Lithium-ion batteries were out of reach due to high prices for many decades. But with the cost of these batteries now falling sharply, energy storage is becoming a viable solution for a variety of applications in the energy industry (Maloney 2017). The price of lithium-ion batteries fell from about $200 per watt-hour to about $0.40 per watt-hour between 1991 and 2005. The batteries in smartphones, cell phones, and electric vehicles have become omnipresent these days—pushing up demand and causing economies of scale. In a recent study, investment bank Lazard says it believes that over the next five years, the price of lithium-ion batteries will fall by about 50% (Maloney 2017).

The falling prices that led to energy storage growth and triggered a change in the electricity sector. The industry is moving away from the central station model that has existed for a century to a system where there are two types of flowing energy, where consumers can also produce. Customers with solar panels on the rooftop can sell excess electricity back to their utilities in many states (Maloney 2017).

Without having to build a large substation, battery storage could “end up distributing the solution” by strategically relieving stress at a variety of choke points, says Frank Jakob, senior project manager for renewable energy and energy storage at Black & Veatch (Maloney 2017). “Battery storage is to the traditional utility what Uber is to the taxi industry,” says Jakob. “If you don’t adapt, you will be left behind.” B&V is pursuing several requests for proposals in Arizona, California, and Nevada that seek large energy storage projects to defer more costly investments or to extend the capabilities of wind or solar projects (Maloney 2017).

15.2.4 Competition: Ovo Energy

Stephen Fitzpatrick—the founder and CEO of British energy company Ovo Energy—has a vision for the future of energy, where homes buy and sell energy when the demand (and price) is at its lowest, where cars do not just charge themselves, but also act as roaming batteries that store energy, and where all this is controlled by intelligent software that adjusts to your needs and even the weather (Smith 2018).

"When I think of the energy market of the future, really I think of a mesh of distributed energy assets, with each home at the centre of its own energy market," Fitzpatrick told Forbes (Smith 2018).

He unveiled three technologies which could turn that vision into a reality. The launch of Tesla's battery for solar energy storage kick-started a revolution in home energy storage. Fitzpatrick believes that Ovo can do even better, with its own new home energy storage system. He says, "As we move from centralized to distributed energy systems, each home must also become a kind of energy reservoir." The main difference between Ovo's battery and Tesla's is that Ovo's battery can work even for homes that do not have solar panels. Instead, the battery is smart enough to buy energy from the grid when it is cheapest during the daytime, which can then be used in the evening when prices rise. This smart buying and selling is all powered by VCharge, an intelligent energy "platform" which takes signals from the energy industry like supply, demand, and price, along with indicators of future supply and demand like the weather, to make energy decisions at a local level (Smith 2018). "You can see in 20 years time the energy market will be much more about software than power," he told Forbes.

The third technology is Ovo's "bidirectional" electric vehicle charger, which Ovo claims is one of the first in the world, which has been developed in partnership with Nissan (Smith 2018). This will allow Nissan Leaf owners to not just charge their cars but also sell energy back to the grid during peak times, which Ovo said could lead to savings of more than £250 ($354) a year.

15.2.5 Decentralizing Energy

Fitzpatrick believes, "Energy companies that specialize in the creation of very large centralized systems, managing the engineering of power stations and networks is shrinking. The reason is that solar, wind and geothermal energy doesn't have the same economies of scale that coal, gas and nuclear have—so the solar panel on your roof is just as effective as the panel on a solar farm." Fitzpatrick believes that energy giants should be panicking as they will soon be "displaced by new localized energy" unless they adapt to a more clean, green, local future. 4.5 Global Markets.

15.2.5.1 Virtual Power Plant in South Australia

Tesla Virtual Power Plant (VPP) in South Australia (SA) is the world's largest VPP providing 50,000 low-income homes with 250-MW/650-MWh of power (Tesla Virtual Power Plant Takes Shape in Australia, Darrell Proctor and Sonal Patel 2018). Each home would have a 5-kW solar panel system and a 13.5-kWh battery storage unit from Tesla Powerwall 2. The VPP is expected to ensure grid stability by shifting demand away from the larger grid during peak time (Tesla Virtual Power Plant Takes Shape in Australia, Darrell Proctor and Sonal Patel 2018). Tesla has said the VPP project would take about four years to complete. A solar panel and Powerwall 2 test installation on the first 1100 homes is expected to be completed by 2019. The project is designed to store in the Tesla batteries energy generated from the solar panels. Excess energy is transmitted to the grid and is available for use elsewhere in SA.

Residents are not charged for the equipment; that cost is covered by selling electricity to the grid. Tesla said installing the system in an additional 24,000 public housing units will be the next phase. Depending on the outcome of the trial phases, the company said it could make the system available to private homeowners as early as next year. Tesla said that the VPP could provide as much power as a gas-fired turbine or coal-fired power plant and solve the power outage problem (Tesla Virtual Power Plant Takes Shape in Australia, Darrell Proctor and Sonal Patel 2018). According to Tesla, "Powerwall can detect an outage, disconnect from the grid, and automatically restore power to your home in a fraction of a second. As long as the battery has storage in it at the time, you will not even notice the power went out." Government officials in SA have said the VPP can provide as much as 20% of the state's average daily power requirement (Tesla Virtual Power Plant Takes Shape in Australia, Darrell Proctor and Sonal Patel 2018).

15.2.5.2 India—Need for Solar Energy Storage

In India, the largest greenhouse gas emitter after the USA and China, renewable energy currently accounts for only 13% of India's total installed capacity of 2.75.912MW, or 36.471 megawatts (MW) (Bhaskar 2015). India's Prime Minister Narendra Modi is seeking Tesla's technology for long-term storage of solar. Since solar electricity can only be generated during daytime, the Indian premier is looking for an effective storage solution. India is suitable for generating solar power because the country receives 5–7 (kWh) solar radiation per circle for 300–330 days in a year. And with India announcing the most ambitious plan of solar power generation in the world, the real game-changer can be a cost-effective template for Indian conditions (Bhaskar 2015). Modi's government plans to add 100,000MW of solar power by 2022. Of these, 40,000MW each is planned from rooftop and distributed generation projects.

The only problem for India is the cost of storage. The cost of solar power in India is less than a dollar per kWh, but the price of the Tesla Powerwall to installers ($3500 for 10kWh and $3000 for 7kWh not including the inverter and installation costs) is way too high and causes concerns for countries like India.

15.2.6 Strategic Partners for Sales and Marketing

Tesla has a series of partners to help market the Powerwall or incorporate the product into their energy strategies (Laposky 2015). Some of them include:

Treehouse

TreeHouse is an enhancement shop for a green home. "I think it will be as common to have a battery in your home as having a water heater or a dishwasher in the near future," said Jason Ballard, co-founder and president of TreeHouse (Laposky 2015).

SolarEdge

SolarEdge, a global leader in the Photovoltaic (PV) inverter market, and Tesla have partnered with the global residential solar market to jointly develop a PV storage and backup power solution. Building on the proven DC optimized inverter from SolarEdge and the leading automotive grade battery technology from Tesla, the solution will require only one SolarEdge inverter to manage both PV and storage functions. The system is designed for effective outdoor deployment and provides remote monitoring and troubleshooting to maintain low running and maintenance costs (Laposky 2015).

Amazon

Amazon would test the energy storage batteries from Tesla for Amazon Web Services (Laposky 2015).

Target

Target will pilot a test to incorporate Tesla Energy storage as part of its energy strategy in selected stores. David Hughes, senior group manager, energy management says, "Tesla's cutting-edge technology offers unique benefits to powering these stores, most importantly relieving stress from the electrical grid at peak times, furthering Target's investment in designing and operating energy-efficient and sustainable buildings" (Laposky 2015).

Home Depot

Home Depot has partnered with Tesla and General Electric (GE) to help build solar facilities in 50 stores as its alternative energy portfolio continues to expand (Deagon 2017).

Home Depot said the project will reduce the demand for electricity grid in each solar-powered store by about one-third a year, equivalent to powering 2,300 average US homes a year. Six of the locations will also have Tesla Powerpacks to store energy and dispatch additional power as needed (Deagon 2017).

15.2.7 Musk's views on Tesla's future

In a recently published interview of Elon Musk (Eric Johnson, Nov 2, 2018) (Johnson 2018),

Musk says that he burnt out a bunch of neurons this year as running both SpaceX and Tesla was incredibly difficult. He said that Tesla has been fighting incredibly competitive car companies—Mercedes, Audi, BMW, Lexus, etc. And among all the American car companies, the only ones that have not gone bankrupt yet are Tesla and Ford (Johnson 2018).

It is monumentally difficult to make a car company profitable. There have been many attempts to create a car company and they have all failed, even those with a strong customer base, thousands of dealers, and thousands of service centers; they have already invested the money on the plants, like GM and Chrysler, in the last recession and all went bankrupt. It was hardly through the last recession that Ford and Tesla did. Ford's not making it in the next recession; there is a good chance. So it is much harder to be successful as a startup, a car company, than if you are an established, entrenched brand. Tesla is still alive, it is unbelievable (Johnson 2018).

Musk thinks transport electrification, and there is also an important part of Tesla that is solar and stationary batteries, because you need to generate electricity with solar in a standard, sustainable way and then store it at night when the sun goes down with batteries, and then use that energy from the sun to power cars. Without Tesla, this would still happen. A transition to sustainable energy would still take place, but it would take a lot longer. History will obviously judge this, but I would say 10 years, perhaps 20 years (Johnson 2018).

He thinks it is probably fair to say that Tesla has developed sustainable energy for at least five years, conservatively, and perhaps closer to 10 years, and then if we continue to make progress, we can drive it forward by 20 years. This could be the world's difference (Johnson 2018).

For the future of sustainable transport and energy generation, Tesla is extremely important. The fundamental purpose, Tesla's fundamental good, is to speed up the advent of sustainable transport and energy production (Johnson 2018).

The roof is integrated with the solar tile roof. You do not even realize that this is solar. And of course we have got the traditional solar retrofit, so we are working on, you know, continuously improving the retrofit solar aesthetics. Then we have the storage system for the Powerwall battery. We have the Powerpack, which is used on an industrial scale for utilities. On the stationary storage front, we will have some other exciting announcements. On the stationary storage side, we have a large product that I believe will be very compelling for utility customers (Johnson 2018).

15.2.8 Elon Musk as a CEO:

Musk's social media tweet in August 2018 about taking Tesla private, caused a huge fall of about 19% in Tesla's shares. Rumors are that Musk is overworked and falling short of his responsibilities as the CEO of the company. Tesla being a public company, corporate directors are the ultimate bosses. The stockholders empower them to oversee all aspects of operations, including management. If Tesla directors are concerned that Musk is spreading too thinly or putting his health at risk, then they have the power and responsibility to do something other than whisper to journalists (Ovide 2018). They can force Musk to step down, take a leave of absence, or delegate some responsibilities to other executives. According to Bloomberg (Ovide 2018), Tesla directors cannot and should not simply wring their hands about Musk and do nothing.

Tesla and Musk are so closely intertwined that Musk is both the reason for Tesla's success and the source of its possible failure. This puts everyone involved in the company in a difficult spot. Belief in Musk has been the primary reason for Tesla's rich market valuation and support from stock and debt holders despite years of cash burn and missed production targets that have attracted the attention of securities regulators (Ovide 2018). His company's confidence in Musk and trust are so connected that any attempt to put guardrails on Musk seems to jeopardize Tesla's valuation. And the value of the company is the basis for Tesla's ability to secure the cash it needs to remain in operation and meet the aspirations of Musk (Ovide 2018).

15.3 SWOT and PESTLE Analysis

A SWOT (strengths, weaknesses, opportunities, and threats) analysis can help to identify and understand key issues affecting your business. PESTLE analysis is also a concept in the principles of marketing. Companies use this concept as a tool to track the environment in which they operate or plan to launch a new project/product/service, etc.

To evaluate Tesla's venture in energy business, we have performed SWOT and PESTLE analysis (Kissinger 2018a), (Kissinger 2018b).

15.3.1 Analysis

15.3.1.1 SWOT Analysis

Tesla's Strengths (Internal Strategic Factors)

Tesla's strong brand can support strategic expansion in the global market. Tesla has strengths and capabilities of the business as a competitive player in the renewable industry as:

1. Highly innovative processes
2. Strong brand
3. Strong control on production processes

Tesla Inc. is known for its high rate of innovation, especially in introducing the world's first fully developed products using renewable source of energy and also electric cars. This internal strategic factor is a strength that empowers the company to develop competitive and profitable products.

The internal element of strong control over production processes is focused on vertical integration and centralization and hierarchy in the organizational structure of Tesla. For example, the company manufactures many of their product's components. This factor is a strength that minimizes issues linked to the involvement of third parties.

Tesla's Weaknesses (Internal Strategic Factors)

Despite its strong brand as a manufacturer of electric vehicles and energy products, Tesla Inc.'s performance and potential future growth suffer from the following major weaknesses:

1. Limited market presence
2. Limited supply chain
3. High prices

Tesla has a small presence on the market. For example, in the USA, the company produces most of its profits and has a small presence in China and the developing world. This internal strategic element is a vulnerability that restricts business growth based on overseas markets' rapid economic development. Moreover, Tesla's products are relatively more expensive. The high prices prevent the company from rapidly growing its customer base and market share.

Opportunities for Tesla Inc. (External Strategic Factors)

Tesla Inc. has major opportunities to improve its financial standing and competitiveness in energy markets, as follows:

1. Global sales expansion
2. Global supply chain expansion
3. Business diversification

Tesla needs to consider the opportunity for global sales expansion in relation to its weaknesses. This opportunity is based on the significant economic growth of countries where the company's market presence is insignificant. For example, by expanding the Asian renewable energy markets, the company can increase its revenues. Also, through diversification, the company can improve its performance. This external strategic consideration includes setting up or acquiring new companies to reduce the automotive market's exposure to risk. This element of the SWOT study by Tesla points to the benefits of international expansion.

Threats Facing Tesla Inc. (External Strategic Factors)

While Tesla's company has shown considerable profitability, the following challenges must be addressed to sustain resilience despite changing conditions in the energy industry:

1. Aggressive competition
2. Fluctuations in material prices
3. Dealership regulations

In this SWOT analysis, the volatility within commodity prices is another hazard. In particular, this external factor illustrates the fluctuating and increasingly rising cost of lithium, a component used in the energy storage products of the business. The organization is also facing the threat of restrictions on the dealership. Currently, Tesla sells its products directly to customers without involvement in the dealership, which increases prices for sales. Many states like Virginia and Texas, however, forbid direct sales of the goods of the company, forcing those sales to go through dealerships.

15.3.1.2 PESTLE Analysis

Political Factors Affecting Tesla's Business

The following political external factors are important for Tesla and the automotive and energy solutions industries in this case of external analysis:

1. Governmental incentives for energy products(opportunity)
2. New global trade agreements (opportunity)
3. Political stability in the majority of major markets (opportunity)

Tesla Inc. has the ability, through government incentives, to improve its financial performance. This external consideration is directly related to the company's activities and goods' reduced carbon emissions. Major markets' political stability makes the remote or macro-environment favorable to Tesla's generic competitive strategy and intensive strategies for growth, including market penetration.

Economic Factors

The growth rate of the solar energy market determines the growth opportunities of the solar panel business of the company. Tesla needs to address the following external economic factors affecting the automotive market:

1. Decreasing battery costs (opportunity)
2. Decreasing renewable energy costs (opportunity)
3. Economic stability issues (threat)

The quality of Tesla's business benefits from lower battery costs. This external factor, for instance, translates into the quality of the electric car products of the business. When renewable energy solutions become more popular, the company is growing. Economic stability issues, however, threaten the financial performance of the company, particularly in Europe and Asia.

Social/Sociocultural Factors Influencing Tesla Inc.'s Business Environment

Tesla Inc. Research examines how the product aligns with its target markets' social trends. Managers of the company must ensure the application of strategies to maximize the business benefits of such external factors. In Tesla's business, the external sociocultural factors are as follows:

1. Increasingly popularity of low-carbon lifestyles (opportunity)
2. Increasing preference for renewable energy (opportunity)
3. Improving wealth distribution in developing markets (opportunity)

Tesla Inc. has growth opportunities based on the growing popularity of low-carbon lifestyles and rising preference for renewable energy. Moreover, Tesla has an opportunity to improve its financial performance based on the growing distribution of wealth in developing markets. This change in wealth distribution raises the population of the relatively expensive goods of the company's potential buyers.

Technological Factors

The development of the automotive and energy solutions business of Tesla depends on the technologies available. For example, the technology of materials engineering determines the efficiency and cost efficiency of the batteries of the company. The following external technological factors are important in the automotive business of Tesla Inc.:

1. High rate of technological change (opportunity and threat)
2. Increasing automation in business (opportunity)
3. Increasing popularity of online mobile systems (opportunity)

The high rate is an incentive for Tesla to develop the quality of its goods. However, in terms of the potential rapid obsolescence of technologies used in its products, the same external factor threatens the company. However, in this case of PESTEL/PESTLE analysis, increasing business automation is a trend that creates opportunities. For example, by further automating its business processes, Tesla has growth opportunities. Therefore, the growing popularity of digital mobile systems will prompt the company to incorporate such systems increasingly into its automobiles. As shown in this part of Tesla Inc.'s PESTEL/PESTLE analysis, the technological condition of the remote or macro-environment highlights opportunities for growth based on technological enhancement.

Legal Factors

Management decisions and business development are influenced by laws and legal structures. Under legal constraints, Tesla's advertising mix or 4P is enforced. The management of human resources and business partnerships of the organization are also subject to legal restrictions. In this situation, Tesla Inc. must include the following legal external factors in business strategies:

1. Expanding international patent protection (opportunity)
2. Energy consumption regulations (opportunity)
3. Dealership sales regulation in the USA (opportunity and threat)

Tesla has opportunities to expand its business overseas safely, taking into account the expansion of international patent protection. The business also has a chance to grow through direct sales, which is permitted in many US states. However, based on Tesla Inc.'s SWOT analysis, this external factor is also a threat, as other states do not allow direct sales and require dealerships to deal with market customers.

Ecological/Environmental Factors

In this case, the following ecological external factors affect Tesla's market:

1. Climate change (opportunity)
2. Expanding environmental programs (opportunity)
3. Rising standards on waste disposal (opportunity)

Ecological considerations are important factors in the industrial environment of Tesla Inc. The company, for instance, has opportunities to market its energy products based on climate change issues, growing sustainability policies, and increasing waste disposal standards. The electric vehicles, batteries, and solar panels of the company are considered suitable for dealing directly with these external factors related to business sustainability and environmentally friendly products.

15.4 Findings

Tesla identified the need to generate and store power through solar panels in a standard, sustainable manner by taking control of energy with solar and storage in order to tackle the alarming ecological conditions caused by the mass use of nonrenewable energy. In order to create world a better place, Tesla started its venture in energy sector which was much appreciated.

Tesla Inc. has always succeeded as an innovative automotive and energy solutions business and has the strengths needed to maintain profitability in the long term. Tesla's long-term competitive advantage will not be the car; it will be the factory. The positive outlook holds despite challenges in expanding the business. Elon

Musk's leadership and popularity are among the factors behind this performance. The company is also able to improve its operations on the global market by tackling the competitive landscape found in Tesla Inc's Porter's Five Forces report. Furthermore, the company needs to evolve constantly to take into account the patterns shown in this PESTEL/PESTLE analysis. All companies in the automotive, battery/ energy storage, and energy generation industries are affected by these trends. The firm must therefore also consider its market position compared to other car manufacturers and suppliers of energy solutions.

SWOT and PESTEL/PESTLE analysis of Tesla Inc. shows that there are a variety of opportunities that facilitate further growth of the business in the energy sector. Free trade agreements, for example, promote international expansion.

Tesla aims to be a sustainable energy powerhouse with a new energy paradigm and wants to create a self-dependent ecosystem of products. Therefore, it is recommended that the organization extend its activities internationally. It is also recommended that the company increase its marketing aggressiveness, especially in countries other than the USA, to increase its market share. This move could reduce market-based risk in view of Tesla having limited sales operations in overseas markets and increasing the current business ROI. Tesla already has two Gigafactories: Gigafactory-I in Reno, NV (batteries), and Gigafactory-II in Buffalo, NY (solar panels).

The Gigafactory-I began production of battery cells in 2017. Ultimately, it will produce enough batteries to power 500,000 cars a year. In the meantime, Tesla's SolarCity subsidiary runs the second plant, manufacturing solar photovoltaic modules and solar shingles for Tesla's solar roof brand.

Tesla is planning for "probably four" and more battery Gigafactory in locations that would "address a global market," including one in Europe and Shanghai in China as estimated battery demands will be increasing by 2025 (Jeff Desjardins 2018).

Besides being known as the leading electric vehicle manufacturing company with innovative technologies and autonomous vehicles, Tesla has been making progress on becoming one of the largest energy companies generating and storing solar energy. Building the Gigafactory that produces batteries and solar panels is a huge step for Tesla to jump into the sustainable energy market. With the goal of making solar power affordable and easily available for homes and business, Tesla is aiming to become the largest and most innovative company for sustainable energy.

Acknowledgement Tugrul Daim's contribution to this book chapter was prepared within the framework of the Basic Research Program at the National Research University Higher School of Economics.

References

Battisti G, Giulietti M (2015) Tesla Is Betting on Solar, Not Just Batteries. Harvard Business Review Digital Articles, 2–4. Retrieved on 11-20-2018 from http://stats.lib.pdx.edu/proxy.php?url=http://search.ebscohost.com/login.aspx?direct=true&db=buh&AN=118667139&site=ehost-live.

Bhaskar U (2015, September 21) Modi may seek solar battery fix at Tesla. Retrieved on 11-20-2018 from https://www.livemint.com/Industry/JHwNSXB9fR9uGLkFOTYmoK/Narendra-Modi-may-seek-the-solar-battery-fix-at-Tesla.html

Deagon B (2017, August 17) Home Depot Taps Tesla, GE For Solar-Power Expansion. Investors Business Daily, p. 17. Retrieved on 11-20-2018 from http://stats.lib.pdx.edu/proxy.php?url=http://search.ebscohost.com/login.aspx?direct=true&db=buh&AN=124666598&site=ehost-live

Douris C (2017, October 25) The Bottom Line On Electric Cars: They're Cheaper To Own. Retrieved from https://www.forbes.com/sites/constancedouris/2017/10/24/the-bottom-line-on-electric-cars-theyre-cheaper-to-own/#523c624b10b6

EDIT9 (2016, March) Green Energy Can't Compete With $30 Oil. Investors Business Daily, p. 1. Retrieved on 11-20-2018 from http://stats.lib.pdx.edu/proxy.php?url=http://search.ebscohost.com/login.aspx?direct=true&db=buh&AN=113430131&site=ehost-live

Gara A (2016) Elon Musk Deserves Some Leeway As Tesla Stalks Vertical Integration With SolarCity. Forbes.Com, 1. Retrieved on 11-20-2018 from http://stats.lib.pdx.edu/proxy.php?url=http://search.ebscohost.com/login.aspx?direct=true&db=buh&AN=116349294&site=ehost-live

Kissinger D (2018a, September 12) Tesla Inc. SWOT Analysis & Recommendations. Retrieved from http://panmore.com/tesla-motors-inc-swot-analysis-recommendations

Kissinger D (2018b, June 25) Tesla, Inc. PESTEL/PESTLE Analysis & Recommendations. Retrieved on 11-20-2018 from http://panmore.com/tesla-motors-inc-pestel-pestle-analysis-recommendations

Johnson E (2018, November 02) Full Q&A: Tesla and SpaceX CEO Elon Musk on Recode Decode. Retrieved on 11-20-2018 from https://www.recode.net/2018/11/2/18053428/recode-decode-full-podcast-transcript-elon-musk-tesla-spacex-boring-company-kara-swisher

Lambert, F., Fred, & Electrek. (2018, September 07). Elon Musk hints at a 'Tesla Smart Home' with more efficient air conditioning. Retrieved on 11-20-2018 from https://electrek.co/2018/09/07/tesla-smart-home-elon-musk-efficient-air-conditioning/

Laposky J (2015) Tesla Looks To Disrupt The Home Energy Biz. TWICE: This Week in Consumer Electronics, 30(10), 61. Retrieved on 11-20-2018 from http://stats.lib.pdx.edu/proxy.php?url=http://search.ebscohost.com/login.aspx?direct=true&db=buh&AN=102753362&site=ehost-live

Maloney P (2017) Power Banks Shift Energy Industry. ENR: Engineering News-Record, 6–7. Retrieved on 11-20-2018 from http://stats.lib.pdx.edu/proxy.php?url=http://search.ebscohost.com/login.aspx?direct=true&db=buh&AN=124399307&site=ehost-live

Ovide S (2018, August 17) Even Elon Musk Seems to Be Pleading for Tesla's Board to Act. Retrieved on 11-20-2018 from https://www.bloomberg.com/opinion/articles/2018-08-17/elon-musk-tesla-interview-even-he-seems-to-want-the-board-to-act

Patel S (2018) Tesla Bet and Delivered 100-MW/129-MWh Energy Storage System Within 100 Days. Power, 162(1), 12–13. Retrieved on 11-20-2018 from http://stats.lib.pdx.edu/proxy.php?url=http://search.ebscohost.com/login.aspx?direct=true&db=aph&AN=127065144&site=ehost-live

Proctor D, Patel S (2018) Tesla Virtual Power Plant Takes Shape in Australia. Power, 10. Retrieved on 11-20-2018 from http://stats.lib.pdx.edu/proxy.php?url=http://search.ebscohost.com/login.aspx?direct=true&db=buh&AN=131464331&site=ehost-live

Roth R (2018) Solar Panel Installation in the US. IBISWorld Industry Report OD4494. Retrieved on 11-20-2018 from IBISWorld database.http://clients1.ibisworld.com/reports/us/industry/default.aspx?entid=4494

Smith O (2018) Britain's Ovo Is Taking On Tesla To Forge The Future Of Energy. Forbes.Com, 1. Retrieved on 11-20-2018 from http://stats.lib.pdx.edu/proxy.php?url=http://search.ebscohost.com/login.aspx?direct=true&db=buh&AN=129187601&site=ehost-live

Tesla Completes Energy Storage Project for Southern California Edison. (2017). Power Engineering, 121(3), 10. Retrieved on 11-20-2018 from http://stats.lib.pdx.edu/proxy.php?url=http://search.ebscohost.com/login.aspx?direct=true&db=aph&AN=121696734&site=ehost-live

Tesla Plans to Triple Energy Storage Deployments in 2018. (2018). Power Engineering, 122(3), 56. Retrieved on 11-20-2018 from http://stats.lib.pdx.edu/proxy.php?url=http://search.ebscohost.com/login.aspx?direct=true&db=aph&AN=128570678&site=ehost-live

Tesla Ventures Into Solar Power Storage for Home and Business. Cardwell, Diane, (2015, May 05). Retreived on 11-20-2018 from https://www.nytimes.com/2015/05/01/business/energy-environment/with-new-factory-tesla-ventures-into-solar-power-storage-for-home-and-business.html

Tesla Powerpack, Retrieved on 11-25-2018a from https://www.tesla.com/presskit

Tesla Powerpack, Retrieved on 11-25-2018b from https://www.tesla.com/powerpack

Tesla Motors, Inc (2015, March 12). from https://hbr.org/product/tesla-motors-inc/MH0032-PDF-ENG

Tesla Virtual Power Plant Takes Shape in Australia, Darrell Proctor and Sonal Patel. Retrieved on 11-20-2018 from PSU Library online http://web.b.ebscohost.com.proxy.lib.pdx.edu/ehost/detail/detail?vid=3&sid=e3089abf-3c48-451f-b43e-8f5e5170d661%40pdc-v-sessmgr05&bdata=JnNpdGU9ZWhvc3QtbGl2ZQ%3d%3d#AN=131464331&db=aph

Jeff Desjardins (April 28, 2018) Here's what the future of Tesla could look like https://www.businessinsider.com/heres-what-the-future-of-tesla-could-look-like-2018-4?r=UK&IR=T

The Bottom Line On Electric Cars: They're Cheaper To Own, Constance Douris, Retrieved on 11-20-2018 from https://www.forbes.com/sites/constancedouris/2017/10/24/the-bottom-line-on-electric-cars-theyre-cheaper-to-own/#713a1a5710b6

Chapter 16
Future of Transportation: Hyperloop

Aayushi Gupta, Alex Tacco Melendez, Anju Babu, Catalina Reyes, Lipishree Vrushabhendra, and Tugrul U. Daim

16.1 Introduction

The current transportation and transit systems in the USA are reaching a critical focal point in its major urban areas. Carbon emissions, congestion, traffic mortality, and aging infrastructure are just a few of the problems that need to be urgently addressed by creating a sustainable system that integrates all transport modes to meet the economic and environmental mobility needs of today and tomorrow.

It has been 100 years since the last disruptive change in the transportation industry happened. According to Inrix statistics research, we are having a major problem with traffic congestion, the number of cars on the streets keeps increasing and the chaos on the roads is getting worse every year. This Inrix research, published by Forbes Statista (McCarthy and Richter 2018), shows how only in one year, 2017, people in Los Angeles spent 102 h stuck in traffic, almost 4 days and a half just waiting in the car. A critical problem that does not seem to have a clear solution.

The inability for people to use a transportation method that allows them to reach long distances faster is one of the weaknesses of our current transportation modes. Germany, France, and Japan are trying to find ways to make their trains travel faster. However, they have been fighting the problem of friction for decades. Rolling and air resistance are the two major components they have not been able to fix.

A. Gupta · A. T. Melendez · A. Babu · C. Reyes · L. Vrushabhendra
Portland State University, Portland, OR, USA

T. U. Daim (✉)
Portland State University Technology Management Doctoral Program, Portland, OR, USA

National Research University Higher School of Economics, Moscow, Russia

Chaoyang University of Technology, Taichung City, Taiwan
e-mail: tugrul.u.daim@pdx.edu

T. U. Daim, D. Meissner (eds.), *Innovation Management in the Intelligent World*, Science, Technology and Innovation Studies,
https://doi.org/10.1007/978-3-030-58301-9_16

Safety is another component we need to mention. We often see cars, trains, trucks, ships, and planes' accidents. According to the National Transportation Safety Board, 39,339 people died in 2016 in a transportation accident (CO_2 and other greenhouse gas emissions n.d.). The question here is; Could a new transportation mode help to decrease this number?

The last two components to mention are the increasing amount of carbon footprint emissions and the lack of transportation modes using sustainable energy sources. The emissions of CO_2 have never stopped increasing, there are some countries that contribute more than others, as well as other industries. This is a major global problem that now is taking the attention of the majority of people, most of them with intentions to help to solve this issue by proposing disruptive solutions. One of them, the Hyperloop model. In this paper, we are analyzing the implementation of the Hyperloop system which is the fifth mode of transportation after air, rail, road, and water. As a brief description, the Hyperloop is a steel construction medium vacuum pressure tube that accelerates capsules through the tube at up to 760 mph on proposed air bearings. It is meant to be propelled by solar power in a low-pressure environment.

16.2 Current Hyperloop Industry

The Hyperloop industry is a burgeoning one with whole new possibilities when it comes to the development, implementation, and technology of the system. The complexity of the technology and implementation requires close coordination between the different parties at work. In the end, the purpose is to develop an entire ecosystem that provides an alternate transport option to the passenger or end customer.

The first Hyperloop system is scheduled to be deployed in 2022. In the first year of deployment, it is expected to generate a revenue of US$1.35 bn. This is expected to grow at a compounded annual growth rate (CAGR) of 47.2% for the next 4 years and reach US$6.34 bn. by 2026.

16.2.1 Major Players

16.2.1.1 SpaceX

The first proponent of Hyperloop as an idea was SpaceX CEO, Elon Musk. He envisioned this as the fifth and most efficient mode of transportation. He came up with a proposal for Hyperloop that detailed the technology, implementation, and business model. The idea and research results were made open to all so that developments could happen fast. They built Hyperloop system of approximately

1-mile length and 6-foot diameter in California. SpaceX conducts Hyperloop Pod Competition to encourage functional prototype development and student innovation.

16.2.1.2 Virgin Hyperloop One

Virgin Hyperloop One is the company in focus for the project. The details of the company are given in the "Company in Focus" section.

16.2.1.3 Hyperloop Transportation Technologies (HTT)

HTT is a crowdfunded company in collaboration with investing platform JumpStartFund. HTT has conducted feasibility studies in different countries across the globe, viz., Austria, Slovakia, Hungary, France, and India. Recently, they signed an agreement to conduct a feasibility study for a route between Cleveland and Chicago.

16.2.1.4 Others

Apart from these major players, there are other companies such as TransPod, DGWHyperloop, Arrivo, Hardt Global Mobility, and Hyper Chariot.

Considering the complexity and high capital investments required for the project, it is possible that no one company, but partnerships will thrive better in the design and implementation of Hyperloop as an alternate mode of transport.

16.2.2 Hyperloop One

Hyperloop One Technologies, Inc., started in a Los Feliz neighborhood garage in Los Angeles. Co-founders Josh Giegel and Shervin Pishevar presented the first components of the Hyperloop project and initial business model on a whiteboard. The company changed its name to Hyperloop One to underscore its status as the first and only company building a full-system Hyperloop. Hyperloop One went on to establish an Innovation Campus in LA's downtown arts district. Shervin recruited Rob Lloyd, former president of Cisco Systems, to join the company as CEO. Rob Lloyd's goal is "To make Hyperloop three times more effective than any other transportation technology on the ground today."

Brent Callinicos, former Uber CFO, joined as CFO and COO in October 2016. The Hyperloop One team is mainly comprised of the world's leading experts in engineering, technology, and transport project delivery, who are working in tandem with global partners and investors. The total financing raised by Hyperloop One until now ever since its founding in 2014 is $245 million.

The company's vision is "Reinventing transportation by developing the world's first Hyperloop, integrated structure to move passengers & cargo between two points immediately, safely, efficiently and sustainably."

Hyperloop One used an effective strategy to involve people's view with the technological advancements, by organizing *Global Hyperloop One Challenge*. This challenge started with a call for ambitious proposals to create Hyperloop networks that link cities and regions around the world in May 2016. More than 2600 teams registered, and it was then narrowed down as the semifinalists to the 35 strongest proposals. The Challenge attracted wide support from members of government and spawned bold ideas from some of the most imaginative businesses, designers, and urban planners in the world. The final analysis was challenging but they chose the ten routes as Global Challenge winners along with their group of expert judges.

These routes encompass the USA, the UK, Mexico, India, and Canada. As a direct outcome of the Global Challenge, Hyperloop One and the Colorado Department of Transportation, supported by AECOM, entered into a public–private partnership that will begin a feasibility study in Colorado.

16.3 PESTEL Analysis

A PESTEL analysis is a framework used to analyze and monitor the macro-environmental factors that have an impact on an organization. PESTEL analysis has two basic functions (Developing multi criteria decision making model in... n.d.). The first is that it allows identification of the environment within which the company operates. The second basic function is that it provides data and information that will enable the company to predict situations and circumstances that it might encounter in the future (Developing multi criteria decision making model in... n.d.). PESTEL analysis is therefore a precondition analysis, which should be utilized in strategic management.

PESTEL stands for the following factors (J n.d.).

- P—Political
  What is the political situation of the country and how can it affect the industry.
- E—Economic
  What are the prevalent economic factors.
- S—Social
  How much importance does culture have in the market and what are its determinants.
- T—Technological
  What technological innovations are likely to affect the industry and market structure.
- E—Environmental
  What are the environmental concerns for the industry.

- L—Legal

  Are there any current legislations that regulate the industry or can there be any change in the legislations for the industry.

16.3.1 Political

16.3.1.1 Drivers

The technology roadmap and the PESTEL analysis have been integrated to identify the political factors that could be the market drivers for Hyperloop.

One of the most important political factors that could help drive the market is that Hyperloop is a vision to improve transportation and national security. This is due to the economic stability and national security advantages that Hyperloop promises in this age of twenty-first century. A rapid transport of goods and services is accomplished through Hyperloop that will strengthen supply chain networks and complex interconnected critical infrastructure sectors that thrive on speedy conveyances and systemic resilience. Hyperloop also provides a strategic advantage as it offers the ability to move resources, people, medical supplies, and sensitive material to key locations in minutes versus hours, and hours versus days.

Therefore, all the aforementioned factors constitute together in sustaining local and regional economies. And this could happen even in the face of natural or man-made disasters. But according to the popular daily Baltimore, this technology can only be translated into the above improvements when a consensus among political leaders and all the Hyperloop companies is achieved. Therefore, this is one of the most important issues that needs to be addressed at the earliest.

Currently, Hyperloop One has managed to initiate the process of negotiation and discussion in proposing the following routes.

1. Dubai–Abu Dhabi

   Hyperloop One has received support received from the Dubai Roads and Transport Authority (RTA) and therefore unveiled the initial design of the Dubai Hyperloop Pod as part of UAE Innovation month. This is the phase 1 of their entire project and they are now working on Phase 2 toward exploring the evaluation and development of a wider Hyperloop network in the UAE.

2. Mumbai–Pune

   Hyperloop One their intent to build first Hyperloop route in India and have signed a historic agreement with the Indian State of Maharashtra.

3. Los Angeles–Las Vegas

   The company plans to have the Hyperloop built to connect LA and Las Vegas. The team is led by Steve Hill, executive director of the Governor's Office of Economic Development and this also includes support from the state's Department of Transportation. The 454-mile system would carry freight and passengers and run along I-11.

16.3.1.2 Gaps

However, there are gaps identified in the roadmap of the development of Hyperloop wherein out of the 11 routes proposed in the USA from the Global Challenge, three routes have to be finalized. And to finalize these three routes all the states, cities, and municipalities involved should arrive at a consensus. As the northeast Hyperloop will pass-through city centers, tunneling is required under places where lots of people live and work. Therefore, as discussed earlier a consensus of finalizing the three routes in the USA has to be achieved. But it could be speculated that this consensus is going to take a long time. This is because, infrastructure projects have often slowly progressed and such examples are (Building infrastructure for Hyperloop doesn't work like that n.d.):

Eg.1. New York and New Jersey have struggled for over 20 years to reach an agreement to build a single tunnel under the Hudson River.

Eg.2. California is still working to acquire all the land it needs for the first part of its high-speed rail project. This project started building in 2015, yet the land required for the rail project to begin is not allotted.

Therefore politically, the gap in the roadmap of the Hyperloop development in the USA is that the process to reach a political consensus among all bodies related to this infrastructure project might take a longer time that may result in Hyperloop being far from reality.

16.3.2 Economic

16.3.2.1 Energy Consumption and Aging Infrastructure

Petroleum-based fuels account for 97% of the transportation energy consumed in the USA, making this sector vulnerable to potential world supply disruptions (Environmental Protection Agency 2018). A shortage of oil supply would cause barrel prices to increase; therefore, causing inflation and consequently an economic recession since there are many industries that depend on this resource.

This issue is basically the result of implementing decades-old policy related to transportation that has focused on promoting automobile usage through massive highway infrastructure (Mills n.d.). This problem has become critical in megacities where the population is reaching 10,000,000 inhabitants.

In addition, aging infrastructure cannot be restored individually since the effective logistics of goods and services require optimal connectivity of inter- and cross-modal transportation and transit systems (Kaewunruen et al. 2016). Therefore, it is essential that all transport modes (air, rail, road, maritime) have the ability to connect to each other. For instance, the growing population of a city might force the relocation of its airport to a safer and more extensive area. The construction of this airport does not only consider the expenses of the new facilities, but also the costs of connecting roads, transportation systems, accommodations, etc.

A challenge faced by politicians is to achieve public support by generating social and environmental benefits such as reducing carbon emission, congestion, traffic mortality, improving urbanization and land uses, choices of job opportunities, lifestyles, etc. (Kaewunruen et al. 2016).

16.3.2.2 Costs

According to the Hyperloop Alpha paper written by Elon Musk, the total cost of the Hyperloop passenger-only version (as opposed to the passenger plus vehicle version) is under 6 billion dollars which are less than 9% of the total cost of the proposed passenger-only high-speed rail system between Los Angeles and San Francisco (Musk 2013). The reason that Hyperloop is much cheaper compared to the California rail project is that the tubes can be built above the ground on pylons in prefabricated sections that are later dropped in place and joined together. By building Hyperloop on pylons, land acquisition would be kept to a minimum since they would only need to purchase "air rights" (Taylor et al. 2016). In addition, there is an assumption that the system could be built following alongside the California Interstate 5 Highway (with only minor deviations).

It has been estimated that Hyperloop could transport 15 million people from Los Angeles to San Francisco every year (round trip). Elon Musk suggests amortizing the cost of 6 billion dollars over a period of 20 years. Therefore, the total cost of the project is divided by 300 million people transported throughout that timeframe, and the price of 20 dollars is estimated for a one-way trip ticket.

The total cost (6 billion USD) of the project estimated by the Alpha paper does not take into account operating and maintenance costs. This would substantially increase the total cost of Hyperloop and public funding would be necessary to make the project a reality. In the present, there seems to be a general presumption against government interfering in new technology initiatives in the United States (Taylor et al. 2016). Consequently; governance, business model, and fare policy matters need to be discussed since the system would not be fully private.

16.3.2.3 Potential Markets

According to Musk, the Hyperloop will be designed to connect cities that are less than 900 miles apart, beyond that distance, air travel ends up being faster and cheaper, the construction costs of the guideway begin to erode any cost-effectiveness over aviation (Musk 2013). Markets between major urban areas would increase significantly. For instance, the Hyperloop could connect Los Angeles to San

Francisco, or New York City to Boston bringing more opportunities for employment and business.

16.3.2.4 Transportation Innovation

Aging infrastructure systems represent significant risks to people by not being able to provide maintainers early warnings about potential hazards so that they can be managed in a timely manner. Therefore, it is necessary to create new infrastructure under safe, smart, reliable, and automated systems. The challenge is to enable an intelligent transportation and transit system through the integration of the Internet of Things (IoT) to simultaneously improve asset condition monitoring, and response prediction of systems management, maintenance, and operations to provide a safe and seamless transportation experience for the users (Kaewunruen et al. 2016).

"Big Data" would be retrieved through the implementation of smart sensors, smart materials, wireless technologies, and on-board monitoring technology such as infrastructure-to-infrastructure, infrastructure to-vehicle, and intermodal interactive communication. This information would be used as a predictive technology to enhance decision-making models and create low-carbon urban environments (Kaewunruen et al. 2016).

16.3.2.5 Education Is the Key

It is essential to train and enhance research skills and capabilities for engineers and professionals so that they can understand and manage risks associated with climate change, natural disasters, human-made hazards (Kaewunruen et al. 2016). Industry and academia need to work together through joint scholarly work, case studies, and guest lectures to enable technology adoption at a greater rate.

16.3.3 Social

16.3.3.1 Technology Roadmap: Social Aspects

A technology roadmap analysis was done on identifying the drivers, gaps, and feasible solutions in terms of social aspects. The drivers that affect the social acceptance of Hyperloop are the sense of safety & security and convenience. There are increasing concerns over the health and safety effects due to the high-speed acceleration and the ionizing radiations of the pod. However, the convenience, speed, and safety concerns over existing modes of transportation act as positive drivers for Hyperloop technology implementation.

For overcoming the gaps of safety, security, and health concerns, the government participation by the implementation of regulation in the form of safety certificates after rigorous testing should be there. If a compliance certificate is issued and the prospective customers are made aware of this, the concerns can be alleviated.

16.3.3.2 The Hyperloop Advantage

Hyperloop got the world's attention with the innovative technology and the myriad benefits it offers. It claims to carry passengers at speeds that were previously unheard of. Living humans traveling at a sonic speed of up to 780 mph is indeed an interesting concept in itself.

16.3.3.3 Technology Adoption

It is important for the companies and decision-makers to know-how the technology would be adopted by customers belonging to different demographics. As per the technology adoption curve, depending on the time of adoption, the customers can be classified into five; viz., Innovators, Early Adopters, Early Majority, Late Majority, and Laggards.

1. Innovators—constitute roughly 2.5% of the population. They are tech enthusiasts who are passionate about experimenting and staying on top of any information about the technology they are interested in. As Hyperloop is a cutting-edge technology with an active fan base constituted of mainly the innovators, these risk-takers would be the first ones to experiment with the technology by taking a ride.

As far as countries are concerned, even though most of the major Hyperloop companies are based out of North America, UAE was the first to embrace Hyperloop implementation in the country.

Marketing Strategy—The Hyperloop companies do not need to market the technology and information to Innovators as they might already be aware of it. However, the companies can focus on converting these enthusiasts into advocates of the technology by individual social media targeting.

2. Early Adopters—These are visionaries who are enthusiastic about new technology and experimenting. However, they are selective about what they use and advocate. They constitute about 13.5% of the total population and are looked upon by peers for advice on adopting new technology and related. The US could be thought of as an early adopter country as the Hyperloop system is already given permission for testing. Once the testing is done successfully and regulations are in place only, the development would scale up.

Marketing Strategy—It is important to communicate clearly to the early adopters as they have the role of influencers in society. Along with the regulatory compliance, the companies should focus on the overall experience the passenger might experience in the Hyperloop.

3. Early Majority—This group forms the largest part of the population. They are knowledgeable and are sought out by their peers for doing the right thing at the right time. This population will be ready to experiment, only if all the facts that concern them are known and found to be safe. They believe in taking calculated risks.

Marketing Strategy—For Hyperloop companies to attain their financial targets, it is essential that this population is targeted right and is on board. The companies should focus on dispelling any fears or concerns regarding the safety and health factors. Information sharing, mainstream advertising, and focusing on a great experience would contribute to attracting this group.

4. Late Majority—This population forms a major part of the population, as much as the early adopters. They are conservatives who are either complacent with the current modes of transportation or are skeptical about the new technology.

Sometimes, it is not a mindset but the lack of accessibility is the reason behind the late adoption. The complexity and high capital requirement of the structure make it infeasible for deployment at all locations. If the customer is not located at an accessible location or would not have any use for such high-speed or long-distance travel might not opt for it. This would be the case of countries as well, that have a strict regulatory framework that could work against the Hyperloop deployment.

Marketing Strategy—Bringing in the late majority population will allow the companies to scale up the profits from the system. As they might be concerned about the safety of the system and detrimental health effects, it is important that they know all they need to know about the compliance of the system with the safety regulations. Educating about technology and building awareness would work positively for persuading the late majority.

5. Laggards—These are the part of the population with a high level of skepticism. They do not get persuaded easily and would even detract those who would like to use the system. Sometimes, the reasons for lagging behind the technology would be a genuine concern—such as health issues or claustrophobia. It could also happen that they do not have the economic viability to use the system. They are low-risk takers and might find it difficult to adapt to the new technology.

Marketing Strategy—If the concern is genuine, then there is nothing much companies can do to make the population adopt the technology. Although not a positive picture as far as the companies are concerned, mass advertising and being ubiquitous might help.

16.3.4 Technological

Hyperloop is devised as a fifth mode of transportation, has the potential to replace short and medium distances of today's air and train travel with significant gains on overall efficiency, energy consumption, and total cost of ownership. The Hyperloop could be imagined as a large tube, which is immune to weather conditions and operates with a low-pressure environment inside, a partial vacuum. Inside this tube, people and goods are to be transported in capsules or pods, which hover magnetically and are driven by electromagnetic propulsion. Hyperloop pods are therefore the basic units of Hyperloop. Pods would travel through the Hyperloop one at a time, leaving every 30 s or so at rush hour and spaced 23 miles (37 km) apart on average (How Hyperloop works n.d.). Passengers can enter and exit the tube at each end and via branches along the loop. Each passenger pod is designed to hold 28 people seated in 14 rows of two, along with a luggage compartment in one end, and larger pods can hold a car. The maximum pods height would be 6.11 ft (1.10 m) and width of 4.43 ft (1.35 m).

Renewable energy is key for the Hyperloop business model. The Hyperloop is devised as an ecosystem, including sources of renewable energy, too. As such, Hyperloop tubes could be plastered with solar panels (Hyperloop: the future of transportation n.d.). Wind and geothermal energy could be sourced along the tracks and within the tubes themselves, regenerative energy sourced from the electric propulsion and braking system will play a key role, too.

16.3.4.1 Current Level of Technological Aspects

There are many technological aspects in making Hyperloop a reality now. The vacuum system now has larger pumping ability as compared to the previous testing phase (Technology roadmapping n.d.). The propulsion and sled tests have been successfully tested and have worked efficiently. Magnetic levitation can now be used in production level and the magnetic braking is fully tested on Hyperloop and is ready to be efficiently utilized. Hyperloop One installed almost 1000 ft of the linear motor in a 1640-foot-long tube capable of reducing the air pressure down to the equivalent of 200,000 ft above sea level. Top speed was aimed to be around 250 mph. The Hyperloop system would get its power from motors and batteries developed for the Tesla Model S electric car, along with solar panels placed on the roof of the tubes. They have recently worked on solar power efficiency and it has increased drastically as compared to previous tests of 25% (O., G., & M. 2015).

The Hyperloop with pods that whiz through steel tubes mounted on pylons, or pillars are designed to withstand earthquakes (How Hyperloop works n.d.). Those pylons, made of reinforced concrete, would be spaced every 100 ft and stand 20, 50, and 100 ft (6, 15, and 30 m) high, depending on the terrain.

A technical problem centers on the pods moving through a tube containing air. It is reported that if the walls of the tube and pod are close together, 'the capsule will behave like a syringe'. In other words, the pod would push the entire column of air in the system instead of letting it flow past. The result is that the pods would have to travel very slowly, or engineers would have to build a massive tube to make traveling quicker. In that case, passengers would be traveling several thousand miles per hour, subjecting their bodies to crushing G-forces when going around the slightest bend. The team thus, decided that the air pressure inside the system should be one-sixth the pressure of the thin atmosphere on Mars, which significantly reduces drag on the speeding pods (How Hyperloop works n.d.). In addition, situating the Hyperloop in the median of I-5 for the most part is a cost-cutting decision because it allows the developer to avoid buying land from those living along the route.

There are many equipments to test these technological aspects. At 50 ft long and 12 ft wide, the Big Tube, a three-and-a-half ton carbon steel vessel was used to validate welds, openings, tube design, vacuum pass-through, and manufacturing automation. The Levitation Rig is another unique test stand designed and built by the Hyperloop One team. The test stand is housed in an 18-cubic meter environment chamber that is capable of achieving pressures down to 1/1000 of atmospheric pressure. The rotor achieves surface speeds of up to 300 m per second. These speeds are necessary to simulate Hyperloop cutting-edge levitation systems for use on our test vehicles. The Blade Runner is the only known test rig of its kind. It was designed, fabricated, and built by the team to test scaled axial compressor blades and aerodynamic structures in environments down to 1/1000 of atmospheric pressure (Hyperloop One n.d.). Powered by two 2000 CFM vacuum pumps, the Blade Runner lets the Hyperloop One team conduct long-duration tests while adjusting flow variables in speeds ranging from subsonic through supersonic regimes.

The company established the Apex Test and Safety site in the desert outside of North Las Vegas, Nevada. At a live Propulsion System Open Air (POAT) test, the Hyperloop sled accelerated to 136 mph in 2.2 s, braking into a sandbank and validating the design of the motor and power electronics system.

Metalworks was opened in North Las Vegas, Nevada which became the first Hyperloop manufacturing plant in the world. The 105,000 square foot facility serves as a tooling and fabrication plant to create Hyperloop components. With DevLoop (First tube tested successfully from August 2016–May 2017) construction complete, the first images of the first full-scale Hyperloop test track were revealed at the Middle East Rail event in Dubai, UAE.

In Phase 2 testing, Hyperloop One achieved historic test speeds traveling nearly the full distance of the 500-m DevLoop track in the Nevada desert. The Hyperloop One XP-1, the company's first-generation pod, accelerated for 300 m and glided above the track using magnetic levitation before braking and coming to a gradual stop (Hyperloop One n.d.).

In Phase 3 testing, Hyperloop One achieved test speeds of 387 km per hour.

The company is now working aggressively to meet the goal of having three production systems in service by 2021.

16.3.5 Environmental

16.3.5.1 Renewable Energy

This is key factor in the Hyperloop model, because the ideal of the technology is to run 100% on renewable energy by creating more electricity than the system actually consumes. This is planned to be done by manufacturing the tubes and the entire system with solar panels. There are also some rumors that wind and geothermal energy might be used to help with the propulsion and braking system of the model.

16.3.5.2 Environmental Impact

Hyperloop One finished on December 15 its third testing phase. However, the team still has a long way to go. They are working non-stop to achieve their goal which is to have the first Hyperloop system completed by 2021. The impact that this model will generate to the environment is still unknown and we will have to wait until the system and more data is released to evaluate the impact that this disruptive technology will have on the environment. For now, we will share the available theoretical information we have found.

Regarding Noise Pollution, it is expected that the air pressure made by the capsules in the tube will generate the tube to swing and most likely there will be some noise. The noise is predictable to be comparatively small to what other transportation modes emit. Hyperloop plans to transport 840 passengers per hour, which will reduce the number of cars in the morning commutes by 400–550 less cars (Is the Hyperloop the greenest track for rapid transit? n.d.). This is a clear example of how Hyperloop's' impact could be beneficial to the environment by reducing the emissions of carbon footprint, since the transportation industry causes 31% of the emissions in the USA.

16.3.5.3 Transportation Efficiency

According to researchers, Hyperloop could affect positively the number of vehicles on the roads. They are looking that by 2040 the system will reduce in California almost 10 million the number of travel miles per day as well as the number of flights. The effect in the Cargo industry will be also noticeable because since the shipment process will be faster and most likely cheaper there will be an incredible reduction on ships in the ocean, truck on the roads and cargo planes.

16.3.6 Legal

The legal process involved in developing the Hyperloop transportation system will require bringing in new regulations and there are two competing policy concerns that affect the regulatory process. The two competing policy concerns are:

16.3.6.1 Passenger Safety

All transportation service providers, generally have the duty of providing the highest safety possible to its passengers. Therefore, in the case of Hyperloop, the safety policy largely shapes the regulatory landscape.

16.3.6.2 Economic Development

The current classifying freight method in the USA is the NMFC which stands for the National Motor Freight Classification system (Regulations could slow down Hyperloop n.d.). For Hyperloop to run toward completion, a new classification system will be required that pertains to cargo claims and insurance as well as how freight is priced. Therefore, there are wide-ranging effects in re-engineering a classification system for a new mode in this process (Regulations could slow down Hyperloop n.d.).

The gaps, therefore identified when analyzing the legal factors include the regulatory structures for Hyperloop which do not currently exist yet. These structures need to be highly customized for the fifth mode of Hyperloop transportation. In addition the decision of who is in charge of this transportation is also in question as it is still not clear if the Federal Railroad Administration, which handles high-speed rail is taking charge of the Hyperloop transportation or is it the Federal Highway Administration, which manages the roads. Finally, there is no clarification made about who determines the safety standards (Regulations could slow down Hyperloop n.d.).

16.4 Conclusions

The milestone of conducting a full flight test of the Hyperloop in Q4 2017 has been missed by Hyperloop One. Just by December 15th (Q4 2017) they finished the third phase of testing of the Hyperloop, that means the first full flight test to be conducted still has a long way to go as the regulations of a new classification system for freight pricing still needs to be established, the milestone of cargo trips to begin from LA to San Francisco in 2020 could be still under speculation. As these two important milestones are not achieved by Hyperloop One due to political and regulatory factors, the milestones discussed in the literature might still be pushed further in the timeline. Therefore, it is expected that to become a reality and transportation of the future, Hyperloop might still be a few years away.

Hyperloop One has to put efforts in the political and legal fronts to develop Hyperloop in the planned routes. It would be easier for the company to rather build public–private partnerships, instead of waiting for the government through a 15- to 20-year process to reach a consensus. Also, the company should actively pursue projects in countries with friendly regulatory environments and economically viable routes instead of contending with overbearing regulators.

The hype around Hyperloop technology and its benefits may have gotten the prospective customers excited to use it. But, to establish it as a preferred mode of transport, the companies should focus on meeting the safety requirements, and provide a top-notch overall user experience.

The technological advancements taking place are huge that make a great difference and will continue the same in the upcoming years. But there is still, lot to work on and to achieve further advancements in the innovation. The phase testing process has achieved good results, setting new records with every phase. These new achievements can set the roadmap on the right path and can turn this mode of transportation into reality.

Once the system is finished, Hyperloop has the potential to become the best environmentally friendly transportation mode. However, it is also important to keep in mind the amount of pollution and contamination that this project will generate during the construction and testing phases. These are factors that will need to be included in the environment impact report to leverage the importance and benefits of having a fifth transportation mode versus the damage this project could cause to the environment.

Finally, the project's costs have been underestimated since operational and maintenance expenses have not been considered thoroughly. Therefore, a fare ticket of 20 USD for a one-trip may not be accurately estimated making it necessary to seek agreements with the US government for subsides.

Acknowledgment Tugrul Daims contribution to the book chapter is based on the study funded by the Basic Research Program of the National Research University Higher School of Economics (HSE) and by the Russian Academic Excellence Project "5-100."

References

Building infrastructure for Hyperloop doesn't work like that (n.d.). https://www.wired.com/story/infrastructure-hyperloop-nope/. Accessed 11 Mar 2018

CO_2 and other greenhouse gas emissions (n.d.) Accessed 15 Mar 2018

Developing multi criteria decision making model in... (n.d.) Accessed 15 Mar 2018

Environmental Protection Agency (EPA) (2018, February 6) DRAFT inventory of U.S. greenhouse gas emissions and sinks: 1990–2016. Accessed 15 Mar 2018

How Hyperloop works (n.d.). https://science.howstuffworks.com/transport/engines-equipment/hyperloop2.ht. Accessed 12 Mar 2018

Hyperloop One (n.d.). https://hyperloop-one.com/. Accessed 11 Mar 2018

Hyperloop: the future of transportation (n.d.). https://medium.com/thebeammagazine/carl-brockmeyer-43377e2729de. Accessed 10 Mar 2018

Is the Hyperloop the greenest track for rapid transit? (n.d.) Accessed 9 Mar 2018

J (n.d.) What is PESTLE analysis? A tool for business analysis. Accessed 11 Mar 2018

Kaewunruen S, Sussman J, Matsumoto A (2016, February 24) Grand challenges in transportation and transit systems. Accessed 14 Mar 2018

McCarthy N, Richter F (2018, February 9) Infographic: America's most congested cities. Accessed 11 Mar 2018

Mills L (n.d.) Transportation sustainability in the United States. Accessed 9 Mar 2018

Musk E (2013) Hyperloop Alpha. Accessed 10 Mar 2018

O., G., & M. (2015, July 25) Technology roadmapping: The integration of strategic and technology planning for competitiveness. Accessed 10 Mar 2018

Regulations could slow down Hyperloop (n.d.). https://www.freightwaves.com/news/2017/10/19/regulations-could-slow-down-hyperloop. Accessed 12 Mar 2018

Taylor C, Hyde D, Barr L (2016, July) Hyperloop commercial feasibility analysis. Accessed 15 Mar 2018

Technology roadmapping: linking technology resources to... (n.d.) Accessed 9 Mar 2018

Chapter 17
R&D Management in Rare Disease Focused Biotechnology Companies: The Case of Shire

Amir Shaygan, Tania Lilja, Bobby Romanski, Rasnia Tabpla, John Bauer, Hussain Almohameed, and Tugrul U. Daim

17.1 Introduction

2016 was a transformative year for the Shire, becoming the leading global biotechnology company in rare diseases. In a letter from Shire's current CEO, Dr. Flemming Omskov stated that "responsibility and responsible leadership permeate everything we do in order to address significant unmet medical needs and improve people's lives with breakthrough medicines." Throughout 2016, Shire completed several milestones that furthered their mission and global leadership, most notably, their acquisition of Baxalta. Regarding the partnership with Baxalta, Dr. Ornskov stated that "the possibilities are tremendous for our patients, healthcare partners, and, importantly, our people, with opportunity for additional value creation for our shareholders" (Paul et al. 2010).

Shire's global presence includes its manufacturing and R&D centers. Currently, Shire's manufacturing facilities are in Cambridge and Lexington Massachusetts. Along with manufacturing, these sites include warehouse facilities, laboratories, and

Around 2 years after this study was done (August of 2017), on 8 January 2019. Shire was acquired by the Tokyo based multinational Pharmaceutical Company Takeda for $62 billion. Some of the figures in this study were used from Shire's website which does not exist anymore. Shire was studied as a R&D management project at the department of Engineering and Technology Management at Portland State University located in Portland, Oregon.

A. Shaygan · T. Lilja · B. Romanski · R. Tabpla · J. Bauer · H. Almohameed
Portland State University, Portland, OR, USA

T. U. Daim (✉)
Portland State University Technology Management Doctoral Program, Portland, OR, USA

National Research University Higher School of Economics, Moscow, Russia

Chaoyang University of Technology, Taichung City, Taiwan
e-mail: tugrul.u.daim@pdx.edu

T. U. Daim, D. Meissner (eds.), *Innovation Management in the Intelligent World*, Science, Technology and Innovation Studies,
https://doi.org/10.1007/978-3-030-58301-9_17

distribution operations. Additional warehousing and distribution facilities are in Florence, Kentucky, and North Reading, Massachusetts, and laboratory and office Shires offices and laboratories outside of the US include Sao Paulo, Brazil, Dublin, Ireland Wayne, Basingstoke, UK, and Nyon, Switzerland. The prioritization and rationalization of Shire's development portfolio resulted at the end of many of the R&D programs run by Basingstoke, UK, resulting in the elimination of R&D roles in Basingstoke and the relocation of certain positions. The company also announced plans to relocate its international trade hub from Nyon, Switzerland to Zug, Switzerland, in 2013. The Shire also announced in October 2013 that it would halt the construction of a new factory in San Diego and close its site in Turnhout, Belgium.

In seeking to acquire Baxalta, Shire is moving forward with a strategic focus that was formed in 2013 when the company repositioned itself as a biopharmaceutical specialty company focusing primarily on specialized and rare diseases. On April 30, 2013, the company named a new CEO, Flemming Ornskov. Ornsko set forth a new strategic focus for the Shire, which included integrating three separate segments (Specialty Pharmaceuticals, Human Genetic Therapies, and Regenerative Medicine) into four business units based on the therapeutic area of the company's in-line products (rare disease, neuroscience, gastrointestinal, and internal medicine) and also in ophthalmic to support the development of Shire's ophthalmic pipeline candidate as well as creating a single R&D unit with a focus on rare diseases. The Shire announced in November 2013 that its preclinical pipeline would focus solely on rare diseases and discontinued other programs that did not fall within that jurisdiction.

17.2 R&D Strategy

Shire increases their absorptive capacity by implementing open innovation processes, hiring people who are open-minded, able to work with different cultures and knowing that innovation needs to be accessed globally, improving their dynamic capacity and interpersonal skills, building more strategic alliances and active involvement in innovation networks and developing managerial skills to make better use of them (Shire 2017a). Shire's strategy includes the following—a broad pipeline in the treatment of rare and specialty diseases, a culture of innovation and calculated risk-taking, creative external partnerships that drive the success, core expertise related to enzyme replacement therapies, and the recognition that they can't be experts in all technologies, so partnering with the right external experts helps broaden their portfolio and meet customer needs (Table 17.1).

Building an internal research portfolio around high trust goals in diseases with major unmet medical needs, focusing exclusively on the rare disease field is priority thereby focusing on illnesses where the underlying cause is identified is the cornerstone of Shire's research portfolio. They can thus start with an understanding of the disease—meeting patients and families to understand their daily struggles and characterize the phenotype of the disease. The next Shire looks at the disease's

Table 17.1 Pipeline summary (Biocentury 2017)

Pipeline information						
Pipeline summary						
Disease category	Preclinical	Phase I	Phase II	Phase III	Market	Totals
Totals	16	19	17	12	55	97
Hematology	3	2	–	1	15	21
Neurology	1	2	1	3	14	18
Endocrine/Metabolic	1	4	2	–	9	14
Autoimmune	3	2	3	–	3	9
Inflammation	1	1	1	2	2	8
Cancer	2	3	2	2	3	7
Infectious	–	–	2	3	2	7
Ophthalmic	1	2	2	–	1	6
Cardiovascular	1	1	1	–	2	5
Dermatology	2	–	–	–	1	3
Gastrointestinal	–	–	–	1	2	3
Transplant	–	–	3	–	–	3
Hepatic	–	1	1	–	–	2
Musculoskeletal	–	–	–	–	1	1
Other	–	–	–	–	1	1
Pulmonary	–	–	–	–	1	1
Renal	1	1	–	–	–	1

underlying biology and identifies a molecular target that forms the basis for possible treatment. Internally, its core strength is focused on protein engineering. Nevertheless, if the best target for the disease cannot be achieved through protein interference, Shire complements its internal efforts to apply cutting-edge approaches to these specific programs through strategic partnerships with world-class innovation providers. This helps the Shire to discover new treatments across a wide range of rare diseases and improve them. The Shire takes a hypothesis-driven approach with a focus on making critical go / no go decisions throughout each phase of pipeline development to effectively advance these novel approaches (Shire 2017a).

17.2.1 *Importance and Reasons for Focusing on R&D Productivity*

The overall productivity of R&D as it relates to pharmaceutical discovery and testing is critical, as its associated monetary and time costs are high, and ROI can only be possible after approval of the drug candidate by regulatory government agencies. Due to the recent increase in FDA standards, making it more difficult for drug candidates to be approved, R&D must also increase productivity proportionally to the same or greater level for its host company to survive in an already high-risk high-reward market.

The productivity of R&D is made up of its effectiveness and efficiency. The effectiveness in terms of Shire's products is determined by the health outcomes of the patients after approval, which will not be discussed in this study. The efficiency of R&D is the amount of resources needed to achieve a milestone (Paul et al. 2010) In this section, we will focus on how Shire creates decisions that significantly improve R&D productivity by reducing the count of higher attrition drugs in the pipeline while simultaneously increasing the count of drugs that successfully exit the pipeline and into the market (GEN 2017).

During this era of investor pressure on executives to produce profits quickly, the pharmaceutical companies were commonly trying to push as many of their "phase III" candidates into the market at the expense of the potentially more successful candidates in the earlier stages of the pipeline. To remedy this situation, "The quick win, fast fail drug development paradigm" (Paul et al. 2010) was created to illustrate that weak phase II and III products should cease being developed and their resources transferred to strengthen products in earlier stages of the pipeline. In other words, divesting the unnecessary risks such as the phase III low hanging fruit that does not yield value and investing in strong seeds that are reasonably likely to weather the entire drug process, will increase R&D efficiency.

17.2.2 Deciding How to Increase R&D Productivity

Success in phase II has the most effect on the capitalized cost of launching a new drug. To exploit this, phase I candidates must have an increased probability of completing phase I and be plentiful so that there is a healthy queue of them ready to be chosen for phase II. Referring to our earlier mention about companies unnecessarily pushing phase III candidates through the pipeline. Phase III is significantly outweighed by phase II relative to "cost per launch" and therefore Shire's decision-making should focus their resources on creating good candidates for phase II.

To determine whether the Shire is using "The quick win, fast fail drug development paradigm," published in 2010, we derived a count clinical phases I, II, and III initiated by Shire pre and post-November 2013, which as mentioned earlier, is the month that "Shire announced that its preclinical pipeline would focus only on rare diseases, and it discontinued other programs that were not within that purview" (Shire 2017b).

17.2.3 Decision Methodology

All of the information used in these derivations were acquired by downloading a complete list of 444 clinical trials sponsored by Shire from 1994 to 2017 from clinicaltrials.gov. The list of drug names in each trial along with its corresponding data were sorted in alphabetical order and trials were removed that used a placebo, combination of drugs, did not use pharmaceuticals, or were one of the rare trials in a transitory phase or was a phase that was being repeated. This revealed a count for each phase I, II, and III. The count was then separated into two groups depending on whether the trials had a "start date" before or after November 2013. The counts of each phase were then divided by the total number of counts for all phases in order to determine the percentage of drugs assigned to each phase.

17.2.4 Results and Discussion

After 2013, the phase I pipeline is 28% larger than before 2013. We also see that the 'phase II' pipeline is similar in all years and that the "phase III" pipeline decreased 21% relative to before 10/2013. We believe that the likely reasons for this change are explained by 'Paul et al. (2010)' and earlier in this section about how Phase I candidates should be plentiful in order to keep the queue full of good candidates and that phase III candidates should be more likely considered for cancellation due to phase III's high cost and the prevalence for pushing bad drug candidates to the final stages. In conclusion, funds typically used for underqualified phase II candidates, should be diverted to preclinical and phase I development to prepare excellent and numerous candidates for phase I (Fig. 17.1).

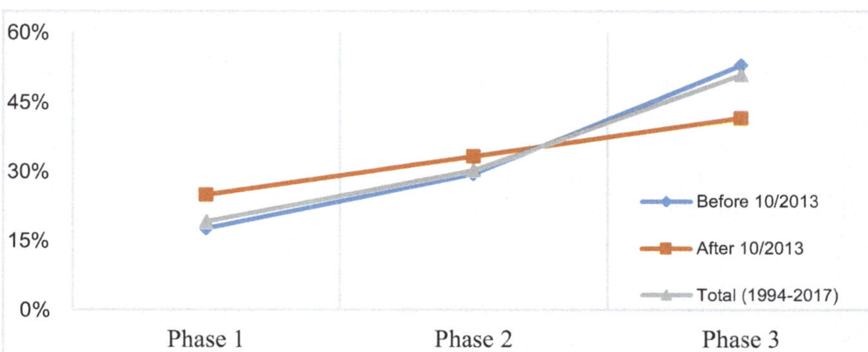

Fig. 17.1 Percentage of total drug candidates in each clinical trial phase (using Biocentury data)

17.3 Technology Transfer in Shire

For a company to effectively conduct its businesses, it is evident that they need to merge with other company's especially if they are operating at a global level. This is the case of Shire Company, as a global biotechnology industry the company distributes its products in over 100 countries. The company mainly focuses on rare diseases and specialized conditions. Core therapeutic areas such as Hematology, Immunology, Neuroscience, Lysosomal Storage Disorders, Gastrointestinal/Internal Medicine/Endocrine, and Hereditary Angioedema; a—oncology franchise; and an evolving, creative ophthalmic pipeline mainly benefit from shire products. With all these tasks at hand, it is obvious that the company ought to find help especially in the safe distribution of its products. Despite the need for help, challenges are encountered and in results forcing Shire Company to make decisions on how to deal with them (Shire 2017c).

The Shire saw it necessary to optimize its independent supply network. This would also help in achieving its main goal which are safety and quality delivery of products. While going about the optimization of their supply chain shire in 2013 saw it necessary to buy a rare disease firm ViroPharma. The purchase was at 4.4 billion together with a product Cinryze which brought a half-billion dollars' profit to its portfolio. It was a good investment since until then Cinryze was being produced by a Dutch manufacture Sanquin Solely. Tings worked at their advantage since at the time, the Dutch company was under FDA investigation that led to strictness in its production. The drug has a blood plasma nature and a high rate of contamination which makes it a bit tricky to manufacture. Afterward shire started to build a supply capability for the drug following its access to Cinryze manufacturing technology after collaborating with Sanquin. The next agenda on shires strategy was the acquisition of Baxalta which had plasma fractioning capabilities. This would enable the company to produce 30% of Cinryze from within leading to a $226 million (30%) rise in annual sales. Ultimately the number of patients would increase, and shire will be able to achieve its goal of safely delivering products through improving the supply chain (Shire 2017c; United States Product Patent Information 2015).

Through forming strong partnerships with research organizations, manufacturing, analytical testing laboratories, and packaging companies that are reputable for high-quality principles, shire will ensure that products fulfill their intended use. In so doing, robust technology transfer mechanisms are to be established to ensure qualified environments that are validated are used in meeting the expected high standards. Due to lack of access to shires tech transfer strategy, the tech transfer 5 stage planning in Cormican and O'connor (2009) will be used instead (Cormican and O'Connor 2009).

Technology transfer is the acquisition of new technology externally and transferring it to your organization. It is an essential part of companies seeking growth, especially in their products. Searching innovation opportunities is necessary for product innovation, especially in the current economic world. To ensure that one's company thrives in the current market acquiring new technologies and products is vital. Furthermore, ensuring that the new technologies in place work a company is expected to put the transfer process into action. Inadequate information exists on best practices or guidelines for tech transfer.

17.3.1 How Shire Transfers Technology

As a global company shire deals with several companies. Through such dealings, the shire has been seen to have good commercial execution and reaching its financial goals. One of the companies involved is Kamanda, the company runs its programs in Europe. Shire tasked it with overseeing IND for the acute Graft-Versus-Host Disease (GvHD) treatment candidate Alpha-1 Antitrypsin (G1-AAT IV). Another company that is seen to deal with shire is Baxter which later changed to Baxalta. In 2016 the two companies completed a $32 million merger. Before this, Baxter had an agreement with Kamanda on supply, distribution, and license agreement for its IV AAT. This transfer later leads to shire being the exclusive distributor due to the agreement it had with Kamanda (GEN 2017).

The definition and interpretation of tech transfer exist in several ways. Our framework focuses on "transfer and integration of external product technologies." Tech transfer has various processes involved they are selection, analysis, adaptation, integration, and absorption. Additionally, it has key benefits which include:

1. Swifter market entry and simplified product launch.
2. Extension of product lifecycle and maintenance of income streams.
3. Being able to exploit rapid changes in technology.
4. Less time used in product development.
5. Minimal research and development failure are encountered.
6. Covers for lack of skilled individuals.

There are five stages involved in the framework including (1) preparation of transfer team—involves team that comprehends the technology being assembled. They are expected to conduct analysis and be present at the location where the product will be. (2) Generation of a training plan which involves coming up with details relevant in the transfer process, (3) a validation plan—checking of the products, equipment's of installation, the process involved, and product happens here, (4) detailed planning including budget allocation, timelines, and sequence of transfer and (5) equipment and information transfer (Cormican and O'Connor 2009).

17.3.2 Shire's Difficulties in Technology Transfer

The inability to predict whether types of technologies and certain arrangements will be common in the future are a major obstacle for technology transfer. Such are public–private partnerships that are long-term with government and government agencies that pertain to technology transfers that support local manufacturing capacity and technical expertise that also include emerging markets. Such endeavors bring the risk of affecting the company's material results of operations. They may occur through loss of exclusivity in manufacturing and technical capabilities incase such a model becomes popular. Furthermore, another risk presents itself since public–private partnerships might do business with governments and government agencies. Additionally, instances like sovereign immunity, political shifts, and changing economic, political-legal, and social dynamics may occur.

Another challenge involves shires future revenues being affected. This may happen through them experiencing increased pricing pressures, government regulations that limit patient access, and market developments resulting from operations. The fact that some products used by shire come from a single manufacturing source puts it at a risk of stopping marketing or development of products f such a source is disrupted. Also, such a challenge may occur since shire relies on third-party contract manufacturers to manufacture other products. This is regardless of shire conducting its own manufacturing operations.

Regulatory agencies are another challenge faced by shire. Delays increase in operating cost, lost sales in products, research activities being interrupted, and delayed launches may occur because of extensive oversight by regulatory agencies. Such endeavors are mandatory for approval of manufacturing sites, ingredients, and processes involved to happen. On the other hand, timely response by shire to market forces and managing production capacity may be hindered by some therapies that involve lengthy and complex processes.

Uncertainty in research and development processes which take a considerable amount of time and expenditure and no guarantee of regulatory approval. Financial conditions and result operations being affected through the failure of achieving strategic objectives regarding the acquisition of NPS Pharmaceuticals, Inc., Dyax Corp. ("Dyax") or Baxalta Inc. ("Baxalta"). Damaged reputation that may result from a failed marketed product. Such may happen if the product has side effects causing it to be withdrawn from the market and chances of legal action being taken are high.

Information technology threat that may result in loss of sensitive or confidential information, cyber-attacks security breaches, and data loss. Since shire depends on information technology mostly, the risk is high especially because its revenues, finances, and result of operations may be affected. Increased borrowing cost and decrease business flexibility that may be because of financing Baxalta acquisition. Additionally, integration of Baxalta and Dyax into shire may lead to operating efficiencies, cost-saving and, revenue enhancements, synergies, or other benefits not being realized in the required time.

17.4 How Does Shire Manage Intellectual Property?

Intellectual property rights (IPRs) are the tool to keep R&D efforts to be most efficient. It protects the achieved results including failure results and results during R&D processes (Kaiser 2010). It is not necessary to be the final products or services. To prevent copying products, services, ideas, concepts, and other information from their work, the company should do the intellectual property. Also, they require significant investment. Hence, they can be some valuable company assets. Intellectual property includes patents, trademarks, copyrights, registered designs, trade secrets, and domain names such as shire.com.

The Shire has granted several patents belonging to the products below:

- ADVATE® (Antihemophilic Factor [Recombinant]) and BAXJECT III® Reconstitution System
  - Patented and/or made under the US Patent Numbers: 5,733,873; 5,854,021; 5,919,766; 5,955,448; 6,100,061; 6,313,102; 6,475,725; 6,555,391; 6,586,573; 6,649,386; 6,936,441; 7,087,723; 7,094,574; 7,247,707; 7,253,262; 7,381,796; and 8,545,476.
- HYQVIA® (Immune Globulin Infusion 10% [Human] with Recombinant Human Hyaluronidase)
  - Patented under U.S. Patent Number 7,767,429, under license from Halozyme, Inc., a wholly owned subsidiary of Halozyme Therapeutics, Inc.
- MYDAYIS™ (Mixed Salts of a Single-entity Amphetamine Product)
  - Patented under and/or used under U.S. Patent Numbers: RE 41148; RE 42096; 6,913,768; 8,846,100 and 9,173,857.
- XIIDRA® (Lifitegrast Ophthalmic Solution) 5%
  - Patented under, used under, and/or made under U.S. Patent Numbers: 7,314,938; 7,745,460; 7,790,743; 7,928,122; 8,084,047; 8,168,655; 8,367,701; 8,592,450; 8,927,574; 9,085,553; 9,216,174; 9,353,088 and 9,447,077.

However, some of the products marketed above were sold under the name of Baxalta Incorporated, and its subsidiaries (www.strategic-alliances.org/blogpost/1143942/277595/Academia-and-Industry-Partnerships-Creating-a-Seamless-Fit%2D%2DPart-I?tag=Shire+Pharmaceuticals. https://www.shire.com/research-and-development/collaborations).

17.4.1 *Shire's Intellectual Property Management*

The company's statement on IP on their website states that the Shire respects others and does not copy intellectual property form any company, so they do not expect others to infringe them as well. It continues to state that the Shire would preserve their IPRs and protect their business secrets by not speaking or disclosing confidential business material and information and takes steps and be aware of new ideas including technological or medical advances or unique solutions to protect these works by intellectual property laws. According to the annual report 2015, Shire believes that the company's success depends on its ability and partners and licensors' ability to protect their intellectual property rights. They need to obtain, maintain, enforce, and defend their IPRs to be able to conduct their business (Shire 2015).

Shire's strategy is to register the IPRs such as patents and trademarks. However, the IPRs might not be enough to protect their work, therefore, the company uses unpatented know-how and technological innovations protected by NDAs (Non-disclosure agreements) with the third parties, including employees, consultants, advisors, and partners, to maintain their competitive position. The company also relies on various trade secrets which would not allow third parties to make competing products or impact Shire's ability to develop, manufacture, and market its own products. Also, they believe that their commercial partners, licensors, and third-party manufacturers intend to enforce those IPRs that they have licensed to the company.

17.5 Alliances, M&A, and Strategic Investments

Joe Sypek, PhD, director and external science lead, comparative immunology at Shire's role is to target and assimilate new academic alliance and partnerships. This combination of new partnerships, in turn, improves the early-discovery stage pipeline in the rare disease area within discovery biology research. Shire's milestone-based agreements are dependent on contingent investments for each gene target if specified research, regulatory, clinical development, commercialization, and sales goals are met.

"We've tried other models," Sypek said. "Each institution has nuances. Each has upfront money and needs money to start up. So, we start with initial payments and set the budget, year to year." "We do milestones because we need to get meaningful data. We want data that is robust and statistically significant. If it does not work out, the principle investigator (PI) can take the project and partner with someone else," Sypek continued. "Treatments are an internal project that require regular lab meetings. Both parties must be committed to getting to goals, but all projects have regular meetings where we try to pour all necessary resources together for success." (Shire 2015)

When building a program, if it does not have a molecule, Shire might outsource and pay for its development, even if it is outside of the budget. In 2012, Shire entered a broad, 3-year research collaboration in rare diseases with Boston Children's Hospital, and since then has expanded to other pediatric hospitals.

Shire could take advantage of the change and their coping mechanisms were always key to the success of their business. When they had problems with Sanquin in terms of FDA regulations and investigations, they turned the disadvantage to a great advantage by using Sanquin's technology side and Baxalta's area background and experience to expand their supply chain network and take more control over products related to blood plasma. They used the experience of Baxalta to facilitate and smooth the transfer of technology as the Shire had no hematology experience or background.

Shire is constantly looking for partners to help itself grow its business. As part of their goal to leverage innovative treatments to target unmet patient needs, Shire engages in several partnerships with leading academic centers, technology providers, and biotechnology companies. These partnerships enable the Shire to access a wide range of innovation aligned with its strategic needs and combine the expertise of our partners with Shire's development and commercialization capabilities. They also partner with hospitals, in-license molecules, engage in dedicated ways with charitable foundations, acquire compounds and experts and bolster and construct a robust in-house R&D program concurrent with the outsourced R&D programs.

At the same time, there are always challenges to alliances in technology companies specially in high-velocity and high-risk/high-reward markets such as biopharmaceuticals. According to Sypek, central to the challenges are the cultural differences between academia and industry. But the goal for both parties is to find a cure to address the disease." You can work for years in a lab, but it is the research collaboration that allows a breakthrough [to be] possible. Today, academia seeks out industry partners. The boundary walls are not as high as they use to be. They are more in tune with working with industry. NIH budgets can be tight, and there are always questions about what might happen to funding. That is where the industry might be able to step in and fund research and materials." he added (Shire 2015).

Shire's plan of change is to focus on improving and marketing rare new disease drugs for specific conditions in order to provide their goods with substantial unmet patient needs. M&A has been a major force behind Shire's growth over the past 20 years, supplying much of its current product portfolio (58/97). M&A activity will continue to be a strategic goal as the Shire tends to construct its pipeline and increase patient access to future treatment by purchasing other companies or products that are always a major decision. A decision-making process with multicriteria is needed to ensure understanding of the opportunities and potential risks. A decision-making process with multicriteria is needed to ensure understanding of opportunities and potential risks. The Shire dedicates key roles to this type of due diligence and has invested in training to ensure that this is one of the core capabilities of Shire. They focus not only on the company or product they want to purchase, but on how we are going to integrate them into Shire.

The change that accompanies an acquisition can provide many new opportunities but can also be challenging for some. The Shire is committed to communicate openly with existing and new staff on the impact of any acquisition. The Shire works thoughtfully to integrate new employees into the Shire organization in a way that makes them feel valued and ensures they understand our way of working, our expected standards of behavior, and their approach to Responsibility. At the same time, it is important to listen to and learn from our new members of the organizations.

The Shire is open to new ideas and strives to adopt and implement the best practices wherever they originate. The Shire first looks for companies/technologies to acquire (such as solutions in protein synthesis), and if no solution exists in that realm, they will partner instead with other R&D firms or existing pharmaceutical solutions After a lengthy 6-month courtship, London-based drug maker Shire announced plans to buy Baxalta in a $32 billion cash and stock offer, giving the Shire a better foothold in treating rare diseases in 2016. This would allow the merged company to generate about 65 percent of its total annual revenues from its rare disease products—revenues rising to over $20 billion by 2020, with annual top-line double-digit compound growth. The joint venture will consist of more than 22,000 workers across more than 100 countries, as well as more than 50 drug development programs spread through early, mid, and late-stage ventures. Shire adds gastrointestinal /endocrine disorder, hereditary angioedema (HAE), neuroscience, and lysosomal processing disorders to the combined company goods. Baxalta—which is now an indirect wholly owned subsidiary of Shire—is contributing products in its specialty areas of hematology, immunology, and oncology. "Upon the completion of our combination with Baxalta, Shire is now the global leader in rare diseases, with the number one rare diseases platform based on both revenue and pipeline programs," Shire CEO Flemming Ornskov, M.D., M.P.H., declared in a statement (Market Watch 2017).

"As we launch our combined company today, we have a talented and experienced extended leadership team in place to guide the organization in achieving our goals," Dr. Ornskov added. "Working together, the possibilities are tremendous for our patients, healthcare partners, and, importantly, our people, with opportunity for additional value creation for our shareholders" (United States Product Patent Information 2015).

Shire PLC said net profit dropped in the first quarter of the year on May 2, 2017, despite more than doubling its revenue, largely due to expenses related to Baxalta's $32 billion acquisition. Net profit fell 11 percent to $375 million on March 31, while revenue fell from $1.71 billion a year earlier to $3.57 billion (Market Watch 2017).

The decrease in income was attributed to a significant increase in production costs, which increased from $248.6 million a year to $1.33 billion in the first quarter. The Shire clarified that most of this was due to one-off expenses related to the acquisition, although it also caused a decline in the gross margin of the business after Baxalta was purchased. Shire's revenue has doubled roughly after finalizing its Baxalta acquisition. The contentious contract, originally refused by the management of Baxalta, has offered Shire's portfolio new drugs for conditions of hemophilia,

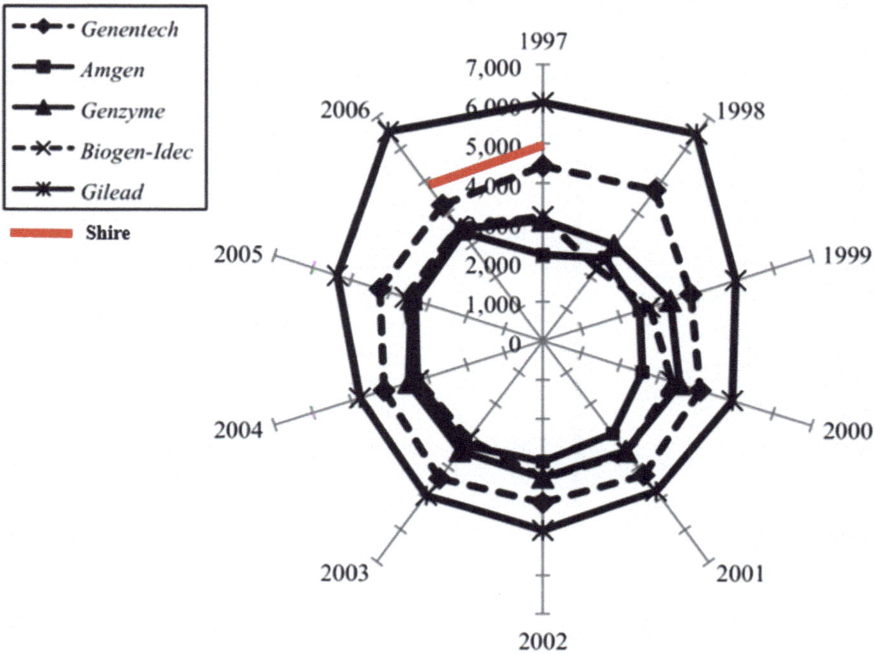

Fig. 17.2 Benchmarking spider plot

leukemia, and immunodeficiency. But the higher costs of producing Baxalta drugs—because of blood plasma—have affected the gross margin of Shire as well (Market Watch 2017).

CFO Jeff Poulton explained that compared to the mid-1980s before the deal, Shire expected its gross margin to be 75.5 percent in 2017. Growth in revenue came from a broad sweep of the portfolio of Shire. Drug sales purchased through the Baxalta deal increased to $1.61 billion by 8 percent. Shire's "legacy" medicines, including ADHD medications and rare diseases such as hereditary angioedema, created $1.81 billion in sales, up 11 percent from the previous year.

In order to benchmark the Shire against other top pharma companies, we considered the role of proximity and knowledge excellence in companies' performance according to Ahn et al. (2009) (Ahn et al. 2009). To do this, the information about all the partnered drugs of the Shire with other companies was mined from literature and reports, and their physical proximities in terms of Kilometers from two headquarters were measured. Furthermore, Shire's average distance from its partners as compared to the top five pharma companies studied in Ahn et al. (2009) (Fig. 17.2 and Table 17.2).

As mentioned in Tsai et al. (2011), long-term strategic partnerships have been favored by enhancing mutual trust and understanding and enhancing the quality of R&D work and results (Tsai et al. 2011). Long-term partnerships would lead to

Table 17.2 Physical distance from partnerships

Shire's distance with partners (Km)			
Cosmo	4181	Kyowa Hakko Kirin Co.	10,766
Pfizer	300	Nogra Pharma Ltd.	4181
Mochida	10,766	Nektar Therapies	4324
Eleison	1929	Verdura Group	5159
MediBIC	10,766	Halozyme	4133
Ipsen Group	5545	Xenetic	0
PharmaEngine	12,433	GSM	5226
Endo International plc	440	Leadiant BioSciences	620
Bayer AG	5727	Lee's' Pharma Holding	12,821
OncBioMune	2225	Neos Therapeutics	2500
Sanofi	5545	Shining	10,766
AmGen Inc.	4179	UCB	5619
Kamada Ltd.	8887	Grunenthal	5698
Parion Sciences	967	Intellect Neurosciences	282
Insmed	344	J&J	341
Sangamo Therap	4309	Average	4870.29

decreased costs and decreased risk as companies are more in their "comfort zone." In high-velocity markets such as biopharmaceutical number of alliances has been shown to be 2–2.5 times more important compared to geographical proximities of alliances stressing the primacy of scientific excellence over physical proximity (Ahn et al. 2009). Strategic selection of complimentary tech (knowledge) is the most important strategic factor to consider. Shire's success is another testament to the fact that staying close to your partners and cost reduction through doing business with companies you know is not guaranteed to lead companies to success. It is the way companies select, assimilate, and exploit the knowledge and technology of other companies and transform and change them to fit their own needs.

Multinational biopharmaceutical firms grapple with intense financial pressures due to an increasingly cost-constrained and highly regulated healthcare environment, finite patent expiration on blockbuster drugs, generic competition, decreases in effective market exclusivity from new innovations, and a proliferation of smaller markets due to the escalating genetic segmentation of patient populations. Specifically, due to dramatic cost reductions in DNA sequencing following the development of "next-generation" platforms, molecular diagnostics are increasingly being cost-effective enough to be used as a standard medical test, both prospectively for risk assessment and confirmation of diseases—and increasingly, as therapeutics for rare diseases.

Pharmaceutical companies are forced to reassess their drug development plans and business models in the midst of these innovations. The role of technology managers is not only to handle the technology's financial aspects, but also to effectively manage human resources, asset management, and strategic alliances for faster and better development. Strong dynamic capabilities can be created through the accumulation of experience, the articulation, and codification of knowledge, and the adaptive ability to change the way problems are solved as the environment changes (Zahra et al. 2006; Eisenhardt and Martin 2000). In the case of biopharma firms, more efficient, prolific, and versatile staff can lead to better new product development and a more efficient research and development pipeline. Acquiring knowledge or technology without prior knowledge of what is going to be done with that resource is extremely risky and can damage companies in non-repairable ways. In the literature, factors such as number of employees, revenues, number of pipelines and marketed products and retained earnings are strongly correlated with an enterprise value in rare disease focused biopharma companies. These correlations seem to be weaker as a company's market capitalization size decreases, indicating that there tends to be increasing returns to scale (Ahn et al. 2019).

All in all, companies, that choose the right resource based on their scenario planning and decision-making models, and eventually transfer them in a successful way (no matter how far they are in terms of partnerships) can gain great benefits from their new integrated resources. Shire is working with many companies inside the USA and globally to gain new markets and opportunities to target rare diseases gaining financial gain and helping people at the same time.

17.6 Conclusion

In high-velocity markets such as biopharmaceuticals, it is imperative for companies to be active in terms of new product development and keeping a broad and versatile portfolio. This intensifies the need for a consistent and well-thought technology and drug sensing, seizing, and exploiting. Companies like the Shire must sense new areas of improvement, assimilate those areas and then, try to achieve it through internal R&D or external partnerships and acquisitions. In case of mergers, acquisitions, and partnerships, the way the company manages the transfer of those technologies and products into their own portfolio is a delicate and sensitive matter. Other than the cultural and infrastructural differences, companies should make sure that the technology that they are acquiring or the partner that they are making alliances with fits the strategies of the company. Just because a product or technology seems attractive in terms of market and opportunities does not mean that it will fit into company's agenda. Therefore, there should be a decision-making system considering both the qualitative and quantitative aspects of the decision-making environment.

Moreover, there is a need to secure and protect the intellectual property provided by the company and not using any other company's IPs without permit. From the IP agreements point of view, in time of initiation, both sides of the agreement should make sure that they are on the same page in order to any contradictions and problems further down the road.

Finally, the primacy of knowledge compared to the proximity of partners was tested in the case of Shire and as mentioned in Ahn et al. (2009), the number of partners was more important compared to how close or far they are from each other.

This study stresses the importance of R&D management in the pharmaceuticals industry. Furthermore, concepts like technology transfer, M&A, partnerships, IP protection in product management, and technology integration play significant parts in the management of research and development in biotech companies. Shire was selected as it possessed a specific type of company in its industry. It was labeled as knowledge leverage which means they have a high proportion of externally acquired research and development and are extrovert in terms of innovation management. Furthermore, the company is not big enough to be considered big pharma and not too small to be considered a biotech startup. This size helps the Shire avoid corporate rigidity and bolsters its capacity to maintain flexibility in terms of portfolio and research and development management.

Acknowledgments Tugrul Daims contribution to the book chapter is based on the study funded by the Basic Research Program of the National Research University Higher School of Economics (HSE) and by the Russian Academic Excellence Project "5–100."

References

Ahn MJ et al (2009) Death of distance? Biotechnology agglomeration patterns, alliance proximity, and firm performance. Int J Innov Technol Manag 6(03):247–264

Ahn MJ, Shaygan A, Weber C (2019) Impact of genomics on biopharmaceutical industry: rare diseases as disruptive innovation. Int J Innov Sci 11(2):241–260. https://doi.org/10.1108/IJIS-01-2018-0006

Biocentury (2017) Shire Biocentury Report, 2017, [Online]. http://bciq.biocentury.com/companies/shire_plc

Cormican K, O'Connor M (2009) Technology transfer for product life cycle extension: a model for successful implementation. Int J Innov Technol Manag 6(03):265–282

Eisenhardt KM, Martin JA (2000) Dynamic capabilities: what are they? Strateg Manag J 21 (10–11):1105–1121

GEN (2017) Shire transfers IND for GvHd candidate to Kamanda. 2017, [Online]. http://www.genengnews.com/gen-news-highlights/shire-transfers-ind-for-gvhd-candidate-to-kamada/81254465

Kaiser L (2010) Management of intellectual property in research and development: a search for systems from the viewpoint of research and technology organizations. Int J Innov Technol Manag 7(3):263–272

Market Watch (2017) Shire after Baxalta, [Online]. http://www.marketwatch.com/story/shire-profit-hurt-by-baxalta-acquisition-costs-2017-05-02

Ornskov F (2016) CEO Letter, Shire. [Online]. https://www.shire.com/who-we-are/responsibility.

Paul SM et al (2010) How to improve R&D productivity: the pharmaceutical industry's grand challenge. Nat Rev Drug Discov 9(3):203–214

Shire (2015) Shaping what's next. Shire's Annual Report

Shire (2017a). How we operate: quality. 2017, [Online]. https://www.shire.com/who-we-are/how-we-operate/policies-and-positions/quality

Shire (2017b) Investors relations: disclaimer. 2017, [Online]. http://investors.shire.com/disclaimer-Baxalta-acquisition.aspx

Shire (2017c) Manufacturing: product safety. 2017, [Online]. https://www.shire.com/products/manufacturing/product-safety

Tsai K-H, Hsieh M-H, Hultink EJ (2011) External technology acquisition and product innovativeness: The moderating roles of R&D investment and configurational context. J Eng Technol Manag 28(3):184–200

United States Product Patent Information (2015) Doing business with integrity; protecting company assets, The Shire Code of Ethics, [Online]. https://www.shire.com/legal-notice/product-patents

www.strategic-alliances.org/blogpost/1143942/277595/Academia-and-Industry-Partnerships-Creating-a-Seamless-Fit%2D%2DPart-I?tag=Shire+Pharmaceuticals. 2a. https://www.shire.com/research-and-development/collaborations

Zahra SA, Sapienza HJ, Davidsson P (2006) Entrepreneurship and dynamic capabilities: a review, model and research agenda. J Manag Stud 43(4):917–955

Chapter 18
Biogas: Converting Waste to Energy

Asmitha Velivela, Husam Barham, John Bauer, Jon Roschke, Tugrul U. Daim, and Dirk Meissner

18.1 Introduction

According to the US Energy Information Administration (EIA), 10% of the USA total energy consumption and 13% of electricity generation was coming from renewable resources in 2015 (U.S. Energy Information Administration 2016). The International Renewable Energy Agency (IRENA) estimates that if renewable resources reached 27% of the US energy mix, it would save the US economy between \$30 and \$140 billion a year in terms of reduced health effects and CO_2 emissions (IRENA 2015).

Biogas generated by a process called anaerobic digestion (AD) is a prominent source of renewable energy, that is characterized by being efficient, clean, and sustainable (energytrust.org 2015), that gained international momentum in the last few years as the technology behind it has become more advanced and efficient (BioCycle 2015). In Germany, for example, electricity generated from biogas is serving 7.9 million houses and is the source of 4% of total electricity generation in that country (BioCycle 2015), this technology was adapted in the USA on small scale, mainly in farms and sewage treatment facilities (EPA 2016a; Center for Climate and Energy Solutions 2011).

A. Velivela · H. Barham · J. Bauer · J. Roschke
Portland State University, Portland, OR, USA

T. U. Daim (✉)
Portland State University Technology Management Doctoral Program, Portland, OR, USA

National Research University Higher School of Economics, Moscow, Russia

Chaoyang University of Technology, Taichung City, Taiwan
e-mail: tugrul.u.daim@pdx.edu

D. Meissner
National Research University Higher School of Economics, Moscow, Russia

T. U. Daim, D. Meissner (eds.), *Innovation Management in the Intelligent World*, Science, Technology and Innovation Studies,
https://doi.org/10.1007/978-3-030-58301-9_18

The Pacific Northwest region has been actively pushing for more usage of renewable energy in the energy source mix in that region, with the states within the region (Washington, Oregon, Idaho) spending billions of dollars (rnp.org 2016) and issuing incentives and policies (dsire-usa 2016) to support the adaptation of renewable energy. However, most of the generated renewable energy is coming from two sources only, wind and solar, while other types of renewable energy resources like biogas were getting less attention and support (rnp.org 2016).

18.1.1 Biogas and Anaerobic Process

Biochemical conversion is one of several processes for converting biomass into heat or fuels. The biochemical conversion process through anaerobic digestion is a natural fermentation process in which microorganisms break down biodegradable material in the absence of oxygen for the production of biogas. These microorganisms are bacteria that can only exist in oxygen-free environments. In the anaerobic process, complex organic compounds, including proteins, carbohydrates, and lipids, are converted to stable gases, namely carbon dioxide and methane. The produced methane and carbon dioxide-rich biogas is a renewable energy source, and the nutrient-rich solid by-product can be used as fertilizer (International Energy Agency 1987).

The anaerobic process of methane production occurs in four stages: hydrolysis, acidogenesis, acetogenesis, and methanogenesis. In the first stage of hydrolysis, bacteria transform proteins into amino acids, carbohydrates into monosaccharides (sugars), and lipids into fatty acids (Johansson and Burnham 1993). In the second stage of acidogenesis, acidogenic bacteria converts the first stage products into volatile acids, hydrogen, and carbon dioxide. In the third stage of acetogenesis, acetogenic bacteria converts the second stage products into acetate, hydrogen, and carbon dioxide. Finally, in the fourth stage of methanogenesis, methanogenic bacteria convert the acetic acid into methane biogas and carbon dioxide (Johansson and Burnham 1993).

There are several environmental factors that affect the anaerobic process including temperature, pH and alkalinity, and toxicity. Though the temperature needed for anaerobic digestion can be as low as 0 °C, the production of methane is greater at higher temperatures (Ostrem 2004). An ideal temperature range for optimal methane production is between 35 °C and 37 °C. The level of acidity also affects the efficiency of methane production, and pH levels must be monitored and maintained in a pH range of 6.5–7.5, where 7 is neutral. Methanogenesis is the fourth stage of the anaerobic digestion process in which acetic acid is converted into methane biogas and carbon dioxide. In this stage, the toxic ammonia, sulfide, and heavy metals can negatively impact the rate of methane production (Ostrem 2004).

18.1.2 Biomass Sources

Input sources, called feedstock, of the anaerobic digester process for methane production, include organic and non-organic material from municipal waste, animal manure, and industrial, institutional, and commercial waste. Animal manures, wastewater solids, food scraps, and by-products of food production are the most commonly digested materials. Municipal solid waste (MSW) includes household, commercial, industrial and institutional waste, including garbage, food scraps, and non-hazardous industrial waste from breweries, sugar plants, fruit processing, and meat processing. Industrial waste from agricultural, pharmaceutical, and technological industries can also be digested once treated and diluted. Household waste includes food waste, wastewater, and sewage, and agricultural waste is organic and non-organic material produced from dairy farming, horticulture, and livestock breeding (Kumar et al. 2014).

18.1.3 Municipal Wastewater Treatment

Wastewater treatment plants are an emerging source of renewable energy. Anaerobic digestion at wastewater treatment plants use an existing waste stream, and typically converts 40–60% of the organic semi-solid sewage to methane and carbon dioxide. The wastewater treatment process starts with water piped into the facility from the municipal sewer system and is filtered through a settling and thickening process, where water is removed to create a dewatered sludge (Wong 2011). This sludge is piped into digester tanks with constant mixing and heating. Following the four-stage process, the biosolids are broken down in the anaerobic process by different types of bacteria to produce a biogas mixture of approximately 60–70% methane and carbon dioxide. To generate electricity from the methane in the biogas, the gas is cleaned, compressed, and burned in a gas turbine, in which mechanical energy is converted into electricity. In conjunction with a combined heat and power system, the biogas can be used for heating the buildings in the treatment facility, increasing energy efficiency. Currently, in the USA, 30–60% of the energy usage of municipalities is used in wastewater treatment facilities. Thus, on-site anaerobic digestion systems to generate electricity can have significant economic benefits for municipalities (Wong 2011).

18.1.4 Anaerobic Digestion Advantages and Disadvantages

The process of anaerobic digestion provides a series of advantages. These advantages help society to yield income and other perks. It is evident from the introduction to this process that anaerobic digestion of solid organic waste provides a great scope of providing a renewable energy source for the production of usable energy from heat and electricity. This energy can be utilized round the clock and even has better efficiency. The other leftover product is high in nutrient content and is considered to be used fertilizer, fiber and in some countries, it is even used for the production of liquor (Arsova 2010). This process produces methane and other gasses, which have less carbon dioxide emissions compared to other sources of energy. This is considered one of the environmental factors for the development of this technology by many scientists and industrialists (de Mes et al. 2003).

This process can be treated as an additional source of income for farmers and beverages industries. The produced methane can be used for the production of power and heat. The leftover organic compost can be used as fertilizers and for other products, which yield high gains for rural areas (ad-nett.org 2016). This process helps in creating a lot of employability options for skilled and efficient labor who are capable of running and managing the plant.

There are also a few negative points in this technology. Research scholars from around the world are taking these cons as a serious challenge and working on to minimize them. The technology is new and requires highly talented labor actually to implement the technology in rural areas. This requires upgradation of technology and acquiring new technology for the usage of methane gas for heat and power production (Spuhler 2011). Markets also need to be upgraded to the use of solid waste compost and commercialization of this technology. The anaerobic digestion is only for the treatment of organic waste, and other non-organic wastes are removed for recycling or disposal. This persists the problem of solid non-organic waste treatment. There is always a problem of the production of quality compost. This quality compost depends on the inputs given to the digester. As the quality of the compost decreases the quality of output methane gas and the organic by-product also degrades which leads to less economic gains (Spuhler 2011). This process produces sulfurous components when wastes from industries are treated. The anaerobic treatment of this sulfurous content can lead to odor nuisance (Naik et al. 2013). This has to be avoided by post aerobic treatment and removal of Sulfur contents before the actual process (de Mes et al. 2003).

18.1.5 Global Approaches

Many countries around the world utilize biogas technologies to meet some of their energy demands. The world's largest biogas energy producer in Germany, accounting for a quarter of the world's biogas installed capacity. Germany generated 18,244 GWh in 2012 and is expected to expand to 28,265 GWh by 2025. By comparison, the USA is the second-largest biogas producer (as ranked by capacity installed), yet the USA only generated roughly half that of Germany at 9072 GWh in 2012. The USA is expected expand to 20,936 GWh by 2025 (Stephan 2013). The key driver for the growth of biogas in Germany has been impressive support by the government. Thanks to the Renewable Energy Sources Act (EEG), feed-in tariffs provide considerable financial compensation for the energy produced by biogas plants in the country as well as bonuses for biogas Combined Heat and Power (CHP) plants (Stephan 2013).

Turkey is a country that holds the potential for growth in the biogas field. While the installed capacity for the country is relatively low (132.9 MW in 2012), Turkey has generated electricity using various biogas technologies, including landfill gas projects and urban wastewater treatment sludge power plants (Ozcan et al. 2013). Turkey imports 98% of its natural gas from other countries for electricity generation, and thus energy independence serves as the main driver to adapt to biogas and other renewable energy sources. Many areas of Turkey are rural and dependent on farms for survival. Animal waste is plentiful in these areas, though the collection of waste can be difficult. However it is estimated that 36% of the total land area in Turkey is farmable land, so the use of the fertilizer by-product would be beneficial as well. Two-thirds of the farms in Turkey manage animal and crop production so the complementary nature of the resource is very advantageous for people throughout the country (Avcioğlu and Türker 2012). Odor and environmental pollution were drivers for Turkey's farmers to consider using anaerobic digesters, and the small-scale of these local farms allowed for quicker payback and easier investments. While the payback period can be 5 years for a biogas facility with an installed capacity of 500 kW, these small-scale plants at local farms can see a quicker payback in as little as 8–10 months (Avcioğlu and Türker 2012). The need for governmental support and financial incentives still is seen as a major barrier however, as even the small-scale operations need financing structures in place to aid in the installation and high upfront costs, even relative to smaller operations (Avcioğlu and Türker 2012).

In developing countries, biogas is often not used in commercial operations, but instead can be easily used on the small and local scale. 90% of energy production in developing countries is estimated to be from biomass sources, and biogas plays a key role (Surendra et al. 2014). Nigeria offers an example of a country that has not seen commercial biogas facilities, but farmers use biogas on the individual scale for cooking and lighting. If the organic material has low energy content, the biogas has to have the carbon dioxide and other incombustible gases separated to make it more storable and portable in order to justify any commercialization efforts (Olugasa et al. 2014). This can be a task that proves to be more difficult that it is worth a small poor farming family in rural Nigeria. If the gas is to be stored, the storage vessels must be compatible with the pressure of the gas, yet another complication that most Nigerian farmers prefer to avoid altogether. However, Nigeria has a surplus of animal and human wastes (as most countries do) and the renewable and complementary nature of the resource in farms and cities alike justifies the local use of its energy potential at households throughout the country, especially in light of the exploration for crude oil that occurs along the delta of the Niger River and the environmental degradation that inevitably follows.

In developing and underdeveloped countries worldwide, waste management is a major issue at both the local and national levels. As more areas are urbanized following a surge in population, biogas facilities offer a clean and sustainable approach to handling the cities' waste. The use of existing biomass materials can improve human health, the local environment, and the socio-economic conditions in these changing countries, as well as the agricultural productivity that is seen after using the nutrient-rich fertilizer by-product that comes with anaerobic digesters (Surendra et al. 2014). Health benefits are also found by replacing traditional fuel sources with cleaner-burning methane for cooking and lighting indoors. Local forests can be impacted as well when populations use wood for fuel as an estimated 54% of deforestation in developing countries is attributed to fuelwood.

Carbon trading potential is also considered as a way for developing countries to reap the benefits of using biogas technologies. Assuming the cost of a household biogas plant is around 1000 USD, roughly 11 million such plants could be installed with the revenue generated by carbon trading alone (Surendra et al. 2014). With this plentiful and locally viable resource, developing countries could see improved waste management, clean energy production, and local job opportunities around the globe (Surendra et al. 2014).

Challenges and barriers still exist for developing countries however. Upfront costs can be out of reach for poor farming families, and financing options in many countries favor fossil fuels over renewable fuels (Surendra et al. 2014). Local knowledge and expertise are also needed for the installation, operation, and maintenance of these facilities, and locals in these countries may lack access to education to be able to master the technology. Water is also essential for a properly functioning biogas facility and some remote, rural areas may not have access to enough. Again, governmental policy and incentives are seen to play a major role in whether biogas technologies thrive or fail (Surendra et al. 2014). Micro-financing opportunities could also support growth in the sector and basic public education would improve the success rates as well. With greater attention and continued research, the biogas industry could see significant growth both in rural and urban applications in developed and underdeveloped countries.

18.1.6 The Gresham Case

Sewage treatment plant in Gresham city, in Oregon State, is the first sewage facility in the Pacific Northwest to reach energy net-zero status (greshamoregon.gov 2016). They were able to achieve this goal mainly by using an anaerobic digestion process to generate biogas from sewage and FOG (Fat, Oil, and Grease), extracted using FOG traps in the sewage near restaurants and other businesses that generate an excess of those materials. The biogas is used to generate electricity and heat needed to operate the plant. And while this process covers more than 92% of their needs, they also installed a PV farm to cover the rest (greshamoregon.gov 2016; veolianorthamerica.com 2015). The plant is now generating an average excess of 20–25% electricity, that is being given for the utility for free, to support a utility program that offers reduced fees for senior citizens and poor people. Also, in the visit, the team learned that the cost of generating electricity from biogas is 3.5 cent per kWh, and 8 cent per kWh from the PV panels. Biogas generates an average between 750 and 800 kWh and the PV panels generate in average between 50 and 80 kWh, although the panels capacity is 400 kWh.

In conclusion, many anaerobic digestion systems, including at the Gresham wastewater treatment plant, have been implemented to produce a net-zero facility and have achieved competitiveness with conventional energy sources. However, many other applications are struggling to become viable without government incentives, especially as the cost for natural gas is decreasing and fracking becomes a more prevalent and mainstream technology. Despite the recent decline of petroleum prices contributing to biogas production options being unattractive, anaerobic digesters are gaining traction for being economically viable in municipal wastewater treatment. This industry application is significant, as 30–60% of the energy usage of municipalities is used in wastewater treatment facilities (EPA 2016c).

18.2 Analysis

18.2.1 Barriers to Adaptation

Several barriers preventing the adaptation of biogas in the Pacific Northwest can be identified which come as barriers based on organizational, personal, and technical perspectives.

18.2.1.1 Organizational Perspective

- *Lack of governmental support*: the states of the Pacific Northwest region has shown a strong support for renewable energy, however, most of that support goes to wind energy (rnp.org 2016), please refer to table.
- *High initial capital investment*: the anaerobic digestion process requires building big digesters on a sizable land; it also requires special piping equipment, especially if the target is large scale production of electricity (Moser et al. 1997; Yorgey et al. 2011).
- *High operational cost*: food scraps and FOG are the best sources for the anaerobic digestion process (Davidsson et al. 2010), however collecting those requires a fleet of garbage trucks and personnel to operate them, which is expensive (Yorgey et al. 2011).
- *Fracking gas prices*: recent fracking gas discoveries led to increased production of natural gas in the US, and as a result, natural gas is becoming very cheap, and that affected the burgeoning renewable energy sources ability to compete on commercial bases, including biogas (energy.gov 2016).
- *Becoming regulated*: in Gresham's visit, we were told that the plant can expand to produce more electricity and sell the excess to the grid, but the fear of getting regulated alienate them from doing so (Hill 2016a).

18.2.1.2 Personal Perspective

- *Low recycling efficiency*: food scrap is the main source for biogas that can be acquired through recycling, and while recycling is gaining ground in the USA and increased significantly in the last few decades, it is still not enough, and people do not recycle all of their garbage (EPA 2016b).
- *Fertilizers Awareness*: One of the anaerobic digestion process important by-products is a liquid material that can be used as a fertilizer, as explained earlier in the literature review, the resulting product is classified as class B fertilizer, which can't be used with all types of plants, and currently, there is a lack of awareness about when and when not to use it by farmers in the region, that causing them to avoid using it, please refer to Appendix for more details about the difference between class A and class B fertilizers, and hence, facilities that currently generating biogas, have challenges disposing of this by-product, instead of the expected demand on it (Hill 2016a).
- *Illegal dumping*: Sewage is a source for biogas that has a challenge with illegal dumping, as some people dump hard items in the sewage, and when such items go to the digester, they can cause damage to the pipes and the digester itself (Hill 2016a).
- *Lack of engineers and technical personnel* specialized in the anaerobic digestion process in the region (Hill 2016a).

18.2.1.3 Technical Perspective

- The *lack of a steady large source*: The anaerobic digestion process can be applied to any organic source; however, food scraps and FOG (Fat, Oil, and grease) are the best sources, as they can generate more biogas than any other source (Davidsson et al. 2010), however, such sources need big cities with high population densities to provide a steady amount that can allow for steady electricity supply, and the Pacific Northwest does not have much density expect in Seattle (statemaster.com 2016).
- *Facility location*: In Gresham's visit, we learned that pumping sewage to the anaerobic digesters could consume much energy, however, if a plant is built in on a location where gravity can naturally let the sewage goes to the digester, without pumping, then much energy can be saved and used to generate electricity back to the grid (Hill 2016a).
- *FOG smell*: FOG is a great source of biogas, but it has a strong bad odor, and while there are chemicals that can reduce the odor, they are bad to the environment (Beyer 2013).
- *Different sources need different processes*: each source of biogas (landfill, food scraps, farm waste, sewage, and so on.), and this means either more investment in building several digesters or using fewer sources than is available.

- *Climate*: generating biogas using the anaerobic digestion process can be faster and more efficient in warmer weather areas (statemaster.com 2016), however the Pacific Northwest is considered a relatively cold region (Hill 2016b).

18.3 Discussion and Recommendations

Gap analysis to evaluate the current capabilities in the Pacific Northwest, and what is the gap to adapting biogas in the region reveals several needs for action discussed in the following.: Based on the gap analysis, the following are recommendations on how to overcome the biogas adaptation barriers in the Pacific Northwest, classified by the organizational, personal, and technical perspectives.

18.3.1 Organizational Perspective

First, governmental support to anaerobic digestion becomes economically viable in part, from increased governmental incentives, enabling the investment costs to become competitive against conventional energy generation. Investments in renewable energies in the Pacific Northwest between wind, solar, geothermal, and biogas vary considerably. Washington has doubled Oregon's investment in biogas development. Despite Oregon's significant biogas potential, biogas development projects are hindered by a lack of incentives and project funding (rnp.org 2016). In Oregon, Federal and State programs provide incentives through tax benefits only when the project becomes operational, neglecting financial support for construction. Biogas production incentives would increase the value of biogas energy, and increase financing opportunities during construction (Weisberg and Roth 2011). Through dairy farms, MSW, wastewater treatment plants, and food processing manufacturing, Oregon has the resources to support feedstock for 12 times the current capacity. With sufficient financing and incentives, biogas investment and development can grow in Oregon and lead the Pacific Northwest in biogas energy production (Weisberg and Roth 2011).

Second, deregulation regards to independent power producers and the requirements and cost to implement and maintain grid connection will reduce the investment risk, and further enhance the economic viability of biogas production for the generation of electricity. Third, finding a market for the class B fertilizer by-product can be achieved by signing agreements with fertilizer manufacturers, so biogas plants become a supplier for class B fertilizer to them, which they can process further to become a class A fertilizer that they can sell commercially. Fourth, food distributors and retailers dispose of huge quantities of unsold food. We recommend that the government issues mandate that such food be provided to biogas plants instead of disposing of it.

18.3.2 Personal Perspective

First, farmers and the general public need to be better educated in regards to the difference between Class A and Class B biosolids. The by-products from the anaerobic digester process can be used as fertilizer, but both the EPA and the DEQ recognize a difference in the quality of the product between the classes (EPA 2016c; nwbiosolids.org 2016). Farmers are not familiar with these differences and may not know about class B fertilizer and some of its benefits. With better education, the demand for fertilizers may be increase and class B biosolids could avoid landfills and instead be put to use (Hill 2016a; lystek.com 2016). See Appendix for more information on the difference between Class A and Class B biosolids. Second, a stronger culture of composting may increase the total amount of organic material available for anaerobic digestion. If composting became the norm in places like apartments, individual houses, etc., food waste could be limited in the Pacific Northwest and biogas facilities could benefit from more materials and consequently production. This culture will open doors for the municipal solid waste anaerobic digester. One way to achieve that is using normative behavior influence; if every house knew how much do they fare in comparison with the neighborhood in terms composting amount they recycle every week, which might encourage them to do better.

18.3.3 Technical Perspective

First, there should be more awareness about the impact of illegal dumping on the sewage system in general, and on operations similar to the anaerobic digester process; many people think that if they flush something in the toilet, it will magically disappear! This is not the case, and perhaps a media campaign showing the side effects of illegal dumping would deter most people from continue doing so. Second, more research should be conducted to create a unified process anaerobic digester process that can accept different types of sources, as that will reduce the cost and increase the source material amount.

Third, location can play an important role to reduce cost and increase efficiency; there is a need for locations that are close enough to cities, where food scraps and FOG is coming from, but not close enough to make the smell a problem, such locations should be also on areas where the temperature is the warmest around cities; so, we recommend conducting a study to identify such locations and offer incentives on using such locations to investors. Fourth, concerned energy organizations (like the Energy Trust of Oregon) should work with universities to incorporate more educational programs and classes related to the anaerobic digestion process to overcome the shortage of specialized people in this field.

18.4 Conclusion

Biogas is an important renewable energy source that is not getting enough attention in the USA, and while the technology has improved in the last few decades and many countries start to adapt it, it still did not get the momentum in this part of the world.

In this case study we identified the barriers preventing biogas effective implementation, after reviewing biogas and the anaerobic digestion process used to generate it, looking at the pros and cons of adapting this energy source, and how it is being used in other countries, and, our visit to the sewage treatment plant in Gresham, a regional leader in adapting biogas, which allowed us to learn more about the challenges facing adapting biogas as a source of renewable energy.

We conducted a gap analysis, that led us to offer recommendations that we believe if implemented would significantly reduce the adaptation barriers, allowing biogas to be an important and viable sustainable and clean source of energy in the Pacific Northwest.

There are a number of current and potential methods for improving biogas production in anaerobic digesters. One current method of adding fats, oil, and greases (FOG) to anaerobic digesters has shown to greatly improve methane production (Hill 2016a). However, more research is needed in containing or reducing the strong odor from the FOG additive. As populations increase around municipal wastewater treatment facilities, the strong odors will present issues for greater growth of anaerobic digestion for methane production.

Better methane production efficiency can be achieved through future research in optimizing anaerobic methane production stages. Each stage requires specific bacteria for sequentially converting reaction by-products into eventual methane and carbon dioxide. The rate limitations of the conversion process of bacteria per volume of feedstock can be improved through a pretreatment process to increase waste degradation (Karlsson et al. 2014). Overcoming some of the reaction rate limitations will greatly increase methane production, and maximize the energy potential of input feedstock.

More research should be conducted to appropriately incentivize the investment of biogas production in Oregon and the Pacific Northwest. Current Federal and State incentives financially support biogas projects, after construction and after the system comes online and starts producing energy. This is insufficient support for initial investment. Greater incentives through attractive financing will help augment the cost of investment prior to the production of energy, including the costs of construction and installation (Weisberg and Roth 2011). Finally, improving the quality of the fertilizer by-product will have significant benefits to biogas producing facilities. High-quality compost that meets the requirements for agriculture can be sold for profit, thus further incentivizing development, by increasing overall economic value (Arsova 2010).

Acknowledgments Dirk Meissners contribution to the book chapter is based on the study funded by the Basic Research Program of the National Research University Higher School of Economics (HSE) and by the Russian Academic Excellence Project "5–100."

Appendix

Class A Versus Class B Biosolids as Used for Fertilizer

There are two classes of biosolids that are distinguished by their pathogen reduction levels, according to the EPA and Oregon DEQ.

Class A biosolids must be reduced to very low levels of pathogens, as they are allowed for use in areas that are open to the public (homes, golf courses, etc.). Class A biosolids are allowed for use in small quantities by the general public with no buffer requirements, crop type, crop harvesting, or site access restrictions. When larger quantities are used, restrictions may be in place (EPA 2016c).

Pathogen reduction is less complete for Class B biosolids. However, Class B typically has more nutrient value, particularly nitrogen, which can be more beneficial for certain crops like wheat or hay (nwbiosolids.org 2016).

An energy-intensive heat treatment is used to meet the regulations necessary to label biosolids as Class A, and the cost can often outweigh the benefits. Most biosolids are left as Class B, as even Class A biosolids have received a poor reaction from the public before (Hill 2016a). In 2006, 91% of biosolids in Oregon were left as Class B, while only 4% were treated to be Class A (nwbiosolids.org 2016).

References

ad-nett.org (2016) The advances in agriculture. [Online]. http://ad-nett.org/. Accessed 07 Jun 2016.

Arsova L (2010) Anaerobic digestion of food waste: current status, problems and an alternative product. Columbia University, May.

Avcioğlu AO, Türker U (2012) Status and potential of biogas energy from animal wastes in Turkey. Renew Sust Energ Rev 16(3):1557–1561

Beyer K (2013) Anaerobic digestion of FOG for Optimal Methane Production. San Diego State University

BioCycle (2015) Anaerobic digest. JG Press 56(7):17

Center for Climate and Energy Solutions (2011) Anaerobic Digesters | Center for Climate and Energy Solutions. [Online]. http://www.c2es.org/technology/factsheet/anaerobic-digesters. Accessed 31 May 2016.

Davidsson Å, Bernstad A, Aspegren H, la Cour Jansen J (2010) Assessment of Biogas Production from Source Separated. Fat, Oil and Grease (FOG) from Households. Presented at the 3rd International Symposium on Energy from Biomass and Waste.

dsire-usa (2016) Database of State Incentives for Renewables & Efficiency®. DSIRE. [Online]. http://www.dsireusa.org/. Accessed 31 May 2016.

energy.gov (2016) Shale Gas 101 | Department of Energy. [Online]. http://energy.gov/fe/shale-gas-101. Accessed 07 Jun 2016.

energytrust.org (2015) Willamette Valley Biogas Plant converts food waste to energy.

EPA (2016a) Guidelines and permitting for Livestock Anaerobic Digesters. [Online]. https://www.epa.gov/agstar/guidelines-and-permitting-livestock-anaerobic-digesters. Accessed 07 Jun 2016.

EPA (2016b) Advancing sustainable materials management: facts and figures. [Online]. https://www.epa.gov/smm/advancing-sustainable-materials-management-facts-and-figures. Accessed 07 Jun 2016.

EPA (2016c) Frequently asked Questions about Biosolids. [Online]. https://www.epa.gov/biosolids/frequently-asked-questions-about-biosolids. Accessed 07 Jun 2016.

greshamoregon.gov (2016) City of Gresham: City: Wastewater Treatment Plant. [Online]. https://greshamoregon.gov/city/city-departments/environmental-services/wastewater-division/template.aspx?id=4330. Accessed 07 Jun 2016.

Hill P (2016a) Gresham Sewage Treatment Plant. Interview, 29 Apr.

Hill M (2016b) Typical weather on the Pacific Coast. [Online]. http://traveltips.usatoday.com/typical-weather-pacific-coast-109818.html. Accessed 07 Jun 2016.

International Energy Agency (1987) Ed., Ch. 4 Biomass Energy. In: Renewable sources of energy. IEA: OECD; OECD Publications and Information Centre [distributor], Paris, France: Washington, DC, pp 199–210.

IRENA (2015) Renewable energy prospects: United States of America. [Online]. http://www.irena.org/remap/irena_remap_usa_report_2015.pdf. Accessed 07 Jun 2016.

Johansson TB, Burnham L (eds) (1993) Renewable energy: sources for fuels and electricity. Island Press, Washington, DC

Karlsson A, Ika Björn A, Yekta SS, Svensson BH (2014) Improvement of the Biogas Production Process. Biogas Research Center—Sweden.

Kumar N, Dureja G, Sandeep K (2014) To make a biogas energy from different sources & creating awareness between human begins—case study. Int J Mod Eng Res 4(3):1510–1516

lystek.com (2016) What are Class A, Class A EQ and Class B Biosolids?. [Online]. http://lystek.com/what-are-class-a-class-b-biosolids/. Accessed 07 Jun 2016.

de Mes TZD, Stams AJM, Reith JH, Zeeman G 2003 Methane production by anaerobic digestion of wastewater and solid wastes.

Moser M, Mattocks RP, Gettier DS, Roos K (1997) Benefits, costs and operating experience at seven new agricultural anaerobic digesters. epa.gov.

Naik N, Tkachenko E, Wung R (2013) The anaerobic digestion of organic municipal solid waste in California. The Berkeley Center for Green Chemistry, 15 May

nwbiosolids.org (2016) Biosolids Fact Sheet Oregon Association of clean water agencies. [Online]. http://www.nwbiosolids.org/pubs/OR_BiosolidsFactSheet%209_09p.pdf. Accessed 07 Jun 2016.

Olugasa TT, Odesola IF, Oyewola MO (Apr. 2014) Energy production from biogas: a conceptual review for use in Nigeria. Renew Sust Energ Rev 32:770–776

Ostrem K (2004) Greening waste: anaerobic digestion for treating the organic fraction of municipal solid wastes. Department of Earth and Environmental Engineering Fu Foundation of School of Engineering and Applied Science, Columbia University.

Ozcan M, Ozturk S, Yıldırım M (2013) Turkey's municipal solid waste and urban waste water treatment sludge electrical energy potential. In International Conference on Renewable Energies and Power Quality (ICREPQ'13), Bilbao (Spain), vol. 11

rnp.org (2016) Renewable NW Reports & Fact Sheets | Renewable Northwest. [Online]. http://www.rnp.org/node/RNP-reports-and-fact-sheets. Accessed 31 May 2016.

Spuhler D (2011) Anaerobic Digestion (Organic Waste) | SSWM. [Online]. http://www.sswm.info/content/anaerobic-digestion-organic-waste. Accessed 31 May 2016.

statemaster.com (2016) Population density statistics—states compared—People data on StateMaster. [Online]. http://www.statemaster.com/graph/peo_pop_den-people-population-density. Accessed 07 Jun 2016.

Stephan D (2013) Germany remains the world's leading biogas energy producer. 17 Jan. [Online]. http://www.process-worldwide.com/germany-remains-the-worlds-leading-biogas-energy-producer-a-391244/. Accessed 07 Jun 2016.

Surendra KC, Takara D, Hashimoto AG, Khanal SK (2014) Biogas as a sustainable energy source for developing countries: opportunities and challenges. Renew Sust Energ Rev 31:846–859

U.S. Energy Information Administration (2016) How much U.S. energy consumption and electricity generation comes from renewable energy sources?. [Online]. http://www.eia.gov/tools/faqs/faq.cfm?id=92&t=4. Accessed 07 Jun 2016.

veolianorthamerica.com. (2015) How the City of Gresham uses biogas and solar energy to fuel wastewater operations | Planet. 20 Jul.

Weisberg P, Roth T (2011) Growing Oregon's Biogas industry: a review of Oregon's Biogas potential and benefits. American Biogas Council, Feb

Wong SC (2011) Tapping the energy potential of municipal wastewater treatment: anaerobic digestion and combined heat and power in Massachusetts. Massachusetts Department of Environmental Protection, Jul.

Yorgey G, Kruger C, Frear C, et al (2011) Anaerobic digestion in the Pacific Northwest, Washington State University.

Chapter 19
Assessing Barriers to Electric Assist Cargo Trike Delivery Technology: Implications in Last Mile Logistics in the United States

Jesse Fritz and Tugrul U. Daim

19.1 Introduction

This case focuses on a transportation manufacturing company in Portland, Oregon, which works with a German-based electric cargo trike company. Their goal of the partnership is to launch a high capacity electric-assist cargo trike (EACT) as the preferred last mile delivery solution for high population density areas. The product is an electrically assisted human-powered tricycle capable of hauling up to 400 pounds of cargo nearly 30 miles per battery charge. This is the manufacturing company's second-generation pilot with units currently in beta testing by highly regarded logistic service providers (LSP's), in the United States and Canada. The technology has shown to be versatile in solving last mile delivery (LMD) in controlled environments such as college campuses, large venues, as well as in less controlled and highly volatile urban environments in Europe.

According to the global logistics market report in 2018–2022, the industry is forecasted to grow at a rate over 7%-year with $357B increase in revenue. Last mile delivery market revenue in the United States is currently $40B. The home food delivery market in the United States is forecasted to reach $100B by 2025. A major area of focus during this period is the adoption of the Fifth Party Logistics (5PL) distribution model, meaning a switch from supply chains to supply networks. The 5PL model is often associated with e-Commerce and relies tremendously on

J. Fritz
Portland State University, Portland, OR, USA

T. U. Daim (✉)
Portland State University Technology Management Doctoral Program, Portland, OR, USA

National Research University Higher School of Economics, Moscow, Russia

Chaoyang University of Technology, Taichung City, Taiwan
e-mail: tugrul.u.daim@pdx.edu

T. U. Daim, D. Meissner (eds.), *Innovation Management in the Intelligent World*, Science, Technology and Innovation Studies,
https://doi.org/10.1007/978-3-030-58301-9_19

integration of new technology such as Big Data analytics, Blockchain security/ contracting, and the Internet of Things (IoT's). The final trickle down of goods to end users in the 5PL model is also critically dependent on efficient, profitable, and reliable last mile delivery. While a solely economic perspective primarily fosters the expansion of market shares and the reduction of operation costs, a holistic perspective fosters also alternative transportation modes, such as cargo bikes, private car use, or even walking distance as well as logistically enabled sharing and circular economy businesses (Gruchmann et al. 2018). Consumers are driving increases in services provided by big names in e-commerce such as Amazon and Walmart, which directly drives LSP's to find new delivery solutions. Doorstep delivery once considered only for consumer goods is rapidly evolving to include same day delivery of everything from groceries to medicines. The end user market is now expecting orders to be 100% accurate as well as just in time (JIT). For logistic companies to take full advantage of the 5PL model, an efficient and reliable method for last mile delivery must be developed. By 2021, 51% of satisfied metropolitan consumers are expecting deliveries multiple times per week, but this forecast drops to 16% for dissatisfied customers (Jacobs et al. 2019). With such a huge swing in utilization, and same day delivery being the closest option to immediate customer pickup, to it is easy to see why customer satisfaction for home delivery is so important.

The trend in urban logistics is pointing to reducing costs with lighter easier to navigate and operate vehicles with high cargo capacity. Increased emission policies and development of new electric vehicles are likely to boost the light-duty vehicle segment. The focus of this case is to use global examples to show how the electric cargo trike technology can be integrated into LMD logistics model in North America, particularly in seller arranged delivery models and Intermediary delivery models. Global successes, implications, and policy trends will be used to identify barriers to this technology adoption in the United States with regard to social acceptance, environmental policy, economic feasibility, user integration, and vehicle regulations. Barriers are gaps or shortcomings that block the goal of meeting market drivers and must be resolved for the technology to come to fruition. Porters 5 forces analysis will be used to compare other emerging technologies, such as drone delivery and buyer arranged pickup models, to evaluate the competitiveness of the market and give an indication if entering the market would be a profitable endeavor. Industry expert ranking of the identified barriers will be used to show the most critical gaps to the technology adoption that need to be addressed to fully utilize EACT's in the United States. Lastly, a conclusion will be made as to how large logistics companies and private delivery services will be able to determine resources needed for closing the gaps in the technology roadmap in order to implement this technology on a large scale.

The EACT is a technology push approach to adoption. While the market demand is essentially creating opportunities for innovative concepts to be introduced, the EACT attempts to sidestep many traditional aspects of vehicle regulation and use associated with LMD. Technology push is considered as a technological innovation motivated by manipulating the current landscape of the industry. The EACT is to be considered as a bicycle-type vehicle and is attempting to eliminate the licensing and insurance requirements of motorized vehicles yet the size and weight of the vehicle will require some roadway travel in addition to bike paths and car-free zones.

A concept very similar to last mile logistics also using large deployment of new electric vehicles is first and last mile transportation. The model also relies heavily on new micro mobility technology and vehicles such as bikes, scooters, and cars. Just as last mile delivery refers to efficient and sustainable means of short route logistics, micro mobility refers to efficient modes of transportation for people to reach other forms of larger transportation such as buses and trains to relieve traffic congestions while navigating the city. Many cities across the United States have pilot programs experimenting with micro mobility as well as last mile logistics. Many of the barriers facing electric micro mobility are also directly relating to last mile delivery due to the introduction of new vehicles, routes, and safe usage/best practices. Jeanette Shaw, Senior Director of Public Affairs—Forth Mobility, states “It is a popular view among key developers in this area that shared electric bikes and scooters is the gateway to scale up into larger platforms such as the electric cargo bike.” Key players in last mile delivery include traditional delivery companies include UPS, FedEx, DHL, and the US Postal Service as well as technology companies including Google, Uber, Instacart, and TaskRabbit, several of which use crowdsourcing for deliveries (Lee et al. 2016). The UPS electric cargo bike model is seen below.

19.2 Analyzing the Competition: Porters 5 forces

> “Developing a strategy in a newly emerging industry or in a business undergoing revolutionary technological changes is a daunting proposition. In such cases, managers face a high level of uncertainty about the needs of customers, the products and services that will prove to be the most desired, and the best configuration of activities and technologies to deliver them.” Michael Porter

19.2.1 Threat of Substitution

19.2.1.1 Robots

For this case, robots are considered as ground traveling vehicles without a human operator/programmer. Robot deliveries are currently more adaptive for small to medium-sized controlled environments with well-maintained walking paths, clearly defined boundaries, and large numbers of technology users. College campuses and/or shopping malls could be considered prime targets for this technology because of medium density population in a small to medium area. Student bodies would also likely consider robot delivery a cool status symbol, possibly utilizing robot delivery even if it was faster and cheaper to use different delivery modes. Most lower-cost robots also have limitations for moving over obstacles or climbing stairs. If a tree limb fell and blocked the robot path to the delivery location, the delivery would be delayed or even possibly cancelled. If there was no path for a robot to reach upper floors of a building, the customer would still need to go the robot at ground level to retrieve the delivery. Robot applications have advantages of reliably working all hours of the day and create very little noise pollution. Modern robot designs are also highly mindful of aesthetics.

Autonomous delivery vehicles such as cars could also be considered robots, but they would face many similar challenges of placing packages at doorsteps because of infinite home landscaping designs and terrain. This is referred to as the last feet challenge. At least in early usage of this type of technology, some sort of customer assistance should be anticipated to aid a robot in properly placing a package into an acceptable "delivery zone" or even help unloading the robot manually. The long-term outlook on this technology as a profitable service could have less potential as consumers may begin to own their own autonomous vehicles that they could send out for pickup instead of requesting a delivery.

19.2.1.2 Drones

Drones in this application take on a common form typically with 4 or more vertically oriented propellers that allow the craft to hover and fly. Other drone designs are available but are applied more to longer range deliveries. Drones can be automated but are currently considered aircraft and require a human programmer to input and review flight paths. Drone delivery resolves almost all the limitations of robot delivery save for noise. Drones are scalable, fast, not constrained by ground obstacles, and are able to use straight-line paths from source to delivery site. A major disadvantage of drone delivery is the perceived nuisance of noise and privacy infringement multiplied by the number of drones in use. Personal use of recreational drones has shed a negative light on the technology through spying and encroaching on other personal property. There have been several instances of private citizens, who felt threatened by drone use, shooting them out of the sky. Malfunction of drones can lead to injuries to people if they drop out of the sky or the flight path directed them through highly populated areas. Once the technological limitations are resolved, regulatory restrictions are relaxed, and public concerns around safety and privacy are addressed and minimized, drones could have a significant impact on the landscape of last mile delivery (Lee et al. 2016).

On April 19, 2019, a quadcopter drone made a 2.8-mile flight in just 10 minutes to successfully deliver a human kidney between 2 Baltimore area hospitals. Organ transportation is highly time critical as success of the transplant relies heavily on the freshness of the organ. Historically organ transportation can occur on roadways using Ambulance with traffic override authority or through air using the equivalent of life flight helicopter or airplane. The cargo trike could possibly be used when on roadway options are allowed, but without the traffic override it would need special pathways or dedicated routes to make feasible. Joseph Scalea, Transplant surgeon at the University of Maryland School of Medicine states, Drone delivery could cut the time organs spend in transit by 70 percent. Robert Graboyes, a senior research fellow at George Mason University adds, across rugged terrain, traffic-clogged cities, icy roads, or flooded regions, a drone may become the quickest and surest way to get medical goods to where they are needed.

In April 2019, Wing was the first to gain FAA approval to commercially deliver packages using drones. In October 2019 Christiansburg, Virginal became home to Wing's first commercial drone home delivery service. Wing, A division of Google, delivered the FedEx package from a nearby launching hub at a business park to a residential address. Also, in October 2019, UPS's Flight Forward drone delivery subsidiary became the first to receive FAA certification as a drone airline allowing unlimited number of drones, with an unlimited number of pilots, while also exceeding the 55-pound drone cargo limit. The airline's first flight was launched from WakeMed Hospital with FAA exemption for flight outside visual range of the pilot.

19.2.1.3 Self-Service lockers

Pick up and drop off locations (PUDOs) utilizing self-service parcel locker technology are very easy to implement and have proven to be an efficient method to reduce delivery costs. Eliminating the need for LMD is referred to as up to last mile delivery. PUDOs are not necessarily always associated with same day delivery but still provide both the retailer/LSP and consumer with conveniences of matched timing and cost savings. PUDO's accommodate consumers who chose to shop online but also prefer not to receive at-home deliveries. A major limitation of PUDO's is parcel capacity. Once all the lockers are filled, packages will be refused and continue a route until the delivery vehicle circles back around or an alternative location is determined. UPS has taken advantage of this through an aggressive expansion of its Access Point network into thousands of retail stores including CVS, Michaels, and Advanced Auto Parts (Forde 2019). Now, retailers can integrate HubBox into their existing e-commerce platforms—such as Shopify, Magneto, or SAP—enabling them to offer customers the option to choose an Access Point for delivery automatically at checkout (Forde 2019).

19.2.2 Threat of New Entrants

The threat for new entrants into the electric trike delivery model is currently relatively low. Without crowdsourcing options and sub hubs to allow private individuals to contract package delivery using electric trike technology, the model will be capitalized on by only the largest retailers and LSP's. Moreover, many new entrants to the market are still in early stages, and it is still not clear whether their business models are sustainable in the long run (Lee et al. 2016).

The large players in the technology testing have control of product flow into local consolidation areas and access to customer delivery needs. Combine the infancy of the technology, the high capital required to pilot test the model, and the unknown if the models will even prove to be sustainable, it is easy to understand why this is a major barrier for new entrants. In addition, customers value the reliability of traditional delivery providers such as UPS, USPS, and FedEx and have more trust in them, particularly when shipping valuable or time-sensitive items (Lee et al. 2016).

19.2.3 Bargaining Power of Customers

Customers in this regard are the users of the cargo trike technology such LSP's and private contractors. The bargaining power of buyers can be regarded as a medium to high due to the burden of maintenance and operation costs due to switching product delivery modes. There are not laws, policies, or regulations that are forcing LSP's to change, rather the business case is strictly cost based. This is a common feature in the transportation industry, such as the maritime, rail, and highway modes. It is common for these companies to keep financials confidential so knowledge of actual cost reductions will likely only be known by individual companies through private testing. The full benefit of integrating EACT's into LMD's may not be fully publicized until a large-scale deployment is seen by reputable LSP's. Without knowing the real value of cargo trike delivery modes, price points, and profit margins will be difficult to calculate and leave the door open for the LSP's to drive their purchase price as needed.

19.2.4 Bargaining Power of Suppliers

Next, in terms of supply chain, the raw material for producing cargo trikes and the raw material for making microhub-related equipment have a low monopoly, so the market power of the production factor supplier is weak although these changes when referring to the electrical components. EACT's are a unique application requiring custom components for optimal efficiency. Typical electric bike components have shown to be too light for high capacity applications and electric motorcycle components have shown to be too heavy or inefficient. High-quality EACT's use custom components specifically designed for the size and weight of the trike. This currently creates high bargaining power for the few suppliers of these custom components that are critical for optimal operation of the trike as high efficiency is known to be a strategic differentiation between these products. Component supply competition should be expected to increase as the adoption of the EACT technology increases and electric drive imitators emerge.

19.2.5 Rivalry Among Existing Competitors

Competition refers to rivalry among EACT manufactures. There are currently few recognized names in EACT delivery as well as vehicle manufacture. The players in this market are well defined based on the natural segmentation of the market. Each LSP, private delivery contractor, and EACT manufacturer appears to operate within their niche segment. For this reason, rivalry is currently low but should be expected to increase with technology adoption increase and front runners in the LMD market and EACT manufacture emerge (Fig. 19.1).

19.3 Global Cases

The percentage of consumers shopping for groceries online in the United Kingdom, France, Germany, and The Netherlands is relatively close to that of the United States. On average these consumers have low satisfaction with the delivery services due to price of delivery, lack of same day delivery, and deliveries arriving late (Jacobs et al. 2019). To meet future societal and environmental requirements with response to climate change, a collaborative effort to reduce CO_2 emissions is a major force driving the electrification of LMD logistics across the EU. Much like in the United States, European consumers are also increasing demand for same day delivery through ever-increasing utilization of e-commerce. European LSP's are facing the same struggle in finding profitable and sustainable models for LMD while meeting customers' requirements and societal acceptance. e-Cargo trikes deployed from LSPs or crowd sharing is a holistic approach that is gaining attention. Although this satisfies social concerns for acceptance, large LSP's may not be realizing quite the reduction in costs they anticipated. A solely economic perspective primarily fosters the expansion of market shares and the reduction of operation costs, a holistic

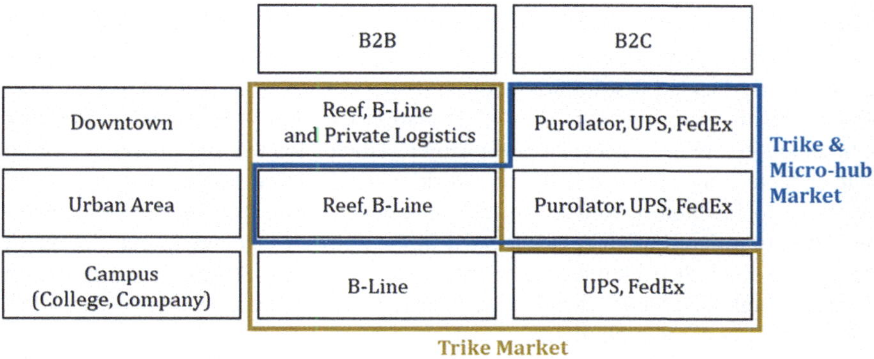

Fig. 19.1 Market Segmentation of LSP's and private contractors

perspective fosters also alternative transportation modes, such as cargo bikes, private car use, or even walking distance as well as logistically enabled sharing and circular economy businesses (Gruchmann et al. 2018). Even with this holistic approach over the last 9 years, UPS seems to still be in the analysis phase of whether electric-and-pedal assisted trikes can totally replace traditional delivery trucks in dense urban areas. UPS also operates e-bike (trike) delivery programs in several major cities including Hamburg, Paris, Berlin, London, Dublin, and Rome.

19.3.1 Germany

Rytle is a German-based company and is also a subsidiary of a larger transportation equipment company named Krone. The EACT has been developed and tested for many years. Several different prototypes of vehicles have been beta tested by large LSP's as well as private contractors. From previous research, it is known that the success of innovation diffusion depends on factors, such as the early adopters or the spread of information within the social system under consideration of basic economic conditions (Heinrich et al. 2016). Even though the technology has been developed for many years, there remains a gap in the performance and economic feasibility for full large-scale adoption. The technical and economic viability, ease of use and low complexity are decisive points for increasing the acceptance of the cargo bicycle as an alternative mode of transport for commercial use (Heinrich et al. 2016). The decision to substitute conventional motorized vehicles is based on the existence of a trustworthy, workable alternative. By now, the technology for electric cargo bicycles is still at the beginning and there is an urgent need for improving the performance of vehicles (Heinrich et al. 2016).

19.3.2 London

Trials in London have similar results but also indicate some difficulties with lack of or improperly located distribution centers. These centers, also called consolidation centers and/or micro hubs, act as refilling station for cargo trike vehicles. Refilling stations are essential to keep the lightweight vehicles loaded and operating within their capable range for a full day of work. Supply chain reconfiguration can be necessary to facilitate urban deliveries by cycle—ideally, this requires the implementation of a distribution center located in the delivery catchment area (Leonardi et al. 2012). Such distribution centers bring additional costs, especially when located in areas in high land values therefore such centers need to be as small and "no frills" as possible (Leonardi et al. 2012).

The testing, in this case, was carried out by an office supply company. Another barrier arises when the company is unwilling to disclose financial results of the trial and simply states that they were pleased with the success related to environmental and economic terms. If testing companies do not disclose exact financial benefits of electric cargo trike tests, it will be difficult to prove economic feasibility on a general level and would require each company interested in the technology to perform their own testing, likely delaying the technology adoption for many years. The observation of the situation in London, however, will need to be completed with similar evaluations in other cities and countries, before general lessons can be drawn on the economic profitability (Leonardi et al. 2012).

19.3.3 Poland

In Poland, the technology was extremely well bolstered by laws relating to environmental sustainability. The electrically assisted (zero emission) cargo trike use becomes much more attractive with laws supporting the use rather than local policies. The level of enforcement associated with laws will influence regulations more than any political lobbying. It is the responsibility of local authorities to shape transport policy in accordance with the concept of sustainable development, which is defined in the Environmental Protection Law of April 27, 2001 (Journal of Laws No. 62, item 627), in which sustainable development means such a socio-economic development involving the process of integrating political, economic, and social activities, maintaining a natural balance and durability of basic natural processes, in order to guarantee the possibility of satisfying the basic needs of individual communities or citizens of today and future generations (Nürnberg 2019).

Yet even with this level of government support, there is still an issue of proper infrastructure to accommodate the EACT usage. Useful and accommodating paths and unloading zones remain as a barrier to usage. Although the delivery of goods to city centers often having historical buildings is necessary to maintain the economic and social functions of cities, delivery vehicles in many places in the urbanized area are struggling with the lack of infrastructure necessary for proper functioning such as lack of parking spaces enabling loading or unloading (Nürnberg 2019).

19.3.4 Korea

The Korean case adds the aspect of customer satisfaction related to price and delivery times. The technology must be able to prove its effectiveness in function, reliability, and meet consumer expectations. The expected demand is suggested in a function of the price, guaranteed lead time, and lateness penalty (Ko et al. 2018). Ko suggests that changing the vehicle or micro hub location independently is inadequate. Rather both systems will need innovative solutions to create a truly effective model. The hub and spoke models have been researched for many decades but are mainly based on using existing vehicles and modes of delivery. Existing hubs are highly optimized for current vehicles and located in appropriate locations for those vehicles. Therefore, profit maximization through cost reduction from other processes is needed instead of cost minimization through changing already existing networks (Ko et al. 2018).

19.3.5 Canada

The cities of Montreal, Quebec and Vancouver, British Columbia recognized some shortcomings in expecting change being solely driven by the private sector and have taken the lead by playing proactive roles reducing CO_2 emissions and transforming congested downtown areas. Transportation is considered the second largest contributor to carbon emissions in these areas and the congestion from stop and go delivery trucks is considered a safety hazard to pedestrians and bicyclist. The short-term vision is to reduce CO_2 emissions back to 2005 levels by 2030 and recreate human-centric living conditions in areas of high population. The longer-term vision of the current government is to become zero emission by 2050. The ministry of environment is admittingly candid about the effort involving actions before knowledge but justifies the goal through a commitment to results. In the greater Montreal area, there are already 50 streets that are car free for a total length of 8 kilometers, with more projects in the pipeline for 2020. The ministry has also donated an old bus depot to become a pilot consolidation testing area in the heart of the downtown. Known as Project Colibri, the depot receives products in the traditional fashion using large delivery trucks from multiple leading LSP’s. The packages are then loaded onto various electric 4-wheel vehicles, e-assist cargo trikes, and human-powered delivery bikes.

19.4 Barriers to Technology Adoption and Integration in the United States

Seth Shultz of Streets for all Coalition and Ride Report describes the current global micro mobility and micro transportation agenda as a space race of innovation to create ride and drive cities to help combat climate change at a speed required to make a difference. Yet while many countries are bolstering social, environmental, and regulatory change through integration of new LMD business models using lightweight electric assist cargo vehicle concepts, there are still many barriers impeding the use of this type of vehicle in the United States.

19.4.1 User Acceptance Barriers: Ability to Integrate

Experiments with urban consolidation areas in Europe have shown to reduce costs and are widely accepted by consumers. Consolidation areas could also be used as sub-hubs to allow utilization of private delivery contractors using the EACT. Currently, most large warehouses and distribution centers are located on outskirts of cities where property and taxes are cheaper to build large storage structures. The distance to distribution warehouses makes electric trike deliveries infeasible hence the current crowdsourcing services are using standard cars and trucks for delivery. If consolidation areas are located in the range of electric delivery trikes and combined with an interface to tap into consumer orders, then private contractors could use Uber/Lyft style apps to build out their cargo box and map delivery routes all while the consumer tracks the progress in real time. Large retailers and LSPs will benefit from efficient ways to get more products to more customers doorstep, they do not necessarily need to provide the specific service. Sixty-four percent of consumers are indifferent if their delivery is made by the retailer, private individuals, or third-party couriers (Jacobs et al. 2019). In 2018, Walmart began pilot testing Spark Delivery, a crowd-sourced delivery platform that allows Walmart to learn even more about the full last mile delivery process. From a social point of view, this new design in urban logistics will increasingly become one of the most meaningful forms of competitive advantage, as it can cater to customers' insatiable appetite for greater simplicity and convenience by adding a layer between service providers and end consumers (Akeb et al. 2018). Although from global examples it has been shown that without specific and accommodating hub infrastructure and EACT pathways, these crowdsourcing efforts will likely utilize traditional fossil-fueled vehicles. An additional barrier for the crowdsourcing models comes from local laws ability to abruptly alter the current models as seen in California's proposed AB-5 law.

California AB-5 classifies independent contractors as "workers" and can only be considered independent contractors if:

(A) Workers are "free from the control and direction" of the company that hired them.
(B) Their work falls outside the usual business of the company.
(C) They are engaged in work in an independent business of the same type as the company's.

19.4.2 *Social Acceptance Barriers*

The introduction of any new technology with social implications should be strategic in nature to create buy in from the general population. People and cars will need to share space with any type of new LMD vehicle. Strategically introducing the new electric-assist trike vehicle out in public and demonstrating the function is key to prevent extreme polarization of opinions. The goal is to engage people's interest and spark progressively critical discussions about the know what, know why, and know-how of the technology. As seen with many electric scooter programs across the country, the mass opinion of people is that they love them or hate them. These programs partially fell short on a social level due to lack of general knowledge sharing as to the purpose of the programs. The general public will need to know what these vehicles are, where they can go, what they can do, that they are safe, and that the technology aims to provide a sustainable last mile delivery service of consumer goods. Bicycles requirement to follow the rules of the road is a major concern even in a bike-friendly city such as Portland, Oregon. Therefore, insurance and licensing requirements should also be addressed when considering viable commercial delivery services.

19.4.2.1 Forth Mobility

Forth Mobility is a local advocate for electric, smart, and shared mobility. While Forth is not necessarily focused on last mile delivery solutions, many of the barriers they have identified in sustainable mobility directly relate to EACT's. They address social concerns of new types of transportation devices by putting the new vehicles in the public eyes and offering hands-on educational workshops about the vehicle's benefits and safe operation. In addition, Forth Mobility aims to bridge political barriers by advocating for policies and laws that are mutually beneficial for consumers, businesses, and government. They tie together business and community through demonstration of new technologies in real-world projects. An EACT is currently on display in their storefront showroom in the heart of downtown Portland.

19.4.2.2 University Campus

In November 2019, Portland State University facilitated a new EACT delivery service in partnership with the Portland Bureau of Transportation (PBOT) and UPS. The UPS branded trike uses a TruckTrike brand model manufactured in Portland, Oregon. The last mile delivery model is anticipating servicing the PSU campus as well as extending into surrounding neighborhoods. UPS calls this initiative the “UPS Urban Solutions e-Bike”. The goal of PSU/PBOT delivery service partnership is to determine if they can replace at least one of the two fossil-fueled cargo vans currently servicing the PSU campus area.

> “This is another way in which we get to participate with the city on experimenting with new ways to really do things in a better safer more sustainable fashion”
> Ian Stude—PSU Transportation & Parking

There are is a growing number of groups and businesses that are highly interested in making the theme of sustainable transportation work. Their major focus to increase adoption is listening to what communities will accept, how they will support to make it work, and how they can remove negative extremities associated with the new and unknown.

19.4.3 Economic Barriers

Last mile delivery is the most expensive step in the supply chain making up to 41% of supply chain cost, over double the next highest cost of warehouse sorting at 20% (Jacobs et al. 2019). Research can help approximate cost comparisons of different vehicles and delivery modes but actual numbers form LSP beta testing will likely remain confidential. Regulatory restrictions of size, weight, and power directly affect the capacity and range of EACT while the actual cost of the vehicle and efficiency of delivery is determined by engineering design. Because of the great cost of LMD, all proposed solutions are being highly criticized. Due to different municipal policies and regulations, one design does not necessarily work in every region. Currently, electric cargo trikes are designed to specific region requirements creating somewhat of moving target in terms of economic performance. Decreasing power, size, or capacity of EACT independently can skew efficiency in multiple directions. By tweaking original optimized designs to meet local requirements can make a cargo trike overpriced, over efficiently, or under-efficient. This creates a constant struggle for designers because EACT delivery must be able to prove profitability in order to be considered a sustainable solution. Companies trying to make their mark with a vision to change the LMD industry must have a consistent and sustainable business model based on a proven vehicle performance and payback. Without a generalized business model and specific financial benefits, it will be very difficult for LSP’s and subcontractors to justify the investment in “experimental” vehicles.

19.4.4 Environmental/Political Policy Barriers

Cities across the United States are incredibly diverse in vision, policies, and speeds at which they employ their goals and vary greatly in level advancement toward sustainability. Standards between cities and states should be standard yet the speed of action between states and cities is also highly varied. In addition to climate change issues, there is a huge shift from the norm of the last 100 years of designing cities around cars back toward historical tradition of designing cities around people. The gap between lagging and advanced cities are essentially limiting how efforts toward LMD is being approached. Efforts to influence issues related to e-cargo trike are forced to remain segregated, occurring individually within municipalities. Even cities with a vision of smart city technology view of transportation still usually operate on a long-term land use strategy, but the speed of disruptive technologies of LMD vehicles are developing faster than most cities can adapt causing struggle to integrate effectively. Currently, the best approach to guide policy evolution is to learn by doing. Municipalities that recognize what we have done in the past is not necessarily the best path forward, and are interested in embracing the shift, also have an opportunity to rebuild deteriorating infrastructures around these futuristic models creating urban sustainability by easing congestion and reducing carbon footprints through the electrification of transportation of people and goods. These cities will also realize some cost-saving benefits by adapting, planning, and building to future models. Bridges, paths, and roadways that may no longer be suitable for heavy motorized traffic could be repurposed to accommodate the transportation of people and goods using light EACT's at a fraction of the cost of rebuilding to the original purpose. Environmental impact, pollution, and urbanistic considerations can lead to a change in the use of private vehicles and the application of new technologies used in dense city centers more and more often (Bányai et al. 2018).

Cities have the responsibility to manage the right of ways, making sure people do not get hurt, and the technology is safe to use. Policies that do not take into account the complex interactions within the chain may yield suboptimal outcomes, based on inaccurate projections of the likely effects (Hensher and Puckett 2004). Examining transport management from a purely cost perspective may initially identify road transport as the cheapest alternative, but only by including aspects such as environmental emissions and resource consumption, which are transparently presented using decision support systems, additional economic and ecological potentials can be leveraged (Gruchmann 2019). Ensuring efficient urban freight transport is a fundamental and daunting task for local policy makers (Gatta and Marcucci 2016). Policy makers are keen to know, before a policy is implemented, the likely reactions so to gauge how much of the objectives set will be achieved (Gatta and Marcucci 2016). Policy makers typically ignore the chain nature of goods distribution and view freight operators as an obstacle to policy implementation rather than core participants (Stathopoulos et al. 2012).

19.4.5 Regulatory Barriers

Since EACT regulations are determined by local and/or state government, vehicle developers and end users need to fully understand what the limitations are for each location intended for use. Features such as throttle, turn signals, pedal assist, size, weight, power, speed, and even software controls can deem the vehicle allowable or not. Each authority has their own opinions on what these vehicles should be limited to so large LSP's operating in multiple states and cities have a difficult, if not impossible, task of finding one preferred vehicle to integrate across the United States. Even if one vehicle could be determined local authorities also determine when and where these vehicles are allowed to operate. Late last year the city of Atlanta banned the use of electric scooters and bikes at night between 9 pm and 4 am due to safety concerns. Although safety and infrastructure are associated with the user's ability to integrate in this case. Below are a few examples of inconsistent regulations found in the United States. NY and Oregon disagree on allowable power as well as sidewalk usage. To add complexity, California offers different classes of e-bikes with different requirements and speed limits.

19.4.5.1 NYDOT Regulations

Section 1. The definition of "bicycle" in subdivision (b) of Section 4-01 of Chapter 4 of Title 34 of the Rules of the City of New York is amended and a new definition of "pedal assist bicycle" is added to such subdivision to read as follows:

Bicycle. A "bicycle" shall mean every two- or three-wheeled device upon which a person or persons may ride, propelled by human power through a belt, a chain or gears, with such wheels in a tandem or tricycle, except that it shall not include such a device having solid tires and intended for use only on a sidewalk by pre-teenage children. For the purposes of these rules, the term bicycle includes a pedal-assist bicycle as defined in this section.

Pedal-assist bicycle. A "pedal-assist bicycle" shall mean a bicycle equipped with fully operable pedals and an electric motor of less than 750 watts (one horsepower) whereby such electric motor engages only when the operator is pedaling and the rate of speed of the bicycle is less than 20 miles per hour, and disengages or ceases to function when (1) the operator applies the brakes, (2) the operator stops pedaling, or (3) the bicycle achieves a speed of twenty miles per hour. A pedal-assist bicycle shall not be equipped with any throttle capacity or have any additional motorized equipment affixed to it.

19.4.5.2 Oregon Regulations

Oregon Law (ORS 801.258]) defines an electric-assisted bicycle as an electric motor-driven vehicle equipped with operable pedals, a seat or saddle for the rider, no more than three wheels in contact during travel. In addition, the vehicle must be equipped with an electric motor that is capable of applying a power output of no greater than 1000 watts, and that is incapable of propelling the vehicle at a speed greater than 20 miles per hour on level ground.

Bicyclists may use e-bikes in the same matter as traditional bicycles except sidewalk riding is prohibited and rider must legally use a helmet.

19.4.5.3 California Electric and Motorized Bicycle Laws (Croll 2020)

Motorized bikes (also called electric bicycles) are similar to mopeds, but California law treats them differently. A motorized bicycle is defined by having pedals and an electric motor with fewer than 750 watts. There are three different classes of electric bikes:

Class 1 electric bicycle: A bicycle with an electric motor that activates when the rider is pedaling and deactivates once the bike reaches 20 miles per hour

Class 2 electric bicycle: A bicycle with an electric motor that can propel the bike without the rider pedaling. The motor cannot be capable of providing assistance when the bicycle reaches the speed of 20 miles per hour.

Class 3 electric bicycle: A bicycle with a speedometer and a pedal-assist electric motor that stops providing power once the bike reaches 28 miles per hour. You must be at least 16-years old to operate Class 3 electric bicycles.

19.4.6 Barrier Assessment

Identified technology barrier perspectives and criteria from the literature review were filtered and categorized into a comprehensive table (Tables 19.1, 19.2, 19.3, and 19.4). Hierarchical Decision Modeling (HDM) was chosen to assess the identified barriers for EACT from a multi view perspective. Among the Multi-criteria decision models, HDM provides the opportunity to combine existing data with judgment quantification (Yildiz 2018). Transportation industry experts from sales, manufacturing, project management, acadamia, LSP's, operators, advocacy groups, and policy makers participated in the pairwise comparisons of the HDM. After filtering the results for greater than 15% consistency, 19 expert opinions were tallied into the final results (Fig. 19.2).

The final test value for agreement of 2.93 is above the benchmark value of 1.96 which indicates an acceptable level of agreement of 99% for this study. The top two ranking perspectives from the model are Economical Feasibility (0.275) and Vehicle Regulations (0.224). This makes sense in respect that regulations, or so many different regulations, create many difficulties in vehicle and business model

Table 19.1 Technology perspectives and criteria

Barriers to electric-assist cargo trike technology adoption				
User integration	Social acceptance	Economic feasibility	Environmental policy	Cargo trike regulations
Lack of infrastructure	Lack of dedicated paths	Capacity	Lack of emissions policy	Power limits
Lack of proof of value	Lack of knowledge	Range	Lack of energy incentives	Size limits
Lack of crowd source	Lack of insurance reqmt.	Efficiency	Lack of car-free zones	Weight limits
Lack of micro hub(s)	Lack of licensing reqmt.	Cost	Lack of sustain-ability law	Feature restrictions

development. One might expect Environmental Policy to rank higher since this is a major driving force seen in the global cases, but this could be indicator of US complacency with a historic lack of policy.

The top-ranking criteria are Cost (0.1), Size Limits (.07), with Business Model, Range, and Efficiency (0.06) all tied. Similar to the perspectives, these criteria make sense during early pilot phases of the technology when users' requirements are considered, and regulations hinder the delivery of those requests. The two lowest criteria are licensing requirements and crowdsourcing are likely a low concern since the technology is not yet even past pilot testing phases.

19.5 Conclusion and Discussion

Social, political, and economical acceptance of new e-cargo trike technology shows promise to help solve the sustainability of last mile delivery as the mode can be utilized by retailers, LSP's, private contractors, and even crowdsourced. Maintaining the e-cargo trike classification of e-bike will keep the technology deployment timeline to minimum as anyone who can legally operate a bicycle may operate the e-cargo bike. In addition to recognizing drivers and barriers in a technology roadmap, a good technique also identifies resources that help the adoption of technology. Several resources were identified during this study that both LMD LSP's and vehicle manufacture may attempt to partner with and bolster the progress of EACT adoption.

Ride Report (www.ridereport.com) is a real-time data monitoring service that claims to empower smart city progression by facilitating the use of sustainable forms of micro transportation and micro mobility. This service also offers to help scalability and crowdsourcing opportunities by monitoring vehicle usage, locations, and compliance with regulation.

Populus (www.populus.ai) provides a data platform for cities to manage the future of electric mobility through real-time data analyzation of shared scooters,

Table 19.2 Level 1 results of the HDM

Level 1—Technology barrier perspectives						
	User integration	Social acceptance	Economic feasibility	Environmental policy	Vehicle regulations	Inconsistency
Expert 1	0.01	0.04	0.61	0.04	0.21	0.07
Expert 2	0.12	0.13	0.36	0.27	0.12	0.02
Expert 3	0.23	0.13	0.18	0.14	0.32	0.01
Expert 4	0.33	0.09	0.13	0.09	0.36	0.14
Expert 5	0.27	0.17	0.37	0.1	0.09	0.03
Expert 6	0.07	0.05	0.12	0.12	0.65	0.13
Expert 7	0.13	0.24	0.32	0.14	0.17	0.11
Expert 8	0.18	0.22	0.22	0.22	0.17	0.02
Expert 9	0.15	0.05	0.5	0.1	0.2	0.07
Expert 10	0.21	0.16	0.18	0.21	0.24	0.06
Expert 11	0.09	0.21	0.39	0.06	0.25	0.07
Expert 12	0.2	0.19	0.25	0.15	0.21	0.02
Expert 13	0.12	0.05	0.29	0.44	0.1	0.05
Expert 14	0.2	0.2	0.2	0.2	0.2	0
Expert 15	0.21	0.13	0.32	0.16	0.19	0
Expert 16	0.29	0.12	0.19	0.17	0.23	0.02
Expert 17	0.42	0.14	0.29	0.06	0.08	0.08
Expert 18	0.07	0.27	0.13	0.27	0.27	0
Expert 19	0.12	0.17	0.18	0.33	0.2	0.01
Mean	**0.180**	**0.145**	**0.275**	**0.172**	**0.224**	**0.048**

bikes, and cars. Standardizing how cities collect and use data from first and last mile transportation of people should also provide a framework and pave additional paths for the larger electric trike delivery vehicles. If major paths of people movement can be mapped and proven safe to use, certainly these routes should also be attractive for

Table 19.3 Level 2 results of the HDM

Level 2—Technology barrier criteria											
	Infrastructure	Business model	Crowdsource	Micro hubs	Dedicated routes	General knowledge	Insurance	Licensing	Capacity	Range	Efficiency
Expert 1	0.01	0.04	0.01	0.04	0.02	0.01	0.01	0	0.09	0.01	0.07
Expert 2	0.05	0.02	0.03	0.03	0.05	0.04	0.02	0.03	0.05	0.14	0.08
Expert 3	0.07	0.06	0.05	0.05	0.05	0.04	0.02	0.02	0.04	0.05	0.05
Expert 4	0.03	0.07	0.09	0.14	0.04	0.03	0.01	0.01	0.03	0.04	0.03
Expert 5	0.08	0.09	0.05	0.05	0.06	0.05	0.03	0.03	0.06	0.08	0.1
Expert 6	0.02	0.02	0.01	0.02	0.02	0.01	0.01	0.01	0.04	0.02	0.03
Expert 7	0.02	0.03	0.04	0.04	0.06	0.04	0.06	0.07	0.05	0.13	0.05
Expert 8	0.05	0.04	0.04	0.04	0.05	0.05	0.07	0.05	0.03	0.07	0.02
Expert 9	0.03	0.09	0	0.03	0.03	0.02	0.01	0.01	0.07	0.06	0.15
Expert 10	0.05	0.05	0.05	0.05	0.04	0.04	0.04	0.04	0.05	0.04	0.04
Expert 11	0.01	0.02	0	0.06	0.04	0.07	0.06	0.04	0.13	0.12	0.04
Expert 12	0.05	0.05	0.05	0.05	0.05	0.05	0.05	0.05	0.04	0.07	0.07
Expert 13	0.07	0.02	0.01	0.03	0.03	0.01	0.01	0	0.03	0.03	0.03
Expert 14	0.03	0.11	0.02	0.04	0.01	0.02	0.12	0.05	0.04	0.03	0.07
Expert 15	0.04	0.1	0.04	0.03	0.04	0.01	0.05	0.03	0.04	0.04	0.19
Expert 16	0.08	0.07	0.05	0.1	0.02	0.02	0.04	0.04	0.04	0.04	0.05
Expert 17	0.09	0.28	0.01	0.04	0.02	0.07	0.04	0.02	0.03	0.11	0.02
Expert 18	0.01	0.03	0.01	0.02	0.08	0.09	0.04	0.06	0.05	0.02	0.03
Expert 19	0.03	0.03	0.03	0.03	0.06	0.04	0.03	0.04	0.05	0.04	0.05
Mean	0.04	0.06	0.03	0.05	0.04	0.04	0.04	0.03	0.05	0.06	0.06
Minimum	0.01	0.02	0.01	0.02	0.01	0.01	0.01	0.02	0.03	0.01	0.02
Maximum	0.09	0.28	0.09	0.14	0.08	0.09	0.12	0.07	0.13	0.14	0.19
Std. Deviation	0.02	0.06	0.02	0.03	0.02	0.02	0.03	0.02	0.02	0.04	0.04
Disagreement											

(continued)

Table 19.3 (continued)

Level 2—Technology barrier criteria										
	Cost	Emission policy	Energy incentives	Car Free zones	Sustainability law	Power limits	Size limits	Weight limits	Feature restrictions	Inconsistency
Expert 1	0.43	0.01	0.03	0	0.01	0.02	0.13	0.01	0.05	0.14
Expert 2	0.08	0.03	0.07	0.05	0.12	0.02	0.02	0.03	0.05	0.01
Expert 3	0.04	0.04	0.04	0.03	0.03	0.07	0.09	0.06	0.1	0.01
Expert 4	0.03	0.02	0.01	0.04	0.01	0.05	0.12	0.11	0.08	0.04
Expert 5	0.13	0.02	0.03	0.04	0.01	0.02	0.04	0.01	0.02	0.01
Expert 6	0.03	0.02	0.04	0.02	0.04	0.1	0.16	0.15	0.24	0.05
Expert 7	0.09	0.02	0.04	0.01	0.07	0.03	0.06	0.04	0.04	0.05
Expert 8	0.1	0.06	0.05	0.06	0.05	0.11	0.02	0.03	0.01	0.01
Expert 9	0.22	0.01	0.03	0.05	0.01	0.03	0.06	0.09	0.01	0.05
Expert 10	0.06	0.05	0.08	0.05	0.04	0.1	0.05	0.05	0.04	0.01
Expert 11	0.1	0.01	0.02	0.02	0.02	0.02	0.13	0.05	0.06	0.08
Expert 12	0.08	0.02	0.04	0.05	0.04	0.06	0.04	0.09	0.03	0.01
Expert 13	0.19	0.21	0.02	0.16	0.04	0.04	0.01	0.04	0.01	0.1
Expert 14	0.06	0.03	0.03	0.08	0.06	0.06	0.06	0.05	0.03	0.03
Expert 15	0.05	0.02	0.08	0.03	0.02	0.06	0.06	0.06	0.02	0.02
Expert 16	0.06	0.05	0.04	0.06	0.03	0.08	0.05	0.03	0.07	0.01
Expert 17	0.13	0.01	0.03	0.01	0.01	0.02	0.04	0.01	0	0.1
Expert 18	0.02	0.08	0.03	0.12	0.04	0.03	0.15	0.07	0.02	0.08
Expert 19	0.05	0.08	0.08	0.1	0.07	0.05	0.04	0.06	0.04	0.01
Mean	0.1	0.04	0.04	0.05	0.04	0.05	0.07	0.05	0.05	
Minimum	0.02	0.01	0.01	0.01	0.01	0.02	0.01	0.01	0.02	
Maximum	0.43	0.21	0.08	0.16	0.12	0.11	0.16	0.15	0.24	
Std. Deviation	0.09	0.05	0.02	0.04	0.03	0.03	0.04	0.03	0.05	
Disagreement										0.036

Table 19.4 Consistency results of the HDM

Source of variation	Sum of square	Deg. of freedom	Mean square	F-test value
Between Subjects:	0.1	19	0.005	**2.93**
Between Conditions:	0	18	0	
Residual:	0.59	342	0.002	
Total:	**0.69**	**379**		
Critical F-value with degrees of freedom 19 & 342 at 0.01 level:				**1.96**
Critical F-value with degrees of freedom 19 & 342 at 0.025 level:				**1.77**
Critical F-value with degrees of freedom 19 & 342 at 0.05 level:				**1.62**
Critical F-value with degrees of freedom 19 & 342 at 0.1 level:				**1.45**

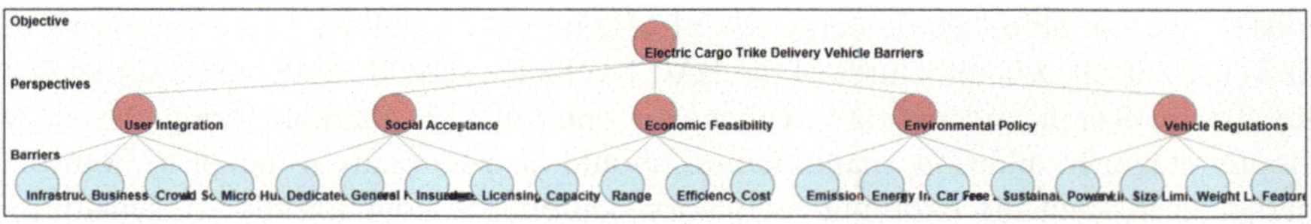

Fig. 19.2 The HDM model

overlaying cargo delivery trike routes into surrounding neighborhoods. The data should also provide insights into technology adoption within the neighboring areas to help prioritize the development of the routes and maximize utilization of the technologies in a timely manner.

Urbanism Next (www.urbanismnext.org) boasts to lead the way when it comes to the application of technological innovations in smart cities. Their goal is to collaborate with multiple professional disciplines to frame the future of smart cities and better prepare for upcoming technological change. It is considered a resource for cities and public agencies to access the latest in policy and regulation in order to facilitate standardization of policies. Urbanism Next is launching a new module for urban goods delivery set for June 2020.

Increasing consumer usage of online shopping combined with expectations of faster and more frequent deliveries of last mile parcel packages is directly driving the need for new last mile delivery technology. LMD providers are struggling to find ways to keep up with the demand as the current delivery models sacrifice profit margin to maintain customer satisfaction. To meet consumer demands, we are seeing major disruptions in delivery technology and emergence of new last mile delivery business models. Large retailers and LSP's are fiercely competing to establish profitable and sustainable solutions to last mile logistics. Facing uncertainty in governmental regulations, which adds challenges to profitability of new delivery modes, force key LSP's to explore all possible holistic solutions simultaneously.

Regarding electrical assisted cargo trikes, the consensus among experts in this study is that economic feasibility and vehicle regulations are the key perspectives that hinder this technology adoption in the United States. Inconsistencies between local governance and ever evolving EACT regulations ultimately create a moving target for technology developers to aim for. The current tactic for developers of this technology is to customize EACT and add configurations per individual local regulations. This customization adds difficulties for the EACT developers' efforts to bring the technology costs down to aid in technology adoption. Cost of EACT technology is the top-ranking barrier criteria among the experts. The next highly ranked barriers are size limits, efficiency, range, and correlation of a proven business model.

A focus on increasing consistency of vehicle regulation at a national level will eliminate multiple barriers for EACT last mile delivery technology in the United States. Efforts by the consumer society and industrial operators could essentially be mooted without mutually beneficial policies and supportive legislature required to bolster a sustainable electric cargo trike LMD model as well as future variations of the vehicle itself. Manufactures of the EACT vehicles should expect to be somewhat flexible in design and options available if entering this market during the early adopter stage. In addition, manufactures should also be ready to adapt to both the market needs and the evolving regulatory compliance concurrently. A sensitivity analysis of this HDM model could also be created using the results to help identify shifts in the perspectives as the top barriers are eliminated and the technology adoption progresses forward.

Acknowledgments Tugrul Daims contribution to the book chapter is based on the study funded by the Basic Research Program of the National Research University Higher School of Economics (HSE) and by the Russian Academic Excellence Project "5-100."

References

Akeb H, Moncef B, Durand B (2018) Building a collaborative solution in dense urban city settings to enhance parcel delivery: an effective crowd model in Paris. Transport Res E: Log 119:223–233

Bányai T, Illés B, Bányai Á (2018) Smart scheduling: an integrated first mile and last mile supply approach. Complexity:2018

Croll M (2020, March 6). California Laws for Mopeds, Scooters and Other Motorized Bikes. Retrieved from https://www.valuepenguin.com/california-moped-scooter-insurance-laws

Forde M (2019, September 18) "UPS and HubBox partner on last-mile delivery, BOPIS solutions." Retrieved 2020, Jan 1, from https://www.supplychaindive.com/news/ups-hubbox-partner-last-mile-delivery-bopis/563169/

Gatta V, Marcucci E (2016) Behavioural implications of non-linear effects on urban freight transport policies: the case of retailers and transport providers in Rome. Case Stud Transport Pol *4*(1):22–28

Gruchmann T (2019) Advanced green logistics strategies and technologies. In: *Operations, logistics and supply chain management*. Springer, Cham, pp 663–686

Gruchmann T, Melkonyan A, Krumme K (2018) Logistics business transformation for sustainability: assessing the role of the lead sustainability service provider (6PL). Logistics 2(4):25

Heinrich L, Schulz WH, Geis I (2016) The impact of product failure on innovation diffusion: the example of the cargo bike as an alternative vehicle for urban transport. Transp Res Proc *19*:269–271

Hensher DA, Puckett S (2004) Freight Distribution in Urban Areas: The role of supply chain alliances in addressing the challenge of traffic congestion for city logistics. "Walmart Tests New Last-Mile Grocery Delivery Service." Business Wire, 5 Sept 2018. www.businesswire.com/news/home/20180905005099/en/

Jacobs K, Warner S, Rietra M, Mazza L, Buvat J, Khadiker A, Cherian S, Khemka Y (2019) The last-mile delivery challenge. Capgemini Research Institute

Ko SY, Cho SW, Lee C (2018) Pricing and collaboration in last mile delivery services. Sustainability *10*(12):4560

Lee H, Chen Y, Gilla B, Rammohan S (2016) Technological disruption and innovation in last-mile delivery. Stanford GSB Value Chain Initiative in Collaboration USPS

Leonardi J, Browne M, Allen J (2012) Before-after assessment of a logistics trial with clean urban freight vehicles: a case study in London. Procedia Soc Behav Sci *39*:146–157

Nürnberg M (2019) Analysis of using cargo bikes in urban logistics on the example of Stargard. Transp Res Proc *39*:360–369

Stathopoulos A, Valeri E, Marcucci E (2012) Stakeholder reactions to urban freight policy innovation. J Transp Geogr *22*:34–45

Yildiz B (2018) Assessment of policy alternatives for mitigation of barriers to EV adoption. Portland State University, Portland, OR

The manufacturer's authorised representative in the EU is Springer Nature Customer Service Centre GmbH, Europaplatz 3, 69115 Heidelberg, Germany. If you have any concerns regarding our products, please contact ProductSafety@springernature.com

Printed and bound by CPI Group (UK) Ltd, Croydon, CR0 4YY

30/09/2026

02225508-0011